MEDITATIONS

ON THE

MYSTERIES OF OUR HOLY FAITH.

HIC MAGNVS VOCABITVR QVI FECERIT, ET DOCVERIT
IHS
Venerabilis P. Ludovicus de Ponte
Soc. Iesu Vallisoletanus, obijt magna cũ
opinione Sanctitatis Vallisoleti in Collegio
S. Ambrosij decimo sexto Februarij Anno M.DC.
XXIV. Ætatis suæ Septuagesimo.

MEDITATIONS

ON THE

MYSTERIES OF OUR HOLY FAITH:

TOGETHER WITH

A TREATISE ON MENTAL PRAYER.

BY THE VEN. FATHER LOUIS DE PONTE, S.J.

BEING THE

TRANSLATION FROM THE ORIGINAL SPANISH BY JOHN HEIGHAM.

REVISED AND CORRECTED.

TO WHICH ARE ADDED

THE REV. F. C. BORGO'S

MEDITATIONS ON THE SACRED HEART.

TRANSLATED FROM THE ITALIAN.

IN SIX VOLS.—VOL. VI.

Permissu Superiorum.

SAINT LOUIS

LIBRI SANCTI PRESS

MMXXIII

NIHIL OBSTAT
GEORGE PORTER, *SJ.*

IMPRIMATUR
✠ HENRY EDWARD,
Archbishop of Westminster

*Originally published by
Richardson & Son, 1852*

SECOND PRINTING

ISBN 979-8-8690-1149-7

TABLE OF CONTENTS OF VOL. VI.

THE SIXTH PART OF THE MEDITATIONS ON THE MYSTERIES OF OUR HOLY FAITH.

III.—FOR THE PERFECT IN THE UNITIVE WAY.

B.—THE INTRODUCTION,

1. The meditations which hitherto have been laid down have been principally on the mysteries which appertain to the humanity of Jesus Christ our Lord, and to the works which He wrought in and by the same, before and after His Resurrection; although many others have been inserted with them on certain mysteries proper to the divinity, because of the connexion that there is between them, inasmuch as they proceed from one and the same Person, who is jointly both God and Man. But those meditations which we shall put down hereafter, shall be principally on the mysteries which appertain to the Divinity and Trinity of Almighty God, and to the works which proceed from Him for the benefit of men; and these by reason of their connexion shall be intermixed with other mysteries which concern the humanity. And although as St. Thomas says, these are more in accordance with our feeble nature;(1) yet those of the divinity are much more excellent of them-

(1) 2, 2, q. xxii. art. 3, maxime ad 2; et q. cviii. art. 4.
Vol. VI.—I.

selves, on which principally the angels and the blessed spirits feed, as also perfect men who live in bodies here on earth, and in spirit have their conversation above in heaven; and, with continual meditation and contemplation of celestial things, augment and perfect the burning love of Almighty God, and perfect union with Him, which is the end of the unitive way, as has been said in the Introduction to the fifth Part.

2. This St. Basil declared most excellently well, answering to a question which his monks put to him, to know with what affection they were to serve Almighty God, and in what this affection consists, to whom he answered in these words:—The good affection of the soul I suppose to be a vehement desire of pleasing God—and that, insatiable, stable, and immoveable; and it is obtained by a vigilant and continual contemplation of the greatness of the glory of Almighty God, and with a grateful repetition and frequent remembrance of the benefits which God has given us, whereby that is engendered in the soul, "thou shalt love the Lord thy God, with thy whole heart, with thy whole soul, and with thy whole mind," as he did who said, "as the hart panteth after the fountains of waters, so my soul panteth after Thee O God." With such affection, therefore, of mind, is God to be served, and that to be performed which He said by the apostle,—" Who then shall separate us from the love of Christ? Shall tribulation, or distress, or famine, or nakedness, or danger, or persecution, or the sword?" (2) Thus says St. Basil, in which words this holy doctor briefly teaches us the principal end of the contemplative life in its highest degree, and the principal means that there are whereby to obtain it, and the fruit which is drawn from them. And at the same time, also, he declares the perfection with which the

(2) S. Basil. in Reg. Brev. clxxv.

works of the active life are to be exercised, viz., by joining with them the inward devotion and fervour of the spirit, which consists in bearing a great affection to the things belonging to the service of God, with desire to please Him in them, not the world, nor our flesh, nor ourselves, but God alone, and for His love, accompanying our desire with these four following conditions:—i. That it be not lukewarm nor remiss, such as is that of the slothful, which ends only in desire, and converts itself, as the Holy Ghost says, into torment and death, (3) but that it be *vehement,* strong, and effectual, such as the desire of the fervent is, which ends in works, doing them with integrity and perfection.—ii. That it be *insatiable,* that is to say, not to content itself with that little which it does, or suffers, although it spare itself in nothing, but that it extend the desire to a great deal more; and that it not only feels not irksomeness or loathing in good works, but that it have such a hunger, that it never thinks itself satisfied with them, so that his desire be like " fire," which " never says, it is enough."(4)—iii. That it be *stable;* that is to say, —that it be not changeable, fleeting from one thing to another, like to the slothful, who as the Holy Ghost says, " the sluggard willeth, and willeth not;"(5) for with levity he attempts various exercises of virtue, leaving some for weariness, and then setting upon others, without firmness or stability in the good he has begun, which stability is very necessary to attain to the summit of that perfection at which he aims.—iv. That it be *constant, and that he persevere in it until death,* without loosing it, relenting, or becoming lukewarm by temptations or persecutions, opposing himself with invincible valour and courage, after the manner that the thirsty hart breaks through

(3) Prov. xxi. 25.

(4) Prov. xxx. 16.   (5) Prov. xiii. 4.

the bushes and briars, running until he find some fountain of water, at which he may allay and quench his thirst. The desire with which Christ our Lord fulfilled the will of His Father for our redemption, had all these properties, as appears by what has been said in the third and fourth Part. This sole consideration is sufficient to awaken in us the like affection, since there is great reason for the disciple to imitate his master, and it is most just, .that I employ myself in His service with the same affection that He employed Himself for my profit.

3. But leaving this consideration, on which already much has been said, the glorious St. Basil puts here two others, which greatly aid our present purpose, by which, by little and little this affection is obtained, with the properties before related.—i. The first is the contemplation of the greatness of God, of His excellencies and perfections, for which He is worthy to be beloved, praised, served, and obeyed, with a kind of infinite affection, if so it were possible. But because this cannot be attained, yet every one of them moves and obliges us to procure an affection the most vehement, insatiable, constant, and persevering, that we can, as Ecclesiasticus says, " Glorify the Lord as much as you can, for He will yet far exceed, and His magnificence is wonderful." (6)   ii. The second is the contemplation ot the innumerable benefits which we receive from His holy hand, which He gives to us, with a love so vehement, insatiable, and constant, that He is never wearied with doing us good, nor satisfied with giving us His gifts, nor yet will He ever cease on His part to give them to us for all eternity. Thus He obliges us by the law of gratitude, to desire to repay His infinite benefits with infinite services, if the same were possible for us, since all is little to repay the much we owe to Him.

(6) Ecclus. xliii. 32.

4. Hence this holy doctor infers, that with these considerations, there is engendered in the soul the perfection of the love with which Almighty God will be loved, when He desires us to love Him with our whole heart, with our whole soul, with our whole mind, and with all our strength, so that all our powers, both interior and exterior, and all the senses and members of our body, occupy themselves after such a manner that they may be in the love of Almighty God, concurring to the work of love with insatiable vehemence and perseverance. For the memory and the understanding only love when they remember, think and ponder the things that provoke to love. (7) The imagination and the appetites of the soul likewise love, when they bud forth imaginations and affections, which awaken and give life to love. The senses love, when the eyes, ears, tongue, and taste, only desire to see, hear, taste, and speak of those things which are directed to this love; and all the corporal members love when they all serve in the works of the love of God. And finally, all our powers love, when all employ themselves in loving God, with all that intensity of which they are capable, and in overcoming the difficulties which oppose them, and in resisting the temptations which divert them from loving, so that charity may in such sort be " rooted" in the soul, that nothing created can " separate" it from the same, nor the " waters of many tribulations "quench" it, nor " floods" drown the flames thereof; (8) but that they may increase and ascend so high, that they may move us to imitate the heroic and exemplary virtues of the divinity, of which mention shall be made in the Sixth Meditation, after the manner that Christ our Lord, as He was

(7) S. Th. 2, 2, q. xliv. art. 4 et 5.
(8) Ephes. iii. 17. Rom. viii. 39. Cant. viii. 7.

Man, imitated them, who, with great reason might say to us, " Be ye followers of me, as I am of my Father."

5. All this, and the end of these meditations, the unitive way embraces; for, although it be true, that love and affection, as we have said, is the gracious gift of the Holy Ghost, who, without many discourses, is wont to bring some of His elect into the " cellar" of His wine, and to inebriate them with the fervent wine of His love, and to delight them with the experimental knowledge of His immense charity; yet, on our part, being assisted with His help, we approach to this cellar, flying with the two wings of these two sorts of meditations, viz., of the perfections of God and of His benefits. These meditations are so mixed one with another, on account of the connexion which exists between them, seeing that in this life we cannot attain to know the greatness of Almighty God, but by His works, and by the benefits and gifts which proceed from Him; and because in these gifts many attributes of God jointly shine forth, therefore, in the meditation of one of them some things must be inserted which appertain unto the other.

THE MANNER OF MEDITATING THE DIVINE BENEFITS, WITH AFFECTIONS OF GRATITUDE.

1. It remains now to declare the manner how to meditate the divine benefits, concerning which, five things are principally to be considered to know the infiniteness of them, and to be grateful for them as we ought.

i. The first is, *the infinite greatness of the benefactor,* who is God, whose excellence and perfections we will speak of in the manner they shall be set down in the ensuing Meditations. whence it will follow, that every gift, how little soever it appear, yet it is greatly to be esteemed, because He is infinitely great who gives it; and so David said, "I will extol Thee, O God, my King, and I will bless Thy name for ever, yea, for ever and ever. Every day will I bless Thee, and I will praise Thy name for ever, yea, for ever and ever. Great is the Lord, and greatly to be praised, and of His greatness there is no end." (9)

ii. The second is, *the infinite greatness of the love with which He bestows the benefit*, which, for this cause is to be esteemed very greatly; for giving the gift with love, together with the gift He gives Himself, and enters Himself into the thing which He loves, so that, whatsoever He gives, although the thing be very little, He gives it in such a manner that He desires to give others much greater, as He said to David, by the mouth of the prophet Nathan:— "If these things be little," which I have bestowed upon thee, "I shall add far greater things unto thee;" (10) because He neither wants power nor will, as we shall hereafter see.

iii. The third is, *the greatness of the benefits themselves,* which, after a certain manner, are likewise infinite, either in number or in excellence. For some benefits there are which comprehend innumerable goods, as with the benefit of creation and preservation of the world, and that of His providence over it. Others there are which contain within them an infinite excellence, as the benefit of the Incarnation, Redemption, the institution of the Blessed Sacrament and glorification, for all which we are to give thanks to Almighty God, as Isaias said:—"I will remember the tender mercies of the Lord, the praise of the Lord for all the things that the Lord hath bestowed upon us, and for the multitude of His good things to the house of Israel, which He hath given them according to His kindness."(11) And, as St. Bernard says,—"No gifts of Almighty God

(9) Ps. cxliv. 1. Eccles. xliii. 31.   (10) 2 Reg. xii. 8.
(11) Isa. lxiii. 7.

ought to be passed over by us without praise and thanksgiving, 'Non grandia, non mediocra, non pusilla;' Neither great, nor mean, nor those that are little, (12) for the little are infinite in number, and although in respect of others they are but little, yet in other respects they are very great."

iv. The fourth is, *the infinite baseness of the person on whom the benefit is bestowed*, who is a miserable, contemptible, and ungrateful man, and truly unworthy that Almighty God should be mindful of him, and confer any benefit upon him, which caused holy David to say:— "What is man that Thou art mindful of him, or the son of man that Thou visitest him?" "Man is like to vanity; his days pass away like a shadow." (13) Whence I will gather, that, comparing my baseness with the greatness of Almighty God, I am unworthy to take His praises into my vile mouth, saying with St. Augustine:—" Who am I, O my God, that presume to praise Thee? I am dust and ashes, a dead and stinking carcase, worms and rottenness; how shall, therefore, darkness praise light, death life, and a worm his infinite creator?"(14)

v. The fifth is, *the infinite liberality of God*, in bestowing the benefit, giving it gratis and freely, without expecting any profit from the man to whom He gives it, and without meriting it, but infinitely undeserving for his innumerable sins and ingratitudes: so that although he be so great an enemy to God, yet God is not weary with bestowing upon him new benefits every day. These five things Christ our Lord taught us how to ponder, calling to memory the benefit of the Incarnation, saying:—" God so loved the world as to give His Only begotten Son ;" (15) which sentence (as was said in Meditation xvi.,

(12) Serm. li. in Cant.   (13) Ps. viii. 5.   Ps. cxliii. 3.
(14) In Soliloq. cap. 10.   (15) Joan. iii. 16.

Part 2,) contains five words, and in every one of them something of what we have here said is to be considered. For He that gave the benefit is an infinite God. The manner was by loving. The receiver of it is the world, full of abominations. The benefit was His Only-begotten Son, even as infinite as Himself. And He gave Him gratis, without our merits, and therefore says,—"He *gave* His Only-begotten Son."

2. Pondering, therefore, these five points in every divine benefit, we ought duly to answer with gratitude to God for the same, whereunto, as St. Thomas says, (16) inclines first, the virtue itself of gratitude, for God is the first and supreme Benefactor, towards whom principally we are to exercise the three proper acts of gratitude, which are, to acknowledge and greatly to esteem the benefit itself, for the reasons before alleged; to praise Him for it, publishing His liberality to the end, that all may praise and glorify Him; and lastly, to do Him some services, not for profit, but gratis, although we expect from God no other new benefit, because those suffice we have already received. And to the end that our gratitude may be complete, it ought to be according to the counsel of St. Paul, universal, "for all things," without omitting any; and not only for those which I myself receive, but for those which all *other creatures* receive. (17)

3. And it is to be noted that in the world there are three several sorts of creatures, some which both *can and will*, render thanks to Almighty God, for the benefits received from Him, requiting this debt according to their power; such are the angels, the saints of heaven, the souls in purgatory, and the just on earth.—Others there are which *can, but will not* render thanks, either from igno-

(16) 2, 2, q. cvi. art. 6; et q. cvii. art. 1.
(17) 1 Thess. v. 18. 1 Tim. ii. 1.

rance, as the idolaters and other infidels do who know not God, or from malice, as wicked Christians do, amongst whom may also be numbered the devils and the damned, on whom Almighty God heretofore bestowed great benefits.—Other creatures there are, which *neither will nor can* be thankful, because they want the use of understanding; such are the heavens, the elements, the planets, and brute beasts. For all the benefits, therefore, which are granted to these creatures, we are to give thanks to Almighty God, joining ourselves with those of the first kind, supplying the ignorance and malice of the second, and the impotency and impossibility of the third, yet inviting them to praise Almighty God, because by this means I rather animate myself to praise and glorify Him, and whet my desire that all who can and ought should praise Him. Wherefore, as the apostle says, in every place and time I will praise God, with those words which he himself oftentimes used, especially to the Corinthians, saying:—" Thanks be to God for His unspeakable gift." (18) These words the Church uses frequently at the end of the mass and canonical hours, the more to provoke us to the practice thereof, for, as St. Augustine says:—" What thing can we better carry in our hearts, and deliver with our mouths, and write with our pens, than ' Deo gratias,' ' God be thanked?' Nothing can be said more briefly, nor heard more gladly, nor understood more highly, nor be practised with more utility." (19)

4. In what has been said we have shown the diligence which on our part we are to use in these meditations, to obtain their end, co-operating with the divine grace, in which we are principally to put our trust, distrusting our own diligence, saying after we have done all, that we are

(18) 2 Cor. ix. 15. ' Ephes. v. 4. 2 Thes. i. 3.
(19) Epist. xvii. ad Medit.

unprofitable servants, we have done that which we ought to do, nor are we worthy of so sweet and sovereign a reward, as is the gift of contemplation; it suffices to have endeavoured to obtain it for the glory of that Lord who desires to give it, and will give it to us, either in this life, if it be expedient for us, or in the other, where we shall clearly contemplate Almighty God, and love Him with all our powers, world without end, Amen.

MEDITATIONS ON THE MYSTERIES OF THE DIVINITY, TRINITY, AND PERFECTIONS OF ALMIGHTY GOD, AND OF THE BENEFITS NATURAL AND SUPERNATURAL WHICH HE BESTOWS UPON US.

I.—MEDITATIONS ON THE EXISTENCE AND ESSENCE OF GOD.

MEDITATION I.

OF THE BEING OF ALMIGHTY GOD.

THE ground and foundation of all the truths of our holy Catholic faith, is, as the apostle says, to " believe that" God " is," that is to say, to believe and understand, with great firmness of faith, that within this visible world, there is a Sovereign Spirit, supreme and invisible, the beginning and end of all things, who created them by His omnipotency, governs them by His wisdom, and directs them to Himself, as to their last end, and this Spirit we call God.(1) To understand this truth aright, besides the light of faith, the same God has given us numerous masters, and preachers, to teach us, and put us in mind of this faith for our own profit, as shall appear in the ensuing points.

POINT I.

1. First, I will consider how all the creatures of the world are preachers of this truth; for the heavens, with

(1) Heb. xi. 6.   S. Th. 1, p. q. ii. art. 3.

their planets and stars, the air with its birds, the water with its fishes, the earth with her living creatures, plants and other mixed bodies, all confess that they made not themselves, nor the order which they have in them to have been by chance, nor by their own disposition, but that Almighty God made them such as now they are, and if they had tongues they would cry out with a loud voice, and say with the Psalmist:—"Ipse fecit nos, et non ipsi nos;" "He made us, and not we ourselves." (2) And as upon beholding a beautiful image, or a palace curiously built, we forthwith reasonably infer that there was some skilful painter and architect that made them, and framed these works for some certain end; and we immediately conceive a desire of knowing who he is, and make enquiry after him; so, likewise, when we behold the beauty of creation, and the perfect order of all its parts, we may understand, as the holy Scripture says, that it is God who made them, and who arranges them in such order and harmony, for some great and glorious end; and we ought to conceive a desire of knowing and understanding who He is, and of loving and serving Him as He deserves. In this spirit I ought to behold all the works of creation, and hear the voices with which they speak to me.

2. Sometimes, therefore, I will lift up the eyes of my soul to the *heavenly bodies*, and to the order they observe in their motions, as the sun, the moon, and the other planets and stars; for, as David says:—" The heavens show forth the glory of God, and the firmament declareth the work of His hands; day to day uttereth speech, and night to night showeth knowledge;"(3) and the seasons in their change declare His infinite wisdom, and I will rejoice that there is a God, who preserves and governs all these. At other times I will follow the counsel of Job, where he

(2) Ps. xcix. 3

(3) Ps. xviii. 1.

says:—"Ask, now, the beasts, and they shall teach thee, and the birds of the air, and they shall tell thee; speak to the earth, and it shall answer thee, and the fishes of the sea shall tell thee"(4) who made them, who gave them their beauty and fruitfulness, and the knowledge which they have of the various seasons, and of those things which are profitable or hurtful to them. And I will imagine that I hear them immediately answer me:—This which we have is none of ours, there is a God who gave it to us: "Who is ignorant, that the hand of our Lord hath made all these things?"(5) And at this answer I will inwardly rejoice, and beseech this same God to open my ears to hear the voices of these creatures, and to move me by their means to know Him and to love Him with my whole heart; and I will also call upon the creatures themselves, to praise and magnify this great God, who is in the midst of them, in those first words of the Canticle:—"All ye works of the Lord, bless the Lord, praise Him, and super-exalt Him above all for ever."(6) O city of Sion, rejoice and sing songs of praise, because the great and powerful, "the Holy One of Israel,"(7) is in the midst of thee.

Colloquy.—O my soul, ascend by contemplation above this Sion and looking-glass, the world, and beholding all the works of creation, praise, bless, and glorify with great gladness and thanksgiving the immense God, who is in the midst of them. O infinite God, I give Thee all the thanks that I am able, for the testimony which Thou hast given of Thyself, in all the things which Thou hast created, and for the benefits which Thou showerest down from heaven, "giving rains and fruitful seasons, and filling our

(4) Job xii. 7.   (5) Ibid. ver. 9.
(6) Dan. iii. 17.   (7) Isa. xii. 6.

hearts with food and gladness."(8) Open, O Lord, the eyes of my soul, that they may not rest contented with the sight of temporal things which I perceive with my bodily eyes, but that they may ascend to contemplate the eternal, which are not seen, and Thee, the invisible God, who art above all, to whom be honour and glory, world without end. Amen.

In this affection of gratitude I ought to pause, and give thanks to our Lord, for the knowledge which He has given us of this truth, and for the multitude of witnesses that He has created, to give testimony of it.

POINT II.

Secondly is to be considered, that *within ourselves* also there are many things, which preach to us, and bear witness of the existence of a God; so that if by consideration I enter into that *abbreviated world*,—man, and particularly into myself, I may come, by the knowledge of that which is within myself, to know that there is a God. Such a result it was, probably, that caused David to exclaim:— "Thy knowledge is become wonderful to me, it is high, and I cannot reach to it."(9)

1. First, I find engraven within myself the *light of nature*, according to that expression of David :—" The light of Thy countenance, O Lord, is signed upon us,"(10) a light and splendour which issues from the face of God, and discovers to us that which is God, and Him who is the chief good, from whom all good proceeds. This light is accompanied by a natural inclination, which solicits us to that which is conformable to reason, and to the rule of all goodness, which is God Himself, and inclines us to love Him, honour Him, and obey Him; and when our sins do not put out this spark, or extinguish the splendour of this

(8) Act. xiv. 16.   (9) Ps. cxxxviii. 6.   (10) Ps. iv. 7.

light, we often perceive within ourselves certain flashes, as it were, of light, which discover this truth to us, and fill our hearts full of joy.

2. Secondly, I observe within myself such great *beauty*, and such a *variety* of *powers*, and of senses both outward and inward, together with such a multitude of bones, veins, arteries, and other innumerable parts, and such an admirable order in the disposition of them all, that they themselves seem to cry aloud and say, that they were not made by chance, or by themselves, but that God was the supreme artificer, from whom all proceeded, according to those words of David:—" All my bones shall say, Lord, who is like to Thee?"(11)

Colloquy.—O infinite God, my bones, my arteries, my veins, my eyes, my ears, and every part and particle of each of my members and senses, declare and affirm this, that Thou art God, and that there is none other like to Thee ; none who can give them the being they have, but that Thou alone canst give it to them.   O that they were all changed into tongues, to testify this truth to the whole world, and to praise, glorify, and bless Thee for it !   Amen.

3. But above all, the noble *spirit* which there is within our body, proclaims that there is another supreme Spirit within this world, although in no way confined to it.   For if I enter by consideration into myself, I shall see the nobility of my soul, by the admirable works which proceed from her three powers, memory, understanding, and will, together with the freedom with which she exercises them: for these powers are not bound to the body, but issue forth out of it, and roam through the round world, the sea, and the air, and pierce the heavens, discovering the secrets of nature, which the senses cannot perceive.   Hence proceed

(11) Ps. xxxiv. 10.

innumerable arts and sciences, all wonderful inventions, and prudent systems of government, by considering which we come to know that our soul is a *spirit, invisible*, and *immortal*, and *independent* of the body, in which it is enclosed; so that although the body be dissolved and perish, she still subsists and remains, and retains her natural inclination and desire for immortality. All this clearly preaches and proclaims that God is a spirit, *invisible* and *immortal*, from whom all other spirits proceed, and that He is in the midst of this world, giving being and life to all things; not in the same manner as the soul inhabits and directs the body, but in another far higher and more elevated manner; governing all creatures, and communicating to them all their arts, sciences, skill, and natural inclinations, but without any dependance upon them; for although the whole frame of the world should be dissolved, yet God shall remain for ever and ever.

Colloquy.—O God of infinite majesty, now I am forced to confess that the knowledge is wonderful which I have of Thee by what I discover in myself. If, in a thing so gross as my body, there is a spirit so noble as my soul, which gives it being and life, and governs it, and in it and by it, performs such stupendous works, how much more necessary is it to acknowledge that Thou art in the midst of this extended world, who art that supreme spirit by whom we all " live, and move, and are!" Since, therefore, Thou art my being and my life, I will also call Thee my soul, and rejoice to have Thee for my God, and love Thee much more ardently than myself. O that all knew and loved Thee more than their own life and soul, since Thou art the true life and soul of all, to whom be glory and praise, for ever and ever! Amen.

POINT III.

Thirdly, I will reflect, that it is not only the beauty, concord, and order that prevail in this great world, and in the little and abbreviated world of man, but also all the *tumults, disagreements,* and particular *inversions* of *order,* together with all the *miseries* and *calamities* from which men cannot free themselves by their own strength, that tell us that there is a God.

1. Thunders, lightnings, and thunderbolts, snow, hail, ice, winds, and tempests, the waves of the sea, the inundations of floods, earthquakes, sicknesses, wars, and *all such things* as *afflict* us, continually cry out to us, that there is a God, who can remedy all these evils. So that, naturally, as soon as we see ourselves oppressed with any of them, we remember God, and lifting up our eyes to heaven, ask relief of Him, who alone can help and relieve us: for even reason itself suggests to us that there is one who can do this, according to those words of king Josaphat to God: —" As we know not what to do, we can only turn our eyes to Thee."(12)   Even sins also, and the injustices and aggrievances which the good suffer, cry out in like manner, that there is a God to whom it belongs to punish these vices, and to reward virtues, because there is no power on earth that does this completely and exactly.

2. Moreover, the *war* and *contradiction* which I feel within myself, from the rebellion of my flesh against the spirit, and of my passions against reason, cries out that there is a God, by whose power I may subdue those enemies whom I cannot subdue by my own. With this consideration I ought to comfort and encourage myself, as well in my own calamities as in those of others, and in private as well as in public miseries, and take occasion from the

(12) 2 Paral. xx. 12.

evils of the world, to come to the knowledge of that supreme good, which there is in the midst of them, to whom it belongs to redress them.

Colloquy.—O my soul, open thine eyes, and turn them upon the world without thee, and upon what is within thee, beholding all things, whether prosperous or adverse, and then immediately open thine ears, to hear that which they say to thee; and thou shalt hear them all cry out, that in the midst of all there is a God who can give prosperity, and can deliver from adversities those who cannot deliver themselves. Encourage thyself with this good news, and study, with the apostle, to show thy fidelity by fighting " on the right hand, and on the left," in prosperity, and in adversity, serving Him in all, who shows Himself to be God in all, and therefore deserves to be praised by all. Amen.

3. From these considerations I will gather of how much importance it is to have a *lively faith*, and a *clear perception* of this truth, together with a *continual remembrance* of it; since it is the bridle of all vices, and the spur of all virtues; and on the contrary, the want of this faith, or the deadness of it, or the forgetfulness of this truth, are the causes of all the sins that are in the world, and of all the remissness and imperfections of which men are guilty in the service of God. And therefore David, as soon as he had said:—" The fool hath said in his heart, there is no God," immediately added, " they are corrupt, and are become abominable in their ways, there is none that doth good, no not one."(13) If in any commonwealth, men knew that there were no king, or judge, or administration of justice, they would immediately let loose the bridle, and would burst forth into a thousand outrages, one against

<hr>

(13) Ps. xiii. 1.

another. The very same mischief arises from the forgetfulness that there is a God, as we are reminded in the
book of Job.(14) And therefore holy Scripture, in the Law,
in the Psalms, and in the Prophets, insists very strongly
on the necessity of our not forgetting God, but being
always mindful of Him; for by reminding ourselves that
there is a God, we shall be kept from sinning, and we
shall live contented, joyful, and confident; and we shall be
encouraged to exercise all virtues, according to that saying
of David:—" I remembered God, and was delighted, and
was exercised, and my spirit swooned away."(15)

4. Hence I will conceive great compassion towards sinners, who confess with their *mouths* that there is a God,
" but," as the Apostle says, " deny Him in their *works;*"
(16) and will reflect how great an evil one mortal sin is,
seeing that, as far as the sinner is concerned, it is a denial
of Almighty God, and a practical assertion that there is
no God to be obeyed, or who can chastise such a sin. But
I, on the contrary, must assert this truth with heart,
tongue, and deeds, rejoicing that there is a God, and rendering Him thanks for the belief and knowledge that He
has given me of this truth; and I must endeavour to
retain it always in my memory, employing creatures to
awake and rouse me up out of my forgetfulness, that upon
the sight of them I may immediately remember that there
is a God, from whom both they and I have our being, to
whom be honour and glory, world without end. Amen.

(14) Job. viii. 13.   (15) Ps. lxxvi. 4.

(16) Tit. i. 16.

MEDITATION II.

ON THE ETERNITY OF THE BEING OF ALMIGHTY GOD, AND HOW HE ALONE IS
HE THAT IS.

POINT I.

FIRST is to be considered, how it is not only a most
certain truth that God is, but also that this God *necessarily
was*, and *ever shall be*, because His essence is to be. Accordingly, when Moses demanded of God His name, God
answered him:—"*I am who am.*"(1) "Thus shalt thou
say to the children of Israel: *He who is*, hath sent me to
you." As if He had said:—My proper name is, to be *He
that is*, and my essence is, always to be, without the pos-
sibility of ceasing to be, just as it is not possible for man
not to be reasonable, or for a stone not to be a body.

1. God, therefore, was before the world was; so that if
by the imagination I could conceive millions of millions of
years before the world began to be, yet before all these
God was, and ever has been. And therefore in holy Scripture He is called "Antiquus dierum," "the Ancient of
days,"(2) because every created thing whatever is new and
recent, and He alone is so ancient, that no beginning of
His being can be found.

2. Moreover, He has always *continued the same*, without
any kind of change, as He Himself says by Malachias:—
"Ego Dominus et non mutor." "I am the Lord, and I
change not."(3) I neither decay nor grow old, but always
continue in one and the same state of being, so free from
change, that not so much as the shadow of it can once
touch me: "with whom there is no change, nor shadow
of alteration."(4)

3. In this being *He will remain everlastingly;* nor are

(1) S. Th. 1 p. q. iii. art. 4; et 11; et q. x. art. 2 et 3. Exod. iii. 14.
(2) Dan. vii. 9.   (3) Mal. iii. 6.   (4) Jac. i. 17.

we able, even in imagination, to suppose or conceive an end to it after millions of millions of years. This caused David to say:—" Thou art always the self-same, and Thy years shall not fail."(5) And therefore God is, and is called *eternal;* and His eternity consists in this, that His being neither had a beginning nor can have an end, nor admits of any succession or change, but absolutely ever was, is, and ever shall be, as He has ever been. With these thoughts I will excite myself to emotions of great joy and thankfulness, for this eternal being of Almighty God, singing that song of the four holy living creatures:—" Holy, holy, holy, Lord God Almighty, who was, and who is, and who is to come."(6)

Colloquy.—O Holy of holies, firm, stable, and unchangeable in Thy being, which is altogether holy, visit me with Thy grace, and make me understand who Thou art, and what Thy eternal being is, in order that my soul, being illuminated by Thy light, may praise Thee, glorify Thee, and ever bless Thee throughout all eternity. Amen.

4. Hence, also, I will learn how *abominable* a thing *self-will* is, of which St. Bernard says:—"That as far as it can, it seeks to kill and destroy God, and would have God cease to be, and not be what He is, in order that He might not know its wickedness, nor be able to chastise it. Yet this madness is what all sinners utter by their actions, when they give themselves up to their own wills, contrary to the will of God."(7) I ought then to feel compassion for them, while I deplore the many times that I myself have fallen into the same folly; and, on the other hand, I should rejoice that God our Lord has such a being, as that none can destroy or dissolve it, or take away anything from

(5) Ps. ci. 28.　　　(6) Apoc. iv. 8.　　　(7) Serm. ii. de Resur.

what belongs to His wisdom and omnipotence, since all His attributes are eternal and unchangeable, as His being itself is.

POINT II.

1. Secondly is to be considered, that it is in such a manner of the *essence* of God to be *He that is*, that this cannot be said of any other whatever besides Himself.

i. To God alone it belongs to be of Himself, and all other things receive their being from God; so that He is the beginning without beginning, on whom all things depend for their being, while He depends on none. And therefore the apostle says, that God " only hath immortality;"(8) for it belongs to Him alone, of His own nature, not to die, nor cease to be. All other things, even heaven itself, the sun, moon, and stars, and even the very angels, have no being of themselves, but are capable of not being, and are of themselves as things vain and destitute of being, according to those words of the apostle:—" Vanitati enim creatura subjecta est;" " for the creature was made subject to vanity:" and "all of them shall grow old like a garment," (9) and shall come to perish, if God do not always give them being, and preserve them in it.

ii. This truth well pondered, will lead to the principal foundation of the spiritual life, for upon it is grounded that *profound humility* which we ought to feel in the presence of God, and which is felt by the angels, the blessed spirits, the Virgin our Lady, and even by the soul of Christ our Lord. I have, therefore great reason to study to attain the same humility, by considering that as God alone is *He that is*, even so I am *he that is not*, because of myself I have no being, and cannot have any but from God, and if He ceases to give it me, I should return into

<hr>

(8) 1 Tim. vi. 16. (9) Rom. viii. 20. Ps. ci. 27.

nothing. And as Almighty God said to Adam:—"Dust thou art, and into dust thou shalt return," because he was made of earth, and was to be turned into earth again; so in like manner I ought to imagine that Almighty God has said to me, Thou art nothing, and into nothing thou shalt return; for I was made of nothing, and of myself am merely nothing, and should speedily return into nothing, if Almighty God did not preserve me, although I know that by His will the being of my soul will never be turned into nothing.

If, then, I am nothing as to my *being*, which is the foundation of my other perfections, the same is to be understood of all the rest; and therefore of myself, and of my own nature, it does not belong to me either to be, to know, to will, to work, or to move; nor have I any stability, or strength, in any thing or quality of my own, but all are subject to vanity and change, and would all end in death and turn to nothing, if Almighty God did not preserve them; according to those words of the prophet David:—"Behold, Thou hast made my days measurable, and my substance is as nothing before Thee."(10) By his *substance* he means his whole being, his powers and virtues, and whatever strength and energy is displayed in anything that he possesses, either within or without himself, all which of its own self is nothing in the presence of God, apart from whom it has no being.

2. Upon these two truths, therefore, of *my own nothingness*, and the *essential being* which God *has of Himself*, I will ground all the affections of the spiritual life. Some of these affections will be directed towards God, such as to *love* Him as the author of my being, to *reverence* Him for the supreme prerogatives that He has of Himself, to trust in Him as the source of all virtue, and of all strength

(10) Ps. xxxviii. 6.

and stability in it, to praise Him and thank Him for the being which He imparts to me, together with the other affections of *resignation* and *obedience*, which are justly due to so great a God. Other affections will be directed towards myself, such as to despise myself, as being nothing of myself, to distrust my own strength, and not to presume on it, nor attribute to myself any good, which either is in me, or in what is done by me, but to give the glory of all to Almighty God, and to drown all the motions of pride, presumption, and vainglory, in the abyss of this nothingness.

Colloquy.—O eternal God, whose essence it is *to be* in a manner wholly Thy own! I rejoice that Thou alone art He that is, and that nothing has any being except from Thee. Clear, I beseech Thee, the eyes of my soul, that they may acknowledge the being which Thou possessest of Thine own essence, and the not being and nothingness which I have of my own self: that upon these two truths, as upon two firm and unchangeable poles, the wheel of my whole life may be moved, till I arrive at the rest of the life eternal, where I shall see Thee, and enjoy Thee, and be made partaker of Thine eternity. Amen.

POINT III.

Thirdly is to be considered, how it is also of the essence of Almighty God, to be *He who is*, inasmuch as His simple being, without any mixture or addition, *contains in itself*, with a special identity and unity, in a most eminent degree, and without any limitation, the *perfections* of all things that exist, and other perfections infinitely greater and more excellent than we are able to understand, in such a manner, that in comparison with Him, all things created, and all things that may be created, are as nothing, and as if they were not, and had no being. And there-

fore, as Isaias says :—" Behold the Gentiles are as a drop
of a bucket, and are counted as the smallest grain of a
balance,"(11) before God, and, in a word, are in His presence as if they were not, as nothing, and as things destitute of being. Hence I will conceive a high idea of the
sovereignty and majesty of the being of God, before whom
things which have so noble a being, are so eclipsed, and
are as if they were not. This shall be further considered
in the fourth meditation, and in others that follow.

From this consideration, likewise, I will learn, how
small a value I ought to set on all created things, especially those visible things which rob me of my heart; since
in the presence of the divine being they are like a drop
of water which cannot quench my thirst, or satisfy the
least part of my desires, and are also as changeable as the
beam of a balance, which easily inclines, now to one side,
now to another, with every grain added to or subtracted
from the balance.

Colloquy.—O eternal God, whose peculiar name is
He that is, I rejoice in the sublimity of this name,
which is so peculiarly Thine, that it cannot possibly
be made to apply to any other than to Thee.   O
name adorable, name ineffable, concealed from Abraham, Isaac, and Jacob, and manifested to Moses as a
special sign of love!(12)   Manifest to me, O my God,
the inestimable riches of this name, in order that I
may reverence Thee, adore, love, and serve Thee, as
is justly due to a Lord of such supreme being.   O
my soul, if God alone is *He that is,* and contains in
Himself all the perfection of being, why dost thou not
unite thyself to Him, that so thy being may share in
the nobleness and stability of His? Why dost thou
spend thyself upon creatures which in themselves are
destitute of being, and which cannot give thee that

(11) Isa. xl. 15.   (12) Exod. vi. 3.

which thou desirest, since they themselves have it not? Henceforth, O eternal God, I will esteem whatever is created, "as dung" and dirt, "loss"(13) and detriment, vanity and nothing, in comparison with the blessedness of uniting myself to Thee, to love Thee, and serve Thee, for all Thine eternity. Amen.

MEDITATION III.

ON THE INFINITY AND INCOMPREHENSIBILITY OF THE BEING OF ALMIGHTY GOD.

To enter with more security upon the knowledge of the greatness of the being of Almighty God, so as not to drown ourselves in our reasonings upon it, it is necessary to remember that He is infinite and incomprehensible, and that it belongs to His greatness that no one less than Himself should be able to comprehend all that He contains.(1) For the better understanding of the subject, I premise, that, as there are two ways or methods of making a picture, one by painting, the other by engraving, in the first of which the picture is produced by adding various colours and lines upon the surface, in the second, by taking away with the pencil many little particles of it, until the figure is left engraved; so in like manner, as St. Dionysius (2) teaches, there are two methods of knowing God, and of forming in our soul a true and proper conception of the image of His divinity. One is affirmative, by ascribing to Almighty God the excellencies and perfections that are found in the creatures, but in a much more perfect degree, and saying that He is good, wise, powerful, strong, &c. The other is negative, by excluding from the idea of Almighty God the limitations and restrictions which we

(13) Philip. iii. 8.   (1) S. Th. i. p. q. vii. art. 1; et q. xii. art. 7.
(2) De Myst. Theol. cap. iii. et Divin. Nom. cap. vii.; et ibid. S. Th. lect. iv.

observe in the creatures, as things unworthy of His greatness; and therefore saying that He is infinite, immense, incomprehensible, ineffable, &c. This latter method of knowing Almighty God is that which will be employed in the present meditation, because it teaches us more of His infinite greatness, and opens the way for us to the former method, which shall be followed in the succeeding meditations.

POINT I.

The first shall be to consider that God our Lord is *none of all those things* that are *capable of being perceived* by the *five senses*. He is therefore neither white nor red, nor of any colour; He is not bright, or beautiful, after the manner of the things which we see here; He is not like the heaven, the sun, or the stars; nor like the fire, air, or water; nor like a lion, an eagle, or any kind of body; for all these things, which are perceived by the senses, are unworthy of God, who infinitely exceeds them all; and it is a great and manifest injury to compare Him with them on any footing of equality. And therefore Isaias asks:—"To whom, then, have you likened God, or what image will you make for Him?" (3)

Colloquy.—O Holy of holies, let "all my bones" be turned into tongues, and cry with a loud voice:—"Domine, quis similis tibi?" "Lord, who is like to Thee?" (4) There is none like to Thee amongst those that are called gods; nor can their works be compared to Thine. Thou art not beautiful like the things of earth, but adorned with another beauty, which the angels of heaven cannot comprehend. Thou dost not shine like the light of the visible sun, but with another brightness and light, that is "inaccessible."

(3) S. Th. i. p. q. iv. art. 3. Isa. xl. 18, 25.
(4) Ps. xxxiv. 10; et lxxxv. 8.

Thou art not great with the greatness of quantity, which belongs to bodies, but with an essential greatness, which exceeds all spirits. Thou art not sweet or pleasant with the sweetness of music or corporal meats, but with another sweetness and deliciousness which far exceeds the capacity of all spiritual things. O infinite God, who can be like Thee? I rejoice in This, O. my Lord, and exult in soul that Thy being is so infinite, that there is no comparison between it and anything whatever of all that Thou hast created. O that I loved Thee with so perfect a love, that no earthly love could be compared to it!

POINT II.

1. Secondly is to be considered that God our Lord is *none of all those things* that can be *conceived* or *comprehended* by the imagination or understanding of men, or even of angels; for all such things are *finite* and *limited*, and therefore far removed from the sublimity and majesty of the being of God, who is infinite, and without limit. God is not good, or wise with that kind of goodness and wisdom which men and angels can comprehend; for this is imperfect and limited, and infinitely inferior to that which belongs to God. His goodness and wisdom, is such that we cannot comprehend it, nor find any name for it that will fully answer to it; so that it is *incomprehensible* and *ineffable*; and the same may be said of His other divine perfections. It would therefore be a foolish thing to compare His excellencies with those of any man or angel on terms of equality and perfect similitude; but we ought rather to say with holy David:—" For who in the clouds can be compared to the Lord? or who among the sons of God shall be like to God?" (5) That is to say, none of those who dwell above the clouds, or of those who "are the *sons of God*" by

(5) Ps. lxxxviii. 7.

grace, can be compared with Almighty God, or placed on an equality with Him; for they are all at an infinite distance from Him, and He Himself far above them all.

2. Hence I will proceed to reflect, that, in order to know the greatness of the being of God with that kind of knowledge of which I have spoken, I must leave, as St. Dionysius tells Timothy, (6) the things that are perceived by the senses, and by weak and imperfect understandings, and must bid farewell to the imaginations, reasonings, and limited knowledge of the understanding, and learn that God is not a substance, or a spirit, or such a being as I can figure to myself, but a Being infinitely excellent, infinitely great, absolutely supreme, and highly exalted above every substance, and every spirit, and every being; whom I know not, and whom we all know not; who is to me, and to all creatures, as a cloud of obscurity and darkness. Accordingly we read in the Scripture:—"That Moses went to the dark cloud, wherein God was." (7) Again David says:—"Clouds and darkness are round about Him;" (8) and Solomon:—"The Lord said that He would dwell in a cloud." (9) And St. Paul declares still more plainly:—"That He inhabiteth light inaccessible, whom no man hath seen, nor can see," (10) so as to comprehend what He contains in Himself. In this so wise an ignorance, and in this so bright a darkness, although " *inaccessible*," I must endeavour to take my rest and repose, thinking very highly of Almighty God, rejoicing that He is infinitely greater than I can imagine or conceive, full of admiration and amazement at His incomparable greatness, and supplying the defect of my knowledge with the excess of my love, desiring with my whole heart to love Him, and serve Him, and sighing to see Him.

(6) De Myst. Theo. cap. i.   (7) Exod. xx. 21.

(8) Ps. xcvi. 2.   (9) 3 Reg. viii. 12.

(10) 1 Tim. vi. 16.

Colloquy.—O invisible God, when shall I see Thee, not through a glass, in a dark manner, but "face to face?" (11) O that I knew Thee as Thou knowest me, in order that I might love Thee as Thou lovest me! Since, however, my knowledge is so imperfect, and remains so far behind, my love shall be more ample, and shall reach much further: and I will love Thee as much as I am able until I see Thee as I desire.

POINT III.

1. Thirdly, I will consider that the infinity of the being of God is such, that all the *perfections* which Holy Scripture ascribes to Him are also *infinite;* so that our understanding cannot sound or dive to the bottom of them, or imagine any end or limit to them. As the prophets say:—" Great is the Lord, and greatly to be praised; and of His greatness there is no end;" (12) and so neither has His *duration* any end, nor His *extent*, nor His *bounty*, nor His *wisdom*, nor His *power*, because He is infinite in all of them. And after I have imagined as much as I am able to imagine, He is infinitely more than I either have, or can imagine. Thus, if I imagine God to endure for some millions of years, and then add as many more, and after that again as many more, after I have added as many as I can possibly imagine, there will still be an infinity remaining; for, as one of Job's friends exclaimed:—" Behold God is great, exceeding our knowledge, the number of His years is inestimable," (13) and cannot be counted. In like manner Almighty God fills this whole world, and can fill millions of other worlds much greater than this; and after I have imagined as many worlds as I am able, there are an infinity more, which God can fill with His immensity. And the same is to be said of His wisdom and omni_

(11) 1 Cor. xiii. 12.   (12) Ps. cxliv. 3.
(13) Job. xxxvi. 26.

potence, and of every one of His perfections. Of every one I must have so exalted an idea as to believe that that which I do not understand of it is much more than that which I understand: and in this ignorance I will rest, rejoicing that there are so many things in the being and perfections of Almighty God which I cannot comprehend.

2. Hence it follows that the being of Almighty God ought to be freely and fully confessed to be *incomprehensible* and *ineffable* as God Himself is; so that no creature can comprehend either that which is in Him, or that which is in His bounty or wisdom, or in any other of His attributes and perfections, or apply any name to them that will fully come up to them; for God, as the prophet Jeremiah declares, is "great in council, and incomprehensible in thought." (14) It is evident that this must be so; for every creature is finite, and limited; but that which is finite cannot comprehend that which is infinite, any more than I can grasp or enclose the whole world with my fist, or take up all the water of the ocean in a vessel of small capacity. "Hardly," as the Wise man says, "do we guess aright at things that are upon the earth: and with labour do we find the things that are before us. But the things that are in heaven who shall search out?" (15) I ought therefore to confess, and to glory in the confession, that I have a God so great, that none can comprehend Him: for if I could comprehend Him myself, He would be a very limited and imperfect God, or, to speak more plainly, no God at all.

3. To this purpose I will take an example of the highest order of angels, the Seraphim. These have six wings, by which is signified that they fly in the knowledge of God, and of the things which He created in the first six days of the world, and that they soar to a greater height

(14) Jer. xxxii. 19.   (15) Sap. ix. 16.

than the other angels; (16) yet nevertheless, when they are in the presence of Almighty God, they fold up four of their six wings, and with two of them they cover the face of God, to signify that they cannot comprehend the height of His divinity; and with two others they cover His feet, to signify that they cannot comprehend all the works which proceed from Him; and they fly with only two, proclaiming some of the great wonders of God, which they do know. But they magnify God much more by folding their four wings, than by flying with the two others, or than by the words which they utter; for they thus confess that that which they do not know of Almighty God is infinitely more than that which they know.

Colloquy.—O incomprehensible and ineffable God, I rejoice that the Seraphim themselves find themselves, as it were, blind and dark in Thy presence, and confess that Thou surpassest all their knowledge, and that They cannot comprehend Thee. O that I had those six wings of these inflamed Seraphim, and could turn them all into wings of love, to employ all my strength in loving Thee, although I cannot comprehend Thee! Amen.

POINT IV.

Fourthly, is to be considered, as a foundation of our faith, the singular *favour* which Almighty God does us in *revealing to us some of the most secret mysteries* of His infinite being and perfections. For His Divine Majesty, knowing that it was not possible either for men or angels to attain to them all, nor even to search out many of them which are to be seen in the creatures themselves, was pleased, out of His infinite bounty and mercy, to reveal some of them to us, for His own glory, and for our

(16) Isa. vi. 2.

good; amongst which there are many so sublime, that we cannot attain to understand how they are, since they far exceed our shallow capacity, and all the powers of reason, and the light of nature. This consideration ought to move me to exceeding joy to see that I have a God so excellent and infinite, that His being, and the works which proceed from Him, far surpass everything whatever men or angels can attain to, or investigate. Moreover, I ought to draw three other holy affections and purposes from the same foundation.

1. The first affection is, that of *gratitude* towards God our Lord for having revealed to us in His holy Scriptures, by means of His prophets, the secret things of His divinity, according to that saying of David :—"The uncertain and hidden things of Thy wisdom Thou hast made manifest to me."(17) But especially we that live under the law of grace are bound to render greater thanks to Him for having given us His Only-begotten Son; since, as the glorious St. John says:—He has revealed Him to us more distinctly, (18) than to those that had seen Him. I will therefore give Him thanks for having revealed to us the mysteries of the most holy Trinity, the Incarnation, the Eucharist, the remission of sins, the resurrection of the flesh, and life everlasting; acknowledging that I could not know these, and other like mysteries, except by His revelation.

2. The second affection that I ought to conceive is that of most assured and submissive *faith*, by which I should constrain my understanding to believe that which I cannot comprehend, simply because God has revealed it, without whose revelation it would be impossible to know it. (19) And therefore I ought principally to exercise faith upon those mysteries which are most sublime and secret, delight-

(17) Ps. l. 8.   (18) Joan. i. 18.   (19) 2 Cor. x. 5.

ing to believe them, and to live in this faith, and to guide myself by it. And after the example of the Seraphim, confessing my insufficiency, I will, both with my voice, and with great inward joy, laud and praise Almighty God, Three and One, with the other names which He has revealed to me, saying:—" Holy, Holy, Holy, Wise, Wise, Wise, Mighty, Mighty, Mighty, is the Lord of Hosts;" without attempting to search into more than He has revealed to me; because the curious "searcher of divine majesty," as the Wise man says, " shall be overwhelmed by glory."(20)

3. The third affection is that of great *confidence*, with great joy and gladness of heart, and a steadfast hope that I shall come to see these mysteries clearly which now I believe; thus fulfilling in myself the words of St. Paul:— " We see now through a glass in a dark manner, but then face to face;" for God has revealed them to me with obscurity, for the very purpose, that by believing them with a lively faith, and by obeying His commandments, I may come to see them clearly. Moreover, I ought to have great confidence that He will likewise in this life enlighten my faith, and give me a great understanding of His mysteries, if I dispose myself, by cleanness of heart, to behold them, since He Himself has said:—" Blessed are the clean of heart, for they shall see God." (21)

Colloquy.—O God of hope, fill me with all joy and peace in believing, that hope, and the virtue of the Holy Ghost, may abound in me, world without end. Amen.

(20) Prov. xxv. 27. Ecclus. iii. 22.

(21) Matt. v. 8.

MEDITATION IV.

OF THE UNITY OF GOD IN ESSENCE, AND TRINITY IN PERSONS.

POINT I.

1. The first point shall be to consider the first article of our holy faith, in which we confess that there is no more than *one only God*, in one only essence and divinity, and that it is not possible there should be more Gods than one, (1) so that*there is no more than one Creator, one Governor, one Lord, one first beginning, and one last end of all things. And upon this truth are grounded the principal precepts of our law.

i. First, God is the *chief* and *infinite good*, in whom are contained all possible good, and all possible perfection, so that none is wanting to Him, for if one were wanting He would be imperfect, and would have to beg that one of some one else. From this it follows evidently that there is no more than one God, for if there were more than one, there would be wanting to one some perfection which the others have, and in respect of which He is different from them. And upon this is grounded the commandment of God, that we love Him above all things, " with our whole heart," because He is the chief good, the universal good, and the only good, and worthy to be beloved with chief, universal, and single love, without dividing or parting the heart into other loves that do not tend to the love of Him.

Colloquy.—O infinite good, what great thing do I do if I love Thee above all things, since Thou art the one God, superior to all? and what great thing do I do, if I give Thee my chief universal and single

(1) Deut. vi. 4. S. Th. i. p. q. xi. art. 3. 1 Cor. viii. 4.

love, since all this is little in comparison of that love which Thy chief universal and single bounty deserves? I have the greatest reason to love nothing contrary to Thee, or that is not referred to Thee: since there is nothing good, or worthy of love, except for the goodness that it receives from Thee.

ii. Secondly, God is the *supreme Lord* and governor of His creatures, to whom they are all subject, and whose efficacious will none at all can resist; for if any could resist Him, He would be a very miserable God, without satisfaction or peace in His government, and His kingdom would not last long. (2) From this also it follows that there is but one only God, for if there were more Gods than one they would have different judgments, wills, and powers, and one might will something contrary to another, make war against Him, and contradict Him. Moreover, the world could not possibly continue in that peace and concord in which we see it; for "every kingdom divided against itself, shall be brought to desolation;" (3) and thus the agreement of the heavens, of the elements, and of living creatures, proclaims that there is but one only God, the governor of all. And upon this is grounded the commandment of Almighty God, that we worship Him alone, and fear Him, and serve Him "with our whole soul." For, as our Saviour says, it is impossible to "serve two masters," (4)—since, of necessity they will sometimes command different things, and by seeking to obey the one we shall be sure to displease the other; and so neither is it possible to serve two Gods. I will, therefore, make it my whole care to serve this one God, my supreme Lord, and to render entire obedience to Him alone, and to

(2) Job. ix. 4.   Ps. lxxv. 8.   Isa. xlvii. 3.
(3) Luc. xi. 17.   (4) Mat. vi. 24.

no one else, unless for His sake, to one that is appointed in His place, and whom He wills me to obey.

iii. Thirdly, God is our *supreme lawgiver*, to whom it belongs to prescribe laws to us, because His will and judgment is the rule of what we ought to do; to Him also it belongs to be judge of all, to reward the obedient, and to punish the disobedient; and He likewise is our last end, and our highest good, in the vision and possession of whom we shall find satiety, and the full satisfaction of all our desires. (5)   From all this again it follows, evidently, that there can be no more than one God, one lawgiver, one supreme judge, and one last and final end; for, if there were more than one, they might be contrary in their laws, and in their rewards and punishments; and no one of them, by Himself alone, could ever satisfy our desires, because we should always desire to see the other.   Upon this is grounded the obligation under which we lie, that our intention should be one, pure, and simple, and that we should direct all our works to God alone, as to our last end, seeking only His honour and glory in all things.

2. From all this I will gather, first, a great compassion for all infidels and idolators, who multiply false gods to themselves, to the evident dishonour of the true God, and I will beseech Him to root this vice out of the world, saying to Him:—

Colloquy.—O only and true God, who, upon the " swift cloud" (6) of Thy most holy humanity, enteredst into the " Egypt" of this miserable world, cast down by Thy presence all the " idols" which wordly men adore at this day, and " melt" their hearts within them, affrighting them with Thy holy fear, and alluring them unto Thee with Thy sweet love.   Amen.

3. Next I will consider how great an evil sin is, which

(5) S. Th. i. 2. q. i. art. 5.   (6) Isa. xix. 1.

tends to destroy the unity of Almighty God, and bring in false gods; for carnal men, as St. Paul says, make their belly their God, the covetous their money, the proud their vain honour, and every one takes for this his god, and last end, the object for love of which he leaves the true God. (7) And thus it is that men are every day inventing new gods, which, as the Scripture says, were never known or adored by their fathers. (8)

Colloquy.—O eternal God, the " ancient of days," and the judge of mortal men, "judge Thy own cause," (9) and destroy the multitude of false gods, in order that all, not only with the mouth, but also by their works, may confess and proclaim that there is " one God and Father of all, who is above all," (10) and is in all things, whom let all things praise and glorify, world without end. Amen.

4. After this I will conceive an inward desire *to fix all my intentions*, affections, and inclinations, *upon this supreme God*, so as not to be drawn after other objects, but to rest contented in this one, in which are all, saying to my soul that which Christ our Lord said to Martha: O my soul, " thou art careful, and art troubled about many things; but one thing" alone "is necessary," which is, to love, reverence, and serve one only God, Creator of all things, and one only Father, from whom they all proceed, and one only end, to which they are all ordained, in which thou shalt find true rest and everlasting satiety.

5. Lastly, I will conceive another great desire to love and *do good to all men*, since we have all one God, one beginning, and last end, according to that saying of the prophet Malachy, "Have we not all one Father? Hath not one

(7) Philip. iii. 19. Gal. v. 20.
(8) Deut. xxxii. 17   (9) Dan. vii. 9. Ps. lxxiii. 22.
(10) Ephes. iv. 6.

God created us?   Why, then, doth every one of us despise his brother, violating the covenant of our fathers?" (11)

Colloquy.—O infinite God, One in essence, from whom we all proceed, grant that we may be one in Thee, loving one another as the workmanship of one and the same God, as servants of the same Lord, and as sons of the same Father, and ordained to enjoy the same end, even Thyself, who art the only and chief good of all; to whom be honour and glory, world without end.   Amen.

POINT II.

Secondly, is to be considered, that other principal article of our faith, that while God our Lord is *one* in *essence*, He is *Three Persons*, the Father, the Son, and the Holy Ghost.   I must subdue my understanding to the belief of this truth, although I cannot comprehend how it is.   At the same time I may reflect that God our Lord comprises in Himself everything of good and perfection that we see in the creatures, without any of the evil and imperfection that is in them; and, therefore, He has the good of being *one*, without the evil of being *alone*, and the perfection of being in some sort, *plural*, without the imperfection of being *divided*, for He is one in essence, and in divinity, one in His bounty, His wisdom, His omnipotence, and all His other attributes.   As the three divine Persons are but one God, so have They but one and the selfsame judgment and will, and one and the selfsame power and work, without any difference of opinions, or contrariety of wills, or opposition in works amongst Them, for all think the same, will the same, and are united in the same work, external to themselves, with ineffable peace and concord.

There are, notwithstanding, three distinct Persons, and

(11) Malac. ii. 10.

not one alone, that so God may not want that perfection and joy, which communication and perfect friendship between equals brings with it; and that His bounty, wisdom, and power, may accomplish their desire of communicating themselves infinitely, and after an infinite manner. For thus, the Father, to fulfil His desires, communicates His divine essence, and all His wisdom, and omnipotence, to the Son; and again, the Father and the Son communicate the same attributes to the Holy Ghost, so that, between the three Persons there is an infinite love and most perfect friendship, as between persons not only equal, and alike, but also really and truly one and the same in the substance of their divine being. And in this communication and friendship there is an infinite joy and gladness, each person rejoicing infinitely in the proper personal being of the others.

1. From this consideration I will gather, first, a great *admiration* and profound *reverence* towards the majesty of Almighty God, One and Three, devoutly adoring in this Trinity, that which I cannot comprehend, and animating myself to believe in It, in order that I may understand It. With St. Paul I will exclaim:—" O the depth of the riches of the wisdom, and of the knowledge of God. How incomprehensible are His judgments, and how unsearchable are His ways!" (12) If Thy *judgments* are *incomprehensible*, and Thy *ways unsearchable*, how much more incomprehensible shall Thy being be? And how much more unsearchable Thy *divinity?* Augment, O Lord, my faith, in order that I may so believe in Thy divine Trinity, as to understand It, and so understand It, as also to love It, and at the last come to enjoy It everlastingly. Amen.

2. Secondly, I will conceive a great *joy* for the infinitely

(12) Rom. xi. 33.

perfect union of the three divine Persons with one another, together with an inward desire to be partaker of it, and to imitate it in such a manner as is possible for me, saying:—

Colloquy.—O eternal Father, I rejoice exceedingly in the union which Thou hast with Thy blessed Son. O only Son of God, I rejoice in the love which Thou bearest towards Thy Father. O Holy Ghost, I rejoice in the union and love which Thou bearest towards the Father and the Son. O blessed Trinity, I rejoice in the ineffable friendship which is displayed in Thee. O infinite God, since Thou hast given me faith in this divine union, give me likewise grace, to imitate it after the manner that Thou desirest. Amen.

3. Then I will apply myself to consider the *manner* in which I may *imitate* this holy union, calling to mind that which Christ our Lord, on the night of His Supper, asked of His Father in our behalf, viz., that we might be "one," as they two are one. (13) As, therefore, the Three divine Persons have one and the same desire, and one and the same will, and work in all things with perfect harmony, without any difference, so that, as our Lord said of Himself, " The Son cannot do anything of Himself, but what He seeth the Father doing; for what things soever He doth, these the Son also doth in like manner." (14) Even so I will endeavour to unite myself to God, and to make myself one thing with Him by love, having one and the same desire with His, in all the things that He has revealed to me, and one and the same will in all the things that He has ordained, and performing all my actions after the manner that He commands me, without departing from His holy will in anything, but conforming myself to it with perfect agreement and delight.

(13) Joan. xvii. 11.   (14) Joan. v. 19.

4. This union, so great in itself, I will endeavour *to establish with my superiors*, and those who govern my soul, especially if I be a Religious, conforming my judgment and my will, and the execution of my works, to the judgment and will of my superiors, who govern me in the name of God. And I must aim at maintaining the same union with all my neighbours, in all such things as I lawfully may, conforming myself with them, as St. Paul says, that I be of one meaning, having the same charity, of one mind, agreeing in one. (15) And because it is out of my own power to attain to such union with God and my neighbours, I will crave it of the most holy Trinity, saying:—

Colloquy.—O infinite God, who being Three in Persons, art but One in essence, and dost communicate Thy Divinity without prejudice to Thy unity, communicate to me Thy copious grace, that by it I may come to be one with Thee in the union of perfect charity. O Saviour of the world, offer to Thy eternal Father the prayer which Thou madest for me in the night of Thy passion, that, by virtue of it, I may be made one with Thee, and with all my brethren, as Thou art one with Thy heavenly Father, world without end. Amen.

POINT III.

Thirdly is to be considered the *manner* and *order* of this mystery, as it takes place in Almighty God.

1. The first Person, the Father, knowing and comprehending Himself and His divine essence, with infinitely greater clearness than I see myself in a looking-glass, by this knowledge formed within Himself, a conception and lively image of Himself; and this conception is the Son, who, as St. Paul says, "Is the brightness of His glory, and the figure of His substance," and "the image of the

(15) Ephes. ii. 3.

invisible God." (16) This is He whom St. John calls the "*Word*" of God, the Word which the Father spoke within Himself, and in which He expressed the whole mind of God; and for this cause He is called His "wisdom." And, as the Father produces the Son, therefore, He necessarily loves Him, and delights in Him with infinite love and joy, because He beholds in Him His own infinite goodness. And the Son, after the same manner, loves the Father with infinite love and joy, for the infinite goodness which He sees in Him, and which He receives from Him. And both together, by means of their love, produce a force or impulse of the divine will, which we call the Holy Ghost, and communicate to Him the same divinity, so that He is one and the same God with them. (17) All this is in God, from all eternity; for all three Persons are *eternal*, nor is one before another, nor is the Father more ancient than the Son, nor the Son more ancient than the Holy Ghost, for they are not Father and Son, after the manner of human relationship. Moreover, all the three Persons are *immense*, nor can one be separated from the other; but, wherever the Father is, there is the Son, and there is also the Holy Ghost; and all three are equal, no one being greater than another, for, it is as great a dignity to be the Son as to be the Father, and to be the Holy Ghost, as to be the Son.

2. All the three Persons, therefore, *possess entire and complete blessedness* in the knowledge and love of themselves, and of their divinity; whence it is that they rejoice with an unspeakable joy, and are full, without satiety, and without the necessity of anything out of themselves. So that, although Almighty God, in His eternity, before He created the world, was alone without any creatures, yet was He neither inactive, nor without joy, because His

(16) Heb. i. 3. Colos. i. 15.　　　　　(17) S. Th. i. p. q. xli.

principal work is His own interior knowledge and love, in which His ineffable joy consists; and from this proceed the exterior works which are common to all the three Persons, for the three are together one, Creator, Sanctifier, Glorifier, and one Benefactor, from whom all the works of nature, grace, and glory proceed; and, therefore, all three hear our prayers, accomplish our desires, and fill us with their mercies.

3. From these considerations we may draw affections of great *admiration, love, joy,* and *gratitude,* for the unspeakable excellencies of each divine Person, enlarging on the several properties of each in the way of colloquy, and addressing Them in the following, or some similar terms.

COLLOQUY WITH THE ETERNAL FATHER.

1. First, I will speak to *the first Person,* saying:—

O Father of infinite majesty, beginning without beginning, proceeding from none, and from whom the other Persons proceed, with great reason didst Thou say:— " Shall not I, that make others to bring forth children, myself bring forth?" " Shall I, that give generation to others, be barren?" (18) I rejoice, O my Lord, that Thou hast conceived within Thyself this eternal Word, and hast begotten this Son, so like Thyself, that He is one and the selfsame thing with Thee. Thou hast no need of many sons, since in this one alone Thou displayest Thy infinite perfections, begetting at once the greatest thing Thou couldst beget.

2. O most glorious Father, I rejoice that the joy which Thou hast in begetting such a Son is perpetual, since Thou art perpetually begetting Him, and saying, " Thou art my Son, this day have I begotten Thee." (19) O

<hr>

(18) Isa. lxvi. 9.   (19) Ps. ii. 7.

eternal day, which ever was, ever is, and ever shall be, and shall never cease to be! O divine generation, with which Thou, O sovereign Father, hast begotten, begettest, and wilt beget, a Son, whom Thou lovest so exceedingly. O with what gladness didst Thou say in Thine eternity, that which afterwards Thou saidst at the river of Jordan and on the mount of Thabor: "This is my beloved Son, in whom I am well pleased?" (20) Who, besides Thyself, and the other divine Persons, who are one with Thee, can understand the love with which Thou dost communicate to Him Thy divinity itself? If "a wise son maketh the father glad," (21) what gladness didst Thou receive from such a Son, who is Wisdom itself, and equal in wisdom to His own Father?

3. O heavenly Father, "of whom all paternity in heaven and earth is named," (22) since Thou delightest so much in being the Father of such a Son, by Him I beseech Thee to beget many other sons, of whom Thou mayest be Father by grace and adoption, as Thou art of this one by nature. Oh, that both heaven and earth were full of such sons, in order that Thy divine paternity might dilate itself, and shine both in heaven and earth! O "Father of lights, from whom proceeds the true light," which is Thy Son, "the brightness" of Thy infinite "glory," give me the light of lively faith, that by it I "may know Thee, the only true God, and Jesus Christ," the Only-begotten, whom Thou hast begotten, by whom I shall know Thee, and love Thee, and shall be a son of light in this life, and afterwards obtain the light of glory, by which to see Thee clearly in the life eternal, Amen. (23)

(20) Mat. iii. 17; et xvii. 5.

(21) Prov. x. 1.   (22) Ephes. iii. 15.

(23) Jac. i. 17. Joan. i. 9. Heb. i. 3. Joan. xvii. 3.

WITH THE ONLY BEGOTTEN SON OF GOD.

1. Then I will speak to *the second Person* concerning the properties that belong to Him.

"O Son of the living God, who proceedest from the Father by eternal generation;"(24) I rejoice that Thou art "the *Only-begotten*," so that there never was, and never will be, such an only begotten as Thyself. There are many that are only sons of their fathers. But Thou art "*Only*," and "*Only-begotten*," after so singular a manner, that it is impossible to find another like Thee.

i. Thou art "the Only-begotten" because in Thy divine nature Thou art begotten of a Father *without a mother*, and Thou art so absolutely the "*Only Son*" of Thy Father, that He cannot beget any sons by another, and it is from Him alone that Thou receivest the infinite good which Thou enjoyest: it is not possible that the Father should cease giving Thee so great a good, or that Thou shouldst cease receiving it; He takes infinite delight in begetting Thee, and Thou in being begotten by Him.

ii. Thou art "the Only-begotten," because Thou alone amongst all sons art so perfectly the *image* and *figure* of Thy Father, as to be one thing with Him; so that, such as the Father is, such in all respects, and to the fullest extent, is the Son, and it is the very same dignity to be the Son, as it is to be the Father. O infinite equality! O incomparable similitude, more admirable than imitable, to which none can fully attain, although we may aspire to obtain some share in it!

iii. Thou art also eminently "the Only-begotten," because Thou alone receivest *all* the *inheritance* of the Father, which is the inestimable riches of His divinity; for He

(24) Joan. i. 14; et viii. 42.

reserves none to Himself without communicating it to Thee; but Thou art as mighty as He, with equal power to acquire other sons by adoption, who may be heirs of Thy glory in that share or portion which Thou art pleased to impart to them. O that Thou wouldst make me like Thyself in being a son; since, as the apostle says, if I am a son, I shall also be a "joint-heir" with Thee of the kingdom of heaven. (25)

iv. Finally, Thou art eminently "the Only-begotten," since Thou art *ever in the bosom of Thy Father*, and never departest from Him. I rejoice, O my only good, in this eternal joy and rest which Thou possessest in the breast of Thy Father, penetrating all the secrets of His infinite wisdom, loving with infinite love the goodness of Him, who holds Thee within Himself, and drinking all the torrent of delights which issues from His divine breast. O that I might enter into this divine bosom! O that I might recline upon this divine breast, so as in some measure to be made partaker of the light, and love, and joy, which Thou there receivest! I cannot be satisfied, O Lord, with the bosom of Abraham, the father of the believing, but only with the bosom of Thy Father, who is the Father of the living; and where Thou art I desire to be, since Thou hast said, "Where I am, there also shall my minister be." (26)

2. O my soul, behold the joy which the Father has in enclosing in His breast such a Son, and the joy which the Son has in resting in the bosom of such a Father; enter by faith and contemplation into this bosom, to enjoy the joys of these two, which are one and the same joy, and rejoice with them, joining thy joy to theirs, that they may make thee one with themselves. But what art Thou

____

(25) Rom. viii. 17. Gal. iv. 7.
(26) Joan. xii. 26.

doing, O divine Word, from Thine eternity, in the midst of this breast? Wilt Thou, then, reserve it, so as to have to Thyself alone, none with Thee in it? O ineffable virtue of the Son, who, proceeding from His Father, jointly with Him produces the Holy Ghost, equally divine and almighty with themselves! I rejoice, O my God, in the joy which Thou enjoyest in this production, in which Thou communicatest to Him the same divinity that Thou receivedst from Thy Father, and with the same joy with which the Father did communicate it to Thee. O that it may be granted me to communicate without grudging to others, the good things which I receive from Thy holy hand, so that many may love Thee, as I desire to love Thee, world without end, Amen.

WITH THE HOLY GHOST.

1. After the same manner I will speak *to the third Person*, concerning the properties which belong to Him, saying:—

O sovereign Spirit, who proceedest from the Father and the Son, as from one beginning, with the eternal procession of love; I rejoice that Thou art eminently *Spirit*, and drawest, with an ineffable joy, *spirit* and life from each of the two Persons, from whom Thou proceedest.

i. Thou art the Spirit of the Father, from whom Thou receivest divinity and omnipotence, and the Spirit of the Son, from whom Thou also receivest His own wisdom; and Thou art the Spirit of both, from whom Thou receivest the infinite love with which they love one another; loving them with the same love with which Thou art beloved by them, and rejoicing as much in being beloved by them, as they rejoice in loving Thee, because You all three are one God, one goodness, and one love. O that I were united to Thee in one spirit, that I might be wholly converted into the spirit of love!

ii. Thou art properly *Spirit*, because Thou proceedest by a vehement *impulse* from the loving will of the Father and the Son; while yet Thou remainest within them in unity of essence and love, uniting with the bond of an ineffable affection the Persons from whom Thou dost proceed. O that there may proceed from Thee such an *impulse* of divine love, as may fill my whole will, and, piercing my heart, may carry it away, and join it to Thine, making of two one heart by love.

2. O divine Spirit, who art eminently holy, because Thou proceedest with love, the fountain of *holiness*, which consists not so much in knowing with wisdom, as in loving with great charity: I rejoice in Thy holiness, and in the joy with which Thou receivedst from the Father and the Son, from both of whom Thou proceedest, as a gift, to be liberally communicated to those who are capable of Thee. Give me the infinite gift of Thyself, that, by such a gift I also may become a spirit, like Thee in purity, and in the holiness of charity; and I may be enabled to give myself wholly to Thee, as Thou givest Thyself to me, that so I may enjoy Thy sovereign Deity, world without end, for all eternity.

POINT V.

1. From what has been said in the preceding point, I will consider the form and manner of *mental prayer*, and the interior communication with Almighty God, and its resemblance to that eternal communication which the three divine Persons have with each other.

i. For, as the Eternal Father, knowing His own divine essence, forms a conception and lively similitude of Himself, which is the Word, which always remains within the Father: even so, in prayer I ought to aim at a perfect knowledge of Almighty God, and at forming within myself a *true*, *proper*, and *perfect conception* of Him, the image and representation of that which is in Him, so as to accomplish that saying of St. Paul:—" That we all, beholding the glory of the Lord with open face, are transformed into the same image."(27)   And this knowledge I ought to maintain within myself, with the greatest possible continuity and steadiness.

ii. Moreover, as the Father and the Son, loving themselves mutually, produce that love which is the Holy Ghost, which also remains within God; even so, I, in knowing Almighty God, and in forming within myself this conception of His goodness, ought to *love* Him, and to produce within myself the affection of *love*, with others which accompany it, and to strive to make them remain in my heart as long as I possibly can; for then is accomplished that which the spouse said:—" I found him whom my soul loveth; I held him, and will not let him go." (28)   To *find* Him belongs to the *knowledge* and *desire* which seeks God our Lord, to *hold* Him is proper to the *understanding*, and to *love*, which possesses and enjoys Him.

iii. From these acts proceed the chief *joy* and *delight* of which my soul is capable; for in them consists the blessedness which I can attain to in this life.(29)   By them also is acquired everlasting blessedness, which consists in seeing Almighty God distinctly, and in loving Him and enjoying Him everlastingly.   Whence our communication with our Lord will be perfect, and very like that which the three divine Persons have with each other; for, as the glorious St. John says:—" When God shall appear, we shall be like to Him, because we shall see Him as He is."(30)

(27) 2 Cor. iii. 18.   (28) Cant. iii. 4.
(29) S. Th. 2, 2, q. clxxx. art. 7.   (30) 1 Joan. iii. 2.

iv. Finally, from these acts it will follow, that as the three divine Persons have one desire and one will in all that they work, and work it all jointly for the *good of the creatures;* so I also, by virtue of this interior communication with Almighty God, and united to Him by it, shall always delight to accomplish His will, and to *do good to others*, which is the true fruit of holy prayer. Hence, too, I may understand, that to be thus exercised in prayer is not to be idle, but to be busied and employed in the most noble of all possible occupations, and one resembling that which Almighty God carries on within Himself, although it is wont to be called idle, on account of the stillness which belongs to the contemplation of Mary, and by which it is distinguished from the noise and solicitude of the occupation and life of Martha. Hence the same Lord Himself said by holy David:—"Be still, and see that I am God:"(31) that is to say, disengage yourselves from other things, that you may attend to contemplation, and you shall see that I alone am God, by the glorious things of my divinity, of which I give interior testimony to him that practises it in contemplation.

2. Hence I will proceed farther to meditate on those mystical words in which St. John declares this mystery:—"There are three who give testimony in heaven, the Father, the Word, and the Holy Ghost, and these three are one. And there are three that give testimony on earth, the spirit, and the water, and the blood, and these three are one"(32) in giving this testimony. With regard to these words I will consider, how the three divine Persons, like lawful witnesses, of which three is the prescribed number, give full testimony of all things belonging to Themselves, and that with perfect harmony, being one and the same God. Such testimony They gave in the creation of

(31) Ps. xlv. 11.   (32) 1 Joan. v. 7.

the world, and especially in that of man, whom They made to Their "own image and likeness." And in the baptism and transfiguration of Christ our Lord, They gave similar testimony of His divinity, and afterwards of the truth of His doctrine, of the sanctity of His law, and of the efficacy of His grace, the Holy Ghost cooperating with them for that purpose, as has been already said. But more especially do they give testimony of His excellencies and perfections within the hearts of the just, with admirable signs of His divinity. And hence the same St. John says:— "He that believeth in the Son of God hath the testimony of God in himself," which testimony it is the proper work of the divine Spirit to afford, as St. Paul witnesses.(33) But the last and most clear and evident testimony is that which they give to the blessed in glory, where all see the three divine Persons, since it is impossible to see one without the other; and with this sight of all the three they shall remain satisfied and contented for all eternity.

Colloquy.—O most blessed Trinity, and most glorious Unity, what shall I give Thee for the most evident testimonies which Thou hast given, and givest, and wilt incessantly give us of Thyself? That which I desire is to embrace these three things which give testimony on earth:—"the spirit, and the water, and the blood;" adoring, loving, and imitating the *spirit* of Christ our Lord, washing myself with the *water* which flowed from His precious side, and enriching myself with the *blood* which distilled from His divine veins. O that there may be given me the *spirit* of love, the *water* of tears, and the *blood* of penance, that I may give testimony how much I owe to Thee, and may make myself one with Thee in the union of charity, to praise and glorify Thee in Thy eternal glory. Amen.

(33) 1 Joan. v. 10. Rom. viii. 16.

MEDITATION V.

ON THE INFINITE PERFECTION OF ALMIGHTY GOD.

WE call that perfect which contains all things that it can, and ought to have according to its nature, without wanting any one of them, however little it may be; for if any one of them is wanting to it, some imperfection is the result.(1) The same is likewise called beautiful, because it delights and refreshes the sight both of the body and of the soul. It is also called good, because it moves, affects, and draws after it the will of the beholder. These three names, therefore, in the sacred Scriptures are given to God, and to His works, because of their completeness in all things that their being requires and ought to possess. The force of these terms, then, being presupposed, we will consider the actual properties which they signify.

POINT I.

The first and supreme perfection of our great God, Three and One, is, to be so perfect, that in His own nature He *includes all the perfections and excellencies possible*, without any manner of imperfection; so that nothing at all is wanting to Him of all that belongs to God, nor is it possible to imagine any true perfection of which Almighty God is capable that is not in Him, in all the degrees of perfection possible for Him to have, without any bound or limit whatever.(2) Whence holy Scripture says:—that "of His greatness there is no end;"(3) that "the Spirit of the Lord" "containeth all things;" and

(1) S. Th. 1, p. q. iv. art. 1 et 2.   Ibid. q. v. art. 4, ad 2.
(2) S. Dionys. cap. 5, de Divin. Nom.   S. Aug. in Man. cap. 32.
(3) Ps. cxliv. 3.   Sap. i. 7.   Rom. xi. 36.

that "of Him, and by Him, and in Him are all things;" for in Him is infinite perfection, without the mixture of those imperfections which appear in the creatures. And therefore with great emotions of admiration and joy I will say to our Lord:—"Deus meus et omnia," "My God and all things."

Colloquy.—O my God, God of infinite majesty, I most firmly believe that Thou art " all things," since, in an unapproachable degree, Thou comprehendest the perfection of all things; for all things receive from Thee whatever perfection they have. Thou art " all things" also, because Thou art the beginning and the ending, the idea and exemplar of that perfection, which they all receive from Thee; and they are more perfect in proportion as their perfection approaches nearer Thine. Thou art " all things" to me that I can desire; Thou art my riches, my delight, my honour, and dignity, the portion of my inheritance, and my infinite treasure: (4) in Thee alone, without other things, I have all things, and without Thee all things are as nothing to me. O my soul, if thou seekest after *perfection*, embrace God, and in Him thou wilt find it most pure, without any mixture of imperfection. If thou desirest *beauty*, behold and contemplate Almighty God, because it is wholly in Him, without any mixture of deformity. If thou lovest *goodness*, love God, in whom it shines eminently, without any mixture of malice. O my God, and my all in all, when shall I come to behold Thee clearly in · Thy glory, where Thou art all things to all throughout all worlds? Amen.

This expression contains copious matter for meditation, taken in conjunction with that which the father of the prodigal said to his eldest son:—"Omnia mea tua sunt."

(4) S. Aug. Med. c. 12.

"All I have is thine."(5) In order, therefore, to penetrate more deeply into what it contains, I will consider the different degrees of perfection displayed in the being of created things, reducing them to four or five, which shall form the subject of the ensuing points.

POINT II.

1. In God our Lord are very eminently displayed the perfections of the *first degree* of creatures, which are *corporeal*, but *without life ;* such as the heavens, the stars, and the planets, the four elements and their various compounds; gold, and silver, and all precious stones; for all these God created, and gave them their beauty and splendour, and the properties and virtues by which they produce such wonderful effects.

i. All the perfections of these creatures are found in God, after a manner infinitely more perfect; for what in the creatures, by reason of their imperfection, is devoid of life, is in God with life. "All things," as St. John says, "were made by Him;" and "in Him was life;"(6) that is to say, before they were really made they had *life* in God, because God had living in Himself very eminently the perfection which He was about to communicate to His creatures, and a living idea of them, such as the carpenter has of the house which he is to make.(7)

ii. Hence it is that God our Lord can *do without creatures* what they do, as, for instance, give light without the sun, heat without fire, coolness without wind, and moisture without water, and produce without the earth what He usually produces by means of it, since He contains in Himself the virtue and perfection of all these creatures;

(5) Luc. xv. 31.
(6) Joan. i. 3.   (7) S. Aug. Beda et alii.

and if He makes use of them, it is not from necessity, but to show His infinite bounty, as we shall see hereafter.

iii. Hence also it is that Holy Scripture, to express to us the perfections of Almighty God, applies the *names of these creatures* to Him, calling Him " the sun of justice,"(8) the " morning star,"(9) " a consuming fire,"(10) a fountain of " living water,"(11) a spirit which " breathes where He will,"(12) &c. And the riches of His grace and glory it expresses by the names of gold, silver, pearls, and precious stones; and from the beauty, excellency, and marvellous properties of these things, carries us onward to contemplate the beauty and splendour of Almighty God, and of His excellent properties.

But these names are given to Almighty God in such a manner as to lead me to understand and confess that everything whatever in these creatures is but a shadow or figure, and as nothing in respect of that which is in God our Lord, in comparison of whom the heavens are not clean, the sun does not shine, the moon is not beautiful, and all beauty is deformity. With each of these considerations I should move my heart to affections of admiration, love, and thanksgiving, and of joy at having a God so beautiful and so perfect in all things.

Colloquy.—O infinite God, I rejoice that the sun and moon admire Thy beauty, and acknowledge that theirs is nothing in respect of Thine. O beloved of my heart, if I so much rejoice in beholding the beauty and perfection of these creatures, how much more shall I rejoice in beholding that beauty and perfection of Thine from which they all proceed? Let me therefore love Thee above them all, since Thou art infinitely more beautiful and more perfect than all; and

(8) Mal. iv. 2.   (9) Apoc. xxii. 16.
(10) Deut. iv. 21.   (11) Joan. vii. 38.   (12) Joan. iii. 8.

let me not love any of them but for the love of Thee, from whom they receive all their perfection.

2. Hence also I will gather what madness it is to leave Almighty God, who is most infinitely perfect, for the sake of enjoying the perfection and beauty of these creatures, or for the delight or emolument which I may have in the possession of them, since, as the Scripture says:— "All gold in comparison of" Him "is as a little sand, and silver in respect to" Him "shall be counted as clay,"(13) and all riches reputed as nothing, and the delight which may be taken in them is as water flowing into "broken cisterns," for the sake of which it is most unreasonable to leave the fountain of living water, and the infinite treasure of all perfection. Finally, I will sometimes apply myself to consider the properties of some of these creatures, in order to understand the perfections of Almighty God, who i compared to them, as St. Dionysius did, who reckoned about thirty-four properties of fire, from which he gathered corresponding properties in God, who is called "Ignis consumens," "a consuming fire."(14) This I also will do, and will rejoice that God has all these properties, and many more, and that He can do by Himself alone what He does by means of His creatures.

POINT III.

Similarly it is to be considered, that in God our Lord are also in an eminent manner the perfections of the *second degree* of *corporeal* creatures, those that have a *vegetative life*, and increase and grow, and produce others like themselves, such as trees, plants, herbs, and odoriferous flowers, the properties of which are displayed in the fruits, leaves, and seeds which they produce, through the virtue their

(13) Sap. vii. 9.
(14) Lib. de Cœlest. Hier. cap. 14. Deut. iv. 24.

Creator gave them. In Him all these properties exist in infinite perfection, and He Himself greatly glories in them, saying:—" With me is the beauty of the field;"(15) that is, the beauty of all the trees, plants, herbs, and flowers in the gardens and fields of the whole world; and hence He is sometimes called a lily, at other times a vine, and at other times a tree of life. From all these considerations affections are to be drawn, as has been said in the preceding point.

2. In the same manner also there are in Almighty God the perfections of all *living creatures endowed with sensation*, such as the beasts of the earth, the birds of the air, and the fishes of the sea, the properties of which are innumerable and admirable; for in some greatness is displayed, in others strength, in others swiftness, in others beauty, in others prudence and a kind of wisdom, all of which are found in Almighty God, in infinite perfection. And therefore in holy Scripture He is compared to these living creatures, that from the perfections which we find in them, we may ascend to the knowledge of those which He has in Himself. Thus He is called a lion, for His fortitude; a lamb, for His meekness; a hart, for His swiftness; an eagle, for His care of His offspring. But in Almighty God these perfections exist in such a manner, as not to be mingled with the imperfections which appear in these creatures; for there is in God the fortitude of the lion without cruelty, and the meekness of the lamb without deficiency of understanding, and so of the rest. Whence it appears that from all that I see, perfect and imperfect, good and bad, beautiful and deformed, I may gather the infinite perfection of Almighty God, setting aside, in my conceptions of Him, all that is evil, imperfect, and de-

(14) Ps. xlix. 11.

formed, and ascribing to Him all that is good, perfect, and beautiful, after a far more excellent kind of perfection.

Colloquy.—O my beloved, as I separate in Thee the "precious from the vile," (15) in order thus to know Thee, even so do I desire to separate in myself the precious from the vile, in order thus to be made agreeable to Thee. Grant me, O Lord, to be made partaker, by means of Thy grace, of this high and sovereign division which belongs to Thee by nature, that, being made free from imperfections, I may remain pure and perfect in all virtues. Amen.

POINT IV.

Fourthly is to be considered, how there are in Almighty God all the perfections of the *intellectual creatures*, both men and angels, whom He created to His own image and likeness, and gave them their spiritual being, and with it memory, understanding, will, and freedom of judgment, arts, sciences, virtues, graces, and all the power and excellence displayed in all and each of them.

1. All these are found in Him with infinitely greater excellence; for as He Himself demands in a certain psalm: —"He that planted the ear, shall He not hear? or He that formed the eye, doth He not consider? He that teacheth man knowledge,"(16) shall He want knowledge? And He that gives virtue and sanctity, shall He be deficient in them? Or He that imparts to others the power they have, shall He be impotent Himself? Wherefore when I see the abilities of men in arts and artificial works, as in architecture, the manufacture of glass and paper, weaving, painting, music, and other such things, I will at once ascend to the consideration of the infinite wisdom of Almighty God, from whom all these inventions originally proceeded. And when I see the prudence and

(15) Jer. xv. 19.   (16) Ps. xciii. 9.

forethought of kings and governors in their government, and the exalted virtues which shine in saints and
perfect men, I will lift up my eyes, to consider the infinite
excellences of Almighty God in all these things, and will
praise, glorify, and love Him for them without ceasing.

2. Hence I will deduce,

i. That God is a *pattern of infinite perfection*, which I
should always look upon, in order to admire in Him those
infinite perfections which are inimitable, and to imitate
those which admit of imitation, according to that which our
Redeemer said to His disciples:—" Be you therefore perfect,
as also your heavenly Father is perfect;"(17) as if He had
said, Take care that no perfection of virtue be wanting to
you of all those that you can attain to, even as your Father
is so perfect in all, that none are wanting to Him.

Colloquy.—O most perfect Father, from whom all
perfection proceeds, give me that which Thou commandest, that so I may attain to that which Thou
desirest in me.

ii. Secondly, I will gather, that as the tree is known by
its *fruits, for " a good tree bringeth forth good fruits,*"(18)
so the perfection of Almighty God is understood and
known by His *works;* for, as the holy Scripture says:—
" God saw all things that He had made, and they were
very good" and "*perfect,*"(19) not only the great things,
such as the heavens and elements, but even the very least,
such as ants and worms. After His example, therefore,
I also will take heed to be perfect, and manifest my perfection in all my works, great and little, and endeavour to
follow the counsel of the wise man:—" In all thy works
keep the pre-eminence."(20)

iii. Finally, as imperfect things have recourse for the

(17) Mat. v. 48.   (18) Mat. vii. 17.
(19) Gen. i. 31. Deut. xxxii. 4.   (20) Ecclus. xxxiii. 23.

perfection which they want to the perfect in that kind, as he that wants heat has recourse to the fire, so I, seeing myself to be imperfect, ought to have recourse to Him that is infinitely perfect, in order that He may perfect me, and give me what is wanting to me.

Colloquy.—O infinite God, Thine eyes have seen my imperfection; of Thee have I received what I have, and Thou alone canst give me what I want: perfect, O Lord, in me the work Thou hast begun, and make me so perfect, that nothing may be wanting to me. Amen.

POINT V.

1. Fifthly is to be considered, how all the perfections which we ascribe to Almighty God, although innumerable, as dispersed among the creatures, yet in Him are but *simply one*, and are all contained in Him, as many little pieces of money are contained in one piece of greater value;(21) and thus in Almighty God, His wisdom, His bounty, His charity, His mercy, His omnipotence, His strength, and the rest, are all one and the same thing, without any kind of composition or division, and each perfection is contained in all, and all in each, so that His bounty is His wisdom and omnipotence, and His omnipotence is the same wisdom, and so of the rest. And perchance it was for this cause that the Wise man says:—that the Spirit of God is "one," and "manifold," yet "containing all spirits."(22) Whence it is, that not only in the frame of this world, but also in every work of Almighty God, considered in itself, the conjunction and union of His admirable perfections evidently appears, and by this conjunction and union we may come to know the author of the works to be potent, wise, good, infinite, amiable, &c.

2. Hence I will draw two affections and firm purposes of great utility.

(21) S. Th. 1 p. q. iii. art. 7. (22) Sap. vii. 23.

i. The *first* affection is an inward *desire* to *imitate* this infinite *simplicity* of the Divine Being, by *simplifying* and *purifying* my *intention* as much as possible, so that in all my works, however many, there may shine the purest intention of pleasing God alone, for His own sake. In such an intention are virtually included great perfections; and therefore Christ our Lord said:—"If thy eye be single, thy whole body will be lightsome."(23)

Colloquy.—O most perfect God, enlighten the eye of my understanding, in order that in all the creatures I may behold Thee, their Creator, from whom they receive their perfection. Purify also the eye of my affection, that in all of them I may love Thee, their benefactor, from whom they receive their goodness. Illuminate likewise the eye of my intention, that in all my works I may purely and sincerely seek Thee, their last end, from whom they are to receive their splendour, that so Thou mayest be glorified in them, world without end. Amen.

2. The *second purpose* ought to be, to combine with all my works the display of the *various virtues* that chiefly belong to them, so that each work may be after its manner, "*one*," and "*manifold*," and may contain many "spirits" and affections towards Almighty God. Thus, if I pray, fast, or give alms, this work should be accompanied by the love of God, confidence, obedience, humility, filial fear, and other such affections. And perchance it was for this cause that Christ our Lord called the intention the "*eye*," and its work the "*body;*" thus giving us to understand that as the body has many members and parts, so every work ought to exhibit the exercise of various virtues, and be directed with the eye of a simple and pure intention to the glory of Almighty God.

(23) Mat. vi. 22. Luc. xi. 34.

MEDITATION VI.

ON THE SINGULAR GOODNESS AND HOLINESS OF GOD.

There are two sorts of goodness in the creatures, one *natural*, which consists in having all the parts necessary to the integrity of their nature; of which goodness holy Scripture speaks, when it says:—"God saw all things that He had made, and they were '*valde bona*,' very good;" (1) the other, *moral*, which is proper to the intellectual creatures, and consists in having all the virtues belonging to the state of each, and exercising them in a manner appropriate to it, and this is called by another name, *holiness*. And although these two kinds of goodness may be separated in the creatures, so that the first may be without the second, which depends on the freedom of the will; yet in Almighty God they are joined together, for the second is as natural to Him as the first; although He manifests and more freely exercises the acts of the first in the order of creation, or in the perfections of the creatures. This meditation, therefore, will comprehend both, presupposing what has been said before.

POINT I.

1. Let us consider that God our Lord is infinitely good, and that His goodness chiefly consists in *three things*.

i. The *first* is, that He *contains* in Himself *all* the *degrees* and *kinds* of goodness that are found in the creatures, in such a manner, that there cannot be imagined any goodness which is not found in Almighty God with infinite excellence. Hence our Lord answered Moses, when he besought

(1) S. Tho. 1. p. q. 6.

Him to show him His face and His glory :—" Ego ostendam tibi omne bonum," " I will show thee all good ;" (2) giving him to understand that God is, and contains in Himself, *all good*.

ii. The *second* excellence is, that God has all this goodness *of His own essence*, so that it is neither derived from any other, nor added to His divine nature, nor capable of being taken from it, as things may be added and taken from us; but it is as much a part of His nature to be good and holy, as it is to be God. In this sense Christ our Lord answered the ruler, who called Him good, believing Him to be a mere man:—" Why callest thou me good? None is good but one, that is God,"(3) for God alone is essential goodness.

iii. The *third* excellence is, that the goodness and holiness of Almighty God so far *exceed* the *goodness of all things* created, or that can be created, that in comparison of Him they do not deserve the name of good, and their goodness is as if it were not. In this sense also Christ our Lord said, that none is good but God only, and that one is good, that is, God; and in the same sense the mother of Samuel said :—" There is none holy as the Lord is; for there is no other beside Thee:"(4) that is, there is none that can be called holy but God, for He alone deserves the name of holiness.

2. Hence is drawn the foundation of that *true* and *profound humility* which the saints have in the sight of Almighty God. It is based upon these two last considerations: that all the holiness of men is added to their nature, and is changeable in itself; and that, in comparison with that of God it is even as nothing. And therefore one of Job's friends, comparing the angels with Almighty God,

(2) Exod. xxxiii. 19.   (3) Marc. x. 18. Luc. xviii. 19.
(4) 1 Reg. ii. 2.

said:—" Behold among His saints, none is unchangeable, and the heavens are not pure in His sight."(5)

Colloquy.— O most holy God, to whom alone belongs the name of " Holy of holies," because Thou art the beginning, pattern, and end of all holiness, I rejoice in Thy singular goodness and holiness, which Thou possessest with infinite firmness and stability. I confess, O Lord, that I can attain to no holiness unless Thou give it to me, nor can persevere in it unless Thou preserve me; and however much Thou mayest impart to me, it will be so little in respect of Thine, that, covering my face with shame, I will cry out like the Seraphim :—" Holy, holy, holy, the Lord God of hosts;" thrice art Thou holy, because of the three excellences of Thy holiness. Therefore I beseech Thee to ground me in this profound humility, that so I may be worthy to ascend to a very high degree of sanctity. Amen.

POINT II.

Dwelling more in detail upon what has been said, I will consider, secondly, the infinite virtues of God our Lord, in which His infinite goodness and holiness consist. Of these I will ponder certain peculiar excellencies.

1. The *first* is, that God our Lord possesses *all* the *virtues* that are distributed amongst the saints, as well men as angels, and that *in an infinite degree*, and *without* the *imperfections* and *limitations* to which these virtues are subject in them. So that He has infinite wisdom, justice, fortitude, and temperance; infinite charity, liberality, and mercy; infinite meekness, clemency, patience, with all the rest; and none whatever are wanting to Him, which do not presuppose imperfection in the subject in which they are found. And for this reason He is loudly proclaimed

(5) Job xv. 15; et iv. 18.

to be "omne bonum," "Dominus Deus virtutum;" "all good," and "the Lord God of virtues:" in whom not one or another virtue, but all virtues together, are contained: for all belong to the infinite goodness and holiness of Almighty God, and every one draws others with it, being closely linked with all the rest. And hence it is, that when these virtues reach their full perfection, they are like rings linked together, as they are in Almighty God, whom I ought to imitate in this, and endeavour to excel, not only in one virtue, but in all, saying: O God of virtues, make me like to Thyself in all virtue.

2. The *second* excellence is, that the virtues of God our Lord are an *idea* and infinite pattern of all those which either are or can be in the saints, whose virtues are the more or less perfect the more or less they appear, and are like to the divine virtues, which are so infinite, that none other than God Himself can possibly comprehend them; yet we will search into their immense greatness, and endeavour to arrive at some notion of them, by those which are in the blessed saints.

To this purpose it will very much assist to consider *four sorts of virtues* which St. Thomas proposes, with very grave and spiritual words. Beginning, therefore, from the lesser:—

i. The first are *political* and *moral*, proper to those men who govern their life according to the dictates and rule of reason, and moderate the fury of their passions so as not to decline from this rule.(6)

ii. Other virtues there are of such as *aspire to the divine likeness*, and desire to conform themselves to it, and to accomplish that which Christ our Lord said:—" Be you, therefore, perfect, as also your heavenly Father is perfect." These, by the virtue of prudence, come to despise

(6) S. Th. i. 2, q. lxi. art. 1.

show Thy face, and we shall be saved."(7)   O king of virtues, give me those in which Thy kingdom consists, that by means of them Thou mayest reign in me.   I will also make a canticle of praise to God our Lord for His virtues, and invite and provoke all to praise Him for them, and they themselves also to praise our Lord, saying with David:— "Praise ye the Lord in His holy places; praise ye Him in the firmament of His power; praise ye Him for His mighty acts; praise ye Him according to the multitude of His greatness."(8)   Let all His angels praise Him, let all His virtues praise Him, let His mercy praise Him, and let His holiness praise and glorify Him.   Amen.

POINT III.

1. Thirdly, *the infinite purity and sanctity of God in all His works*, are to be considered, in which He discovers those two parts of holiness and justice which David calls, to "decline from evil, and" to "do good,"(9) i. e., to be exempt from all evil, and to possess all good.

i. For, first the virtues of God our Lord are so pure, that it *is impossible to admit anything contrary or defective*, or which may subtract one tittle from His infinite perfection; so that in God there cannot be either vice, sin, defect, or any imperfection; it being as proper to His goodness to be impeccable, as it is proper to Him to be God. It is not possible that He can sin through ignorance of good, because He knows all things; neither through forgetfulness or inadvertence, because He is mindful of all things; nor yet through imbecility, because He can do all things; nor through surprise of sudden passion, because He prevents all things; nor through fear, for He fears none; nor through malice, because He is the chief good, and the first rule, from which He cannot depart.   Where-

(7) Ps. lxxix. 8.   (8) Ps. cl. 1.   (9) Ps. xxxvi. 27.

fore it is impossible that in Almighty God there should be lying, infidelity, deceit, falsehood, impatience, tyranny, or other sin, or any the least shadow of them, because His Divine eyes are so "pure," that they cannot "look on iniquity,"(10) i. e., with approbation.

ii. Hence it is that God not only cannot sin by Himself, but He *cannot be the cause of sin in others*, by inclining and moving them to it; because this is very foreign to His infinite purity, and would be contrary to the principles of His nature, and to the order of His infinite wisdom and goodness.   Whence also it is, that although God could take upon Him human nature, and subject Himself to all the penalties of this life, yet was it impossible for Him to take the same with subjection to sin.(11)

iii. Hence I conclude that the infinite goodness and sanctity of God shines in the *purity and sanctity of His works*, and that His virtues are not idle in Him, but whenever He works, He discovers Himself in His works.   Hence David said:—"The Lord is faithful in all His words...The Lord is just in all His ways, and holy in all His works;"(12) and this last he repeats twice, to mark that God wills that men should imitate Him with great solicitude in this respect; and therefore he said to his people, "Do not defile your souls, nor touch ought thereof, lest you be unclean," but "be holy, because I am holy;" and with the same words St. Peter exhorts all the faithful, that "in all manner of conversation" they should be "holy."(13)

Colloquy.—O most holy God, who of Thine only goodness hast chosen us, that we might be holy and unspotted in "Thy sight," (14) grant that I may be

(10) Hab. i. 13.

(11) S. Th. 1, p. q. xlix. art. 3; et i. 2, q. lxxix. art. 1.   S. Th. 3, p. q. xv. art. 1.

(12) Ps. cxliv. 14, 18.   (13) Levit. xi. 43.   1 Pet. i. 16.

(14) Ephes. i. 4.

such an one, and drive from me all vice, and adorn me with all virtue and sanctity. O celestial Seraphim, who praise your God with the name of holy, in which He so greatly delights, vouchsafe to come from heaven with some coals of love, and purify my lips like Isaias, as also my heart, that I may be perfectly pure and holy in the presence of my God. Amen.

2. From this consideration I am principally to conceive a great purpose of *withdrawing myself from all kinds of sin*, whether great or little, and from every defect, imperfection, or savour of them, as far as is possible for me, remembering what our Lord said to His people:—" Thou shalt be perfect and without spot before the Lord thy God;"(15) and strive also to imitate on earth that purity which is in heaven, where the Church, as the apostle St. Paul says, shall be glorious, " not having spot, or wrinkle, or any such thing."(16)   This I may, after my manner, accomplish in this life, if I live with care not to fall in little things; and if I shall fall as being feeble, I will presently purge myself of them, so that in any hour and part of the day God may say unto my soul, " Thou art all fair, O my love, and there is not a spot in thee."(17)

3. Finally, I draw from this consideration a great resolution *not to glory in this life of honours*, genealogies, dignities, wit, learning, nor other talents, but principally of virtue and holiness, remembering that God our Lord did glory more in these than in all His attributes in relation to us. For not having a proper name by which to call the third Person of the most holy Trinity, he applied the name of goodness and holiness to Him; and called Him not eternal Spirit, or immense, but Holy Spirit, and the good Spirit. And with the same name will God be named by men, as He was by the Seraphim.

(15) Deut. xviii. 13.   (16) Ephes. v. 27.   (17) Cant. iv. 7.

Colloquy.—O Divine Spirit, who tookest unto Thee the name of holy because Thou greatly gloriest in holiness, grant me that I may glory in the same more than in all things else created, procuring to appropriate this holiness to myself with great solicitude, so to be holy with great firmness and constancy in Thy presence, world without end.   Amen.

MEDITATION VII.

OF THE GREAT INCLINATION WHICH THE GOODNESS OF ALMIGHTY GOD HAS TO COMMUNICATE ITSELF TO ALL, ESPECIALLY TO MEN: AND OF THE MEANS BY WHICH HE COMMUNICATES IT, AND BESTOWS INNUMERABLE BENEFITS UPON US.

This Meditation will be the foundation of all the divine benefits, which spring as a fountain from the infinite goodness of Almighty God, who in His eternity necessarily communicated all His divinity to His Son by knowledge, and to the Holy Ghost by love, and afterwards liberally communicated Himself to His creatures, by all possible means, as shall be seen in the points ensuing.

POINT I.

The first point to consider will be the great inclination which the goodness of God has to communicate itself, and to do good to others; for, as St. Dionysius says, "bonum est diffusivum sui"—"Good is a diffuser and communicator of itself;"(1) and the greater the good, and the greater its ability to communicate itself, the greater is its inclination to do so.   And, as God is the chief good, so has He a great inclination to communicate Himself, by all the means that He may, and in this communication He shows great excellencies. (2)

1. The first excellency is, that He does not communi-

(1) Cap. 4. de Divin. Nom.   (2) S. Th. 3 p. q. i. art. 1.

cate Himself *of necessity*, force, or violence, but of His only goodness, and free will, because He is good, and will follow the inclination of His goodness in doing good. Whence He greatly obliges me to love and serve Him after the same manner, saying with David:—" I will freely sacrifice to Thee, and will give praise, O God, to Thy name, because it is good." (3)

2. The second excellency is, that He does *not* communicate Himself *for His own profit*, but for ours; for, in communicating Himself to others, no good arises to Himself, since He was as blessed before He created the world as He is now, and so David says:—" Thou art my God, for Thou hast no need of my goods;" and presently adds the fruit which he gathered from this consideration, " To the saints who are in His land, He hath made wonderful all my desires in them:"(4) as if he had said, Because I can bring no profit to Thee by my works, Thou hast vouchsafed me this favour, that my will and desires be directed to do good to Thy servants, and to repay Thee the good which Thou dost to me, with the good I do to others.

3. The third excellency is, that He *suffers not this inclination of doing good to be idle*, but exercises it, and imparts His blessings by all possible means, even the choicest. So that, good being diffusive of itself, God Himself diffuses His goodness all that He may, according to the order of His infinite wisdom; and thus obliges me also to diffuse myself in His holy service, and for the good of my neighbours, by doing them all the good that I am able, and that with the greatest perfection that is possible for me. Wherefore, when I pray, I will " pour out my soul," like Anna, " before the Lord," (5) or like David, " pour out my prayer" (6) before Him, and employ all my

(3) Ps. liii. 8.   (4) Ps. xv. 2, 3.   (5) 1 Reg. i. 15.
(6) Ps. xiv. 13. Ps. lxi. 9.

powers therein. And when I love I will pour forth my heart and affections before our Lord, and employ all in loving Him.

Colloquy.—O supreme good, who greatly desirest to communicate Thyself, for if Thou didst not communicate Thyself, it were impossible that any good should be found out of Thee ; communicate to me these excellencies by which Thou dost communicate Thyself, to the end that I may love, serve, and obey Thee, not by compulsion, nor yet from fear, but willingly, and from love : not for mine own emolument, but only for Thy service : not with a penurious and niggardly, but with an ample and generous mind, doing the most that I may in favour of my neighbours, and of Thee, like as Thou hast done in favour of me. Amen.

POINT II.

To particularize this communication of the divine goodness, we must consider, secondly, how He communicated being and natural goodness to creatures, and divided amongst them four degrees of great beauty and perfection, which we have put down in the Fifth Meditation.   For to some He gave only a corporal being, although with great variety of perfections, as is to be seen in the heavens, elements, and mixed bodies.   To others He gave a vegetative life, as to trees, flowers, and plants.   To others a sensitive life, as to beasts, birds, and fishes.   To others a spiritual being, and intellectual life, as to the angels of the three hierarchies; and lastly, all these four degrees He gathered together in man, composed of a body and soul, giving him being as to the heavens and elements, life as to the plants, sense as to the beasts, and understanding as to the angels, for which cause man is called, " Omnis creatura," " every creature, "(7)—an abbreviated world.   So that these four

(7) Marc. xvi. 15.   S. Greg. Hom. xxix. in Evang.   Gen. ii. 6.

degrees of being and perfection are as the four rivers, which flowed from the fountain of Paradise, which signifies the infinite goodness of Almighty God, watering on all sides both earth and heaven; and, finally, all four gather themselves into man, thus making him much like to paradise itself, whence they came. Hence I will draw great affections of admiration and joy, of gratitude and love, for the marvellous manner in which God our Lord communicates Himself to men, admiring the infinite wisdom which He thus displays, rejoicing in His omnipotency, grateful for His liberality, and loving His infinite bounty. (8)

Colloquy.—O supreme Goodness, what thanks shall I give Thee for this variety of perfections with which Thou hast adorned my nature! Now I see with how great reason Thou commandest me to love Thee in this four-fold manner, " with my whole heart, with my whole soul, with all my strength, and with all my mind," since it is but reasonable that all I have received of Thy goodness should employ itself in loving Thee without end. I will therefore love Thee with my whole heart for the corporal being which Thou hast given me. I will love Thee with my whole soul, for the life whereby I live. I will love Thee with all my strength, for the senses and powers which I use. I will love Thee with all my mind, for the spirit and understanding which Thou hast given me. Oh that there did flow forth from my bowels four " rivers of living waters,"(9) full of the fervent affections of love and of joy, of praise and of gratitude, for the four rivers of benefits with which Thou hast all over watered me !

POINT III.

1. Thirdly, I will consider how the divine goodness, not

(8) S. Th. 2, 2, q. xliv. art. 4, et 5.   (9) Joan. vii. 38.

contenting itself with this manner of communication, chose *another most excellent method,* comprising four other degrees, or manners, which far exceed all in the order of nature. i. The first is the supernatural being of grace, by which men and angels come to be " partakers of the divine nature,"(10) sons and friends of the same God; and to this being is annexed charity, with the other supernatural virtues and gifts of the Holy Ghost. ii. The second is the being of glory, by which the just are made perpetually " like" to Almighty God, in the glorious properties which He has, and reign with Him in His kingdom.(11) iii. The third and supreme is the personal being of the same God, who communicated the second Person of the most holy Trinity to the nature of man. And if it had been convenient that the Eternal Father, or the Holy Ghost, should have communicated Their own personal being to another nature; or, that the Son Himself, should have communicated His to many other natures, He would not have omitted to do so, either for lack of goodness, or of an infinite inclination which He has to communicate Himself to His creatures, of which communication we have spoken largely in the Second Part of these Meditations. iv. The fourth manner is the most admirable; because, as it was not convenient that the Son of God should communicate His personal being to many natures, His infinite goodness inclined Him to communicate that divine being, with the two natures, divine and human, to all men, in the most holy Sacrament of the Altar, conjoining them, after an ineffable manner, with the species of bread and wine, and in them we receive Christ, true God and true Man. (12)

(10) 2 Pet. i. 4.   (11) 1 Joan. iii. 2.
(12) S. Th. 3, p. q. iv. et. v.

2. In these four degrees of benefits there are two excellent things which I will ponder.

i. The infinite goodness of God would satisfy its infinite inclination, to diffuse itself by communicating itself to man, and not to angels. By this He showed clearly that His "delights were to be with the children of men," (13) and that He not only created them to His image and likeness, but also ordained that one of them should be the Word itself, who is the image and infinite similitude of the Father, and one God with Him.

Colloquy.—O infinite goodness of our Lord, and supreme Lord! If we men are so much bound to Thee, for having conjoined in us the four rivers of benefits in our natural being, how much more are we indebted to Thee, for having conjoined in our nature these four rivers of incomparable benefits in our supernatural being! If we are so much obliged for having had a created being imparted to us, how much more are we bound for having had the very uncreated Being communicated to us! It seemed little to Thee, O my God, to communicate to us the goods which are external to Thee, and therefore Thou wouldest communicate Thyself also! O that such a manner of goodness were granted me, that I might have a vehement inclination to communicate to Thee whatever I have, employing all in loving and serving Thee, who hast done me so great a good! And since all the rivers which flow from the sea return again to that from whence they flowed,(14) it is meet that all these rivers, which have flowed from the immense sea of Thy goodness, should return to it by thanksgiving, attributing to Thine infinite goodness alone all the good which is found in our nature.

ii. The next thing to be considered is, that Almighty

<hr>

(13) **Prov. viii. 31.**   (14) **Eccles. i. 7.**

God, in His infinite goodness, seeing that it was not convenient to communicate His divine being to all created natures, to satisfy His infinite inclination, chose to communicate it to one, in which were united all the four degrees of being, distributed amongst the creatures of the world; and in such a most fitting manner He communicated Himself to all, and honoured all. For He honoured all bodily natures in communicating His divine being to our body; He honoured all spiritual natures in communicating Himself to our spirit; and for this cause I ought to give Him great thanks, and invite all creatures to praise our Lord, for the part which they have in this sovereign benefit, and animate and encourage myself to become holy, " Corpore et spiritu," " Both in body and spirit," (15) since the infinite goodness of Almighty God so greatly desired to honour and aggrandize both the one and the other. Other manners in which the goodness of God communicates itself particularly to the elect, shall be set down in the ensuing meditations.

MEDITATION VIII.

HOW AMIABLE THE GOODNESS OF GOD IS, AND HOW WORTHY TO BE BELOVED WITH SINGULAR LOVE, BOTH FOR ITSELF AND FOR THE INNUMERABLE GOODS WHICH IT COMMUNICATES TO US, AND FOR THE INFINITE DELIGHTS WHICH IT CONTAINS, AND WHICH FLOW FROM IT.

The principal property of goodness is to be amiable, and by the same the philosophers defined good, saying:— " Bonum est quod omnia appetunt," " Good is that which all love and desire," (1) because it moves our will and appetites to love and desire it. The respects and motives to love goodness are reduced to three heads. For, first,

(15) 1 Cor. vii. 34.   (1) S. Th. 1, p. q. v. art. 6.

goodness is amiable for itself, and for the perfection which it has. Secondly, it is amiable because it is profitable to us, and for the good which it does to us. Thirdly, because it is delectable, and causes delight in him who possesses it; and this is one of the reasons why commonly good is divided into honest, profitable, and delectable, calling that profitable, not only which is the means of obtaining the end, but also which is the cause of any good or profit to us. These three titles shine infinitely in the goodness of Almighty God, so as to render it infinitely amiable, as shall be seen in the points ensuing.

POINT I.

The goodness of God is greatly amiable for itself, and for the infinite bounty and perfection which it contains; for the greater any goodness or beauty is, the more amiable it is. Thus the goodness or beauty which is infinite, will be infinitely amiable for itself, because it is the last end to which all good is ordained, for it is ordained to no other end than to itself.

1. Hence it follows, first, that *God alone can love His goodness as much as it can and deserves to be loved.* He loves it with infinite love, takes delight in it, and rejoices in it with infinite joy. And for this I also ought greatly to rejoice, that the Father, the Son, and the Holy Ghost, satisfy all the love that His infinite goodness requires; and that it is so infinite, that no man, nor angel, can love it with so great a love as it deserves: and to wonder with amazement at this immensity, for it is likewise a kind of love to acknowledge myself overcome, and that I cannot love Almighty God as much as He deserves to be loved.

Colloquy.—O most amiable God, O that I could love Thee as Thou art amiable, and deservest to be beloved! O that my soul were capable of infinite love, to give the same wholly to Thine infinite bounty! O that I did "languish with love"(2) like the spouse, fainting with the desire of love, and sick that I cannot love Thee as much as I desire.

2. Hence, secondly, *I ought to love* this infinite goodness of Almighty God *more than myself* and more than all the amiable things of this life; yea, and with far greater love if it were possible for me. For though I cannot love it with all the love that it deserves, yet it is just that I should love it with all the love of which I am capable, without subtracting the breadth of a hair, and this is what our Lord·signifies, when, with such frequent repetition, He commands us to love Him with our "whole heart," with our "whole soul," with "all our strength," and with "all our mind," (3) i. e. with the greatest love and endeavour possible, esteeming Him more than all that is created, or can be created.

Colloquy.—O great Goodness, give me the greatest love that is possible for me to have, that I may love Thee with all the same. O that the love of all the angels and seraphim, and of all the saints, both in heaven and earth, were laid up in my heart, to love Thee as much as they altogether, although with this I should not be satisfied, for beholding Thine infinite goodness, charity can have no bounds, nor can the fire of love ever say "it is enough,"(4) for Thy goodness continually enkindles and nourishes it more and more.

3. Hence I will gather, in the third place, that the *principal motive of my love ought to be the goodness of Almighty God* for itself, because it is the last end and motive of love, and it were a great disorder to love it

<hr>

(2) Cant. ii. 5.
(3) Deut. vi. 5.   Mat. xxii. 37.   Marc. xii. 30.   Luc. x. 27,
(4) Prov. xxx. 16.

principally for any other thing out of itself, which may blemish the purity of my love. But in this goodness I may discover and imagine infinite titles which God has to be loved, and for which I both may and am bound to love Him. These titles are as many as there are perfections containing His goodness, in Almighty God. And, therefore, His wisdom, omnipotence, liberality, and mercy, are infinitely amiable, for the goodness and perfection which shine in them; and for this cause the spouse says of her beloved, that He is, "Totus desiderabilis," "All desirable and ' all lovely.' "(5) For there is nothing in God that is to be abhorred, but all things in Him are very amiable; even His vindicative justice, by which He chastises sinners for their sins, is desirable and amiable, and worthy to be loved, because in it also shines the goodness of God, since, without it, He would not be entirely good. Wherefore, I ought likewise to rejoice at this, and to joy that God revenges His own injuries, and chastises those who commit them, in this life and in the other; and that He has made a hell and purgatory, like as He made a heaven and paradise, since all appertain to the entire perfection of His divine goodness.

Colloquy.—O Beloved of my soul, Thou art altogether amiable to me, because all is good which is in Thee. O that all were likewise amiable to Thee which is in me! Take, Lord, from my soul all kind of sin and spot, that I may be wholly beautiful in Thine eyes, and amiable to Thy Heart. Amen.

4. Hence, finally I will gather, *how abominable a thing it is to hate a God so good,* and a goodness so amiable and compassionate of the blindness and malice of sinners, who abhor God, either because He forbids unlawful delights, or because He chastises them with His justice, since even

(5) Cant. v. 16.

for this He deserves to be loved, and, therefore, with great reason Christ our Lord said: The wicked "have hated both me and my Father, without any cause"(6) or reason.

Colloquy.—O supreme Goodness, who deservest to be loved with infinite love, and by infinite lovers, if there were so many, suffer not that there be any man that does not love Thee ; open the eyes of those that abhor Thee, for if they knew Thee with a lively faith, never would they hate Thee. O that the day were now come, when I might see Thee clearly, and love Thee above all, because it is impossible to sce Thee and not love Thee.

POINT II.

The second shall be to consider how the divine goodness is infinitely amiable, not only for itself, but also for the great *inclination which it has to do us good*, and for the innumerable and infinite goods which it has bestowed upon us.

1. First, it is amiable for *the four degrees of natural being*, which, as has already been said, it imparts to the creatures, and unites them all in man, as in an abbreviated world. And as these perfections are innumerable, so are the titles and motives likewise innumerable, which I may draw from them to love that most lovely goodness, whence they proceed for my benefit and use. Wherefore, in seeing any creature, I am to imagine, as Hugo of S. Victor says, that God our Lord speaks to me by it these two words:— "Accipe et redde," "receive and render;" or that which the Wise man says:—" Give, and take, and justify thy soul;" (7) which words signify this: Receive of God the good which He giveth thee, and render Him thy love for

<hr>

(6) Joan. xv. 25.
(7) Lib. de Arca. Mor. cap. 4, in ii. Tom. Ecclus. xiv. 16.

the same; receive His gift, and give Him thy thanks; receive His benefit and give Him thy service. "Accipe benignitatem, redde charitatem." "Receive His benignity, and render Him charity;" and if I perform this worthily I shall justify my soul, for I then do what I ought to do; for, as God will receive the thanks for the good which He gives me, so ought I to give Him thanks for the good which I receive.

Colloquy.—O my soul, hear the voices of these creatures, and the counsel of the Wise man, which says:—"Let not thy hand be stretched out to receive, and closed to give;" and since Almighty God opened His hand to fill thee and the whole world with His bounty and benediction, do thou likewise open thy heart, to fill it with love, thy mouth, to fill it with praises, and thy hands, to fill them with services, in thankfulness for such innumerable benefits as thou hast received. Take heed, and be not ungrateful, for if thou close thy hand in giving to God what He doth ask of thee, He will close His, not to give to thee the good which thou dost ask of Him.

2. Hence I will consider how amiable the goodness of God is, as well in itself as for *the innumerable goods of grace and glory* which proceed from it, and how much more amiable, for the singular benefit of the Incarnation of the divine Word, by which He did the last and utmost that He could, to show us by works how much His goodness deserves to be loved.

Colloquy.—O amiable God, if Thou art so worthy to be loved, for having given us so many natural goods, how much more shouldst Thou be loved, for having added so many supernatural goods! And if I ought to love Thee so much for goods that perish, how much more for goods eternal! If Thou art so greatly amiable, for goods which Thou givest us out of Thyself, how much more for giving unto us Thy very self! O that there were given to me a new heart, a new soul, a new spirit, new virtue, and new powers, that with new fervour I might accomplish perfectly the precept of love, and love Thee as Thou desirest to be beloved! O my soul, cast the eyes of thy faith upon the goods of grace which thou hast received, and every day dost receive, and open thine ears to hear the voice of thy Beloved, who says:— "Accipe et redde, da et accipe,—Receive and render, give and receive," receive grace of Me, and render service to Me. O my Beloved, let it be as Thou commandest, but assist me, that I hinder not by my tepidity that which so liberally is offered me by Thy goodness. Amen.

I am to exercise affections of this kind when I receive the sacraments of confession or communion, or when I hear Mass, or a sermon, and finally, when I shall be made partaker of some supernatural good; and imagine that Almighty God says to me, Receive and render, give and receive, that thou mayest justify thy soul, and mayest sanctify it with new signs of sanctity.

3. I will consider, thirdly, how the goodness of Almighty God is also amiable, because *it contains all the profitable good which can possibly be imagined*, without any mixture of imperfection. For, in God our Lord are eminently all those things which are means to obtain our last end; He Himself is the "way, the truth, and the life," since He gives us the means to walk and arrive at the main Truth, and to attain life eternal, which is Himself. Hence holy David said:—"The Lord will give grace and glory." (8) Moreover, all the goods which in this life are means to obtain some good end, are in Almighty God in a very eminent degree, and proceed from His goodness, and,

<hr>

(8) Ps. lxxxiii. 12.

therefore, He is worthy to be loved for them. For if I love meat, because it preserves my life, physic, because it cures my infirmity, money, because I buy with it what is wanting to me; much more ought I to love Almighty God, from whom all these proceed, not that my principal motive is that He may give to me such goods, but for the goodness which He displays in giving them to me with such liberality. Wherefore, from all those things, of which I make use, I must learn how amiable Almighty God is, and labour to love Him for them, in the manner described, and imagine that He likewise says to me the words before recited: Receive and render, give and receive.

POINT III.

1. Consider, thirdly, how amiable the goodness of God is for the third title of good, which we call *delectable*, which is a certain quietness and peace of heart in the possession of the thing it loves, and in the accomplishment of that which it desires, and by another name is called joy, and gladness.

i. First, God our Lord is amiable, for *the infinite joy and delight which He has within Himself;* for as He is Goodness Itself, so is He Delight Itself, and all the perfections which He has are motives of infinite joy to Him, and He takes delight in seeing and loving them. ii. Secondly, He is amiable, for the infinite joy with which He does all His works, and delights Himself in the creation of the heavens and of other things, according to what David says:—"The Lord shall rejoice in His works."(9) iii. He is amiable, since He is the cause of all the delectable goods of this life; for nothing can delight our senses or interior faculties but for the being which they receive from Him; nor can our soul have any delight unless God give

(9) Ps. ciii. 31.

it to her. Wherefore in Almighty God all things are eminently delectable, and in Him are all the delights which we can desire; and although He delights us with His creatures, yet can He alone without them give us the delight which they afford us, yea and other delights incomparably greater; and in this is grounded that promise of His, to give to him that shall leave aught for His love, "a hundred-fold" more than what he leaves, and incomparably greater spiritual gladness for having left it, than he would have had if he had retained it. iv. Lastly, He is amiable, for the singular delight which He has in treating and conversing with us; for which cause the Wisdom uncreated says:—"I was delighted every day, playing before Him:"(10) that is to say, rejoicing and delighting Himself in the works which He did in the whole world, for His pleasures and especial delights are the sons of men, to be with them and to converse with them. v. From all this it follows, that God our Lord desires to be served with alacrity, and that we should converse and treat with Him with great gladness, for every one loves his like, and therefore as He is so glad, and does all that He does with gladness, so it is His will that His elect should live in His service with gladness, and serve Him with gladness, as David says;—" Sing joyfully to God all the earth, serve ye the Lord with gladness, come in before His presence with exceeding great joy."(11) And the more to animate us to this, He promises us for reward the same joy which He Himself enjoys, saying to him that has been faithful in His service:—"Intra in gaudium Domini tui,' " Enter into the joy of thy Lord."(12) With each of these five considerations I will excite in myself great affections of love and joy in the goodness of God, that I may rejoice in

(10) Prov. viii. 30.

(11) Ps. xcix. 1.   (12) Mat. xxv. 21.

God alone, since in Him only shall I find all the causes of
joy and delight which I can desire.

Colloquy.—O my soul, why goest thou begging
delights amongst the creatures, since in God alone
thou shalt find infinitely greater delights than in them
all? Perform with gladness the works of His service,
since He performs with great joy those which are to
thy profit. Give Him all thou hast, "not with sadness, or of necessity,"(13) for He loves "a cheerful
giver," and He will render thee a hundred-fold, ready
counted, in joy and contentment. Rejoice to converse
with Him, since He delights to converse with thee,
filling thee with His own joy. For His " conversation
has no bitterness, nor" His " company any tediousness,
but joy and gladness,"(14) which begins in this life,
and is fulfilled in the other, passing from temporal to
eternal joy.

2. Lastly, I will gather from these considerations how
*detestable a thing it is to love any delight prohibited by
our Lord*, to despise heavenly delights for earthly, and to
leave the infinite and eternal joy for a joy that is limited
and temporal; and I will sorrow for those who fall into
such disorders, and for the times that I myself have fallen
into them, with purpose of amendment, for, as Job says:—
I cannot "delight myself in the Almighty,"(15) if I depart
from His holy service.

(13) 2 Cor. ix. 7.   (14) Sap. viii. 16.
(15) Job xxvii. 10.

MEDITATION IX.

ON THE INFINITE CHARITY AND LOVE OF ALMIGHTY GOD.

Love is a complacency in good, on account of its con-gruity with our nature; its principal acts are three. i. The first is general, and is called benevolence, which is to wish well to another, taking pleasure in the good which he has, or desiring him to have it. ii. The second is a love which we call of concupiscence, loving anything for one's own profit, or for the profit of another, as we love money, meat, and our servant. iii. The third act is of love which is called of friendship between two persons, the one loving the other for the good that is in them, confessing that they love them; and when this good is supernatural, such friendship is called charity. From these three acts of love arises another exterior act, which is called liberality, which is to do good to him whom I love.(1) This presup-posed, we will enter upon the meditation of the infinite charity and love of God, in order to Himself and to all the creatures, but especially towards men, and more especially towards the just, presupposing many things which have been said in the preceding meditations, which appertain to the charity of God, for the connexion they have with His infinite goodness.

POINT I.

1. First is to be considered, how God our Lord loves Himself infinitely *for the infinite good which He has in Himself;* and like as He is essential Goodness itself, so is He love and " charity"(2) itself, and pleases and contents

(1) S. Th. 1, p. q. xx. S. Th. 1, 2, q. xxvi. art. 1, et 4; et 2, 2, q, xxvii. art. 2, q. xxiii. art. 1, q. xxxi.

(2) 1 Joan. iv. 8.

Himself in His own good, and in all the perfections of wisdom, omnipotency, &c., which He possesses. And this love is well ordered, most holy, and most conformable and due to the infinite goodness, sanctity, and beauty of God, and so is very different from that which here we call self-love, by which a man loves himself so inordinately, that he excludes the love due to other things.

2. But I will further consider, how in God our Lord there is an infinite *love of friendship and charity*, because there are found amongst the three divine Persons, with infinite excellency, all the conditions of perfect friendship, which are, equality of persons, union of wills, and community of all things. For what constitutes perfect friendship is, when one friend wills and desires life and all good to another, communicates those things which he himself possesses, takes great delight in conversing with him familiarly, and imparts to him all his secrets; and above all, it is requisite that his love should be of long standing, and have been steadily persevered in, without being extended to many.(3) All this, as has been said in the fourth Meditation, is found betwixt the Father, the Son, and the Holy Ghost, because all three are equal, with infinite equality of perfection, and are chiefly one thing in essence, with unity of will in all things; they have also infinite communication, and all things are common amongst them without secrecy; their love is eternal, it ever was, is, and ever shall be; lastly, it embraces but few, for they are only three, nor is it possible for so infinite a friendship to extend itself to more persons.

3. From this consideration I will deduce great affections of joy and confidence in many respects :—

i. That *God loves Himself* as much as He can, and deserves to be loved, so that His goodness and love keep

(3) Arist. viii. et ix. Eth. S. Th sup. et 2, 2, q. xxv. art. 7.

equal pace; love desiring no greater goodness for its sup-port, and goodness wishing to be loved by no greater love. And since I love Almighty God, reason is that I rejoice to see the desires fulfilled which His charity has of loving, and His goodness to be beloved.

ii. Next I will rejoice, *that* the infinite *love* which God bears to Himself and to His own goodness, *is the cause and origin of the love which He bears to the creatures*, and the friendship which the three Divine Persons have, is the cause and pattern of the friendship which He has with angels and men. And this divine love perpetually solicits and excites Almighty God to love us.

iii. I may have great confidence, that He *will ever love me*, because He loves Himself. For, if St. Paul says of himself, "The charity of Christ presseth us,"(4) i. e., the charity and love which we bear towards Christ is a spur to us and urges us to love our neighbours, how much more shall the charity and love which God bears to His own goodness urge Him to love His creatures, as shall be seen in the points ensuing.

POINT II.

Secondly we will consider the great love that God our Lord *bears to all His creatures*, and ponder some of its more remarkable circumstances.

i. The first is the difference between our love and God's. For, as St. Thomas affirms, our love presupposes that to be good which it loves, or at the least imagines that its object has being and goodness, and in this takes delight.(5) But the love of Almighty God is the cause of the good which it loves, so that together in God are those two acts of love which are called benevolence and beneficence, i. e., to will well and to do well; for Almighty God, seeing in His eter-

(4) 2 Cor. v. 14.   (5) 1 p. q. xx. art. 2.

nity and in His infinite wisdom the goodness of the creatures which He would create, all appearing good to Him, He loved and willed effectually the good of some of them, and determined to give them the being and perfection of which they were capable. Thus, willing to do good to the heavens, to the stars and planets, He gave them all the good they have; and willing good to the creatures of the earth, and to man, He made them with that beauty and comeliness of form which they possess. For, for God to love them, is to will and endow them with all the good and perfection that is in them. And as David said:— "He saved me, because He was well pleased with me;"(6) and so I may likewise say, God gave me this body and this soul, and created me to His image and likeness, because He willed my good. He gratuitously preserves and governs and gives me all the goods that I enjoy, because He still wills my good, and to will my good is to give me the goods which He actually bestows upon me, and this of grace, freely, and only because it is His will to love me, as He says by the prophet Osee:—"Diligam eos spontanee," "I will love them freely."(7)

Colloquy.—O beloved of my soul, I give Thee thanks for this kind of love with which Thou lovest Thy creatures, and me with them. I confess that it is not possible for me to love Thee as Thou lovest me, for I may wish Thee good, but cannot do Thee good, nor give Thee aught which Thou hast not already; but after the manner that I may, I will give Thee what Thou givest me, and serve Thee and give Thee thanks for all; and that which I cannot give to Thee, I will give to my neighbours for the love of Thee.

ii. Secondly, God our Lord loves man incomparably more than all the creatures of this visible world, because

(6) Ps. xvii. 20.   (7) Ose. xiv. 5.

likeness in good is cause of love, and the greater the likeness is, the more vehement is the inclination to love; for likenesses behold one another as one and the self-same thing, and this manner of unity inclines them to will good one to another.(8) And as the other creatures are only a shadow of the being of God, but man His image and similitude, capable of His friendship and familiarity, hence it is that God our Lord loves man much more than all the residue of the visible creatures, on account of this similitude, and so created them for man, ordaining them all to Himself, as to their last end. Hence I will gather the great obligation I have to love God; for if likeness is a cause of love, how much am I bound to love Him who created me to His own image and likeness? If "every beast loveth its like,"(9) and everything desires to be joined with that in which it beholds its own likeness, how shall not I love Almighty God, and rejoice to join myself with Him, since with so great love He hath made me like to Himself?

Colloquy.—O great God, Three and One, who in the creation of man didst manifest the infinite friendship and unity which Thou hast within Thyself, the three Divine Persons saying :—" Let us make man to our image and likeness;" grant that I may love Thee with such love, that all the faculties of my soul may accord, and unite themselves to love and glorify Thee, for the likeness which Thou hast given me, and for the love which Thou hast showed, in giving me this likeness.

iii. Hence proceeds the third remarkable thing which shines in this love, that is to say, that God our Lord loves all the creatures of this visible world except man, not with the love of friendship, because they are not capable of it,

(8) S. Th. 1, 2, q. xxvii. art. 3.   (9) Ecclus. xiii. 19.

but *with the love of concupiscence*, willing them the good they have;(10) not for His own profit, because He, as David says, has need of nothing, but for the profit of men, for the preservation of their life, for their delight and entertainment, and for the other advantages we receive from them. For as they cannot love Almighty God, nor praise Him for the goods which He has given them, He would ordain them to the profit of another creature, which should supply their defect, by loving and glorifying Him for the being He gives to all. Whence I will deduce great sentiments of admiration, and will say with David:—" What is man, that Thou art mindful of him? Or the son of man, that Thou visitest him? Thou hast crowned him with glory and honour, and hast set him over the works of Thy hands. Thou hast subjected all things under his feet, all sheep and oxen, moreover the beasts also of the field, the birds of the air, and the fishes of the sea. O Lord our God, how admirable is Thy name in all the earth!"(11)

Colloquy.—O God of my soul, Thy name is no less amiable than admirable, since whatever is admirable in what Thou hast done for man, Thou hast done it because Thou lovedst him, that he might likewise love Thee, for Thou thus discoverest to him that Thou art exceeding amiable.

2. Hence I will proceed to draw infinite motives for loving Almighty God, from the infinite works of love which He has heaped upon me. For Almighty God, loving these innumerable creatures, loves me likewise in them, and from them His love passes to me; like as a father who loves the garment, the food, and servant of his son, in all this loves his son, because the principal motive he has to love them is his son; even so this our God, and loving Father, loving the heavens, the stars, and the

(10) S. Th. 1, p. q. ii. art. 2. Ps. xv. 2.　　(11) Ps. viii. 5.

planets, loves me likewise, because He loves them, and wills them the good, which He does them, for my sake. And in the same manner, loving the elements, the mixed bodies, the planets, and all beasts, He jointly loves me, because He loves them for me, and does good to them in order to do good to me. Since, therefore, Almighty God loves me in all the creatures in such a manner, it is most reasonable that I should likewise love Him in them all, loving the creatures for the good which He has given them, and for the glory of Him that gave it to them, not using them but for His love and service.

Colloquy.—O eternal God, the lover and benefactor of all creatures, I confess that for a thousand titles I am obliged to love Thee with my whole heart; and since Thou lovest innumerable creatures which cannot return Thee love for love, I am bound to love Thee in their behalf. O that I had as many hearts as Thou hast given me creatures, to the end that with all of them I might love and glorify Thee, and discharge the debt they cannot pay Thee, and with which I stand charged for their sakes. Amen.

POINT III.

The third shall be to consider the *universality* of this noble love of Almighty God, from which no creature is excluded, from the very fact of the being which it has received from Him, according to that of the Wise man, who says:—" Thou lovest all things that are, and hatest none of the things which Thou hast made; for Thou didst not appoint or make any thing, hating it; and how could any thing endure if Thou wouldest not?"(12) Although, therefore, God our Lord hates sin, and the sinner, so far as he is evil, yet He does not hate his nature, nor the good which He imparts to him; and although the sinner

(12) Sap. xi. 25.

is ungrateful, and does not acknowledge his Benefactor, yet God ceases not to love him with this love, i. e., as His creature, and to communicate to him the natural goods which He is wont to give to the grateful. Hence I will draw three lessons.

i. The first is, that of this love which God bears me, for the natural good which He has given me, I will make a plea to beseech Him to *take away the evil* which I have added, saying that of Job:—" Thy hands have made me, and fashioned me wholly round about, and ' dost Thou thus cast me down headlong on a sudden?" (13.)

Colloquy.—O ·my Creator and my Maker, suffer not that I cast myself down headlong into such sins as may provoke Thee to cast me down headlong into hell; destroy, O Lord, that which I have committed through my wickedness, for the love Thou bearest to that which Thou hast made by Thy goodness. Amen.

ii. Secondly, I will conceive a great determination not to hate any of all those things which God loves, but in all things *to conform my love to His*; and although I hate the wickedness of mine enemy, yet will I not hate, but love his person, like as God loves it; and wish him all the good which God both does and desires to give him, remembering what Christ our Lord said:—" Love your enemies, do good to them that hate you...that you may be the children of your Father who is in heaven, who maketh His sun to rise upon good and bad, and raineth upon the just and unjust;" (14) by which He shows that He loves them.

iii. Finally, as this love generally accompanies Almighty God in all His works, according to the saying of the Wise man, that He hates nothing which He has made, or ordained; and, as St. Dionysius says:—" Love is the cause

(13) Job x. 3.　　　　(14) S. Th. 2, 2, q. xxv. art. 6.　Mat. v. 44.

of all things which he does that loves," (15) even so I, if I love Almighty God with fervent love, *am so to imitate Him*, that this love may be the beginning, middle, and end of my works; that they all may begin with love, be accompanied with love; and that I may do them for love of this great God, who so greatly loves me; and thus shall I love Him with my whole heart, soul, mind, and strength, as the precept of love prescribes.

Colloquy.—O my beloved, since Thou always lovest, and always workest with love, and never ceasest to love, or work, because if Thou didst cease, all things would cease to be; grant that I may never cease to love Thee, nor to work for the love of Thee, that thus I may do all my works in charity; for if this cease, I also cease to be in Thy presence, since without the same, "Nihil sum," " I am nothing," (16) and merit nothing; and if I have anything, it is wholly of Thy love.

POINT IV.

1. The fourth will be to consider the *greatness of the charity* and love which God our Lord bears to men, being desirous to contract true friendship with them in all the perfection which friendship between the Creator and the creature can possibly have. In this point we will run over the principal properties thereof, which have already been set down.

i. The first property of friendship is, that it be *between persons in some sort or manner equal;* either with entire equality, as in the case of a great intimacy between two citizens, or with an equality proportionate to the superior condition of the one party, as between a king and his familiar friend, or between a father and his son.

(15) Cap. 4, de Divin. Nom. S. Th. 1, 2, q. xxviii. art. 6.
(16) 1 Cor. xiii. 2.

Whence it proceeds, that when one friend is much elevated in rank above the other, he does all that he can to exalt him; and so, as St. Jerome says:—"Amicitia pares accipit, aut facit." "Friendship presupposes that friends are equal, or makes them equal." (17) And of this kind is the friendship which Almighty God bears towards us; for, seeing the great inequality there was between our nature and His, He would, of His infinite goodness, exalt us to another most excellent being far above our own nature, on which true friendship might be grounded; and gave us, as St. Peter says:—"most great and precious promises" (18) of grace, that by these we might be made partakers of the divine nature, with the greatest conformity that is possible for pure creatures. He not only took us for friends, but also made us His sons, heirs of His kingdom, and blessed and happy as Himself, so far as to say of us:— "You are Gods, and all of you the sons of the Most High." (19) He took our souls, too, for His spouses; and all this of pure grace, and because He is good, and manifests His infinite goodness in admitting His creatures and His servants to be made partakers of that infinite friendship, with which the three Divine Persons are linked together. And although it is not possible to have equality with His infinite excellency, yet His infinite condescension supplies this difference; and so He calls us with names of equality, as is to be seen in the Book of Canticles, where He calls the soul "Sister," and "Spouse;" and attributes to her the same titles of praise with which the soul herself praises Him.

Colloquy.—O most loving God, amiable above all that can be thought, Thou didst me a great benefit in creating me after Thine own image and likeness; but Thine infinite charity would yet exalt me to another

<hr>

(17) S. Jer. in Mich. 7.　　(18) 2 Pet. i. 4.　　(19) Ps. lxxxi. 6.

similitude, much greater, and much higher, in order
to show me greater signs of Thy love.   Now there is
no cause to wonder with David, why Thou hast given
me a natural being, superior to all the things of the
earth, since Thou hast vouchsafed to lift me up to
a supernatural being, like to that which is above the
heavens.   In the first being " Thou hast made" me " a
little less than the angels ;"(20) but in the second
Thou hast made me equal with them, and like to
Thee, the Creator and Sanctifier of all the saints, to
the end that I may love and sanctify Thy name on
earth, as they sanctify it in heaven.

ii. From this first property of perfect friendship arises
the second, which is, for a friend to wish to his friend both
being and life, and liberally to *communicate all the goods
he can himself give him*, for the love he bears him. (21)
In this property Almighty God is pre-eminently our great
friend, for besides that He both wills and does us
good, giving us being and natural life, He also wills us a
supernatural being, i. e., the life of grace, and the life of
eternal glory, together with innumerable goods which
accompany them, so as to say to us:—" Omnia mea tua
sunt," " All I have is thine," because " Amicorum omnia
sunt communia," "all things are common amongst friends,"
and what God has, He wills it for His friends.

Colloquy.—O our Beloved and our Friend, how
well dost Thou accomplish the law of perfect love,
making Thine own goods to be common to Thy
friends!   How shall I accomplish the same law, since I
have no goods of mine own which I may make common to Thee?   " All things are Thine," (22) and
what I have received at Thy hand, this I return Thee ;
my proper will, and my self-love, I will convert into

(20) Ps. viii. 7.
(21) S. Th. 2, 2, q. xxvii. art. 5.   (22) 1 Paral. xxix. 14.

a general love, and perform all that Thou willest, love
what Thou lovest, and will nothing for my own inte-
rest, that all may be for Thee.   Amen.

iii. Hence arises the third property of perfect friendship,
which is *union;* in respect of which it is said, " Amicus fit
alter ego," "a friend is another I," and that friends are one
soul in two bodies, and that the soul is more where it loves
than where it lives, and for this reason they greatly desire
to be united together, and to converse one with another.(23)
This appears much more evidently in the friendship of our
God, who makes us by love "one spirit" with Him, and
puts us within Him, as "the apple of" His "eye,"(24) and
takes pleasure to be with the sons of men, and to converse
familiarly with them, and imparts His secrets to them,
according to that which He said to His apostles:—" I will
not now call you servants; for the servant knoweth not
what his lord doth.   But I have called you friends,'' and
for such repute you, "because all things whatsoever I
heard of My Father, I have made known to you."(25) And
finally, He exalts them to heaven, where this communication shall be more strict and more familiar, because they
shall be continually in His presence, absorbed in His Divinity, beholding Him face to face, and maintaining the most
inward familiarity with Him.

Colloquy.—O most loving God, now I see with how
great reason Thou callest Thyself the spouse of our
souls, and callest them Thy spouses, as He who is one
spirit, and one heart with them, conversing with them
with so tender love, as never spouse bore the like to
his beloved spouse.   Who would ever believe such a
manner of love if Thou didst not reveal it?   And who

(23) S. Th. 1, 2, q. xxviii. art. 1 et 2. S. Aug. iv. Confes. cap. 6, et
2, Retrac. cap. 1.
(24) 1 Cor. vi. 17. Zach. ii. 8.   (25) Joan. xv. 15.

could ever understand such a kind of conversation if Thou didst not impart it to him? O my beloved, what is man that Thou dost so magnify him, or that Thou settest Thy heart upon him? Enclose, Lord, my heart in Thine, and show me the greatness of this love, and make me one with Thee, that I may love Thee as Thou dost me, that so friendship may be most perfect on my part, as it is most perfect on Thine. Amen.

2. From these three properties of friendship I am to draw a great desire to declare the friendship and charity which I bear towards God our Lord, by entertaining *the like charity to my neighbours for His love;* by making myself equal and humbling myself with them, and exalting them by all means I may; by imparting to them both of my corporal and spiritual goods, making myself one, and conversing with all lovingly, in order that they may love Almighty God, and He gain many friends, in whom He may be glorified, world without end. Amen.

MEDITATION X.

ON THE FOUR SINGULAR EXCELLENCIES OF THE INFINITE LOVE AND FRIENDSHIP WHICH GOD BEARS TO MEN, AND BY WHAT MEANS WE MAY IMITATE THEM.

The excellencies of the love of Almighty God towards men, which we have declared hitherto, are founded upon the properties of perfect friendship as it exists amongst men. Now we will ponder other peculiar properties, which cannot be found except in the friendship of Almighty God, which, as it is infinite on His part, so is it also singular, and above imitation. These properties are reduced to four, which the apostle St. Paul calls "Breadth, and length, and height, and depth."(1)   Breadth is its expansiveness, by which it embraces all who desire to contract friendship with Him. Length is its eternal duration, without beginning or end. Height is the excellency of the heavenly goods, to the enjoyment of which it invites them.   Depth is the secrets hidden in this friendship, which are such as cannot be penetrated.(2)   And although something has been said on these points in the preceding meditations, yet they shall be considered more at large in what follows.

POINT I.

1. The first excellency of the singular love of Almighty God toward men is *to be eternal.* This eternity consists in being as *ancient* as God Himself, who from His eternity decreed to love men, and to contract friendship with them, not only in general, and promiscuously, but in particular He knew every one, and willed what lay in Him, to give to every one all the goods of grace and glory, on which true friendship is grounded; although more particularly He loved those whom we call predestinate, so that I may apply to myself that which Almighty God said to the prophet Jeremiah, " I have loved thee with an everlasting love;"(3) as if He had said, From the time that I am God have I loved thee, from the time that I have loved myself have I loved thee, the love I bear thee is as eternal as Myself, as eternal as the love with which I love Myself.

Colloquy.—O eternal lover, who would not love Thee without ceasing?   O that I had loved Thee ever since I was a man, for Thou hast loved me ever since Thou wast God!   O my soul, defer no longer to love God, for even to love Him now, is to love Him

(1) Ephes. iii. 18.   (2) S. Th. ibid. Lect. v.
(3) Jer. xxxi. 3.

late; begin immediately, and love Him, who has ever loved thee. " Ama amorem ab eterno te amantem.— Love that love which loved thee from all eternity." If a friend to be good and secure ought to be ancient, what friend can be more ancient than He that is eternal? Embrace the counsel of the Wise man :—" Forsake not an old friend, for the new will not be like to him." (4)　Leave not the friendship of Almighty God for that of men, for this shall not be like to that; and by how much eternal exceedeth temporal, so much that exceedeth this.

These and other like purposes and affections I am to draw from this consideration, rendering thanks to God our Lord, that He has loved me from all eternity, wishing that I had always loved Him since first I had the use of reason, confiding in so ancient a friend, sorrowing to have forsaken Him, to contract new friendships with His creatures, and finally, purposing never more to forsake Him.

2. Hence I am to ascend to the consideration that the love of Almighty God is always *before ours*, and guides us by the hand, according to what St. John says,—" By this hath the charity of God appeared in us;" (5) not as though we had loved Him, but because He hath first loved us; that is to say, the excellency of the love of God is greatly discovered by this, that He first loved us before we loved Him; for this is a sign that He loved us, not for His own profit, nor yet for our merits, but of grace, and only because He is good, and also to excite our love by His, and to provoke us to return love for love; and so St. John concludes:—" We therefore love God, because He first loved us."

Colloquy.—O my soul, if love produces love, let such a love, and such a God, move thee to love Him,

(4) Ecclus. ix. 14.　　　　　　　　(5) 1 Joan. iv. 9.

who loved thee, and who anticipates thee with His love. O eternal lover, if it were possible that I might love Thee first, before Thou lovest me, it were most just that my love should solicit Thine, beseeching Thee to vouchsafe to love me; but since Thy love doth solicit mine, henceforth I offer it to Thee, with inward desire to love Thee, because Thou lovest me, and daily more and more to love Thee, to the end Thou mayest love me more and more, and augment in me the gifts of love.

3. Then I will consider, thirdly, how the love of Almighty God is eternal, as regards the duration *which is to come*, and firm and stable for all eternity. So that, as His love had no beginning, even so on His part it shall never have an end in relation to man. Hence I may consider how this great God and eternal lover ever loved me, now loves me, and shall love me, as long as He shall be God, unless I myself desert Him. For both His love and His mercy, which proceeds from it, is, "ab æterno in æternum," "from eternity unto eternity," (6) nor is there any created thing which can remove or take from God this love, and in this manner may be understood that which the apostle says:—" Who then shall separate us from the love of Christ?" (7) that is to say, who could bring to pass that Almighty God should cease to love us through Christ? For in all labours and tribulations we overcome by Him that loves us, and by the virtue which His love infuses into us. And so far does the stability of this love extend, that when we, through our own fault, break this friendship, and make ourselves His enemies, He in His infinite charity remains the same, desiring us to return into His favour, and being prepared to admit us anew into His grace, and to forget the injury, if we will ask forgiveness

(6) Ps. cii. 17.   (7) Rom. viii. 35.

for it, saying that of the prophet Jeremiah, "Thou hast prostituted thyself to many lovers, nevertheless, return to Me, and I will receive thee." (8)

Colloquy.—O eternal and immutable lover, give me a love like Thine, from which nothing may separate me. If Thou dost not separate Thy love from me, who can separate mine from Thee? "Shall tribulation, or distress, or famine, or the sword?" None of all these is sufficient, for the love which Thou shalt give me will easily overcome all, in virtue of that which Thou bearest towards me; nor "many waters," nor abundant rivers, can "quench" my "charity," if it be always joined with Thine; for Thine is an infinite fire, which in a moment will consume them. Suffer not, O eternal lover, that I break asunder the thread of Thy friendship by my fault; and if I should be so weak as to break it, let Thy love awake me, and prevent me, that I may return to Thee. Fulfil in me that inclination of charity which is never to "fall away," (9) that, preserving it constantly in this temporal life, it may last for ever in the life eternal. Amen.

POINT II.

1. The second excellency of the love of God is *latitude*.

i. It is infinitely ample and comprehensive, and *embraces all men*, of whatever estate and condition, desires to admit all into its grace and friendship, without excluding any one that desires to be admitted, and thus accomplishes that which the Wise man says, speaking with Almighty God:—"Thou overlookest the sins of men, for the sake of repentance, for Thou lovest all things that are, and hatest none of the things which Thou hast made," (10) and, consequently, hatest no man as an enemy, unless for the sin

(8) Jer. iii. 1.

(9) 1 Cor. xiii. 8.   (10) Sap. xi. 24.

which he has not blotted out by penance. And although it be true that He loves the predestinate with a more especial love, in which sense it is said that He hates the reprobate, because He loved them not so much as the elect; (11) yet, absolutely on His own part, He loves all with infinite charity, desiring all to "be saved," and become His friends, and ceases not to use towards them great cherishings of love, as He did to Judas, in order to reduce them to His friendship, heaping coals of benefits upon the head of His enemy, to convert him into a friend. (12)   And thus with the love of a father, He causes His Son, the sun of justice, to arise upon " the good and the bad," and the rain of His doctrine to be offered to the "just and the unjust," and the dew of His celestial gifts to descend upon all, as many as desire to receive them.

Colloquy.—O immensity of the love of God, which embracest all, and art never filled, because there still remains latitude to receive more! O my soul, rejoice in so infinite a love, and trust to have thy part therein. O immense lover, since the bosom of Thy love is so infinitely ample, admit all mortal men into it; shut up, if possible, the bosom of hell, where Thou art hated, that none may descend thither, and open the bosom of heaven, where Thou art loved, that all may thither ascend, to employ themselves for ever in Thy love. Amen.

ii. I will ponder, secondly, another most singular thing in this love and friendship of Almighty God, which, although it extends itself to many, yet it ceases not to be *as perfect as if it were extended only to a few.* Amongst men, intimate and perfect friendship, as Aristotle says, ought to be between a few, because it is a very rare thing to find many faithful friends in whom one may repose his

(11) Rom. 9. 13.   (12) Prov. xxv. 12.   Rom. xii. 20.

trust. (13) But God our Lord, in His infinite love, contracts friendship with many, by making them faithful, and giving them true charity; and although His most beloved be very many, yet He treats every one with the same familiarity, as He would if He were His only friend. So that the multitude of the friends of God hinders not His familiar communication with each, as is to be seen in heaven, where this friendship is most perfect. And for this cause, in the Book of Canticles, our Lord having recounted three sorts of souls which live in His company, concludes by saying: "One is my dove, my perfect one:" (14) i. e. all souls together which make one Church, I love them as if they were but one, and for the one end of their eternal blessedness and my glory.

Colloquy.—O my beloved, I give Thee thanks for this will, which Thou hast to keep so strict friendship with all and every one, as if he were but one alone. O that my soul were so happy as to be one of these Thy spouses, to whom Thou saidst :—" One is my dove, my perfect one is but one, she is the only one of her mother." Make me Thy dove by innocence, and Thy perfect one by charity, " which is the bond of perfection ;" (15) and grant me to love Thee in this church militant on earth, as our mother, the church triumphant, loveth Thee in heaven. Amen.

2. From these two considerations I am to draw two purposes, in which my love ought to imitate that of Almighty God. i. The first ought to be, not to hate any, nor to hold him for mine enemy, but to love all, enlarging the bosom of my charity, to embrace all men, good and evil, perfect and imperfect, and perform to all the works of a friend as far as I am able. ii. The second purpose is, to

<hr>

(13) 8 Ethic. cap. 6.
(14) Cant. vi. 8.   (15) Colos. iii. 14.

reduce the love of all to the love of one alone, i. e., God; so that, although I love many, yet I love them not as many, nor for qualities peculiar to each, but principally for one only respect and motive, and for one only friend, which is Almighty God, whose all are.

POINT III.

The third excellency is the *height* of the divine love, which discovers itself in the exalted nature of the gifts which proceed from it. These are so infinitely high and sublime that they cannot be greater.

1. First, because they *raise us to the supreme dignity* of sons of God and heirs of His kingdom. Hence, St. John said:—" Behold, what manner of charity the Father hath bestowed upon us, that we should be called, and should be the sons of God;" (16)—as if he had said, Contemplate and ponder the height to which the love of Almighty God has attained, and the admirable effects which it produces, since it has exalted us to the dignity of sons of God, and that with all the excellencies which the sons of such a father ought to have. And what these excellencies are, it is not possible to know in this life, and therefore he adds:—" We are now the sons of God, and it hath not yet appeared what we shall be. We know that when He shall appear, we shall be like to Him; because we shall see Him as He is." In heaven, therefore, only shall we discover the eminence of this dignity of sons, and of the love of Almighty God which has exalted us to it.

Colloquy.—I give Thee thanks, O most loving Father, for the love which Thou hast manifested to me, in accepting me for Thy son; illuminate the eyes of my soul, that I may know what this love is, and

(16) 1 Joan. iii. 1.

being endued with it, may love Thee as a father, and endeavour to be like Thee here in love, so as afterwards to be like Thee in glory. Amen.

2. Secondly, the height of the divine love appears more clearly in this, that Almighty God so loved us, that for our relief *He elevated one man of our nature* so high as to make Him His true Son, not by adoption, but His very natural Son in virtue of the union of the Incarnation; so that a man is the Son of God, in such a manner as to be at the same time a real man, and the real and true Son of Almighty God, equal with the Eternal Father, and one God together with Him. And here the love of God ascended so high, that it could not ascend higher; hence the same Christ our Lord said:—" God so loved the world that He gave His only-begotten Son." And St. John adds:—" By this hath the charity of God appeared in us, because God hath sent His only-begotten Son into the world that we may live by Him."(17) With this divine Man, Almighty God contracted the closest friendship which could possibly subsist next to the infinite friendship of the three divine persons; for, as the latter is grounded on the unity of essence in the Blessed Trinity, so the former depends upon the union of the two natures, the human and divine, in the one and self-same Person of Christ, who is by generation equal with God. And in this consists the stability and security of that love which God bears towards us, who loves us for Christ His Son, and giving us His Son, gives us "all things" likewise "with Him." (18)

Colloquy.—O height of the goodness and love of Almighty God, how incomprehensible are His works, and how unsearchable are His ways! O ineffable love, which, to contract perfect friendship with man,

(17) Joan. iii. 16.   1 Joan. iv. 9.   (18) Rom. viii. 32.

hast raised him to an equality with Almighty God! O most sublime love, what thanks shall I give Thee for such excellent and surpassing works of love, and how shall I praise Thee worthily for them? Let, O Lord, Thine own charity praise Thee, and let the works which proceed from it bless Thee, and above all, let Thy Son, true God, and true Man, glorify Thee, in whom we are all loved with so sublime and surpassing a love. Behold the face of this Thy beloved friend, ancient and new, ancient, inasmuch as God; new, inasmuch as Man; and by Him, Lord, I beseech Thee, vouchsafe to make me Thy friend, renewing me according to the image of this new man, that I may live by Him, and by His means may attain life eternal. Amen.

On the subject of this consideration, more has been said in the second meditation of the second Part.

3. I may likewise ponder the height of this divine love in the mystery of *the most Holy Eucharist*, in which the same Christ, true God and true Man, concealed under the species of bread and wine, enters into us to preserve this love, and augment it in us, and to unite us more intimately with Himself, as has been considered in the eleventh Meditation of the fourth Part, and will be yet farther declared in the four-and-twentieth Meditation.

4. Lastly, I will estimate the height of this divine love by the infinity of the gift which it bestows upon us, *giving us the Holy Ghost*, who is the fountain of love, as shall be seen in the next Meditation. From all these considerations I must conceive a great desire to imitate the height of this divine love, and to return it in such a manner as always to effect great things in God's service, to entertain a pure intention of seeking His greater glory, and to aspire to the gift of an elevated prayer, and sublime contemplation

of His mysteries, and to the perfect imitation of His virtues, according to what St. Paul says:—"I pray that your charity may more and more abound in knowledge and in all understanding; that you may approve the better things, that you may be sincere and without offence unto the day of Christ," (19) replenished with the fruit of justice by Jesus Christ, unto the glory and praise of God. Amen.

POINT IV.

1. The fourth excellency of the love of Almighty God is its depth.

i. This appears in His profound *humiliations* undertaken for the love of men. For the Divine Word being equal to the Father, " emptied Himself, taking the form of a ser-, vant," and " humbled Himself, becoming obedient unto death, even to the death of the cross;" (20) for as perfect friendship desires equality between friends, Almighty God seeing Himself so high, would abase Himself, and clothe Himself with the same nature that they were clothed with. " In similitudinem hominum factus, et habitu inventus ut homo," " being made in the likeness of men, and in habit found as a man," in all things being made like to His brethren. Moreover, as perfect charity does not only show itself in doing good to friends, but also in sustaining labours for them, because there is no " greater love" than " that a man lay down his life for his friends;" (21) the infinite charity of God would also give these signs of love; and because He could neither suffer nor die in His own divine nature, He took the nature of man, and in it sustained most grievous labours and contempts, and, finally, a most cruel death for His friends. What do I say, for His friends? " Because when as yet we were *sinners*, Christ

(19) Phil. i. 9.
(20) Phil. ii. 7.   (21) Joan. xv. 13.

died for us." (22)   Yes, He suffered for His enemies, to convert them into friends, and for those that hated Him, that they might love Him.

Colloquy.—O immense abyss of the love of God! O love, both high and low, who hast lifted up man to the highest God, and hast humbled God to the lowest of men! O patient and benign Love, who, not content to do us good with great benignity, wouldst suffer much for us with great patience! O beloved of my soul, manifest this love to me, and give me a love like to it, which may incline me to humble myself, even to the depth of my own nothingness, and may excite me to suffer even death itself for Thy glory.   Amen.

I may likewise make the same reflections upon the mystery of the most Holy Eucharist, in which the depth of God's love appears, inventing so humiliating a means of honouring and favouring His friends who truly love Him.

2. The depth also of this love of God, discovers itself in the depth of the secret judgments of His divine wisdom, in regard to His *doing good to His friends*, to whose benefit He turns all things, tribulations, afflictions, temptations, and miseries, as well their own as those of others; even the very defects and faults into which they fall by frailty, He converts into their good, taking occasion by them to root them more deeply and perfectly in love. So that the incomprehensible depth of the love of God shines in all the works of justice and vengeance, which He exercises upon the wicked for the profit of the good, and upon the good for their own amendment; and invents a thousand means and most secret ways, springing from the abyss of His eternal predestination, for the salvation of the elect.

3. These are the four excellencies of the infinite love of

(22) Rom. v. 8.

Almighty God, into the full knowledge and understanding of which I shall enter, not so much by long meditations as by the exercise of intense acts of charity. For it is by practice only that I shall be rooted in love. This is the counsel of the Apostle, who says:—" Being rooted and founded in charity," (23) that you may know by experience the properties and excellencies of the infinite love of Almighty God, and may attain to a charity which in its length and duration may extend to everlasting life; in its breadth and extension may embrace all the works of love, and all that can be loved; in the height of its intentions and aspirations, may ascend by its desires to heavenly, and not stoop to earthly things; and in the depth of its humiliation may bear with patience all labours and contempts which may happen to you, for being faithful to your beloved.

Colloquy.—O beloved of my heart, give me a love like Thine in these four conditions, that loving Thee with such a spirit in this life, I may come to enjoy Thee, and to love Thee without end in the other. Amen.

MEDITATION XI.

OF THE DESIRE WHICH GOD OUR LORD HATH TO BE LOVED BY MEN: OF THE COM-
MANDMENT HE HAS GIVEN THEM TO LOVE HIM; AND OF THE HELPS AND
REWARDS HE OFFERS TO SUCH AS KEEP IT.

Though, according to St. Thomas, it is more proper to charity, to love than to be loved; (1) yet Almighty God, whose charity is infinite, does not content Himself with loving us, but also greatly desires to be loved by us; not, for His own profit, but for ours. Hence, as has been said,

(23) Ephes. iii. 17.   (1) S. Th. 2, 2, q. xxvii. art. 1.

He prevents us in love, in order to provoke us to love Him, for to love is a great title to be beloved in return. This desire, together with its efficacy and excellency, appears in various ways, as we shall see in the ensuing points.

POINT I.

1. God our Lord, desiring to be loved by men, *gave them a particular precept*, commanding them *to love* Him with their " whole heart," with their " whole soul," with their " whole mind," with their " whole strength,"(2) i. e. with all perfection of which they were capable, without prescribing any limit to their love.   For the manner of loving God is to love Him without measure or limit, and the greater the love, the better it is.(3)   Whence we learn how infinite the love of God is towards us, for he who desires to be beloved without measure, and commands us to observe no bounds in loving him, shows that he confines himself to no limits in loving us, and doing us good. Thus Almighty God loves those who love Him, and the more they love Him, the more does He love them, and bestow His benefits upon them; for all heavenly gifts and blessings proceed from the love which God bears to us, and we are disposed to receive them, by the love we bear to Him.

Colloquy.—O most amiable lover, since Thou so much desirest to be loved by me without measure, give me what Thou commandest, that I may accomplish what Thou desirest. " Diligam te sicut diligor a te—Let me love Thee as I am loved by Thee," let me love Thee as Thou wilt be loved, and let me love Thee as Thou commandest me to love Thee.   Amen.

2. Hence will I conceive *as great an estimation of this precept of love as Christ our Lord* Himself had, who called

(2) Deut. vi. 5. Mat. xxii. 37.
(3) S. Th. 2, 2, q. xliv. et q. xxiv. art. 5. S. Ber. de diligendo Deo.

it "the first and greatest commandment," and that for many reasons.—i. It is the first in *order*, because it is proposed as the groundwork of the rest, and is the foundation of a spiritual life, and the root of all perfection; whence the apostle desires us to be " rooted and founded in charity."—ii. It is the first in *dignity*, because it commands the exercise of the highest virtue of the Christian life, viz., charity; for charity is greater than faith, hope, and all the other virtues, which, without it, are as dead, according to the saying of the apostle:—" If I have not charity, although I have all virtues and other sciences, ' Nihil sum,' I am nothing."—iii. It is also first in *merit*, for charity is the first cause of all our merits before Almighty God, without which none of our works have any merit before Him, since, as St. Paul says:—" If I should distribute all my goods to feed the poor, and if I should deliver my body to be burned, and have not charity, 'Nihil mihi prodest—it profits me nothing,' "(4) to merit eternal life.—iv. It is likewise the first in *sweetness* and delight, for from charity arises the sweetness of the yoke of Almighty God, and the lightness of the burden of His holy law, and because of it, " His commandments are not heavy:"(5) and its proper effect is joy in the Holy Ghost. v. It is also the first in *efficacy*, since it is the cause of the keeping of the other commandments, and for this reason Christ our Lord said, that upon it depended " the law and the prophets;" and the Apostle says that love is the " fulfilling of the law."—vi. It is the first in *intention*, whence the Apostle said:—" The end of the Commandment is charity," for all the commandments tend to charity, and to this our whole intention ought to be directed, and it ought to accompany all our good works, that so, being done " in charity," their goodness may be perfect.(6)

(4) 1 Cor. xiii. 3.   (5) Mat. xi. 30. 1 Joan. v. 3.
(6) Mat. xxii. 40. Rom. xiii. 10. 1 Tim. i. 5. 1 Cor. xvi. 14

3. For these and other causes I must hold this precept so highly recommended by Christ our Lord in great estimation, and excite myself to its perfect accomplishment, which consists in two things: in removing from myself any thing or affection whatever, that may contradict or cool this charity; and in applying myself seriously to exercise all those things which may augment it.

Colloquy.—O eternal lover, let me love Thee with my whole heart, and mortify all mine own love, that Thy love alone may remain in it. Let me love Thee with my whole will, and denying all other wills, accomplish that which Thou willest. Let me love Thee with my whole soul, by bridling the passions of mine appetites, so that all her affections may go after Thee. Let me love Thee with my whole mind, and renounce mine own judgment, and captivate my understanding in obedience to Thy faith, and in fulfilling Thy will. Let me love Thee with all my strength, and mortify my senses, and apply my powers to the observance of Thy law; and since Thy commandments are not impossible, give me strength to love Thee as Thou desirest to be loved, and make that easy and sweet to me, by Thy grace, which is impossible to my feeble nature. Amen.

All that has been put down in this colloquy is necessary to the perfect accomplishment of this precept: to which, what has been said in the Introduction, and in the eighth Meditation will also conduce.

POINT II.

Secondly we will consider, how God our Lord, desiring to be beloved by us, and having given us a precept to that end, does likewise *give us power to accomplish it* in a most excellent and admirable manner.

1. First, this our infinite lover, out of the desire which

He has to contract love and friendship with us, and in order that this friendship may be perfect on both parts, *infuses into us*, and gives us liberally, *that very charity* by which we love Him. By His inward inspirations also He assists us to love Him, and obliges us to use that charity " which is poured forth in our hearts,"(7) work and exercise divers acts of love for its own augmentation, and for the acquirement of new strength to make progress in love. Hence St. John said:—" Dearly beloved, let us love one another, for charity is of God,"(8) and it is but reasonable that we should use His gift to love Him as He desires to be loved.

2. But the infinite charity of Almighty God passes yet farther. He gives us *the fountain itself of all charity*, the Holy Ghost, the uncreated Charity, living and essential Love, who comes into our hearts to assist us, and preserve, quicken, direct, and excite our charity, and render it efficacious. Whence St. John said:—" We have known, and have believed the charity which God has to us: God is Charity; and he that abideth in charity, abideth in God, and God in him." " In this we know that we abide in Him, and He in us, because He hath given us of His spirit."(9) He, therefore, who has the virtue of charity infused into his soul, has that living and infinite charity, which is God; he is in God, and God is in him, and the bond which unites them is mutual love. Nor has he alone the Holy Ghost, but also the Father, and the Son, according to that which Christ our Lord has said:—" If any one love me, he will keep my word, and my Father will love him, and we will come to him, and will make our abode with him."(10) Whence it follows, that the three divine Persons dwell within the soul of the just man, and as they

(7) Rom. v. 5.   · (8) 1 Joan. iv. 7.
(9) Ibid. 13, 16.   (10) Joan. xiv. 23.

are the living fountain of charity, they pour it forth into his heart, to enable him, after their example, exactly to keep all the laws of true friendship.

Colloquy.—O ineffable height of the love of God! O fountain of living water, which, being in a heart of earth, dost lift it up even to the third heaven, and join it to the most blessed Trinity! O most blessed Trinity, who not only lovest Thine elect, but also wilt take to Thee the name of love, and call Thyself by the name of love, that we may all glory in this virtue! O my soul, rejoice and leap for gladness, for thy God is love. If God is love, what thing is there better than it? If he that is in charity is in God, what thing can be more secure? And if God is in him, what thing is there more delightful? (11) What, therefore, dost thou love, if thou lovest not such a love? And since this God of love will enter into thee, and desirest that thou also shouldst enter into Him, that thou mayest be filled with charity, enter thou into thyself, and behold the example of this infinite love, which thou hast within thee; and love thy God, Three and One, like as He loves Himself, and unite thee with Him by charity, as the divine Persons are united by essence, all three being one and the same essential Love. O my God, manifest Thy charity to me, and give me Thy holy love; let me love Thee, O my Lord, "my firmament, my refuge, and my deliverer; (12) let me love Thee as Thou lovest me, and as Thou wilt that I love Thee, world without end. Amen.

These and similar ejaculatory prayers are frequently to be repeated, so that by sometimes asking for it, and at other times exercising it, we may in a short time obtain the gift of charity; for there are no more effectual means

---

(11) S. Bern. S. Th. in 1 Joan. iv.   (12) Ps. xvii. 1.

to obtain love, than to love and to pray after the manner prescribed.

POINT III.

The third point shall be to consider how Almighty God, in His infinite charity, and from the desire He has to be beloved by us, although it had sufficed to have commanded us to love Him, and although without commandment we were greatly bound to do it, nevertheless to this commandment would *add great rewards*, corporal and spiritual, temporal and eternal, so to oblige us the more to love Him.   Hence in Deuteronomy, having commanded the people to love Him, He added, " that it may be well with thee;" as if He had said,—I do not require thee to love me, for the good which I expect from it, but for the good which thou shalt receive in loving me; and how great this good is may be gathered from three or four particulars.

1. First, the reward of *eternal life* is given to love, so that according to the measure of charity glory shall be given to us.   And although one have done works of themselves very glorious, have converted many souls, and sustained great afflictions, yet if he have not arrived to as great a charity as another who has not done such like things, because he had not power to do them, he shall not have equal glory with him; and so Christ our Lord says: —" He that loveth me, I will love him, and will manifest myself to him:"(13) as if He had said, " For his love I will bestow upon him my blessedness, which is the clear vision of my Divinity; and the more he shall love me, the more clearly shall he see me, and the more shall he rejoice in me, and finally, the higher shall his throne be in the Kingdom of my Father."

2. Secondly, the *gifts and heavenly favours* which are

(13) Joan. xiv. 21.

the rewards of this life, are likewise given according to the measure of love, which disposes the soul to receive them; and so the divine Wisdom says:—"I walk in the way of justice, in the midst of the paths of judgment, that I may enrich them that love me, and may fill their treasures." (14)

Colloquy.—O eternal Wisdom, which showest Thy justice and Thine uprightness in rewarding, and in favouring those that love Thee, help me to walk by the way of justice, and by the paths of perfection, loving Thee with all my strength, that I may be worthy to be enriched with Thy heavenly riches, and replenished with the treasures of Thine eternal goods. Amen.

3. Moreover, this loving God continually prevents us with *innumerable benefits*, as with draughts of love; He draws us to His love and service "with the cords of Adam," and "bands of love;"(15) He nourishes the fire of love with the fuel of His gifts, and blows upon it with the breath of His inspirations; for He came into the world to kindle this fire, and His desire is to have it always burning,(16) so that He may have Seraphim on earth, like as He has in heaven.

Colloquy.—O celestial Seraphim, who are always burning with the fire of love, beseech your God to inflame me with this fire, and to nourish it, that it may ever burn in this life, until it join me with you in the life eternal.   Amen.

4. Finally, that we might be held bound on every side, and constrained by His love, He *threatens us* with terrible punishments if we transgress the precept of love; for love failing, the life of grace fails, and the life of eternal glory will fail, and in its place death and hell will enter.   Hence

(14) Prov. viii. 20.   (15) Ose. xi. 4.   (16) Luc. xii. 49.

St. John says, "He that loveth not, abideth in death," i. e., of the soul, and shall abide for ever in death eternal; and the apostle says, "If any man love not our Lord Jesus Christ, be he anathema, maranatha,"(17) let him be accursed and excommunicated, and in the day of judgment let him be separated from the good who love Him, and cast into eternal fires, which burn those that hate Him. From all these considerations I am to gather the obligation which I have to love God our Lord, principally for Himself, for His infinite goodness, and for the love He bears me, taking this, as St. Thomas says, for a proper motive of my love. For, as St. Bernard says, even when it is pure and disinterested, it wants not its due reward, but obtains so much greater recompense, the less it seeks(18). But that it may be preserved and augmented, I may profit by the three considerations which we have here set down, i. e., the rewards which I expect; the goods I receive; and the chastisements I fear. Of these three things I will make a " threefold cord,"(19) and with it tie myself more strongly to this love, in order that my three enemies, the world, the flesh, and the Devil, may not prevail against me, nor separate me from the love of Jesus Christ.

Colloquy.—O most loving and most gentle JESUS, blessed is he, and blessed shall he be, who loves Thee; and cursed is he, and cursed shall he be, who hates Thee. Who would not love Thee, O my God, since Thou pourest forth so many blessings on him that loves Thee? And who shall hate Thee, since so many maledictions descend upon him who hates Thee? (20) O my soul, lift up the wings of thy

(17) 1 Joan. iii. 14. 1 Cor. xvi. 22.
(18) S. Th. 2, 2, q. xxvii. art. 3. Serm. xxxviii. in Cant. et Tract. De diligendo Deo § dico proinde.
(19) Eccles. iv. 12.
(20) S. Ber. lib. de diligendo Deo § Felix qui meruit.

heart above all that is created, and above thyself also; pass from that which is recompense, pain, or thine own profit, and fly with swiftness to thy Creator. Love Him for Himself, and for His infinite bounty and charity. Love Him because He loves thee, and because He desires to be loved by thee. Gratify Him in what He asks of thee, since He requires it only for thine own good. Praise Him and glorify Him for commanding thee to love Him, and giving thee strength to fulfil what He has deigned to command. O my beloved, what is it to Thee that I love Thee? Or what does it import Thee to hold love and friendship with me? It concerns me, O my Lord, and not Thee; but Thy infinite charity as ardently solicits me as if it was of as great importance to Thee as me. O that, wholly forgetting myself, I could imitate this Thy love, that I might love Thee alone, my only and chiefest good, to whom be honour and glory, and perpetual praise, world without end. Amen.

MEDITATION XII.

ON THE INFINITE MERCY OF ALMIGHTY GOD.

POINT I.

First is to be considered the excellency of God's mercy, compared with His justice, presupposing that these two attributes shine in all the gifts we receive from Him;— justice, in that He distributes and divides them conformably to the order of His infinite wisdom, and to that which the nature of every thing requires, or the merit of every person exacts,—mercy, in that with them He delivers us from the defects and miseries which we suffer, either from the imperfection of our nature or the default of our free will,(1)

(1) S. Th. 1, p. q. xxi. art. 3.

which He does in two ways, either by preventing the misery before it comes, or by delivering us from it after we are fallen into it. It is also the proper office of the justice of God to chastise those who do not profit by His mercy.

This presupposed, I am to consider that although the divine perfections, as they exist in Almighty God, are all equal; yet in order to the effects which proceed from them, one is more eminent than another. And in this respect mercy is greatly eminent, of whose works Almighty God does more glory than of the works of justice, and so the apostle St. James says:—"Mercy exalteth itself above judgment,"(2) and climbs and ascends up above justice. Let us, then, consider how mercy precedes, accompanies, and follows justice in all the works of God.

1. First, mercy always *precedes*, for all the works of justice presuppose some work of mercy on which they are grounded, and before God chastises sinners in justice, He bestows infinite mercies upon them, and pardons them many times, and admonishes them to amend, and to avoid His justice.(3) Whence it is that mercy and forgiveness proceed from Almighty God alone, who of His infinite bounty desires to free us from our miseries; but justice in punishing not only proceeds from God, but also from our own sins, which provoke Him to chastise us. For God, of His own inclination, is far from desiring occasion to exercise His retributive justice; and therefore says, according to the prophet Ezechiel, " Is it my will that a sinner should die,...and not that he be converted from his ways, and live ?" And the Wise man also says:—" God made not death, neither has He pleasure in the destruction of the living...but the wicked in works and words have proved it."(4)

Colloquy.—O most merciful God, since Thou

(2) Jac ii. 13.   (3) S. Th. 1, p. q. xxi. art. 4.
(4) Ezech. xviii. 23, et xxxiii. 11. Sap. i. 13.

delightest not in the perdition of the living, but rather grievest when Thou dost punish, and art glad when Thou rewardest, prevent our sins with Thy mercy, lest they constrain Thy justice to punish and scourge them.   Amen.

2. Secondly, mercy in like manner *accompanies* the works of justice, which never proceed alone, for even in the midst of the punishments which God inflicts, He vouchsafes many mercies, according to the prophet David, " Will God forget to show mercy, or will He in His anger shut up His mercies?"(5)   As if He had said, Although He be exceedingly angry, yet will He not forget His mercy, but with it will temper His anger.   And the like said the prophet Habacuc, " When Thou art angry, Thou wilt remember mercy."(6)   This God does, when He admonishes His enemies to avoid His punishments, and invites them to pardon, and greatly moderates the chastisements which they have deserved for their sins.   Even in hell also the mercy of Almighty God shines forth, for, as St. Thomas says, He chastises the damned, " citra condignum," less than He might punish them according to the greatness of the punishment, which the grievousness of their sins deserve.(7)

3. Hence it is, that mercy is, as it were, *the end* of justice, of which punishments are ordained, in order that the punished may amend him, and make himself capable of the mercy of God; but if he will not, yet at the least that others may take occasion by his punishment to have recourse to the divine mercy; and this never appears and shines more brightly in the good than when compared with the justice, which is executed on the wicked.   Hence St. Paul says:—" God endured with much patience vessels of

---

, (5) Ps. lxxvi. 10.   (6) Hab. iii. 2.

(7) 1 p q. xii. art. 4, ad. 1.

wrath," i. e., the reprobate, "that He might show the riches of His glory on the vessels of mercy,"(8) i. e., upon the elect, in whom is manifested the greatness of the mercy of Almighty God, who delivered them from that misery, into which the reprobate are plunged.

4. Lastly, Almighty God has wrought many *more* excellent works, in order to show His *mercy* in pardoning, than He has in order to manifest His *justice* in punishing, as we shall presently see.   Hence David says, " His tender mercies are over all His works."(9)   From all these considerations I will deduce great affections of joy, confidence, and love, since from what has been said it appears that although we have great reason to dread the justice of Almighty God, yet have we greater to hope in His mercy: and although I ought to embrace them both, lest justice alone should strike so great a fear into me, as to dismay me, or mercy alone inspire me with so great a confidence as to lead me to presume, yet I will still cling more closely to mercy.   For in all my miseries and falls, it is lawful for me, as St. Thomas says, to appeal from the tribunal of justice to that of mercy,(10) as from a lesser tribunal to one which is in some sort greater, and to approach, as St. Paul says, "with confidence to the throne of grace, that we may obtain mercy, and find grace in seasonable aid,"(11) i. e., in time allotted to us for seeking and labouring to obtain grace and mercy.

Colloquy.—O eternal God, I rejoice that Thou art both " merciful and just;"—just, because Thou lovest justice, and Thy " countenance" always beholds "righteousness ;"(12) — merciful, because Thou hast compassion upon the unjust, forgiving them their injus-

<hr>

(8) Rom. ix. 22.   (9) Ps. cxliv. 9.

(10) Iu cap. Ep. S. Jac.   (11) Heb. iv. 16.

(12) Ps. cxiv. 5. Ps. x. 8.

tices, that so they may embrace Thy goodness. But yet more ample art Thou in Thy mercy than in Thy justice, because Thou dost visit the sins of the fathers upon those sons that imitate them unto the third and fourth generation, but showest "mercy to them that love Thee," not to the fourth, but to a thousand generations. (13) O Lord, I worship Thy justice, and submit myself to Thy just correction, but yet desire that Thy mercy may prevail in me, making me a vessel and instrument thereof, that so Thou mayest be glorified in me, and that I may sing Thy mercies in the company of Thine elect, for ever and ever. Amen.

POINT II.

Secondly is to be considered the greatness and extent of the *mercy of God towards all His creatures* and towards all their miseries, which is infinite, because it is founded on His omnipotence, according to the saying of the Wise man: " Thou hast mercy upon all, because Thou canst do all things."(14)

Colloquy.—Rejoice, my soul, that Thy God is so mighty, and so merciful, and that His omnipotence can assuredly relieve every misery on which His mercy takes pity. O omnipotent mercy, and omnipotence infinitely merciful, how well do you agree together for our relief, mutually conferring on each other the *will* and the *power*, and so both together working out our perfection. If mercy were without omnipotence, how could it give me relief? If omnipotence were without mercy, how could it be moved to help me? Wherefore, my soul, consider those words of David:—" God hath spoken once ; these two things have I heard, that power belongeth to God, and mercy to Thee, O Lord."(15) O God of my soul, declare, I beseech Thee, these two things very clearly and efficaciously within my heart; discover to me, by Thy sovereign light,

(13) Exod. xx. 6.   (14) Sap.xi. 24.   (15) Ps. lxi. 12.

the conjunction of Thy mercy with Thy omnipotence, in order that I may serve Thee with gladness, relying upon Thy omnipotent mercy.   Amen.

1. From hence may I discourse upon the greatness and multitude of the mercies of God, pondering some points in particular.—

i. First, as the royal Psalmist says,—" The earth is full of the mercy of the Lord," (16) because *all the creatures* which live in it are subject to some misery, either from some defect of nature, or from the depravity of their own will, and it is God alone that can succour them, and supply a remedy: and, therefore, I may behold the roundness of the earth, as a capacious vessel, all full of the mercies of God, and whatever I see in it, may serve me for an incitement to praise His mercy.

ii. Hence it is that His mercy is such, that it extends itself *even to beasts*, and the rest of the brute creation, according to that of David: "Men and beasts Thou wilt preserve, O Lord.   O how hast Thou multiplied Thy mercy, O God:"(17) which is as much as to say, O Lord, how greatly hast Thou multiplied Thy mercy, since Thou givest not only to man, life, health, and relief in his necessities, but even to the very beasts themselves.

Colloquy.—I give Thee thanks for the mercy which Thou dost show them, though they know it not; and since Thou takest compassion on the " young ravens," (18) giving them to eat when they are in want, and crave after food; much more wilt Thou take compassion on the sons of men, for whose good it was that Thou didst create the beasts.

iii. Hence I may ponder that which Almighty God said to the prophet Jonas:—" Thou art grieved, for the

(16) Ps. xxxii. 5. et cxviii. 64.   (17) Ps. xxxv. 8.
(18) Ps. cxlvi. 9.

ivy withered for which thou hast not laboured, nor made it to grow; and shall not I spare Nineveh, that great city, in which are more than a hundred and twenty thousand persons, that know not how to distinguish between their right hand and their left, and many beasts?" (19) As if He had said, It grieves thee to see that creature destroyed, which thou didst not make, and yet thou desirest the destruction of those whom I made. Thou mournest for the loss of one plant of ivy, which comes forth in one night, and is withered in another, and shall not I mourn over the loss of so many lives, which have endured so many years through my mercy?

Colloquy.—O my God, let Thine infinite mercy, which is incomparably greater than the lives of all creatures, praise Thee, "for Thy mercy is better than lives," (20) seeing it gives life to all things living: and without it there is neither life, nor any means of preserving it. "Let Thy tender mercies come unto me, and I shall live," (21) and for them shall glorify Thy name for ever and ever. Amen.

2. From hence I ought to conceive great confidence in the mercy of Almighty God, seeing that He takes compassion on all my miseries, reflecting that whether they are infirmities of the body, or afflictions of the mind, or any other kind of penalties and persecutions whatever, they cannot be so great in number or enormity, as that the mercy of Almighty God, cannot and will not, deliver me, as far as in Him lies, when it is convenient for me, for if my miseries have no number, much less have His mercies.

POINT III.

Thirdly is to be considered in particular, the infinite mercy of God towards *sinners*, concerning which the Wise man says:—"Thou hast mercy upon all, because Thou

(19) Jonas iv. 9.   (20) Ps. lxii. 4.   (21) Ps. cxviii. 77.

canst do all things, and overlookest the sins of men for the sake of repentance; for Thou lovest all things that are .....but Thou sparest all; because they are Thine, O Lord, who lovest souls:" (22) from which passage we may gather the *properties* of the mercy of God.

1. The first *property* is, that it extends itself to *all men*, of whatever state or condition they may be, without excluding any, as is expressed by the words, "Thou hast mercy upon all," great and little, noble and ignoble, free-men and slaves, for this rule is universal, and admits of no exception; and for this the Wise man gives two reasons: i. The first is, because all sinners are the making and work of His omnipotence, with which His mercy, as we said above, is inseparably joined. ii. The second is, because Almighty God loves souls, and from love springs compas-sion for those miseries to which the object beloved is sub-ject. These two reasons I should often call to mind, as well to animate me to confidence in the divine mercy, as to make me beg Almighty God to employ the same in my behalf.

Colloquy.—O my soul, if the fault which thou com-mittest of thine own accord cast thee down, let the work which God has done by His omnipotency, encourage thee to confidence. If thou wilt blot out by penance the evil which thou hast done, God will certainly repair, by His mercy, the good which He has done, because His mercy cannot be wanting to the work which proceeds from His omnipotence. O lover of souls, who lovest mine because Thou madest it, for Thou wouldst never have made it to hate it, pardon the fault which I have committed, that there may not remain in me any thing hateful to Thee; behold he whom Thou lovest is full of miseries; show, therefore, towards him Thine abundant mercy. Amen.

(22) Sap. xi. 24.

2. The second *property* of the mercy of Almighty God is, that it extends itself to *all sins*, however many and grievous they may be, because no sin can be so *great*, as that the mercy of Almighty God is not infinitely greater to pardon it, nor can they be so *innumerable*, as for His mercies not to be incomparably more innumerable. So that I may make use of these two things joined together, as a title, on which to crave pardon.for my sins, saying with David: " Have mercy on me, O God, according to Thy great mercy: and according to the multitude of Thy tender mercy, blot out my iniquity." O most merciful God, " let Thy mercies speedily prevent us, for we are become exceedingly poor." (23)

3. From hence proceeds the third property of the mercy of Almighty God, which is to *wait for* sinners, that they may do penance, and to invite them to pardon, granting it with great facility when they ask it of Him, and wholly forgetting their sins as if they had never committed them. This is the saying of the Wise man, "That God dissembleth the sins of men for penance," because He acts as if He did not know them, with regard to the punishment of them, waiting for them to do penance for them, and, because as soon as they repent of them, He dissembles them, just as if He knew not they had committed them, casting them, as another prophet says, " into the bottom of the sea," (24) whence they shall never rise into sight again, and separating them from us, as David says, as far as the east is distant from the west; for, as it is impossible to join together these two extremes, even so, the sin which God has once forgiven by His mercy, can never return and join itself to him, who has obtained pardon for it. And that which shows the extent of His mercy still more, is, that He has put no limit to the number of times that He will pardon,

<hr>

(23) Ps. lxxviii. 8.   (24) Mich. vii. 19.

but after He has pardoned most numerous and grievous sins, returns again the second time to pardon as many more, and those, perhaps, much more grievous, and the same He does the third time; and not only " seven times, but till seventy times seven times;" (25) that is to say, times without number. All this the divine mercy does, not to give us an occasion by this of offending Him more freely, but to " lead" us, as St. Paul says, " to penance" (26) for our sins, if we have fallen, with a confidence of obtaining pardon as often as we demand it from our heart.

Colloquy.—O most merciful God, what thanks and praises should we give to Thee for Thine infinite mercy? " I am not worthy of the least of all Thy mercies," (27) how, therefore, shall I give Thee due thanks for them? Let Thy mercies themselves therefore praise and bless Thee for evermore, and I will repeat very often that sweet canticle of David, " Let the mercies of our Lord give glory to Him, and His wonderful works to the children of men." (28)

4. To magnify this point of the divine mercy, I may reflect with great profit on the words of the prodigal son, and of others, the meditations on which are contained in the third Part,(29) drawing from all these considerations a firm determination to *imitate* the mercy of Almighty God, by being merciful towards my neighbours, as He is merciful towards me; for this is another property of the divine mercy, to be especially compassionate towards those who imitate Him, which was the reason that Christ our Lord said:—" Blessed are the merciful, for they shall obtain mercy."

POINT IV.

Fourthly is to be considered the infinite mercy of

(25) Mat xviii. 22.   (26) Rom. ii. 4.
(27) Gen. xxxii. 10.   (28) Ps. cvi. 15.   (29) Medit. xlix.

Almighty God towards *the just*, who love and serve Him, and towards those who are His *elect*, that they may be, as St. Paul says, "vessels of mercy," (30) that is, instruments for making manifest the abyss of His mercies, and all the excellencies comprehended in this perfection of His, in which He so greatly glories.

1. First, the mercy of God towards the elect is *eternal*, without beginning and without ending, for ever since God was God, He took mercy on them, and so long as He shall be God, so long shall His mercy endure, as is expressed by those words of David:—"The mercy of the Lord is from eternity and unto eternity upon them that fear Him:" as we have already said,(31) that His *love* was eternal, because from all eternity God our Lord predestinated them, and determined to deliver them from all their miseries, and most especially from that chief misery, everlasting condemnation, and to give them supreme happiness, which is everlasting bliss; and as far as He was concerned, His mercy had always the same desire for all men, so that, for instance, before I was, God took mercy on me, and foreseeing the miseries into which I should fall, He decreed to deliver me from them, on condition that I would obey Him, intending to persevere in this mercy for evermore. This should kindle in me a most ardent affection of praise and glory in Almighty God, for this His everlasting mercy, in which spirit I may compose a canticle of praise, like that of David, in which he repeats at every verse the following words: "For His mercy endureth for ever:" "Praise the Lord, for He is good, for His mercy endureth for ever: Praise ye the God of gods, for His mercy endureth for ever: Praise ye the Lord of lords, for His mercy endureth for ever. Who alone doth great wonders, for His mercy endureth for ever." (32)

(30) Rom. ix. 23.   (31) Medit. x.   (32) Ps. cxxxv. 1.

Colloquy.—O my soul, praise, glorify, and bless Thy God, because He is so singularly good, and because His mercy has no beginning, and will have no end; rejoice with singular joy, because God is good, and because His mercy towards those that serve Him is eternal. O eternal God, I will " keep Thy law for ever and ever," (33) since Thy mercy to me is eternal, and for ever and ever. Amen.

2. Secondly, the mercy of Almighty God, from the very moment in which the elect person comes into existence, goes before, *accompanies and follows him* at all times, even to his death. For the mercy of God, who *predestinated* him from eternity, afterwards, by little and little, *calls* him, in order to justify him, and justifies him to exalt and glorify him; and so the prophet Jeremiah said: —" I have loved thee with an everlasting love, therefore have I drawn thee, taking pity on thee."(34) If I am dead in sin, the mercy of God prevents and calls me, and I rise again to a new life: if I am in the sleep of slothfulness, the mercy of God comes and awakens me, that I may shake off my sluggishness: if I am to do anything that is pleasing to Almighty God, His mercy prevents and inspires me to do it: if I am to persevere in the good I have begun, His " mercy shall follow me all the days of my life,"(35) for by it I shall overcome all temptations, and shall obtain the final victory and life eternal.

Colloquy.—" Bless the Lord, O my soul, and let all that is within me bless His holy name," (36) who is propitious to thy iniquities, who heals all thy infirmities, who redeems thy life from deadly falling, who crowns thee with mercies and commiserations; His mercy is thy crown, for by it Thou wilt obtain the

(33) Ps. cxviii. 44.   (34) Rom. viii. 30.   Jer. xxxi. 3.
    (35) Ps. lviii. 11.   Ps. xxii. 6.   (36) Ps. cii. 1.

victory, and He will also crown thee in this life with good works, and in the other with great rewards.

3. Hence, thirdly, it is that the mercy of Almighty God towards the elect is *most high*, because it lifts them up to the highest good which He possesses, that is, to the goods of glory. And in this respect David said, with great reason:—that the "mercy of God is great above the heavens," because there it is fully made known to the elect; although even in this life it is also high, because it highly honours them with the sovereign gifts of His grace and protection; and this gave David reason to say:—"According to the height of heaven above the earth He hath strengthened His mercy towards them that fear Him."(37) Now as heaven, always lasting, will always cover the earth, even so His mercy will last always, and protect those who love Him; and in proportion to the height of heaven above the earth is the excess of His mercy above our misery; "For as a father hath compassion on his children, so hath the Lord compassion on them that fear Him, for He knoweth our frame,"(38) and supplies the defect of our great frailty by the greatness of His mercy.

Colloquy.—O my God, and my glory, what shall I say of Thy mercy, how shall I praise Thee for it, and how may I be made a vessel and instrument of it? Thy mercy had compassion on me before I was; it created me that I might be; it prevents me, in order to make me work; it accompanies me when I am working; it follows me till I have finished my work; it surrounds me with blessings; it crowns me with great victories, and gives me a great confidence of obtaining "Deus meus misericordia mea—My God, my mercy," (39) Thou art mercy itself, and all mercy is Thine, because Thou art merciful by Thy

(37) Ps. cvii. 5.   Ps. xxxv. 6.   Ps ci. 11.
(38) Ps. cii. 13, 14.   (39) Ps. lviii. 18.

very nature; but it is also mine, because Thou art not
the object of mercy, who art not subject to
miseries, but I am its object, who am full of miseries,
and Thou alone canst relieve me from them.   O my
mercy, unite me with Thyself in Thine eternal glory,
where Thou mayest always be mine; that, enjoying
Thy happiness, I may be free from all misery, world
without end.   Amen.

POINT V.

1. Lastly are to be considered, the *proofs* which God has
given of His infinite mercy towards men; for He has
made it known in the clearest manner possible, and in an
infinite variety of ways.

i. First, then, mercy has, in us, *two effects.*   One is, to
make us sorry for the evil which afflicts our neighbour, the
other is, to make us deliver him from that evil.(40)   And
because God, by His divine essence, was incapable of the
first effect, so that sorrow could not fall upon Him, yet
His infinite mercy willed that, as far as was possible, this
effect should not be wanting in Him, and therefore He
made Himself true man, that, as man, He might be sorry
for our miseries, and have true compassion on them, as if
they had been His own, being in all things, as St. Paul
says, "like unto His brethren, that He might become
merciful"(41) in a new manner, taking upon Him the
affections of compassion and sorrow, which before He had
not; and that He had them now really is proved by the
tears which He shed at the sight of our miseries, through
His desire to deliver us from them.

Colloquy.—I give Thee thanks, O most merciful
God, for inventing this new manner of showing Thy-
self merciful to man.   O infinite gladness, why wilt
Thou be made capable of sorrow, who art able to

(40) S. Tho. i. p. q. 21. a. 3.   (41) Heb. ii. 17.

afford sufficient relief to my misery without ever feeling sorrow for it? Let Thy mercy, O God, be ever praised for these inventions, which have proceeded from it; and assist me by them, I beseech Thee, so to imitate it in this life, that I may be worthy to obtain it in the other. Amen.

ii. But the mercy of Almighty God went yet further. For not content with having taken this sorrow and inward compassion upon Him, He likewise *took all our miseries and our pains* (sin only excepted), even to death itself, that by this experience He might learn to have mercy after a new manner; for which reason St. Paul said:— " We have not a high priest that cannot have compassion on our infirmities, but one tempted in all things like as we are, without sin;"(42) that is to say, the high priest whom we have will not be so severe as to deal with us only in accordance with His justice, but He will have compassion on us with great mercy, because He has, although always without sin, gone through the experience of those troubles and temptations which we mortals suffer; and from what He has suffered, He has learned to take compassion and mercy on us in our sufferings.

Colloquy.—O most merciful high-priest, although Thou hast not experienced the misery of sin, yet Thou hast made trial of those pains which sin deserved ; and since Thou sufferedst to deliver me from both, deliver me from sin, in order that I may not fall into eternal pains. Amen.

iii. But the infinite mercy of God ended not here, for He invented another new means of exercising mercy towards us, in *the most holy Sacrament* of the Altar, making Himself meat to the hungry, drink to the thirsty, a medicine to the sick, a ransom to redeem those in captivity,

(42) Heb. iv. 15.

a sacrifice to pardon iniquities, and a helper and remedy in all our necessities. Thus we may believe it to be this work which is attributed to the mercy of God by holy David in the mystical sense of those words, where he says: —" He hath made a memory of His wonderful works, being a merciful and gracious Lord; He hath given food to them that fear Him."(43)

Colloquy.—O most merciful God, I have now a new reason for calling Thee *my mercy*, for Thou dost not only mercifully relieve my wants, but Thou art become Thyself their remedy, and the very mercy by which they obtain relief. Let Thy " mercies," O my Lord, give glory to Thee, and Thy " wonderful works to the children of men ;" (44) for Thou hast " satisfied the empty soul," and " filled the hungry soul with good things."

2. From these considerations I will gather, how innu- merable and how boundless the manifestations of God's mercy are, since in every one of these there are so many, that they cannot be comprehended. But from the consi- deration of them all I should conceive a great desire of imitating them for the good of my neighbours, as Christ Himself exhorted us, saying:—" Be ye therefore merciful, as your Father also is merciful,"(45) for He is gentle even towards the ungrateful and wicked; and so, beholding the pattern of divine mercy, which has been set forth in these five points, I will learn another similar mercy, and desire to find opportunities of exercising it, applying to my own intention what the prophet David said:—" Is there any one left of the house of Saul, that I may show the mercy of God unto him ?"(46) that is to say, an exceedingly great mercy, like that of Almighty God, which extends itself to

(43) Ps. cx. 4.

(44) Ps. cvi. 9.   (45) Luc. vi. 36.   (46) 2 Reg. ix. 3.

friends and foes, and grants to all very high and excellent gifts, as a means for their deliverance from the abyss of great evils.

Colloquy.—O eternal God, who art very properly called "Father of mercies," (47) vouchsafe to show Thy mercy to us by making us like to Thee in this respect, that, imitating Thee as sons on earth, we may obtain Thy eternal inheritance in heaven.   Amen.

MEDITATION XIII.

ON THE INFINITE LIBERALITY OF GOD TOWARDS MEN.

POINT I.

First is to be considered, how the infinite liberality of God consists in His *giving* innumerable and excellent *gifts to His creatures*, although He is under no such obligation, and does not expect any payment for them, or to derive any advantage from them.   This the apostle St. James declares, when he says:—God "giveth to all men abundantly, and upbraideth not."(1)   So that the liberality of our God shines particularly in this, that the gifts which He gives us proceed from His bounty and charity, to which this attribute is closely allied.   Now this liberality shows itself principally in five things.—i. In giving *innumerable* gifts of nature and grace proportioned to the capacity of His creatures.—ii. In giving gifts of *infinite value*, for He came to give Himself to them, in the manner of which we spoke when considering the mysteries of the Incarnation, Passion, Eucharist, and coming of the Holy Ghost.—iii. In that He gives *to all*, without any exception

(47) 2 Cor. i. 3.
(1) S. Tho. 1. p. q. xxi. art. 3. et ii. 2, 2, q. cxvii. art. 6. ad. 1. Jac. i. 5.

of persons, to good and bad, to the ungrateful and the illiberal, and even to His own enemies.— iv. In that He gives, not because of any debt which He owes, but simply *because He is good*, and inclined to give: for if liberality began not on His part, no one else could be liberal, according to what He said to Job:—" Who hath given me before, that I should repay unto him?" And so His apostle says:— " Who hath first given to Him, and recompense shall be made him?"(2)—v. In that He gives *without any expectation* or requirement from His creatures *of any payment* or profit for Himself, for He has no need of them, nor of their goods. And if He require gratitude and obedience to His laws, this is because liberality is not contrary to justice, and as He is the supreme lawgiver, and most just, He lays down precepts and laws concerning those things, which we on our part are bound to perform. And even in this He shows His liberality, for His object in His commands and requirements of us is, to have an occasion of giving, and then of rewarding our services with new gifts. We may therefore say without any hesitation, that God alone is liberal, and that there is no one liberal but Almighty God, just as we say that there is no one good but God; and so our liberality, compared with His, is no liberality, for the reason which is expressed in those words of Scripture:—" We have given Thee what we have received of Thy hand,"(3) for we can give Him nothing unless we first receive it from Him, and that which we give, we owe to Him on a thousand titles.

Colloquy.—O most liberal God, I give Thee thanks for all the works of Thine infinite liberality; Thou makest known Thine infinite blessedness, since, as Thou hast said, it is more blessed to give than to

(2) Job. xli. 2.   Rom. xi. 35.
(3) Luc. xviii 19.   1 Par. xxix. 14.

receive. Make me, Lord, liberal in rendering back to Thee what I have received from Thee, in order that I may enjoy Thy blessedness for all eternity. Amen.

2. Hence I should conceive a great *desire of being liberal*, as far as I can be so, to God our Lord, giving Him all those things which He desires and asks of me, either by His precepts, great and little, or by His Evangelical counsels, or by rules of my Religious state, or by the superiors of the Church and of my Religion, or by any one else who may desire anything of me, or by His secret inspirations, or, finally, by the mouth of the poor, and of my neighbours, when weighed down by any affliction, whether of body or soul, which it is in my power to relieve. And all this I will offer to Him, "not with sadness, or of necessity,"(4) as vassals do who pay tribute, and dare not do otherwise, for fear of punishment and death, but with alacrity and willingness, like nobles, who pay what they owe in an honourable manner, and somewhat more than in justice they are bound to do, in order to show the nobility of their disposition and their liberality, for " God loveth a cheerful giver." Finally, in offering anything to God, or giving to the poor, I ought not to act principally from a motive of hope of reward, or for some advantage which I expect from it, but purely out of love, and to imitate, as far as I can, the infinite bounty and liberality of my Creator, in giving Him the thing He most desires, which is my heart.

Colloquy.—O most loving and most liberal Father, Thine is my heart, since Thou hast given it me; take it, therefore, since Thou requirest it of me. And because I cannot give it to Thee with such liberality and perfection as I desire, do Thou vouchsafe to supply my defect, that I may give it back to Thee as

(4) 2 Cor. ix. 7.

Thou requirest.   O my Father, take my heart to Thyself, for it will be much better, and more secure with Thee, than it is with me.   Henceforth I offer Thee my desires, my affections, my actions, and all that is mine; I desire, my beloved, that all the fruit of this tree be " kept for Thee;" (5) I therefore give it to Thee most liberally, in order that Thou mayest eat of it; for Thou conferrest a greater favour in receiving it from me, than I perform service in giving it to Thee.

POINT II.

The second shall be to consider the infinite liberality which God our Lord shows towards *those who are thus liberal towards Him;* for if He be so liberal towards the sparing, how much more liberal will He be towards the liberal, since He says:—" With the same measure that you mete withal, it shall be measured to you again;"(6) that is, in proportion as you are liberal towards me, will I be more liberal towards you.   And this liberality of God towards the liberal is shown in the following particulars.

i. First, in *hearing* their *prayers* and petitions with great promptitude, condescending to them in that manner and in those occasions which is most convenient for them; for in proportion to the quickness and promptness of obedience with which we give to God that which He asks of us, will be the promptness with which He will give us what we ask of Him.

ii. Secondly, if from carelessness or forgetfulness they fail to ask Him for what is expedient for them, He *excites* and solicits *them to demand it,* out of His great desire to give them what they need; for it is the office of the Holy Ghost to inspire us to pray, that so He may have opportunity of displaying His liberality towards us.(7)

(5) Cant. vii. 13.   (6) Luc vi. 38.
(7) S. Greg. lib. iii. Dial. c. 16. Rom. viii. 26.

iii. Thirdly, He manifests His liberality in a still more conspicuous manner, in bestowing upon them the things which they have need of, even *when they ask not* for them, thus preventing their prayers and their desires with the gift of those very things for which their prayers and desires were due. For the necessity of him who is liberal towards God, although he himself hold his peace, cries out for him, and pleads with the divine liberality for relief: and hence He says:—"Before they call I will hear."(8)

iv. Fourthly, He shows Himself liberal, in giving them *abundance of spiritual consolations*, which are so excellent, that they exceed an hundred-fold all they give in return to God. And this liberality Religious especially make proof of who, as they have been liberal, in leaving all things for Christ our Lord, and giving them to the poor; so likewise is Christ most liberal to them, giving them "a hundred-fold" more than what they have left for Him. And whoever with a generous mind offers to Almighty God that which is dear and delightful to Him, shall also in proportion experience the same liberality.

v. Finally, *the gifts and graces are innumerable* which God, in His liberality, imparts to those who are liberal to Him; He receives them under His protection, He helps them in their temptations, delivers them out of their dangers, takes them for instruments of notable works, augments their virtues and merits, and afterwards rewards them with an abundant recompense, fulfilling what He promised when He said:—"Give, and it shall be given to you, good measure, and pressed down, and shaken together, and running over, shall they give into your bosom."(9) For the gifts of the divine liberality infinitely exceed those of ours.

Colloquy.—O my soul, rejoice that Thou hast a

(8) Isai. lxv. 24.   (9) Luc. vi. 38.

God no less liberal than rich. If He were rich, and were not liberal, His riches would serve thee to small purpose ; and if He were liberal, and not rich, His liberality would profit thee very little ; but in the one and in the other He is infinite, and employs both the one and the other to thy advantage. Be thou therefore liberal towards Him who is so liberal towards Thee ; for although it be much that thou givest Him, yet much more is it that thou receivest of Him. "Let not thy hand be stretched out to receive, and shut when thou shouldst give ;" (10) for if thou close thy hand in giving to God what He asks of thee, He will close His hand in giving what thou askest of Him. Stretch forth thy hand, therefore. to give Him all thou hast, and He will open His, and fill thee with bounty and benediction. (11)

POINT III.

From what has been said, I am led to reflect upon *my great niggardliness towards God*, who has been so liberal towards me. For as Christ our Lord, in the midst of His afflictions, was twice athirst, once when He asked drink of the Samaritan, and again when He said on the cross, " I thirst," and both times they refused Him what He desired ; even so I likewise am most niggardly towards Him, for either I deny Him what He asks of me, as did the Samaritan, or I give Him to drink vinegar, mingled with unsavoury hyssop, as did the Jews, doing my works with the mixture of so many imperfections, that He refuses to accept them. This will appear very plainly from the consideration of the five things which Almighty God requires of me, as they are set down in the first point.—i. I am very deficient and sparing in keeping His precepts, and if I keep the greater, I break many of the lesser.—ii. I neglect many of His counsels, observing the rules of my voca-

(10) Ecclus. iv. 36.   (11) Ps. ciii. 28. et clxiv. 16.

tion with many breaches and imperfections.—iii. I resist those which my superiors prescribe me.—iv. I also stifle the divine inspirations, denying Almighty God what, by them, He demands of me.—v. And lastly, I refuse to my neighbours in necessity the corporal or spiritual succour which I might give them.

2. And so by this my parsimony I *restrain*, as far as lies in me, *the divine liberality*, and deserve that Almighty God should deal sparingly with me in the five things in which He shows Himself so liberal to the liberal; if, therefore, He does not hear me, or does not favour me, or impart His gifts to me with the same liberality as to others, the fault is mine, and to me are spoken His words by the prophet :—" Is my hand shortened, and become little, that I cannot redeem?"(12) Or is my liberality and omnipotence so restrained that I cannot save you, and do you the good which I was wont? It is not so, but the sins, and closeness of your hands have closed mine, and been the cause that my justice has restrained my liberality. And even in this God shows Himself most liberal, for it seems grievous to Him to see Himself so straitened, and, as it were, constrained in His justice, by reason of our sins, that He cannot extend His wonted liberality to us.

Colloquy.—O infinite liberality, remove from me, by means of Thy mercy, all the impediments which I oppose to Thy desire ; forgive my sins, that I may be capable of Thy gifts.   Amen.

(12) Isa. l. 2, et lix. 1.

MEDITATION XIV.

This meditation is of great moment, and most important, because it is the foundation of prayer and contemplation, and of that union which is the end of these meditations belonging to the Unitive way.

POINT I.

1. First is to be considered how God our Lord, Three and One, is so immense, that He *fills*, as the prophet Jeremiah says, "*heaven and earth;*" and His Spirit, as the Wise man says, replenishes "the whole world," (2) so that there is no corner in which Almighty God is not; and as He is a pure Spirit, He also penetrates all bodies, and is within them; for He is within the heavens, within the sea, and within the heart of the earth, nor is it possible to imagine any place, or point, in which God is not. Hence, wherever I am, I must imagine that I am in God, as the fishes in the water, and as the birds in the air, saying with David:—"If I ascend into heaven, Thou art there: if I descend into hell, Thou art present: if I take my wings early in the morning, and dwell in the uttermost parts of the sea, even there also shall Thy hand lead me, and Thy right hand shall hold me." (3) So that it is not possible for me to fly from God, nor to hide myself from Him, for in the way by which I fly, there is He, and in the place where I would hide myself, there shall I find Him.

2. But His immensity extends yet farther, for in such a

<hr>

(1) S. Tho. 1. p. q. 8. a. 1, et 2.

(2) Jer. xxiii. 24.   Sap. i. 7.   (3) Psal cxxxvii. 8.

manner does He fill heaven and earth, and the whole world, that He is not tied or bound to the place which He now fills, but is *capable of being in a million worlds besides*, which, if He pleased, He could create above the heavens. And all the place which He now fills, is as point in comparison of the immense place which He could fill; whence Solomon said:—" Heaven and the Heaven of heavens cannot contain Thee." (4)   This consideration is the seed of great affections and virtues, if it be used as it ought, to quicken in us the belief of the presence of Almighty God, in every place, in imitation of Moses, of whom St. Paul says, " He endured, as seeing Him that is invisible." (5) Even so I am to behold Almighty God by faith, to speak with Him in prayer, and to expect succour, and to consult with Him, and do all things before Him, as if I saw Him with my corporal eyes, since, although He is invisible to these, yet is He really and truly present where I am, and the eyes of natural light, and of supernatural faith, ought to supply the defect of the corporal eyes.   Whence it is, that every place may be to me a place of prayer, since God is present in every place, so that everywhere I may speak with Him, according to that saying of St. Paul:— " I will, therefore, that men pray in every place, lifting up pure hands, without anger and contention:" (6) and this especially has regard to the use of ejaculatory prayers.

3. Faith being quickened in this manner, I will break forth into affections of admiration and joy, admiring the immensity of God, and rejoicing that He is so immense, that the whole world cannot contain Him, saying with the prophet: " O Israel, how great is the house of God, and how vast is the place of His possession!   It is great and hath no end; it is high and immense." (7)

<table>
<tr><td>(4) 3 Reg. viii. 27.</td><td>(5) Heb. xi. 27.</td></tr>
<tr><td>(6) 1 Tim. ii. 8.</td><td>(7) Baruch iii. 24.</td></tr>
</table>

Colloquy.—O immense God, who sayest, " Heaven is my throne, and the earth my footstool," both which yet cannot contain Thee, because Thou art " higher than heaven," more exalted than the stars, and deeper than hell; (8) I rejoice Thy immensity, together with Thy glory, is so as to suffer no diminution from the baseness of the place which Thou fillest. Lighten, O Lord, my interior, that I may see with more assurance than if I beheld Thee with my outward eyes. Amen.

POINT II.

1. Secondly is to be considered how God our Lord is in all places, and in all things created, viz., by essence,—presence,—and power. (9)

i. First, God is in all things by *essence*, because, really and truly His divinity is in them, together with all that He has, and works within Himself, because He is indivisible and inseparable. Wherefore I am to believe, that even here, where I am, God the Father, Son, and Holy Ghost, is wholly present. Here the Father is begetting the Son, and the Father, and the Son, are producing the Holy Ghost. Here is His infinite goodness and charity, His mercy and justice, His wisdom and omnipotence, and all the excellencies and perfections of His divinity. And He who is here, the same is, without any difference, also in heaven, who created the world, and governs it; and if here I had light to see Him, here would He make me blessed. O my soul, if thou quickenest thy faith, when thou art alone, thou wilt see that thou art not alone, since the Three divine Persons are with thee; if when alone thou wilt employ all thy powers in the most excellent manner thou art able, then hast thou present with thee,

(8) Isa. lxvi. 1.   Job. xi. 8. et xxii. 1.
(9) S. Tho. 1. p. q. viii. art. 3. S. Greg. in Cant. 5. Quo abiit Dilectus.

the supreme Good to love, the infinite majesty to adore, the sovereign wisdom to converse with, the divine omnipotence to confide in, and the source of infinite gladness wherein to rejoice. Rejoice in the presence of the Father, converse with the Son, speak with the Holy Ghost, enter within this undivided Trinity, and immense Divinity, beholding how on all sides He encompasses thee, and by this means thou shalt always be present with Almighty God, and every place shall be to thee the court of heaven, since, where the King of heaven is, there His court is also.

Colloquy.—O immense King, who art so in all Thy Kingdom by essence, that Thou art wholly in every part, grant that I may also, with an undivided heart, serve Thee as so high a King deserves to be served by all those that are in His presence. Amen.

ii. Secondly, Almighty God is in every place, and in all things by His *presence*, seeing and knowing whatever is in every one. So that God is not here, as a man is in a place in his sleep, or his senses suspended, or distracted, and not observing where he is; neither is God in this world, as our soul is in our body, which sees not what is done within it, but He both sees and knows the place and habitation where He is, so that nothing can be hid or concealed from Him; and although the place of itself be most obscure, yet to God it is most clear, for "darkness," as David says, "shall not be dark to Thee."(10) Wherefore, O my soul, think that God is here, and that He beholds thee. If thou wilt pray in secret, God is there, "who sees thee in secret," and attends to thy prayer to hear it. If temptation molest thee, think that God is looking upon thee, to whose eyes wickedness is "hateful," (11) and he that addicts himself to it. If thou art afflicted, think that

(10) Ps. cxxxviii. 12. Mat. vi. 6.   (11) Sap. xiv. 9.

God beholds thy affliction, and that He knows the season to succour thee. If thou wilt do any good work, consider not that men behold thee, but that God Himself beholds thee, who sees more than all, and many things which others see not; Him, therefore, alone desire to please, since He alone is to judge thee, of those things which He sees in thee.

Colloquy.—O immense God, who art in every place full of eyes, with which Thou dost behold "the good and the evil," (12) clear my sight with Thine, that, considering Thou beholdest me, I may lead a life pleasing to Thee, without doing any thing unworthy of Thy Presence, that so I may come to enjoy the clear vision of Thee. Amen.

iii. Thirdly, God is in every place, and in every thing, by *power*, because He not only beholds what is there, but also, by means of His omnipotence, gives to things the being they have, and helps them in all they do, according to that which St. Paul says, "He is not far from every one of us, for in Him we live and move, and be." (13) No place, therefore, contains God as it contains me, but God contains all places, and sustains all things. If they live, it is because God is in them, giving them life; if they move, it is because God is in them, giving them motion; if they have being, it is because God is in them, and gives it to, and maintains them in it; and if God absent or withdraw Himself from any place, or from any thing, it immediately ceases to be.

2. Hence it is, that beholding all the things of the world, in all I am to *see God who is in them*, by essence, presence, and by power, working in them and by them. And as beholding a man, by the exterior and visible things, which I see in his body, I pass on to regard the interior

<hr>

(12) Pro. xv. 3. et xvi. 2.   (13) Act. xvii. 27.

and invisible soul, which gives him being, life, and motion; even so, beholding all the creatures, I am to penetrate with the eyes of faith to that which is within them, viz., God, not as their soul, or form, but after another more excellent manner, by means of which He gives them being, and whatever else they have.

3. Hence I will *conceive affections of love*, of joy, and thanksgiving, rejoicing to see Almighty God thus united with His creatures, and dwelling in them in so wonderful a manner; and thus the most beautiful objects will not entice me to love them inordinately, nor the most terrible affright me, or cause me to flee from them in dismay. When I see myself near to savage beasts, or to my enemies, I may and ought to believe that I am near to God, and that He is in all things; and hence I shall recover great courage, saying with Job, "Set me beside Thee, and let any man's hand fight against me." (14)

Colloquy.—O Almighty God, "if armies in camp should stand together against me, my heart shall not fear," because I am certain that I am nigh to Thee, without whose will they cannot move their hand.   I will always "set" Thee "in my sight," because Thou art "at my right hand, that I be not moved." (15)

POINT III.

Thirdly, I am to consider more particularly the manner in which Almighty God is *within me*, and how I am, live, and move, in Him.

1. God *encompasses* me *on every side*, as the waters of the sea the fish that is therein; and as the apple is within the eye, so am I enclosed in God; and as the same Lord says, we "are carried by His bowels, and are borne up by His womb," (16) just as a woman with child bears her infant

(14) Job. xvii. 3.

(15) Ps. xxvi. 3.   Ps. xv. 8.   (16) Isa. xlvi. 3.

in her bowels, and serves him for a house, a bed, a wall, sustenance, and all other things. O my soul, dost thou not rejoice, and leap for gladness, at beholding thyself in this manner within thy God? He is the house, out of which thou canst not issue, and within which thou art to live and work for ever. He is thy chamber, in which thou art to take thy repose, and out of which thou shalt find no rest. He is thy bed, in which thou art borne in all thy goings, for unless He carry thee, thou canst not move. He is thy wall, to enclose thee, without which thou shalt have no security. He is thy sustenance and thy life, for in Him thou hast it, and from Him thou receivest it; much more truly than an infant remaining in his mother's womb, receives His life from her.

Colloquy.—O most loving God, and most tender mother, who, wherever I go, bearest me in Thy bowels, grant me always to bear Thee within my own by knowledge, knowing the good that Thou dost me, and loving Thee for the love Thou bearest to me. I am within Thy goodness, transform me therefore into it. I live within Thy charity, inflame me with it. I walk within Thy omnipotency, help me with it; and since I am wholly within Thee, transform me wholly into Thee, to the end that I may live no more to myself, but wholly to Thee for all eternity. Amen.

This consideration I may treat of more at large, dwelling in detail upon the divine attributes. Sometimes I may imagine that God is as a "consuming fire," and that the whole world is full of this fire, within which I myself live, and marvel why I burn not, and why it consumes not, all the evil that is in me, attributing the same to my great coldness by which I resist Him. At other times I will imagine God our Lord as an infinite light, which extends itself through all this world; or as wisdom, and immense beauty, with whose glory and splendour the whole earth is replenished, and myself within this light and beauty, and humbly beseech Him to make me participate in them, and so on with regard to the other divine attributes.

2. Moreover, God our Lord is within me, and with me, much *more intimately than my soul is with my body*, though in a far more excellent manner, by essence, presence, and power, as has already been declared. In me, therefore, is the Father, Son, the Holy Ghost, and the whole divinity, really and truly; and consequently, His infinite goodness is united with me, communicating to me the being and life which I possess; His wisdom, giving me the light and knowledge which I have; and His power is united with all my faculties, helping them in their works and actions; with the eyes, that they may see; with the ears, that they may hear; with the feet, that they may walk; with the memory and understanding, that they may be mindful and understand; with the will and appetites that they may will and perform their appointed functions.

i. And, knowing this indwelling presence, I may, and ought to *behold* Almighty God, *most present within me*, as if I were His house and dwelling, in which He works all that I am, and have, and do, without whose presence I should immediately cease to be, because this inhabitant preserves His habitation, and if He should absent Himself from it, it would presently turn into nothing. I will therefore conceive great affections of joy and admiration, of confidence and love, at seeing myself thus joined, and intimately united with my God. But in particular I must endeavour to convert my heart into a closet and oratory, into which I may enter to pray, and converse with God, for He is within it, and there sees how I pray, and what I ask for; and there also is He powerful to grant my petitions. And in this manner many saints understand that which Christ our Lord said:—" When thou shalt pray, enter into thy chamber," i. e, into thy heart, " and having shut the door," i. e. of thy senses, " pray to thy Father in secret," &c. (17)

ii. I must also acquire the habit of *seeking Almighty God within myself*, for if He is within me, to what purpose do I weary myself in seeking Him without me?   To this end I will purge my soul from all that may displease God thus present within it, and from all that may offend Him, or hinder me from seeing Him, knowing Him, and being united to Him by actual love.   At other times, as St. Thomas says, I will strive to enjoy this presence of God, as the friend rejoices at the presence of his friend, the feeble in the presence of the strong, the poor in the presence of the rich man that is merciful; and to use this infinite treasure which I possess, as the artificer makes use of the instrument which he has in his house, without going forth to seek it; as the rich man avails himself of the money and treasure which he has enclosed in his coffers; and as the hungry refreshes himself with the meats which he has in his storehouse.

Colloquy.—O my soul, thou hast within thee all good things, why dost thou not enjoy them? Within thee is thy sovereign friend and father, rejoice to have Him with thee; unite thyself most closely with Him, and give Him thy whole heart. If thou art poor, thou hast God with thee, who is rich in mercy; run to Him, that He may impart to thee of His riches. If thou art weak and pusillanimous, thou hast God with thee, who is fortitude itself, and united with Him, thou mayest do all things in His strength; wherefore, then, dost thou anxiously seek help of external creatures, when thou hast within thee the omnipotence of the

(17) Mat. vi. 6.   S. Aug. in Conc. in Ps. xxx.

Creator? O my Creator, my God, and my all, perfect in me this intimate union which Thou hast with me, drawing me more closely to Thee with the bonds of Thy grace, that I also may draw Thee more closely to me with the bonds of charity. Amen.

POINT IV.

Fourthly is to be considered how God is, in a more special manner, in certain *places*, and in certain *things*.

1. First, He is in an especial manner in *heaven;* for in other places He, as it were, hides Himself, so as not to be seen, except by faith alone; but in heaven He reveals Himself, and manifests clearly to the blessed His divine Essence, and works most glorious things in those who behold Him. Hence the heavenly Jerusalem is called, " Tabernaculum Dei cum hominibus," "the tabernacle of God with men"(18). For Almighty God dwells therein, and His elect together with Him, and He is with them, and they are His people.

Colloquy.—O most high God, who dwellest in the highest, bring me to this tabernacle in which Thou abidest with Thine elect, that there I may see and enjoy that infinite good which here I have, but do not to the full enjoy, because I see it not.

2. Secondly, God our Lord is especially in those places of the earth, *where He is wont to give some special notice of His presence*, by the wonders which He there performs. Hence when Jacob saw in his sleep " a ladder standing upon the earth, and the top thereof touching heaven...... and the Lord leaning upon the ladder, saying to Him," when he awoke, he said, "indeed, the Lord is in this place, and I knew it not......How terrible is this place! this is no other but the house of God, and the gate of heaven."(19) After this manner is God our Lord in

(18) Apoc. xxi. 3.   (19) Gen. xxviii. 12.

churches and oratories, and in places set apart for prayer and contemplation, and in solitude too, where His majesty is wont to confer particular favours upon us, as He has said:—" I will lead her into the wilderness, and I will speak to her heart."(20)   With what affection, therefore, and reverence ought I to repair to such places, and with what respect for the presence of Almighty God, who is wont there to manifest Himself.

3. Thirdly, God our Lord is especially *in the just* by faith and grace, working in them and with them supernatural works, worthy of eternal life.   Whence St. John says:—" He that abideth in charity, abideth in God, and God in Him;"(21) for he that loves is in the thing loved; and when two love one another, the one is in the other; even so he that loves God is in God, and because God loves him, God is in him.   Moreover, the just is likewise in Almighty God, being within His very bowels, and encompassed and defended by His protection; and God is in Him, for He resides within his soul, and gives it being and life, together with the works of grace and charity.

Colloquy.—O God, who desirest to manifest Thy immense charity by coming to dwell by grace in all those who are capable of receiving Thee, remove from me all the impediments, that Thou mayest enter into my soul, and remain in me, and I in Thee, world without end.   Amen.

4. Besides all this, God our Lord, after another more special manner, is *within some of His friends* in the most secret and profound recesses of their spirit, where He discovers Himself to them with illustrations and inward discourses, and reveals to them the mysteries of His Divinity, with great testimonies and signs of His presence.   Hence they are animated with great courage and confidence, and

(20) Osee ii. 14.   (21) 1 Joan. iv. 16.

replenished with a sense of great security, peace, and inward joy, and with great pledges of eternal blessedness; and they are filled with delight at beholding themselves, by means of the light, enclosed within the immensity of their God, and their God, in all His immensity, dwelling in them, and united with them by a mode of presence so replete with love. This fourth manner we are to reverence with great humility; but the third we must seek with great solicitude, and with all our strength endeavour to perfect it in us; leaving to the divine Providence other things more extraordinary, which He may desire to work in us, and contenting ourselves with the hope of at length attaining to the place where He is seen "face to face," and where He is all things to all, and wholly within all, and all are in Him, engulfed in the everlasting joy of their Lord.

MEDITATION XV.

ON THE INFINITE WISDOM AND KNOWLEDGE OF GOD.

POINT I.

The first point will be to consider how God our Lord in His infinite wisdom knows and comprehends Himself, His divine essence and Persons, His goodness and omnipotence, and all His divine perfections;(1) all His actions, intentions, decrees, dispositions, and all the things which He can ordain and do, so that nothing is hidden from His knowledge. And this knowledge satisfies and fills the infinite capacity of His divine understanding, imparting singular pleasure and contentment, so that nothing is left for Him to desire or learn. And in this consists the blessedness of

(1) S. Tho. i. p. q. xiv. art. 2. et 3.

Almighty God, who yet is not blessed in knowing the things which are external to Him, but in knowing Himself, who is the fountain and beginning of them all. Whence I will conceive a great joy for the wisdom which God has, and for the felicity and contentment He receives from it, with a great desire to participate in this sweet and heavenly wisdom; and I will place my blessedness, not in knowing the creatures, but in knowing Him by means of it; for with this knowledge I shall remain satisfied, and the desires which I have to know shall remain fully contented, since, as St. Gregory says:—" Quid non videt, qui videntem omnia videt?" " What doth not he see who sees Him that sees all things?"(2)

Colloquy.—O my soul, if thou hast so great a desire to know, employ thy study to know God, for once knowing Him well, all thy desires will remain satisfied. If thou desirest to be as God, who knows " good and evil," study to know and to serve God, and by this means thou shalt come to know Him, having part in the good, and none at all in the evil; for although thou dost know all other things, yet if thou dost not know God, what will this profit thee? O most wise God, and most clear fountain of all wisdom, let me know Thee, and what Thou requirest of me, and this knowledge shall suffice me, Thy grace assisting me, that I may love what I know, and perform in work what I understand. Amen.

POINT II.

Secondly, God our Lord has this wisdom by His own very essence, by means of which, as by a most clear looking-glass, sees and comprehends all things, and by Himself ordains and disposes of them. Wherefore, He receives not this wisdom of any other, neither had, nor could have any

(2) lib. 4. Dial. cap. 33.

master or counsellor, nor out of Himself any other book or example in which He might see and learn what He knows, but has all this of Himself, and of His own essence, which, if it be lawful so to speak, is as His master, counsellor, looking-glass, book, example, and idea of all that which He disposes, designs, and executes, and of whatever it is possible for Him to know.(3)

1. Hence it follows that God alone is *essentially and infinitely wise*, without having any measure in His wisdom. And as it is said, that "none is good but God alone:" so may we likewise say that none is wise but God alone, because all others of their own nature are ignorant, and have no knowledge but what they receive from God; and that also which they have is circumscribed and limited, and so little that, compared with the infinite wisdom of God, it is as nothing. Upon this principle the knowledge of myself, humility, in regard of science ought to be grounded, saying with Solomon:—" I am the most foolish of men...I have not learned wisdom."(4) For if I consider the time of my birth, I shall find that I had no knowledge, and that which I have learned since is as little as if it were not, and as if I had learned nothing at all. Wherefore, comparing myself with God, I may say that which sometimes Socrates said:—" Hoc unum scio, me nihil scire." "This one thing I know, that I know nothing;" and "every man," as Jeremiah says, " is made a fool," and ignorant " from knowledge,"(5) compared with God, who is knowledge itself. With this consideration I will repress all affections of vain complacency, of vain-glory and presumption, setting myself in the lowest place of my nothing, and of my total ignorance.

2. Hence likewise it follows that it is great presumption

(3) S. Tho. i. p. q. xiv. art. 4.   (4) Prov. xxx. 2.
(5) Jer. x. 14, et li. 17.

and folly for me to think to penetrate and comprehend this infinite wisdom, because it *infinitely exceeds all the capacity both of men and angels*, and, as St. Paul says, " The things that are of God no man knoweth but the Spirit of God." And for this cause the divine wisdom says:—" Who hath searched out the wisdom of God, that goeth before all things? To whom hath the root of wisdom been revealed, and who hath known her counsels? and who hath understood the multiplicity of her steps?" " It is hid," as Job says, " from the eyes of all living, the fowls of the air also know it not,"(6) which are the angels and celestial spirits.

Colloquy.—O most wise God, who ascendest " upon the Cherubim," which are the fulness of knowledge, and fleet upon the wings of the wind, because Thou surpassest all in the swiftness of Thy flight, and none can attain to understand all that Thou dost know; I reverence the secrets of Thine infinite wisdom, and humbly beseech Thee to discover that part of it to me, which is convenient for me to have, in order to love and serve Thee, now and for ever. Amen.(7)

POINT III.

Thirdly, the divine wisdom alone, without the help of any other, is the *first inventor of all things*, as many as have been in the world, and from it proceed all the sciences, arts, and inventions both of heaven and earth, for Almighty God " hath poured her out upon all His works."(8) And therefore Isaiah says:—" Who hath forwarded the spirit of the Lord? Or who hath been His counsellor, and hath taught Him? With whom hath He consulted? and who hath instructed Him, and taught Him the path of justice,

(6) 1 Cor. ii. 11.   Ecclus. i. 3.   Job. xxviii. 21.
(7) Ecclus. iii. 22.   (8) Ecclus. i. 10.

and taught Him knowledge, and showed Him the way of understanding?"(9)

Colloquy.—"Oh the depth of the riches, of the wisdom, and of the knowledge of God!" Who hath known the mind of the Lord? Or who hath been His counsellor?"(10) I rejoice, O my God, that Thou art the master and counsellor of all, and that none can be Thine; be Thou, I beseech Thee, always mine, that I may in all things be pleasing to Thee. Amen.

1. Hence I will descend to consider *more particularly* the inventions and marvellous dispositions which have proceeded and do proceed from the infinite wisdom of God, and meditate, as David says, " on all Thy works, and employed in Thy inventions,"(11) with affections of admiration and joy, believing, as the apostle says, " by faith... that the world was framed by the word of God, that visible things might be made from the invisible things,"(12) which He had designed within Himself in His eternal wisdom.

i. This may I do first, by reviewing in succession *the six days of the Creation* of the world, and reflecting upon the admirable invention of the divine wisdom in every one of them, as we shall hereafter see.

ii. Then I will consider the invention of the divine wisdom *in the creation of man*, in whom a body of earth is joined to an immortal spirit; and here I will further reflect upon the variety of faces, and of inclinations, and of talents which are found amongst men, and the inventions which have proceeded from them, such as the art of making glass, cloth, linen, and other artificial things, together with the many sciences which so greatly flourish in the world; all of which have proceeded originally from the infinite wisdom of God. Whence the mother of Samuel

(9) Isa. xl. 13.　　　　(10) Rom. xi. 33.
(11) Ps. lxxvi. 13.　　　(12) Heb. xi. 3.

called the Lord, " Scientiarum Dominum," " the God of all knowledge,"(13) for He has them all in Himself, and from Him proceed those that are found in His creatures.

iii. Hence I will ascend to consider the inventions of the divine wisdom, as manifested *in the state and being of grace,* which He has communicated to men; but principally that incomparable one of joining the human nature with the divine, in unity of Person, in Christ our Lord; and the admirable invention of putting Himself in the most Blessed Sacrament of the Altar, with innumerable other methods, which He daily devises in order to deliver His elect from perils, to advance them in virtue, and to bring them to heaven, where He displays marvellous contrivances for giving them perfect felicity.

iv. Hence I will infer that it is the divine wisdom which *directs and accompanies the works* in which His divine attributes are most evidently manifested, i. e., the works of His goodness and charity, of His mercy and justice. For with wisdom goodness is communicated, charity loves, mercy compassionates, and justice rewards and punishes; for so Ecclesiasticus says:—" God had poured out" wisdom "upon all His works;" and David says:—" O Lord, Thou hast made all things in wisdom."(14)

2. All this ought to move me to great *affections of admiration* and gladness, particularly to rejoice that I have a God so exceedingly wise, who can invent a thousand means and ways to attain His proposed end of delivering me from evils, and of communicating to me the goods of nature, grace, and glory as He desires. Whence I will learn to put great confidence in God, even in cases which appear desperate, for the divine wisdom can invent innumerable means and remedies, where I can find none. And in gratitude for all this, I also will endeavour, with His grace

(13) 1 Reg. ii. 3.   (14) Ps. ciii. 24.

and divine light, to discover new means of mortifying and exercising myself in virtue, and of becoming pleasing to Almighty God, because the just "shall eat the fruit of his doings,"(15) and every day will I sing to our Lord "a new canticle,"(16) for the new inventions He displays for my benefit.

Colloquy.—" O God and Lord of all knowledge," I rejoice at the dominion Thou hast over all, as the beginning whence they proceed ; give, me, Lord, the science of the saints, that I may know how to serve Thee in justice and sanctity.   Amen.

POINT IV.

1. In the fourth place we will consider how the infinite wisdom of God disposes and ordains all things in the world, " in mensura, et numero, et pondere," "*in measure, and number, and weight.*"(17)   He comprehends the number of all things, which have been, and shall be, and of all their parts, members, offices, and actions.   He knows the weight of every one of them in the measure of their inclinations, and of their natural and supernatural affections. He scans their proportions in breadth, length, height, and depth; and the measure of their perfection, gifts, and talents.   We may admire, therefore, the symmetry and marvellous arrangement which shines in every one of these things, and in all of them together, by the infinite wisdom of Him who ordained them in such a manner, and after such an order of goodness and perfection.   We may consider this subject by reflecting upon some of those things which the divine Scripture chiefly extols, attributing them to God alone, and to His infinite wisdom.

i. First, as David says, " God telleth *the number of the stars,*"(18) the extent of their inclination to communicate

(15) Isa. iii. 10.   (16) Ps. xcv. 1.
(17) Sap. xi. 21.   (18) Ps. cxlvi. 4.

their influences to the earth, and the measure of their greatness and perfection, and therefore He adds, " and calleth them all by their names," as knowing what is in every one of them. And in the same manner does Almighty God know the number of the motions and revolutions which the heavens are to perform until the end of the world, and consequently the years and days it is to endure, and the last day when this order and harmony of heaven is to rest and to cease for ever, which, as Christ our Lord said:— " No one knoweth, no, not the angels of heaven, but the Father alone."(19)

ii. Descending yet lower to that which passes in the air, Almighty God also numbers the *comets, lightnings, thunders, drops of rain, flakes of snow, the winds and hail ;* of all of which He knows very well the weight and inclination, for " He made a weight for the winds;"(20) and the same may be said with regard to the snow, hail, and lightning, all of which, by the disposition of the wisdom of God, as Job says, go forth with the weight, and in the direction which He gives, and for the end which He has in view. Wherefore I am to have great confidence in the midst of tempests, remembering that they are all ordained by the divine wisdom for very great and excellent ends.

iii. Then will I ponder how God our Lord also in His wisdom, " measured *the waters* in the hollow of His hand, and weighed the *heavens* with His palm," and " poised with three fingers the bulk of the *earth*,"(21) and therefore knows the breadth, the length, the depth, and height which they contain, and the weight of everything. Moreover, He knows the number of all the things which are contained within these elements, and upon the earth, even to the number of the sands of the sea, and of the little sparrows,

(19) Job xxxviii. 33, 37. Mat. xxiv. 36.
(20) Job xxviii. 25. Job xxxviii. 35.   (21) Isa. xl. 12.

since "not one of them shall fall on the ground," without His providence.(22)

iv. But I will dwell more particularly upon that which appertains to *men, whose number God keeps* in remembrance, even from Adam till the ending of the world; the years also, the days, and hours which every one is to live, and the hour when he is to die. He numbers all their bones and hairs, so that not so much as one shall perish without His knowledge and providence. He numbers all their steps, which every one is to make, and all the works, good and evil, which they have done and are to do. He knows the capacity and inclinations of every one, his talents and faculties, and the measure of natural and supernatural perfection, which he has in his soul, and in his actions; for His infinite wisdom distributes all this in weight and measure, weighing the spirits of all, and the works which they do, knowing the weight and value of them.(23)

With this consideration I will cast myself into the hands of God, and of His infinite wisdom, which is infallible, and most assured; determined not to trust my own fancies and apprehensions, concerning the number of years and days of my life, or the esteem and quality of my talents and natural parts, or graces received from God, or the measure of my merits and virtues, but will conclude that what I am in the eyes of God, who sees all things, the same I am and no more.

v. Lastly, I will ascend to consider with regard to the things that are *above the heavens*, how the divine wisdom has disposed them also with order, weight, and measure, so that He knows the number of the angels, which are in all the choirs and hierarchies, and of all the blessed, which now are, and are hereafter to be, in heaven; He knows the

(22) Mat. x. 29.

(23) Ps. xxxviii. 6.   Job xiv. 15.   Ps. cxxxviii. 4.   Mat. x. 30. Luc. xii. 7. et xxi. 18.   Job. xiv. 16.   Pro. xvi. 4.

weight and measure of their natural and supernatural perfections, and distributes to them offices conformable to the order of His infinite wisdom, and the measure of glory according to the measure of their merits.

2. Pondering these things, I will burst forth into affections of admiration at the infinite wisdom of Almighty God, much more than the Queen of Saba, when she saw the wisdom of Solomon, and the distribution and order of the things of his house, and so with much more inflamed affection will I say that which he said. (24)

Colloquy.—The report, O my God, is true which I have heard concerning Thine infinite wisdom, and greater is Thy wisdom and greater Thy works than the report which I have heard. "Blessed are Thy men, and blessed are Thy servants who stand before Thee always, and hear Thy wisdom."(25) O infinite wisdom, who disposest and ordainest all things in number, weight, and measure, set in order, I beseech Thee, in like manner, all things belonging to my soul, and increase in her the number of good works, the weight of fervent affections, and the measure of Thy graces, granting me a measure full, "shaken together," and "running over" of Thy glory. Amen.

POINT V.

Fifthly is to be considered how the infinite wisdom of God is *eternal*, and *immutable, most profound*, and yet most *clear*, and is *without parts*, reaching with one simple glance, from one eternity to another, and seeing whatever is possible to be seen, and known. God, inasmuch as He is God, knows what He knows, and cannot possibly know anything new, because nothing can be new to Him. God knows all things past, present, and to come, and all possible things, and He knows them all most distinctly, and with

(24) 3 Reg. x. 4.   (25) 3 Reg. x. 8.

perfect clearness, without any mixture of doubts, opinions, or perplexities, for He is incapable of ignorance, error, doubt, or delusion, in anything which He knows; and, therefore, Ecclesiasticus says:—"The eyes of the Lord are far brighter than the sun, beholding round about all the ways of men, and the bottom of the deep, and looking into the hearts of men, into the most hidden parts. For all things were known to the Lord God, before they were created:" (26) and so, likewise, they are, after they have passed away; for nothing is hid from Him, who beholds all things, from one world to another, and from "eternity to eternity." (27)

1. This truth we may consider more in particular for our own profit, applying it to things *past, present, future,* and *possible.*

i. First, then, God our Lord, by His infinite wisdom, knows *all things that have been,* from the beginning of the world, up to this present instant, and has them as present to Him, as if they were not past, and, therefore, it is impossible for God to forget anything which He once knows, or the good or evil works which He has seen, or any man, good or evil; although in a different manner He remembers the one from the other, for He remembers the wicked, to punish them for their evil works, which He will never forget, and the good, to reward them for their good works, which He always keeps in His remembrance; for when it is said that He *forgets* the wicked, it is because in just punishment of their wickedness, He takes no notice of them for their good. Applying this to myself, I must believe that Almighty God remembers me and all my actions distinctly, as if I alone were in the world, and has me always present in the memory of His eternal wisdom, from which He never permits me to be blotted out; and

(26) Ecclus. xxiii. 28.   (27) Ibid. xxxix. 25.

I must imagine that He says to me, that which formerly He said to the city of Sion:—" Can a woman forget her infant, so as not to have pity on the son of her womb? and if she should forget, yet will not I forget thee. Behold, I have graven thee in my hands, thy walls are always before my eyes." (28)

Colloquy.—O my soul, forget not God, since God will never forget thee; write Him in thy hands, since He has written thee in His; have before thine eyes the things belonging to His service, since He has before His the things belonging to thy profit. Amen.

ii. Secondly, God our Lord, by His infinite Wisdom, knows everything whatever *that is being done in this day*, and *at this very instant*, throughout the whole world, so that nothing is hidden from Him. He penetrates the secrets of every man's heart, however closely hidden, his imaginations, thoughts, desires, and purposes, good and evil, and all within him, which no one else, whether man or angel, can know, but only the spirit of the man himself, whose thoughts they are. (29) All these, and many more things than man either thinks or imagines, or reflects upon, are penetrated and comprehended by God, to whom alone it belongs to have such comprehension, as He says by the prophet Jeremiah, and the Apostle more fully declares, saying:—" The word of God is living and effectual, and more piercing than any two-edged sword, and reaching unto the division of the soul and the spirit, neither is there any creature invisible in His sight, but all things are naked and open to His eyes." (30)

Colloquy.—O my soul, since the eyes of God always behold what thou dost, let thine always behold the things that are just, and let " thy eye-lids go before

(28) Isa. xlix. 15.   (29) 1 Cor. ii. 11.
(30) Jer. xvii. 10. Heb. iv. 12.

thy steps,"(31) looking first where thou settest thy foot, because God is there beholding thee. Cast from thy mouth the words of the old man, because " the Lord is a God of all knowledge," and penetrates and weighs the thoughts of the heart.(32)

iii. Thirdly, God our Lord, by His infinite wisdom, knows all *things which are to come*, and *are to be done* for all eternity, even those which depend on our free will, and has them as fully present before Him, as if they had already taken place, or were now being done. Sometimes, also, He reveals them to His friends; and it is impossible for anything not to come to pass, which He declares will come to pass, for He beholds it in the manner in which it will take place, as if it were then actually happening. This kind of knowledge belongs so peculiarly to the wisdom of God, that neither man nor angel, can share in it; and, therefore, Isaiah said:—" Show the things that are to come hereafter, and we shall know that ye are gods:" (33) as if he had said, It is an especial mark of the Deity to know things that are to come, and which depend on the liberty and free will of man.

iv. But the wisdom of God reaches still further, for it knows not only all the works which either men or angels will do, but also all that *they can do*, by the use of their liberty, and by the help of the grace which He shall be pleased to give them; and of His infinite wisdom, according to this most profound and secret mystery, He disposes, ordains, or permits the events that actually happen, and passes over others, which might otherwise come to pass. Here I ought to reverence with humility His secret judgments, saying with the Apostle:—" O the depth of the riches of the wisdom, and of the knowledge of God! how incomprehensible are His judgments, and how unsearcha-

(31) Prov. iv. 25.　　(32) 1 Reg. ii. 3.　　(33) Isa. xli. 23.

ble His ways?" "Thy knowledge," O Lord, "is become wonderful to me," it is so vast, and so high, so elevated above me, that "I cannot reach," or attain to it. (34) I therefore adore it with humility, and beseech Thee so to direct my life by it, that I may attain Thine eternal glory, Amen.

POINT VI.

1. Lastly is to be considered how the infinite wisdom of God comprehends and embraces all things that are within the compass of the divine omnipotence, and are *possible to be*, although they never are to be, the number and perfection of which are such that all the things which we have hitherto enumerated, in comparison with them, are as a drop of water in comparison with the whole sea. For the knowledge of Almighty God embraces an infinity of angels, heavens, and worlds, with an infinite variety of differences from those that exist, and with other perfections much greater than theirs; so that if this world should last a million of years, the wisdom of God knows that He could create another world every day, much more perfect than this, and that, when He had created them all, there would still be an infinity more which He could create.

Colloquy.—O incomprehensible depth! O immense sea! O infinite treasure of the wisdom of God! I rejoice, O my Lord, that Thou art so wise as to comprehend all that is to be known, so that nothing can be hid from Thee. I likewise rejoice for the joy which Thou hast in this knowledge, and in the knowledge of Thyself, in whose omnipotence all this is contained. Now, O my God, I confess that all our wisdom is nothing compared with Thine. "And seeing we have heard scarce a little drop" of Thy word, who shall be able to behold the thunder of Thy "greatness?"(35) And if that which Thou hast discovered of Thy wis-

(34) Rom. xi. 33. Psal. cxxxviii. 6.   (35) Job. xxvi. 14.

dom is but as a drop, how immense is that which lies hidden beneath! Thou art great in all, and Thy greatness far exceeds our understanding; but it is our glory to be overcome by Thee, of whom we have received whatever knowledge and greatness we have.

2. Moreover, this infinite wisdom of God our Lord, of which we have been speaking, is *infinitely liberal in communicating itself.* It communicates itself *"without envy;"* (36) nay, with great delight both to men and angels, to Cherubim and Seraphim, and to all the blessed spirits, but above all, to the soul of Christ our Redeemer and Lord, "in whom are hid all the treasures of wisdom and knowledge." But although He imparted to it the knowledge of all things past, present, and to come, for all eternity, as St. Thomas says, yet there remained an infinity which He did not impart, because it is not possible to impart His knowledge wholly to a pure creature.(37) From the consideration of this liberality, I will take occasion to beseech Him to impart His wisdom to me, and to teach me the things which belong to my salvation.

Colloquy.—O most wise God, "send" Thy wisdom "out of Thy holy heaven, and from the throne of Thy majesty, that she may be with me, and may labour with me, that I may know what is acceptable with Thee at all times;"(38) let her go before all my works, as she goeth before Thine; let her accompany me in all I do, as she accompanied Thee in all Thou didst; let her be the final end of my desires and aims, and let her bring me where I may clearly see Thee, by the light which proceeds from her, world without end. Amen.

(36) Sap. vii. 13.   (37) S. Tho. iii. p. q. x. art. 2.
(38) Sap. ix. 10.

MEDITATION XVI.

ON THE OMNIPOTENCY OF ALMIGHTY GOD.

POINT I.

The first shall be to consider, how God our Lord, Three and One, is infinitely powerful to do all things whatever He wills, without any restriction or limitation as to their number, greatness, or perfection; for which reason He is called "Omnipotent," and "Almighty;" and His omnipotence consists in His being able to do all things which His infinite wisdom sees to be possible, and which do not involve inconsistency or contradiction. In this sense the angel said to the Blessed Virgin:—"No word shall be impossible with God;" that is, nothing which either men or angels, or God Himself, can conceive with the understanding, and which does not involve a contradiction. And so God Himself says by the prophet Jeremias:—"Shall anything be hard for me?" as if He had said: Nothing can be hard to me, but "all things are possible" and also easy to me.(1)

Herein may be pondered *three excellences : —*

1. First, God our Lord *can make an infinity of things more than He has made,* because all that He has hitherto made is as nothing in comparison of that which He can make; and after surveying everything whatever that has been made, I may still say with Ecclesiasticus:—"Multa abscondita sunt majora his, pauca enim vidimus operum ejus." "There are many things hidden from us that are greater than these, for we have seen but a few of His works."(2)

(1) Jer. xxxii. 27.   Mat. xix. 26.   Marc. x. 27.
(2) Ecclus. xliii. 36.

Colloquy.— O omnipotent God, I rejoice in this Thy great omnipotence, by which Thou canst do infinitely more than I am able to conceive. If Thou art so wonderful in the works which Thou hast done, how much more wonderful shalt Thou be in those which Thou canst do? "Glorify the Lord," O my soul, as much as ever you can, for His omnipotence "is above all praise."(3)

2. The second excellence is, that Almighty God *can do whatever He will in the things He has already made*, changing, altering, and remodelling them according to His own will. As the same Ecclesiasticus says:—"The Almighty Himself is above all His works;"(4) for He can both make more than He has made, and in those which He has already made He can do what He pleases. He can cause the sun to stand still, as in the time of Josue, or to go back, as in the time of Ezechias, or to give no light, as in the time of the Passion of Christ; He can do what He will in the sea, in the winds, in the earth, and in living creatures of all kinds, like as He did under the old law by His servant Moses, and under the new law by Christ our Lord, when He lived in this mortal life; and He daily works new miracles, and can work far greater than those He has already worked. Considering all this, I may say that which Ecclesiasticus adds:—"The Lord is terrible, and exceeding great, and His power is admirable,"(5) and therefore most worthy to be believed. We ought all, therefore, to give credit to whatever faith has revealed to us concerning His wonderful works and miracles.

3. The third excellence is, that the omnipotence of God can *execute whatever His Divine will determines;* for if God were to will anything absolutely, and yet could not do it, He would be miserable, and so not God. From

(3) Ecclus. xliii. 32, 33.   (4) Ibid. xxx.   (5) Ibid.

what has already been said, we may conjecture what is to come, and what is possible; and, therefore, as God "has done all things whatever He would,"(6) so He will do whatever He wills, and can do whatever He wills, according to what the Wise man says:—"Thy power is at hand when Thou wilt;"(7) when Thou willest to do anything, Thou wantest not power to do it. Accordingly, when the will of God is apparent to me, I cannot doubt of His Omnipotence, and when His will is not apparent, I should say that which the leper said to Christ:—"Lord, if Thou wilt Thou canst make me clean."(8)

Colloquy.—O omnipotent God, I pour forth my soul before Thine omnipotence with all my necessities and miseries, and with all my desires and affections; Thy will is just, and Thou knowest what is most expedient for me; if Thou wilt, Thou canst; if Thou wilt heal me of my infirmities, Thou canst easily do so; if Thou wilt give me what I ask, Thou canst bestow it immediately. I rejoice that Thy omnipotence is placed in the hands of Thy just and loving will, for whatever proceeds from such a will and from such a power, will be good and profitable to me, and also glorious to Thee, to whom be all honour and glory, world without end. Amen.

POINT II.

Secondly is to be considered, that this omnipotency *belongs properly to God alone*, though He liberally gives part of it to His creatures. Here there are three other excellences to be pondered.

1. The first is, that God alone has His power by *nature* and *essence*, and no creature has any except by communication from Almighty God, and for this cause St. Paul

(6) Psa. cxiii. 11.   (7) Sap. xii. 18.

(8) Matt. viii. 2.

calls Him "Only Mighty;"(9) for as to us creatures, we are all powerless, and unable to do anything of ourselves; for we have neither being nor power except what we receive from God.(10)

2. The second excellence is, that God alone, by His omnipotence, can do His works *without any one's help;* whereas no creatures can do anything unless the omnipotency of God works with them: the sun will not be able to give light, nor the fire heat, nor man to move or do anything, unless the omnipotence of God assist and work with them. For this cause Isaiah says:—"Thou hast wrought all our works for us;" and Christ our Lord said: —"Without me you can do nothing."(11) From these two considerations I ought to learn my absolute dependance on the omnipotence of God, and so to ground myself in profound humility, since without His power I can neither be nor act, and to give Him infinite thanks for the assistance which He is wont to bestow on me in all my actions, as we shall see hereafter more at large.(12)

3. The third excellence is, that God *does not confine* His omnipotence to Himself, but *imparts it to His creatures,* in order that every one of them may do whatever is suitable to its own nature. Moreover, He adds both to men and angels another power much higher and more excellent than that which they have of their own nature; for He uses them as His instruments and helpers in many things which properly belongs to His own omnipotence; and this made the apostle St. Paul say:—"I can all things in Him who strengtheneth me."(13) In union, therefore, with the omnipotence of God, I have power to do all things, for God will do all things in me, and by me. God accounts it an honour paid to Himself when we believe this of Him,

(9) 1 Tim. vi. 15. (10) 2 Cor. iii. 5. (11) Isa. xxvi. 12. Joan. xv. 5. (12) Med. xxiii. (13) Phil. iv. 13.

and hope this from Him, and on this faith and confidence
He makes it depend whether any shall experience the gift
itself: and thus Christ our Lord said to a certain man:—
" If thou canst believe, all things are possible to him that
believeth:"(14) for, as St. Bernard says, nothing so much
displays and exalts the omnipotence of God, as His making
those who put their trust in Him omnipotent in the manner described.

Colloquy.—O omnipotent God, I give Thee as great
thanks as I am able, for the share which Thou dost
give Thy servants of Thy supreme omnipotency; I
trust in it, O Lord, since it is Thy pleasure to give it
me, and with it I will do whatever Thou shalt command
me. O my soul, choose for my friend Him who is
almighty, and then with Him thou also shalt be almighty, since according to the law of true friendship
that which we can do by means of our friends, we ourselves also do.

POINT III.

The third shall be to consider, as the conclusion of all
that has been hitherto said, that the omnipotence of God,
together with His *wisdom, goodness,* and *charity, perpetually
employs itself in doing us good,* and is the beginning and
fountain from whence all the divine benefits which we
enjoy proceed and spring. These three attributes are the
" *three fingers*" with which God has " poised the bulk of
the earth," as the prophet Isaiah says, and with these same
three fingers He has also poised the heavens, angels, and
men, and all the creatures of the world, since with these
He created and with these He sustains, governs, succours
them, and brings them to their final end. By His *wisdom*
He knows and determines what He will do; by His *goodness*
and *charity* He wills and decrees what He knows; by His

(14) Marc. ix. 22. Ser. lxxxiv. in Cant.   (15) Isa. lx. 12.

omnipotence He executes what He decrees; and by all three He employs Himself in imparting to us most singular benefits. The Father, by the *omnipotence* which is specially attributed to Him; the Son, by His *wisdom;* and the Holy Ghost by His *goodness;* and all the three Persons by these three perfections; because each one of them has them all in the same entireness, for in Almighty God, they are all one thing.

This is the thought with which I should enter upon the ensuing meditations of the divine *benefits*, which began from the very creation of the world; and I must strive to make the whole framework of my life, as well as of my meditations, rest principally on these three fingers of the *wisdom, omnipotence,* and *goodness* of God, and answer to them with the acts and affections of the three theological virtues, *faith, hope,* and *charity,* which correspond to these three divine attributes. For faith corresponds to the wisdom, hope, to the omnipotence, and charity to the goodness of Almighty God; although, at the same time, each of the three virtues, with its acts, has relation to all the three attributes together.

Colloquy.—O great God, Three and One, as wise as mighty, and as mighty as good, and in all things infinite, enlighten my understanding with Thy divine wisdom, allure my will with Thy sovereign goodness, and strengthen my faculties with Thy admirable power, in order that I may know the innumerable and surpassing benefits which have proceeded from Thee, may love Thee with fervour, and serve and obey Thee with courage, and that world without end.   Amen.

MEDITATION XVII.

OF THE OMNIPOTENCE OF GOD IN THE CREATION OF THE WORLD, AND OF THE
GREATNESS OF THIS BENEFIT.

POINT I.

First is to be considered that first article of our faith, in
which we confess that God our Lord, by His infinite power,
"*in the beginning created heaven and earth*, the sea, and all
things that are in them," and all things in the world, visible and invisible,(1) so that there is nothing great or small
which did not take its beginning from Almighty God, according to that which St. John says of the Divine Word:
—" All things were made by Him, and without Him was
made nothing that was made;"(2) and consequently, I also
am the work of God, and from Him have received my
being.

1. In this article is to be pondered first, how everything
whatever that is not God, *had an origin*, and *began to be*,
not having been before. So that before the creation of the
world, of which Holy Scripture gives the account, there
was nothing out of God; all was nothing; and only God
was; for from Him all things receive the being which they
have. If, therefore, I consider myself as to my origin, I
am merely nothing, not only with regard to the soul, but
also with regard to the body, because that of which I was
made was once nothing; and hence I will excite myself to
render infinite thanks to Almighty God, who, by His
omnipotence, has drawn me out of the abyss of nothing,
and full of profound humility, I will say with the
apostle:—

(1) S. Th. I. p. q. xliv. Gen. i. 1. Psa. cxlv. 5. Apoc. xiv. 7.
(2) John i. 3.

Colloquy.—" O the depth of the riches, of the wisdom," and omnipotence " of God !"(3)   " Who hath first given to Him, and recompense shall be made him." He first gave to all what they have, and to Him all are bound to be thankful for what they possess, because " of Him, and by Him, and in Him are all things," and to Him is due all honour and glory, world without end.   Amen.

2. I will ponder secondly how God our Lord, *freely*, and *purely of His own good will and grace*, created all things, without there being anything to oblige Him to it.   The merits of His creatures did not oblige Him, for there were none to merit; nor did any need of them, or advantage to be gained from them, oblige Him, for He was perfectly happy without His creatures, and stood in no need of them; nor yet did their goodness oblige Him, for it is greatly limited, and cannot oblige any to love them, how much less, then, God!   It was therefore only His own goodness and mercy that moved Him to create them for Himself and for His glory.(4)

Colloquy.—O my soul, praise and glorify Thy Creator, for so vast a benefit as He has bestowed on thee, in drawing so many things, and thee also together with them, out of the abyss of nothing, to give thee the being thou hast; and since He has been pleased to create them and thee of His own free-will, because He was good, employ thy whole being and all thou hast in serving Him freely and with good will, because He is good, and because He made thee without any merit of thine.

3. The third shall be to ponder how God our Lord, in this work of the creation, had *no other pattern or model than Himself*, so that He Himself alone was at once the efficient cause that created all things, the final end for which

(3) Rom. xi. 33.   (4) Prov. xvi. 4.

He ordained them, and the pattern or model from which He drew them. For, discerning by His infinite *wisdom* all the things that He could do, and their different arrangements and orders, He chose by His *free-will* that order of creatures which exists in the world, and by His *omnipotence*, brought it into being; and as He then left an infinity of creatures in the abyss of nothing, and chose to create those which He created, so in like manner He left an infinity of souls in the abyss of nothing, and chose amongst others to create mine, at the time appointed for it. For this I ought to give Him infinite thanks, calling to mind those words of God to Job. When I created the world, " didst thou know then that thou shouldst be born? And didst thou know the number of thy days?"(5)   As if He had said, *Thou* couldst not know it, but *I* knew it, and of my goodness determined to do it.

Colloquy.—O most wise and mighty God, what hast Thou seen in my soul, that Thou wouldst create it, while Thou hast left innumerable others in the abyss of nothing? O final end of all creatures, why didst Thou rather create this miserable creature, than many others, who would have glorified Thee much better than I ? O perfect pattern of all things that can be created, wherefore wouldst Thou create me, rather than others a great deal better, of whom Thou wast equally the pattern ? There is no other cause, O my God, but only Thy pure and holy will; Thy omnipotence created me, and gave me the being which I have solely because Thou wouldst: and since Thou hast dealt so liberally with me, I will serve Thee always, because Thou so wilt; Thou shalt be my last end in all things, because Thou so commandest, and I will behold Thee as the pattern and example of my life, because Thou so ordainest.   Thy will, O Lord, shall

(5) Job xxxviii. 21.

always be mine, because my being and all that I have comes from Thine.

POINT II.

Secondly are to be considered the *particulars* in which the omnipotence of God is displayed in this work of the creation of the world, and more especially the four following.(6)

1. The first is, that He had *no need of any material*, out of which to make this world, as angels and men have for what they build and make; but He made the principal parts of the world *out of nothing*, and gave them their whole and entire being, no portion of them whatever having been in existence before. In this manner He created heaven and earth, and the spiritual substances, such as are the angels and our souls, which can only be made from nothing, that so they may acknowledge themselves absolutely obliged to serve God our Lord with all that they are and have, and to render Him thanks for all, attributing nothing to themselves.

Colloquy.—O Almighty Maker, it is most just that my whole soul should serve Thee, since Thou hast formed it out of nothing. It is most just that I should love Thee with my whole heart, my whole spirit, and my whole strength, since Thou hast given me the whole of them, in order that I should wholly love Thee. O my soul, " what hast thou that thou hast not received? And if thou hast received the whole from God, give the whole glory to God."(7) If thou hast nothing of thyself, glory not except in thy nothingness. Put thy whole confidence not in thyself, who canst do nothing, but in God, who can do all things, and " calleth those things that are not as those that are," drawing them out of nothing, that they may have

(6) S. Tho. i. p. q. xlv.   (7) 1 Cor. iv. 7.

being and power to serve Him and glorify Him, world without end.   Amen.

2. Secondly, the divine omnipotence is displayed in having made *some things out of others*, after the manner that He Himself willed; for although He could have created all living things out of nothing, yet He was pleased to show His power, making fishes and birds out of water; and plants and beasts out of the earth; to give us to understand that He has full dominion and power over His creatures, and changes and converts one into another, according to His own will.   Hence I will learn to submit myself to His dominion, and to rejoice in having a Lord so powerful, to whose will all things are subject.

3. Thirdly, the same omnipotence is displayed in having performed this work of the creation of the world *by Himself alone*, without having any to help Him in it.   " I, the Lord," He says, " that do all these things," " my hand stretched forth the heavens,"(8) I established the earth, and none other with me.   And although after He had created the angels, He might have employed them to produce some material things, yet would He not do so; but chose to perform the whole of this first work by Himself alone, in order that we men, for whom He performed it, might acknowledge ourselves subject, and bound to pay homage to Him alone; that we might adore and serve Him alone, as our Creator and the maker of all things; and might give Him the glory of all, with the elders in the Apocalypse, saying:—" Thou art worthy, O Lord our God, to receive glory, and honour, and power; because Thou hast created all things, and for Thy will they were and are created."(9)

4. Fourthly, the omnipotence of God is displayed in the

(8) Isa. xlv. 7, 12.   Job ix. 8.   S. Tho. i. p. q. lxv. art. 5.
(9) Apoc. iv. 11.

ease with which He made all these things; for upon His merely *willing*, and saying, or commanding, all things obeyed Him without any resistance or delay, so that the very instant in which He said that they should be, they immediately were. Thus when God said:—" Be light made," in a moment light was made: and according to the words of David:—" He spoke, and they were made: He commanded, and they were created."(10) Hence I will conceive, on the one hand, a great admiration of the omnipotence of God, whose efficacious will nothing whatever can resist, and on the other a firm resolution to obey God without *repugnance*, *delay*, or *inconstancy*, in whatever He commands me, with an obedience *prompt, exact, persevering*, and very *perfect*.

Colloquy.—O my soul, why dost thou not submit thyself to the rule and commandment of so powerful a God? Wherefore dost Thou alone resist Him whom all things obey? He gave thee liberty to will or not to will; renounce, therefore, the liberty of resisting Him, and always use that of obeying Him. O omnipotent God, command with such efficacy what Thou willest, that I may never feel repugnance to what Thou commandest. Amen.

POINT III.

The third shall be to consider the manner in which the omnipotence of God accomplished the creation of all things, namely, adorning and perfecting them *by little and little:* for although He could in an instant have created them in all their perfection, yet He was pleased to perform it in the space of "six days," and this for certain ends which He designed for our profit.(11)

1. First, that we might the *better* and more *distinctly*

(10) Gen. i. 3. Ps. cxlviii. 5.
(11) S. Tho. i. p. q. lxxiv. Gen. i. 31.

understand the arrangements of the divine wisdom in the
creation of the world: and that we might learn to meditate upon them, not confusedly altogether, but by little
and little, and by parts, and give thanks to our Benefactor
for the new benefits which He bestowed on us each succes-
sive day.

2. Secondly, that we might the better understand the
necessity of the things which He created, beholding in the
first day the want of the things which He made on the
second, and in the second the want of those that He created
on the third; and so might stir up and move ourselves to
greater love and gratitude for every one of these benefits.

3. The third and last end was, that we might understand
and mark in this first work of the creation, how God our
Lord observes the *same order* in the work of our *sanctification* and *perfection* which He imparts, not all at once and
at one time, but in portions and by degrees, first one
degree and then another, through the whole course of the
six days, which represent the term of our whole life, till
it come to the Sabbath of eternal rest, in which the work
is fully perfect, and we enjoy the reward of our labour.
All which shall be pondered separately in the following
meditations.

MEDITATION XVIII.

ON THE THINGS WHICH ALMIGHTY GOD CREATED IN THE FIRST INSTANT
OR BEGINNING OF TIME.

The end of this meditation, and of those that follow, is
to consider the things which Almighty God effected in the
beginning of the world, and in the first six days of it;
that we may be moved by the consideration of these immense benefits, to love and serve Him who bestowed them;

for which purpose we should sometimes meditate on each day of the week upon the works which He did on that day. But it must be observed, that I shall confine myself to that work which the sacred text itself mentions, leaving to the schools of divines to dispute the particular sense in which such things are said to have been made on such a day, either in whole or in part, because for the purpose of these meditations it matters little that this should be known.

POINT I.

" In the beginning God created heaven and earth. And the earth was void and empty, and darkness was upon the face of the deep, and the Spirit of God moved over the waters."(1)

1. First is to be considered, how " *in the beginning,*" that is to say, in the beginning of time, the eternal Father, by the *beginning*, which is His Son, together with His *Spirit*, which is the Holy Ghost, gave *beginning* to all things, and created out of nothing heaven with all its greatness and roundness, which, great as it is, He holds and weighs, as Isaiah says, " with His palm." He thus displayed His omnipotence in making and supporting this immense vault, so spherical and round, which encompasses the whole earth, without the help of any instrument or prop. But in particular He then created the highest heaven, which we call *empyreal*, that is, *shining as fire*, to comprehend within its circuit, the whole frame of this visible world, and to be the court and throne of His Kingdom, and the perpetual habitation of the Blessed, both angels and men. From this consideration I will draw affections of great admiration, praise, and joy, at the greatness of this work, and at the glory of this place, so full of

(1) Gen. i. 1.

wonder, and will beseech our Lord to bring me to it, since He created it for me.

Colloquy.—O Almighty God, who createdst out of nothing the highest heaven, and placedst Thy especial dwelling in it, giving the earth to " the children of men,"(2) in order that they might there merit some habitation in that heaven ; grant me grace so to lead my life in this valley of tears, that at the last I may come to live with Thee in that paradise of delights. O glorious heaven, praise and bless thy Creator, and let thine inhabitants glorify Him for the greatness and beauty which He has given thee ; for " blessed are they that dwell in" thee, His " house," and they shall praise Him there for ever and ever.(3)

2. Secondly is to be considered how God our Lord did not create this heaven *void* of inhabitants, like the earth, but *full* of innumerable angels, divided into three hierarchies, and into nine choirs, and gave to all of them, in that very instant, all the perfections of nature and grace, which were suitable to each one of them, according to the arrangements of His divine wisdom. (4)   O how beautiful and admirable did heaven become, with that army of heavenly squadrons, so well composed and set in order!   O how great was the satisfaction of the Blessed Trinity, at the sight of those three hierarchies, each with its three choirs, in which were represented the excellencies of the three Divine Persons!   O what satisfaction and joy had these new soldiers at the sight of each other, and every one at the sight of himself, adorned with such perfections! O what exultation did they feel in that first instant, in the knowledge of the Creator, from whom they had received so great a gift.   By this consideration I will excite the angels, who persevered to glorify

(2) Ps. cxiii. 16.   (3) Ps. lxxxiii. 5.

(4) S. Tho. i. p. q. lxi. art. 3 et 4.

Almighty God, at this present time, with the same praises that they gave Him at the beginning, of which our Lord makes mention to His own glory, when He asks: "Where wast thou when the morning stars praised me together, and all the sons of God made a joyful melody?"(5)

Colloquy.—O highest angels, who were the first-fruits of the works of God, created early and in the first morning of this world, praise Him and bless Him, because He was both your Creator and your father, giving you the being of nature and the adoption of the sons of God by grace; and inasmuch as a little after-wards He gave you for your merits a share also in His eternal glory, praise Him with loud songs of joy for this new benefit that He bestowed upon you, and be-seech Him to make me also a partaker of it in your company.   Amen.

In like manner I might address myself to the different choirs of Angels, Archangels, Principalities, Powers, Virtues, Dominations, Thrones, Cherubim, and Seraphim, inviting each choir to praise Almighty God, and to rejoice in the good that they received in their creation, and afterwards in their glorification, according to what has been meditated upon in other places, and will furnish matter for further meditation. (6)

POINT II.

The second shall be to consider, how God our Lord, at the same instant created the *earth*, and placed it as a centre, in the midst of the vault of heaven, and yet made it of such a greatness, breadth, and length, that no mortal man can exactly know or measure its dimensions, which God glories that He alone can do, as Scripture testifies on various occasions. (7)

(5) Joh. xxxviii. 7.

(6) Med. xxxv. p. 1.   (7) Job. xxxviii. 5, 18.   Eccl. i. 2.

1. But that in which His omnipotence is most fully displayed, is, His making a thing of such immense weight hang in empty space, with nothing all about it, and without any prop or material support, and yet, with such great stability, that, as the prophet David says:—" He hath founded the earth upon its own basis: it shall not be moved for ever and ever."(8)   At the same time He supports it with as much ease as one that holds up a very little thing, as Isaiah expresses it, "*with three fingers*," since by His *wisdom, goodness,* and *omnipotence,* He holds it firmly in its place; and, therefore, Job declared, that God our Lord "hangeth the earth upon nothing."(9)   Hence I will gather how much I ought to rely upon the omnipotence of Almighty God, since, by the mere beck of His will, He can confirm and establish me for ever in good, so as not to move either to one side or the other.   For, although the burden of the body is heavy, yet the grace of Almighty God can support it, so as not to weigh down my soul, which, however, it will do, unless I ground myself in humility, by the consideration of my own nothingness, and cast myself entirely into the hands of this our Lord.

Colloquy.—O Almighty God, who bearest up the weight of the whole earth without supporting it upon anything out of Thyself; grant me grace to acknowledge my own nothingness, in order that Thou alone mayest be my stay, and that my virtue may be secure in Thee.   Amen.

2. The second shall be to consider *the abyss of water,* or of clouds, with which Almighty God covered the earth, in the same instant that He created it, in such a manner that it could not be seen.   Here I will take notice of the position which these two elements naturally keep with regard to each other, and how they represent the state of

<hr>

(8) Ps ciii. 5.   (9) Job xxvi. 7.

an earthly man, covered with the waters of miseries and calamities, and so foul and miserable, that he does not deserve to be seen, till Almighty God, in His infinite mercy, takes from him this covering. In this mercy I will put my trust, hoping that in due time He will deliver me, and will say with the prophet Jonas:—" The waters compassed me about, even to the soul, the deep hath closed me round about, the sea hath covered my head, and Thou wilt bring up my life from corruption, O Lord my God." (10)

POINT III.

Thirdly is to be considered how " the earth," at this instant, " was *void* and *empty*, and *darkness* was upon the face of the deep;" so that the whole space between heaven and earth, whether occupied by water, cloud, or air, was all darkness, and without light. (11)

1. Where is to be pondered, first, the *imperfection*, which for the time attached both to the earth and the water, for the earth was *void* and *empty*, and *had not attained the proper end of its creation*, being void of trees and of inhabitants, and all in darkness, for want of light. If, therefore, the earth and the water had had understanding, and a tongue, they would have cried out to their Creator, to crave the perfection which was wanting to them. In all which I may see an image of myself, a man, earthly, and miserable, conceived in sin, by the sin of Adam; and, therefore, in the beginning of my being, void and empty, unable to attain the end for which I was created, void of grace and of virtues, and covered all over with the horrible darkness of ignorance and sin; and the very same misery I incur every time I fall into mortal sin, and, therefore, since I have understanding, and a tongue, I

(10) Jonas ii. 6.

(11) S. Th. i. p. q. lxvi, art. 1, et q. lxviii. art. 7; ait per tenebras, significari aerem, qui est subjectum luminis.

ought to cry out to my Creator, and beg Him to deliver me from this evil, and perfect the work of His own hands. And, moreover, however holy I may otherwise be, I should consider that of myself I am like the void and empty earth, and like the deep, covered with darkness; being mindful, therefore, of the time, when I was such, I ought to be continually crying out to God, upon whom my perfection wholly depends, and beseeching Him to preserve it, and help it forward till it attains its end.

Colloquy.—O my Creator, I am earth, *void* and *empty* of all good, destitute of the fruit of good works, and unable to attain the end which I might attain by their means; and above all my other miseries, I am full of *darkness*, and without light to know my evils, and the remedy of them; come, Lord, in Thy mercy, to draw me out of this my misery, and since Thou hast given me the being that I have, give me the perfection which I want, that so Thy work may remain perfect, world without end. Amen.

2. I will ponder, secondly, the mystical *causes* of this difference in the creation of the earth, and that of the empyreal heaven. One is, that the earth represents that which belongs to man, by his own miserable nature, which is, to be vanity and darkness, and void and empty of all good; but the empyreal heaven represents that which man attains to through the grace of Almighty God, which is, to be, " igneus," that is, of the nature of fire, to shine with divine light, to burn with the fire of charity, and to be full of virtues. Moreover, the empyreal heaven was created to be the perpetual dwelling of the perfect, who have attained their final end, and was therefore created with all perfection, and filled with innumerable inhabitants; but the earth was created to be the habitation of the good, the evil, and the imperfect, and not to be a per-

petual dwelling, but as it were, a passage through, to walk to the final perfection and reward, which is given in heaven; and to represent this, it was made imperfect, void, without inhabitants, and incapable of fulfilling its end. Hence I will gather, that I am placed between earth and heaven, to make me understand that it ought to be my principal care, continually to contemplate the one and the other, that is, what I have of my own, and what I have by divine grace; my present state of a wayfarer and pilgrim on earth, and the eternal state which I hope to attain in heaven. Thus reflecting on my imperfection, I will en-deavour to fulfil the words of David, by walking with such a disposition of "heart," as "to ascend by steps," and increase in virtue in this "vale of tears," in the place where God "has set" me,(12) until I ascend to the high tower of " Sion," and to the place which He has pre-pared for me in His empyreal heaven.

Colloquy.—O eternal God, since Thine eyes have seen "my *imperfect being*,"(13) help me to rid myself of it whilst I live in this place where Thou hast put me, in order that I may attain to the enjoyment of Thee, in that which Thou hast prepared for me, world without end. Amen.

POINT IV.

1. The fourth shall be to consider how the Spirit of our Lord " *moved over* the waters."

i. Here meditate on the *presence* of the Spirit, that is the Holy Ghost, and how to perfect this imperfect work, He *walked upon the waters*, though full of darkness, and endued them with *virtue* and *efficacy*, for the works and things which were to be produced out of them, to adorn and people the earth. (14) By which is represented how

(12) Psa. lxxxiii. 6.   (13) Ps. cxxxviii. 16.
(14) S. Tho. i. p. q. lxvi. art. 1, ad 2, et q. lxxiv., art. 3. ad 4.

it is the office of the Holy Ghost, to succour such as are in necessity, although they are in darkness, and in the shadow of death, and full of many imperfections, and to endue them by His inspiration and inward motions with virtue and efficacy to convert themselves to God, and to make themselves capable of His light and gifts. It likewise signifies, as the Church says, the efficacy and virtue of sanctification, which He was to communicate to the waters, in order by them to cleanse us from our sins,(15) and impart to us the grace and plenitude of all virtues. I will, therefore, invoke this divine Spirit with great affection, saying:—

Colloquy.—O divine Spirit, who movedst upon the waters, dark as they were, come to my soul, which is full of darkness, and impart to it the motion of Thy holy inspiration, that by it she may dispose herself to receive Thy divine light, together with the gifts of Thy grace and charity. Amen.

ii. Secondly is to be pondered, the mystery contained in that word "*ferebatur,*" *walked* and *moved* upon the waters. This expression denotes that although this divine Spirit is in Himself *incapable* of *movement*, and reigns tranquilly in heaven, which is a place of triumph and of reward, where He gives Himself both to be seen and to be enjoyed in everlasting rest; yet in this life He is ever in continual motion, walking with wayfaring men, inspiring them, and moving them to virtue and perfection, and fostering them with His heat and shelter, till they produce that fruit which He desires in them. This His walking and moving is not idle, but is effectual of itself; not that He moves Himself, but that He makes us move ourselves, and thus draws us out of our sloth and idleness, and causes us to walk in the way to heaven; and this He performs

(15) In benedictione fontis Baptismatis.

towards His beloved sons, of whom St. Paul says:—" Whoever are led by the Spirit of God, they are the sons of God."(16)

Colloquy.—O divine Spirit, walk evermore with me, moving me and inducing me to follow Thy will wherever Thy powerful inspiration willeth that I should walk, and to go forward in such a manner as not to return back from what I have once begun.   Amen. (17)

iii. This word "*ferebatur*," further denotes the *continuance* and brooding of this divine Spirit upon the waters,(18) which is expressed by that comparison which the saints and holy Church are wont to use, when they say, that as the hen, by sitting upon her eggs, gives them life by her heat, and brings forth chickens, even so the Holy Ghost *brooded* or *sat* with a like influence upon the waters, to produce from them living creatures.   And in like manner does He sit and brood over souls, to protect them, and to give them life by means of His grace, that they may produce the fruits of living works; nor does He ever withdraw Himself, unless they first drive Him from them, and then that befalls us which befalls those eggs that the hen forsakes, which come to no perfection, and are of no use except to be cast upon the dunghill.

Colloquy.—O my soul, consider what thou dost and what thou thinkest, lest the divine Spirit, in whose presence thy life consists, and upon whose absence thy death ensues, withdraw Himself from thee; apply thyself, therefore, with great continuance and solicitude to His holy service, in order that He may apply Himself with great perseverance to thy salvation.   O divine Spirit, from Thee must all my good take its

(16) Rom. viii. 14.   (17) Ezek. i. 12.
(18) Ecclesia supra Tu super aquas futurus eas, ferebaris.

beginning, because Thou sittest and presidest over all that is good ; suffer me not, I beseech Thee, ever to separate myself from Thee, so that Thou mayest never separate Thyself from me.   Amen.

2. I will ponder, lastly, the *names* which the sacred Scripture here applies to the Creator, namely, "*Beginning,*" "*God,*" "*Spirit,*" and "*Lord.*"—He is "*Beginning,*" because He gives *being* to all things.—He is "*God,*" because of the authority and power with which He governs them.— He is "*Spirit,*" because He perfects and gives *life* to those who are capable of it.—He is "*Lord,*" because He made them and created them. And further, whereas all the Persons of the most Holy Trinity joined in perfecting this work, the Son is signified by the name of *Beginning*, because by His wisdom He gave beginning to the arrangement of everything that ever was created; the Father retains the name of "*God*," because He has His omnipotence of Himself, without receiving it from either of the other Persons; and the Holy Ghost is called "*Spirit,*" because of the office which He performs, of quickening and perfecting creatures by His goodness. All three Persons, however, were concerned in the whole work, and to all three the name of "*Lord*" belongs, because of the dominion that they have over all creatures, by the title of creation. And therefore, as St. Thomas says,(19) it was then that Almighty God assumed the name of Lord, and took possession of His lordship, for it was then that He began to have creatures, slaves, and servants, of which He was Lord, and over whom He had the right of command; for which I will congratulate Him on this new name, with a heart full of gratitude, and say:

(19) S. Tho. i. p. q. xlv. art. 6, et 74, art. 3, ad. 2. The Hebrew text says: ' In the beginning *Gods* created,' to denote the Trinity of P ersons, and Unity of Essence, in the power of working. 1. p. q.xiii. art. 7.

Colloquy.—O eternal God, whose dominion is perpetual and eternal in its power; I give Thee thanks for having vouchsafed to create so many creatures, of which Thou wast pleased to be the rightful Lord. I rejoice, O my God, that Thou art our Lord, Lord of all lords, and the only Lord, from whom all dominion proceeds. And since Thou art my Lord, take care of me, who am Thy creature, and keep possession of me, that so, like a faithful servant, I may always attend to Thy holy service, world without end. Amen.

MEDITATION XIX.

ON THE THINGS WHICH ALMIGHTY GOD DID UPON THE FIRST DAY.

POINT I.

" And God said, Be light made, and light was made; and God saw the light, that it was good, and He divided the light from the darkness, and He called the light day, and the darkness night."(1)

1. First is to be considered, how God our Lord, seeing the darkness in which the world lay, to remedy this, first before all things *made light*, like a person lighting a torch in some obscure and dark house, in order that men might enter into it. And here we may ponder how *miserable* this *world* was, while deprived of this material light, and how many *benefits* this light brings with it.—First, it *discovers the works of God*, and the beautiful things that are visible in the world; and without it we could neither see, nor walk, nor conveniently perform our bodily labour.— Next, it is a cause of great *gladness* and satisfaction in all living creatures, and by it are caused various influences of great virtues for their preservation; on account of all

(1) Gen. i. 3.

which, Almighty God, beholding the light, said of it that
"*it was good*," very suitable for the end for which the
whole world was created, and exceedingly beneficial to all
living creatures. Hence I will gather motives for giving
most humble thanks to God for this benefit of light; and
every day that the sun rises and sends forth its light
anew, I will praise the Creator for it, and for having given
me eyes to see and enjoy it, and for the gladness which I
receive from it, remembering the words of blind Tobias:—
"What manner of joy shall be to me, who sit in darkness,
and see not the light of heaven?"(2) I will also conceive
firm purposes to make a good use of this light, by using it
for the end for which God created it, which was, to see
His works, and to glorify Him for them; and I will grieve
also for such sinners as abhor a thing so good, wishing to
sin with more liberty, according to the saying of our
Lord:—"Every one that doth evil hateth the light...that
his works may not be reproved."(3)

2. Hence I will ascend in meditation to the excellency
of that *spiritual light* with which Almighty God perfects
souls living in darkness and obscurity and in the shadow
of death, and having nothing of themselves but the *darkness* of *ignorance* and of *sin*. This light Almighty God
communicates to them with great willingness, because He
desires that all may know Him, and may see His glorious
works, and together with them may also see what they
ought to do, how to serve Him, and how to walk to eternal light; and by means of this light He communicates to
them the influences of all heavenly graces and virtues, and
fills and replenishes their hearts with gladness. And
therefore Almighty God, beholding this light, also says
that "*it is good*," exceedingly good, and containing in perfection all kinds of good, the becoming, the beneficial, and

(2) Tob. v. 12.   (3) Joan. iii. 20.

the pleasant; for it is the most suitable to the supernatural end of grace, it is the beginning of virtues, profitable to all good works, and delightful in the exercise of them. And if I owe such great thanks to God for the material light, how much greater do I owe Him for this spiritual light, which is incomparably better?

Colloquy.—O " Father of lights," from whom all lights proceed, I give Thee thanks for these two lights which Thou madest to enlighten my body and my soul; a thousand times be Thou blessed for the material light with which I see all visible things, and millions of times be Thou glorified for the spiritual light with which I see invisible things. Behold, O my God, the obscurity of my soul, and have compassion on it; and since Thou art the fountain of light, vouchsafe to " enlighten my darkness" with Thy light. O " brightness" of the " glory" of the Father, the light from which light proceeds, "Light of light," fountain of light, and Day which givest light to the day, draw me out of the darkness in which I lie, and make me a perfect " child of light." Convert my darkness into day, so that I may go forward and increase like the dawn, " even to" the " perfect day" of Thy eternity. Amen.(4)

[After the manner of this colloquy, taken in part out of a hymn of the Church, other colloquies may be made out of the hymns which are sung at the week-day Matins, Lauds, and Evensong, which are full of the praises of this light, and of moving allusions to it.]

POINT II.

Secondly are to be considered, the *circumstances* attending this creation of light; and more particularly the three following. First, that Almighty God made the light on the *first day*, for it is the presence of the material light

(4) Psa. xvii. 29.   Ephes. v. 8.   Prov. iv. 18.

that causes the day, and without it there is no day. In like manner the spiritual light is the first of perfections, and, as it were, the first-fruits of Christian perfection, without which we cannot walk so much as one step; for, as David says:—"It is vain for you to rise before light;"(5) and therefore God our Lord has a special care to prevent us, at the beginning of our life, and when we are in darkness, with some illuminating ray of His most clear light, by which we may walk and labour in His holy service. O "true light, which enlightenest every man that cometh into this world" with the use of reason, prevent me with Thy light, that I may know Thee and love Thee, and help me "to prevent" the light of the "sun," so as to employ the first part of the day in adoring and blessing Thee, for the greatness of the mercies with which Thou preventest me for the relief of my misery. Amen.(6)

2. In the second place God our Lord on this first day made the light *only*, although He could have made many other things. He deemed it sufficient to employ that day on this work alone, and in conducting the light through its course along the whole hemisphere of this world, driving away darkness, and making the day whole and entire. By which He gives us to understand what esteem He makes of the light, and how much we ought to make of the spiritual light, and how we should employ ourselves wholly in seeking to attain it, sometimes spending a whole day, or at least a whole hour of the day, in attending to this alone, to the exclusion, in the meantime, of other affairs, till we have entirely performed our task, and persevering in it to the end, as the light perseveres every day in its course without interruption.

Colloquy.—O divine Wisdom, who camest forth "out of the mouth of the most high, the firstborn

(5) Psa. cxxvi. 2.   (6) Sap. xvi. 28. Psa. v. 5, et lxii. 1.

before all creatures,"(7) and madest "that in the heavens there should rise light that never faileth;" vouchsafe to give me some part of this Thy heavenly light, and cause it to remain so firmly in me, as never to leave me till I receive it completely in Thy glory. Amen.

3. The third circumstance to be considered is, how *all the blessed Trinity*, by a decree of love and joy, created this light, and took satisfaction and pleasure in it. This is implied in those words of holy Scripture :—" God said, Be light made;" that is to say, the Father said by the Son, who is His eternal Word, " Be light made," and in a moment "light was made;"(8) and seeing by His wisdom " that it was good," He approved of it by the spirit of His love, and took pleasure in it. And as it is the property of goodness to communicate itself, He ordained that this light should communicate itself through the hemisphere of the world, as has been said.

Colloquy.—O most blessed Trinity, I rejoice that the delight which Thou hast in the uncreated light, makes Thee take satisfaction in the light that Thou hast created. O supreme Father, for the sake of the love which Thou bearest to Thy Son, say, I beseech Thee, within my soul, " Be light made ;" for then it will immediately be made : and make it, Lord, in such a manner that it may sanctify me, and that Thy holy Spirit, coming with it, may dwell in this house of light, world without end. Amen.

POINT III.

1. Almighty God "*divided the light from the darkness, and He called the light day, and the darkness night,*" willing that in the earth there should be an *interchange* of

(7) Ecclus. xxiv. 5.
(8) S. Tho. i. p. q. xxxii. art. 6, art. 1, ad 3, et q. lxxiv. art 3, ad 3. :

light and darkness, of day and night, in order that man might labour in the day by means of the light, and might rest in the night by means of the darkness, ceasing from labour to give refreshment to the weary body. In this is manifested the sweet providence of this our Lord, who has thus provided that which is suitable for our bodies. Wherefore I will render to Him humble thanks, both for the light and for the darkness, and will invite them to praise Almighty God in those words of the Canticle:—" O ye light and darkness, bless the Lord, praise and exalt Him above all for ever."(9)

2. But ascending from the consideration of this circumstance to the spiritual sense which lies hidden beneath it, I will contemplate the *difference* between Almighty God and men, and between heaven and earth; for God our Lord, as St. John says, "is light" itself, "and in Him there is no darkness"(10) at all, and the Blessed in heaven, by the participation of His grace, are always light without darkness. And in heaven, as we read in the Apocalypse, there is no succession of nights and days, for there are no nights; but on the earth there is vicissitude and succession.(11) For there are some good, who live like " children of light," and who " walk" " as in the day;"(12) and again, there are others evil, who live like children of darkness, and walk as in the night; and the same person is at one time a child of light, and at another time a child of darkness; and between these classes of men also Almighty God makes a division, approving the one and reproving the other; for, as the apostle St. Paul says:—" What fellowship hath light with darkness?"(13)

Colloquy.—Wherefore, O my soul, take heed how

<hr>

(9) Dan. iii. 72.   (10) Joan. i. 9. 1 Joan. i. 5.
(11) Apoc. xxi. 25. (12) 1 Thess. v. 5. Rom. xiii. 13.
(13) 2 Cor. vi. 14.

thou livest, and join thyself to the "children of light," that when the supreme judge shall come to divide them from the children of darkness, it may be thy happy lot to rejoice with the children of light in everlasting glory. Amen.

3. Moreover, on earth there are great *divisions* of light and darkness, days and nights, between *different men*, even among the just, nay, in the very same man at different times; for the same man is at one time in prosperity, at another in adversity; at one time in honour, at another in dishonour; at one time in devotion of spirit, at another in dryness of heart; at one time full of interior illuminations, at another full of darkness and obscurity. This division Almighty God makes for the exercise and trial of His elect, and takes delight in it, because this succession of light and darkness promotes the good of the soul. I also, therefore, ought to rejoice in it, and to give Him thanks for both the one and the other, since His divine providence ordains to give me, in this way, the eternal light of His bliss.

Colloquy.—O Sovereign Father, who, with Thy word, didst divide the light from the darkness; vouchsafe so to illuminate our hearts, that we may obtain the "light" of that divine "knowledge" and brightness, which shines "in the face of Christ Jesus,"(14) and that imitating here the lustre of His light, we may afterwards enjoy His shining glory. Amen.

4. Lastly, I will ponder, that since Almighty God has given names to the light and darkness, calling the light day, and the darkness night; I am bound to *conform myself to those names*, which proceed from His divine wisdom, and to reckon as light, day, virtue, sanctity, and prosperity, those things which God reckons as such, and

(14) Ibid. iv. 6.

calls by such names; and in the same manner to reckon as darkness, night, vice, sin, and adversity, those things to which God has given such names; lest that terrible threatening of the prophet fall upon me:—" Woe unto you that call evil good, and good evil; that put darkness for light, and light for darkness."(15)

Colloquy.—O infinite light, enlighten our hearts with the " light of the knowledge of the glory" which shines " in the face of Christ Jesus," in order that our feeling, speaking, and working, may in all things be conformable to His, since " He that followeth" Him " walketh not in darkness, but shall" always " have the light of life," and by it shall attain to the enjoyment of everlasting glory. Amen.(16)

MEDITATION XX.

ON THE THINGS WHICH ALMIGHTY GOD DID ON THE SECOND DAY.

POINT I.

"And God said, *Let there be a firmament* made amidst the waters, and let it divide the waters from the waters.... and it was so, and God called the firmament, heaven."(1)

First is to be considered, how on the second day God our Lord made or perfected the firmament, that is, everything between the earth and water beneath, and heaven which was first created above, or at least the whole region of the air.

1. Here we may learn the *greatness* of this benefit, by considering the great advantages which come to us from the element of the air. We breathe and live in it; we are surrounded by it wherever we go; it conveys to our eyes

(15) Isa. v. 20.   (16) Joan. viii. 12.   (1) Gen. i. 6.

the forms of things which we see, to our ears the sounds and harmonies which we hear, and to our nostrils the sweet odours which we smell. By the air the light from heaven, and the influences of all the planets, rains, snows, and dews descend. By the air the winds fly abroad, and the clouds are carried, from which proceed many things necessary for our life. For all these benefits I ought to render thanks to our Lord with great affection, and at every respiration by which I draw in fresh air, I ought to breathe forth another expression of praise and love. Sometimes, therefore, I will call upon my ears, my eyes, my nostrils, my heart, and all my inward parts, to praise Almighty God for this benefit of the air which they enjoy, and by means of which they live and perform their offices. At other times I will invite the air itself, and all things that live and move by it, to glorify their Creator.

2. I may likewise ponder the mystery contained in this name of "*firmament*." That the heavens themselves, which, as is said in the book of Job, " are most strong, as if they were of molten brass,"(2) should be called *firmament*, is nothing strange: but the air is the most easily moved and changed of all things on the face of the earth; and yet, to show the divine omnipotence, is called *firmament*, on account of the *firmness* and stability with which it abides, and performs the offices for which our Lord created it, of dividing the waters, filling all empty spaces, and giving us all life continually, for air is never wanting to breathe.

Colloquy.—O most omnipotent God, I rejoice at this demonstration which Thou givest of Thy wonderful omnipotence by joining such great changeableness to such great firmness. Join, O my God, I humbly beseech Thee, to my changeable nature the firmness which proceeds from Thy sovereign grace; so that,

(2) **Job. xxxvii. 18.**

persevering in accomplishing that which Thou commandest me, I may come to enjoy the reward which Thou promisest me, world without end. Amen.

POINT II.

Secondly is to be considered, how God our Lord "*divided the waters* which were under the firmament, from those that were above the firmament," whether by these are meant some waters which Almighty God keeps above the heavens for ends known to His eternal wisdom, or the vapours or waters of the clouds which move in this firmament and region of the air, and are afterwards converted into rain. And to speak of these latter, which we perceive with our senses, in order to have a better understanding of the great benefit which God our Lord bestows upon us by means of them, I will consider various particulars in which His divine providence is here displayed.

1. First, besides that division of the waters that covered the earth, which was necessary, in order that part of it might remain dry and habitable, both for beasts and men, He was pleased on the second day, first to make *another division* of the waters, leaving the more gross and terrestrial upon the earth, and lifting up the others which were more subtle and delicate, into the region of the air, and thus producing the clouds, to water the dried earth when needful, and thus to make it fertile, so as to produce fruits.

2. Again, by means of the air, God in His providence, *guides* and *distributes* these clouds, carrying them whithersoever He will, for the good of men, displaying this mercy at the time that man's necessity cries out for it. And, therefore, it is said in the Book of Job, "Corn desires clouds, and the clouds spread their light, which go round about, whithersoever the will of Him that governs them shall lead them, to whatsoever He shall command them

upon the face of the whole earth, whether in one tribe,"
(3) that is, in one particular religion, " or in" their " own
land," where they were raised, or in another very distant,
"in what place soever of His mercy He shall command
them to be found."(4) Nay, so great is the mercy and love
that He shows in this, that He would be called "the
Father of rain, or He who begot the drops of dew," (5)
because, with a fatherly love, He sends rain upon the
earth for the benefit of those who dwell on it.

Colloquy.—O Father of mercies, I give Thee boundless thanks because Thou callest Thyself also " the
Father of rains," and distributest them with a fatherly
love, not only over the land of the just, but even over
that also occupied by sinners. Rain down upon my
soul the dew of Thy grace, that I may not be ungrateful for so great a mercy, but may ever praise Thee
and serve Thee for it. Amen.

3. Thirdly, the omnipotence and providence of Almighty
God are displayed in this, that while on the one hand He
bears up in the air such an immensity of clouds, charged
with water, on the other hand, when they fall, they do not
come down all at once, but *by little and little*, to water the
earth, and to be sucked in by it. Thus, as Job says:—" He
bindeth up the waters in His clouds, so that they break
not out and fall down together." When they fall with
violence it is God who gives them their " course;" and
when they fall *drop* by *drop*, it is God who numbers all
their drops, and assigns the place where they shall
fall. (6)

Colloquy.—O most wise omnipotence, and omnipotent wisdom, let the clouds and rains praise Thee, and

<hr>

(3) Job. xxxvii. 11.   (4) Job. xxxvii. 13.
(5) Ibid. xxxviii. 28.
(6) Ibid. xxvi. 8.   Ibid. xxxviii. 25.   Ecclus. i. 2.

let the drops of dew glorify Thee everlastingly for the being which Thou givest them, and for the manner in which Thou distributest them over the earth. And since all this is for the good of men, let them all likewise glorify and serve Thee for this so great benefit which they receive from Thee. Amen.

4. I will ponder, fourthly, how the clouds, by the providence of God, serve us likewise *as a shade*, to temper the heat and rays of the sun, from which they receive light, and communicate it to us, tempered and moderated. On this account it is said in Job, " Corn desireth clouds, and the clouds spread their light," as well as the rain, by which they temper the heats and droughts of the earth. All these benefits had their beginning in that which Almighty God did the second day; and since we every day receive and enjoy them anew, we ought every day to praise and serve Him for them.

POINT III.

" And *God called the firmament heaven ;*" that is, He gave the name of *heaven* to the region of the air, because of the resemblance which the air bears to the heavens, in being *raised* above us, and *transparent*, and the vehicle of light, and other influences of the heavens. (7)

1. But raising my thoughts to contemplate the *spiritual meaning* of the works of the second day, I will consider in them the properties of that soul, which God our Lord makes His *heaven*, by the sanctity which He imparts to it. After such a soul has received from His omnipotence the light by which the understanding is perfected, she receives also the *firmness* and *stability* of grace, together with heavenly virtues, by which the will and heart are perfected; and thus she that was before full of change by

(7) S. Tho. i. p. q. lxviii. art. 4.

her natural condition, is made firm and stable by the protection of Almighty God.

2. Hence proceeds the *division* of "the *waters*," that is of the *affections* and *propensities*, which by nature are mingled and confused, but by divine grace are separated from each other, and "*divided;*" so that the affections of earthly things remain in their own *lower* place, subject to the spirit, while the affections of heavenly things ascend to a *higher* place, and command the flesh. And, notwithstanding that there is war, as St. Paul says, between the flesh and the spirit, yet the spirit overcomes the flesh, and remains in the higher place, because the grace of God is its firmament and strength, and firmly divides these affections one from the other. And further from the higher waters of the spirit, there sometimes descend *rains* of comfort, to water the dry and barren earth of our flesh, that it may bring forth the fruits of good works, and that so both "heart" and "flesh" may rejoice "in the living God," from whom the good of both proceeds.

Colloquy.—O eternal God, shall I not love Thee for so many benefits which I receive from Thee? "I will love Thee, O Lord, my strength," "my refuge," and "my firmament;" let Thy grace be a "firmament" to me, by which I may firmly "separate the precious from the vile," in order to become Thy intimate and familiar friend.(8) Send down from heaven the rain of Thy heavenly doctrine, and the dew of Thy most sweet wisdom, that being imbued with this divine moisture, I may produce such fruits of holy works as may remain to everlasting life. Amen.

3. Lastly I will ponder the cause that our Lord *did not praise* the work of this second day, or say, "that it was good," as He said of the work of the day before, and of the

(8) Psa. xvii. 2. Jer. xv. 19.

days ensuing. The principal cause was, because Almighty God does not praise, or take full satisfaction in works, till the time that they are perfect, and completely finished; and, therefore, since the division of the waters began on this day, but was not finished till the day following, God did not say that they were good till the third day, on which this division was completely finished. (9) And this admonishes me to strive to secure *completeness* and *perfection*, both in my life and in my works, since in His eyes an action is not reckoned good and perfect which has a good beginning, if it has a bad ending; nor shall he be saved who begins well, but he who ends well, for "he that shall persevere to the end he shall be saved." (10)

4. We may extend this thought further, if we admit that which certain holy doctors say, that it was on this second day, which we call Monday, that the wicked angels transgressed, and that God *divided* them from the good, leaving the good above the firmament, and casting the wicked into the abyss below, where, like "the giants," they "groan under the waters." These doctors say that God our Lord did not call that which He made on this day, "good," on account of the sin and iniquity which had its origin on this day, by the devils who began well, and ended ill, because they did not persevere, and "stood not in the truth," and in the light which they had received. (11) Hence I will learn to fear my own frailty, from the example of the wicked angels, and to trust in the grace of Almighty God, from the example of the good. And on this day I will praise God with great fervour, for His mercy to the good angels, in giving them perseverance,

(9) S. Tho. i. p. q. lxxiv. art. 3. ad. 3. '   (10) Matt. x. 22.

(11) Albert. in ii. d. 5. Dion. catth. ibid. q. vi. Mag. Hist. suo gen. c. iv. dicit esse traditionem Hebreorum. Job. xxvi. 5. Joan. viii. 44.

and I will rejoice with them for the glory they have obtained, and beseech them to be my defenders against the devils, and my advocates with Almighty God, that He may be my strength, my perseverance, and my crown, world without end, Amen.

5. I may likewise consider another mystical cause for which Almighty God did not give His blessing to the second day, namely, because it was the beginning of *division* of days, and consequently a sign of *dissension* and *division*, the opposite of that unity or union, which is a special mark of charity, and highly acceptable to Almighty God, who pours down His blessing on those who embrace it, while He withholds His favour from those that abhor it, and separate themselves from it. "Behold," says David, "how good and how pleasant it is, for brethren to dwell together in unity, for there the Lord hath commanded blessing, and life for evermore." (12) This being so, I have great reason to make choice of this *one necessary thing*, that I may come at last to enjoy that "*one day*," of which David says in another place:— "Better is one day in Thy courts above thousands." (13) Without doubt the joy of one day in the house of God is of more value than many thousands out of it; and, therefore, I will shun all dissension and division among brethren which deprive us of the divine blessing.

(12) Psa. cxxxii. 1, 3.   (13) Ibid. lxxxiii. 11.

MEDITATION XXI.

ON THE THINGS WHICH ALMIGHTY GOD DID ON THE THIRD DAY.

POINT I.

"God also said: Let the waters that are under the heaven *be gathered together* into one place, and let the dry land appear, and it was so done. And God called the dry land, earth, and the gathering together of the waters, He called seas. And God saw that it was good. And He said: Let the earth bring forth the green herbs, and such as may seed, and the fruit tree yielding fruit after its kind, which may have seed in itself upon the earth: And it was done." (1)

The first shall be to consider, how God our Lord, upon the third day, seeing the earth covered with waters, *gathered together* the waters under heaven into *one place*, and displayed His omnipotence in various wonderful particulars.

1. First, that though the mass of the waters was immense, He collected them all by His mere command, *in a moment*, or in a very short time, into one vast and spacious place, divided into many other places, and thus formed the seas. Led by His omnipotence, the different bodies of water betook themselves all at once each to its assigned place, obeying without resistance His divine commandment, according to what David says, speaking of the earth:—"The deep is its clothing: above the mountains shall the waters stand. At Thy rebuke they shall flee, at the voice of Thy thunder they shall fear."(2) What a spectacle it would have been to see that immense mass of

(1) Gen. i. 9. (2) Psa. ciii. 6.

waters on this day, rushing with the utmost speed to the places which God had assigned them; some to the ocean, others to the south, others to the Mediterranean, and others to other seas.

Colloquy.—O most Almighty God, since Thy command is so powerful, gather together the waters of my affections and thoughts, which are dispersed throughout the whole earth, and put them into one place, assigned by Thy holy will, and let them never depart from it.

2. Another particular in which the omnipotence of God our Lord was displayed was, that whereas the waters had a natural tendency to remain *upon the earth,* as in their natural region, and to encompass it on all sides, as the air encompasses both the earth and the water, yet, as soon as they heard the divine commandment, they immediately *left this region,* and withdrew into the concavities and depths which God had assigned them, where they still remain without resistance, for the common and universal good of other creatures, reckoning the common good their own, and reposing in the place which the Creator gave them.

Colloquy.—O my soul, learn to obey thy Creator by this noble example, which this His creature gives thee; deny thy own inclination, in order thus to fulfil the divine will, and renounce thy own temporal profit, in order to accommodate thyself to the common good of thy brethren. O God of my soul, put me in whatever place it pleases Thee, for in that place will my heart find its true rest. If Thou shouldst remove me from a large and honourable sphere in which Thou hast placed me, and shouldst command me to retire into another more narrow and mean, I will embrace this lot most gladly, because I desire to leave my own inclination, and follow Thine, and to make Thine always mine. I will not seek what is profitable to myself alone, but the common good of my brethren, and with hearty good will yield my own right for their good; for the good of all shall be my good, in obedience to Thee, whose handiwork we all are.

3. Thirdly, the omnipotence of Almighty God is conspicuously displayed in so exactly *detaining* these waters of the sea *in the place in which He put them*, so that they can never issue forth from it, nor " pass the limits"(3) and bounds which He has set them: and all the great risings and swellings, the wonderful ebbings and flowings, to which they are subject, are equally contained within the bounds of the sands, that God has assigned them. (4) God Himself boasts of this, as when He says to Job:—" Who shut up the sea with doors, when it broke forth," with great impetuosity from the abyss of my omnipotence? " I set my bounds around it, and made it bars and doors; and I said: Hitherto thou shalt come, and shalt go no farther, and here thou shalt break thy swelling waves." (5) From this consideration I will conceive not only an admiration of the omnipotence of Almighty God, but also a great *fear* of offending Him, remembering what He says by the prophet Jeremiah:—" Will not you then fear me, saith the Lord: and will you not repent at my presence," of your wicked lives? " I have set the sand a bound for the sea, an everlasting ordinance, which it shall not pass over, and the waves thereof shall toss themselves, and shall not prevail; they shall swell, and shall not pass over it." (6)

Colloquy.—O omnipotent God, who will not greatly fear to offend Thee, and who will not be sorry for having so often offended Thee? Enclose, dear Lord, this sea of my heart, within the wall of Thy protection,

(3) Prov. viii. 29. (4) Psa. ciii. 9.. (5) Job. xxxviii. 8.
(6) Jer. v. 22.

and fasten its gates with the locks of Thy holy fear, that it may never transgress the precepts which Thou hast prescribed me, nor be drawn by the waves of my passions out of the place which Thou hast assigned me. Amen.

4. Hence likewise I will excite myself to place great *confidence* in the omnipotence of Almighty God, who, as Isaias says, "hath measured the waters in the hollow of His hand," and forcibly detains them within an assigned place, notwithstanding their unsteadiness, and although, as many saints say, the sea in some parts is higher than the earth. I may, therefore, steadfastly trust, that, although I am as unsteady as water, and although the propensities of my flesh urge me violently to leave the place where God has put me, yet He will preserve me, and retain me within my bounds, so that I may accomplish His holy will.

POINT II.

Secondly are to be considered the wonderful things which Almighty God did this day upon the earth, to gather together the waters, and to *make the earth fit* for the use of its future inhabitants.

1. First, by an act of His will, He *displaced* in a moment, and *turned over* a large portion of the surface of the earth, which was before exactly spherical, and thus made very deep *hollows* for the waters to gather themselves into, and lifted up very high mountains, like walls, and at the same time produced that remarkable variety of plains, hills, valleys and havens, which we now observe; for the earth obeyed in all things the divine commandment. In the words of David, "The mountains ascend, and the plains descend into the place which Thou hast founded for them." (7)   Hence again I will gather sentiments of admiration, obedience, love, and confidence. On the one hand

(7) Psa. ciii. 8.

I have reason to tremble before this Lord who is so mighty, who, as Job says, "hath removed mountains, and they whom He overthrew in His wrath, knew it not; who shaketh the earth out of her place, and the pillars thereof tremble." (8)   On the other hand I am bound to trust in the word of this Almighty God, who has said:—"If you have faith as a grain of mustard seed, you shall say to this mountain, remove from hence thither, and it shall remove, and nothing shall be impossible to you," (9) for the omnipotence of God, which put mountains in the place where they are, can easily transplant them from this to another place.

2. I will ponder secondly how the omnipotence of God was displayed in making the earth so dry and hard when the waters left it, that He called it "*arida*," "*dry land;*" and that without being many days in doing it, as in the time of the flood, and without making any use of drying winds, such as dried in one night the place where the Red Sea was left uncovered, when the children of Israel passed through it: but the power of God, by a mere act of the will, dried up the earth in the twinkling of an eye.(10)

Colloquy.—O divine Spirit, who art "a consuming fire" and "a burning wind;" consume in my flesh the humours of my earthly affections, and inflame my heart with the love of Thy heavenly virtues, so that the Devil, who loves "moist places," and hates the "dry," may find no "rest" in my soul, but that Thou mayest keep possession of it.   Amen.(11)

3. I will ponder thirdly how God our Lord, by an admirable arrangement, when He gathered the waters together into the sea, and left the earth dry, left at the same time the *sweet waters* of many *rivers* and *fountains*, scattered in

<hr>

(8) Job. ix. 5.

(9) Matt. xvii. 19.   (10) Gen. viii. 14. Exod. xiv. 20.

(11) Deut. iv. 24. Exod. xiv. 21. Matt xii. 43. Job. xl. 16.

various places, and for this purpose made conduits and channels, and as it were veins, within the bowels of the earth, in order that the water that issues from the sea into which "all the rivers run,"(12) only to return, might pass through them. And here there are several wonderful things to be remarked.—i. The first is, the *multitude* ot these rivers, fountains, and wells, so conveniently disposed in every part of the earth, and especially among the highest mountains and rocks, from which they distill and fall into the valleys.—ii. The second is, their *perpetuity* and *continuance;* for though they have run uninterruptedly for so many years, the supply of water does not fail, nor will it ever fail, but there will always be new water running.—iii. The third is, the *sweetness* of these waters, although those of the sea, from which many of them flow, are exceedingly bitter and salt; for the omnipotence of the Creator strains them through the pores of the earth, and so turns their bitterness into sweetness. And here we may see how easy it is to Almighty God to change a thing into its contrary, and to turn *bitter* into *sweet,* for one who faithfully serves Him.—iv. The fourth is, the great *utility* of these waters in various ways. They water and fertilize the earth, which thus has water, not only from heaven, but also from its own fountains and wells. They supply the necessities of men and other living creatures, who preserve their life by drinking them; wash and bathe in them, and use them to resist the violence of fire. And besides this, the waters of many fountains have other admirable properties for healing many infirmities of the body. All this our great God arranged on this day with the providence of a Father; and for these mercies we ought to give Him continual thanks, especially every time that we make use of this benefit, and we ought to invite the sea and earth, the mountains and hills,

(12) Ecc. i. 7.

the rivers and fountains, to praise and glorify their Maker.

4. I will ponder, fourthly, how God our Lord on the same day arranged the earth for different purposes; making some parts of it *fertile*, and suitable for the growth of the *plants* and *trees* which He intended to make; and in other parts forming mines and veins for engendering *gold* and *silver*, *brass* and *iron*, and other *metals*, and compounds necessary for the use and service of men, and distributing these mines accordingly in different parts of the earth, as Job notices.(13) It may be believed that Almighty God made these metals at the time: and for this also I owe many thanks to the Creator, who was so careful in providing us beforehand with things, the want of which would cause great inconveniences: and therefore, every time that I make use of them, I ought to glorify Him who gave them to me. At the same time I may reflect that Holy Scripture does not make mention of the creation of these metals, or of other things hidden in the earth: the mystical cause of which may perhaps be, to teach men how little value they ought to set on temporal riches, in comparison with those that are heavenly; since they are but a part of this earth, and so little esteemed by their Maker, that in recounting the things He had created, He would not reckon them among the rest. Those, therefore, who desire them inordinately, shall fall under that curse denounced by David against the wicked:—" O Lord, divide them from the few of the earth in their life; their belly is filled from Thy hidden stores;"(14) that is to say, separate them from the number of Thine elect, because they have satisfied their covetous desires with the treasures which Thou createdst in the hidden parts of the earth.

(13) Job. xxviii. 1. S. Tho. i. p. q. lxix. art. 2. ad 3.
(14) Psa. xvi. 14.

Colloquy.—O eternal God, who createdst gold, silver, and other metals for my advantage, suffer me not by my evil use of them to convert them to my harm; let not that be a means of offending Thee, which ought to be a means of serving and praising Thee.' Amen.

POINT III.

The third shall be to consider how God our Lord, after separating the waters from the earth, and approving this separation, because it was now perfect and complete, immediately said:—" Let the earth *bring forth the green herb*, and such as may seed, &c." In which two things appear very remarkable.

1. The first is, that although it might have seemed work enough for this third day to have separated the waters from the earth, yet because God saw that the earth, after it had been laid bare, was covered with filth, and still very imperfect, He would not permit it to continue all that day in this state of filthiness and imperfection, or defer to the day following the perfecting and beautifying of it; but at once *began to clothe it* and adorn it with the covering designed for it. In this is represented to us the providence of God towards His creatures, and His readiness to make them perfect. As He took from the earth a garment or covering which concealed it, and made it filthy, and immediately gave it another, which made it beautiful, and pleasing to the sight; and would not suffer it to remain naked for ever so short a time: so likewise He desires to strip us of the garment of the old man, which makes us filthy and abominable, and unfit to be seen either by Himself or His angels, and to clothe us at once with the new garment of His grace and of virtues, that we may become beautiful and pleasing in His eyes; and in this work He desires that there should be no delay on our part, and that we should

not defer till to-morrow that which we can do this present day.

2. The second thing is, that He *would not create out of nothing* the plants and trees which were to adorn the earth, although it was easy for Him to do so, but chose that the earth itself should concur and contribute towards it, and therefore He said:—" Let the earth bring forth the green herb,"..." and it was so done."   Thus while Almighty God was the principal maker, the earth gave what it had, which was itself, that of it, as the material, plants might be made, although with some loss of its own substance· Here we may see clearly represented how God our Lord, although He greatly desires our perfection, yet will He not effect it alone, but would have us assist towards it, and co-operate with His divine grace, by offering Him all that we have, that is, ourselves, our heart, and our whole liberty, for His divine Majesty to do in us and with us what He will, even though it be accompanied with some loss and injury to what belongs to us, that is, to our own will and earthly desires, and by mortifying ourselves, and repairing the evil which we have done.   So that we ourselves, with the assistance of His grace, must, as the apostle St. Paul says, strip ourselves " of the old man with his deeds," and put " on the new," and his deeds.(15)

Colloquy.—O most perfect God, the fountain and origin of all perfection, who, to honour man more, and to preserve his liberty more entire, hast ordained, not to sanctify or perfect him, unless he concurs to his own sanctity and perfection; behold me here, O most merciful Lord, presenting myself to Thee like the unsightly earth, prepared to receive the plants of heavenly virtues.   To Thee, Lord, it belongs to make them by Thy omnipotence, and I, prevented by Thy

-----

(15) Coloss. iii. 9.

grace, give my consent to receive them, whatever it shall cost me ; give me, dear Lord, what I ask of Thee, that I may serve Thee as I ought. Amen.

3. Next I will consider more in detail the things which Almighty God made out of the earth by this His command, dwelling on five remarkable particulars in which are displayed His *omnipotence* and His divine *forethought* with regard to living creatures, and especially with regard to men, for whose sake He ordained all other things.—i. The first of these particulars is, the *infinite number* of the herbs, plants, flowers, and trees which God made upon this day, and how He distributed them through different parts of the earth, and placed each in the *climate suited* to its nature; for some plants require a cold soil, others a hot one, and others a temperate, and in each soil He produced those plants which would naturally thrive in it. Thus it is that the divine providence shows great sweetness in all its works, and is wont in like manner to adapt the gifts of its grace to the good of our nature, in order that grace and nature, being united together, may work with more sweetness and with longer continuance.—ii. The second remarkable particular is, the *facility* and *speed* with which He made all these plants throughout the whole earth, which extends over so many millions of miles, and yet is so full of different sorts of plants. As soon as He said, "Let the earth bring forth," that very instant they were made, and the earth remained clothed and garnished with such variety and beauty, that God Himself, who created these works, glories in them, saying:—"With me is the beauty of the field."(16)—iii. To this is added the third particular, that God our Lord produced all these plants and trees in their *full size* and *perfection*. The tree, which, according to its natural course, would be many years fixing its roots, grow-

(16) Psa. xlix. 11.

ing up, and bearing leaves and fruit, attained to all this perfectly in a single moment. For the works of God our Lord are perfect, and that which men do by little and little, and with great labour, God can perform at once, and with great perfection and facility.

Colloquy.—O most powerful and most perfect Creator, I give Thee thanks for the speed and perfection with which Thou didst effect so many and such great things on this day, with abundance of time remaining, with which Thou mightest have done many other things, if Thou hadst so pleased. Display this omnipotence, I humbly beseech Thee, towards me, and accelerate by Thy divine grace that which my own frailty so greatly retards; since it is a most "easy" thing in Thine "eyes," "on a sudden to make the poor man rich."(17)

iv. The fourth particular is the greatness and infinite number of the *benefits* which men have received by means of this work, for the preservation of their life and the gratification of their senses. The *eyes* are refreshed with the beauty of the flowers and forests which God our Lord made on this day, the *smell* with the most sweet odour that proceeds from them, and the *taste* with the savour of so many fruits and herbs, each having its own particular sweetness; by which also the body is fattened, and nourished, and from which it derives its growth and strength. And although for the preservation of life it would have been sufficient for God to have created wheat of which bread is made, and vines from which wine is made, yet He chose rather to display the liberality of His providence by creating a *great variety* of plants for our sustenance and gratification, to take away, by this variety, the disgust which sameness might have caused, as also that there

(17) Ecclus. xi. 23.

might be different kinds of food to please different tastes. Moreover, to many of them He gave wonderful *medicinal virtues*, for supplying remedies to cure the infirmities of our bodies. And that nothing might be wanting to us, the trees which produce no fruit yield wood and timber for constructing houses, and other artificial things of which we stand in need, and for fuel to nourish the fire with which we warm ourselves, besides many other particular benefits which it would be too long to recount in this place —v. Lastly, that all these things might endure *to the end*, He gave the plants and trees which He made on this day the *power* of *producing seeds*, from which others should spring like themselves, as our eyes daily experience.

With these five considerations, and with each one of them, I will raise up my heart to glorify Almighty God for the things which He created for the preservation and comfort of my life, and for the beasts which enjoy and eat them, and serve me. For although I myself do not eat grass, yet the sheep and oxen which I do eat are fed with it; and although oats and barley are not my food, they are the food of the horse, of which I make use; and therefore it was with great reason that David said, that God bringeth "forth grass for cattle, and herb for the service of men."(18)

Colloquy.—O Life of the living, to whom all things look, waiting to receive food from Thee to sustain their life, and who "openest Thy hand, and fillest" them all " with blessing ;"(19) I give Thee all possible thanks for Thy liberality in opening Thy hand on this day, to adorn the earth, and to supply pasture to the beasts and food and gratification to men. And since Thy bounty goes on every day, and continues Thy benefits, let my gratitude also go on, and continue the service which I owe Thee for them. Amen.

(18) Ps. ciii. 14.   (19) Ps. clxiv. 16.

POINT IV.

The fourth shall be to consider, how God our Lord, on the same day, by a special arrangement, planted in the best part of the earth a most excellent and pleasant garden, which for its excellence was called "*paradise*," or the *garden of delights*, in order that man might be placed there, thus preparing a habitation for him before He created him.(20)

1. The *excellence* of this paradise consisted, principally, in five things.—i. First, that it had the very best *temperature* in the whole world, both of soil and air, without any excess of cold or heat, and without clouds, tempests, and other penalties which we now experience.—ii. Secondly, that it was furnished with *all sorts of trees*, beautiful to the sight, delicious to the taste, and planted in an admirable order and arrangement, the savour and taste of which was such, that man would never have desired the use of flesh and fish, which was afterwards granted him.—iii. Thirdly, that in the midst of it was planted the most sweet and beautiful *tree of life*, the fruit of which had the virtue of preserving from infirmities, from old age, and from corruption, and of prolonging the temporal life of man, until the time that it pleased God to transfer him to the life eternal.(21)—iv. Fourthly, that there was in it a most copious *river* of wonderfully sweet and wholesome water, to water the ground, and to yield most wholesome and delightful drink to man; which river was divided into four others, which watered all the adjoining country.—v. Fifthly, that it was very spacious, and capable of containing many inhabitants; so that although it was a garden, yet it covered a vast extent, like some great province of Spain or France. And in conclusion, all the orchards and

(20) S. Tho. 1. p. q. cii. art. 1. ad 5.   (21) Ibid. lxxix, art. 4.

gardens which have been planted by the great monarchs of the world cannot be compared to this garden, which God planted in His loving providence, to be the dwelling and habitation, not of both good and evil, as other gardens are, but of the good only.

2. But above all, I am to ponder the greatness of the benefit which I received of God in this place of paradise. For it was His will and pleasure to create it, not only for Adam, but also for his posterity, and so even for me, if Adam had not sinned: and therefore, as far as God alone was concerned, He gave it to me also.

Colloquy.—I give Thee thanks, O sovereign Father, for Thy willingness to give man two paradises to dwell in, one earthly and the other heavenly, that he might be translated from the one to the other, if he persevered in Thy service. I beseech Thee, O my Lord, that although I have lost by the sin of Adam that first paradise of earth, I may not lose by my own sins that second one of heaven ; and as Thou hast pardoned me by Baptism my original sin, pardon also my actual sins by the sacrament of Penance. Preserve me always in the earthly paradise of Thy Church, by means of the fruit of the tree of life, which is in it, in order that when death comes, Thou mayest translate me to the heavenly paradise of Thy glory. Amen.

POINT V.

The fifth shall be to consider, how God our Lord, having ended the work of this third day, "*saw that it was good,*" since there was nothing wanting to it of all that belonged to the end of its creation.

1. Upon which is to be pondered, first, that the things which God created for our sustenance are *all good*, and *none* of them *evil* in their own nature, although the use of them may be evil, because His divine Majesty has forbid

them. Thus He forbade our first parents to eat of the fruit of the "tree of knowledge," although it was beautiful and delightful to behold, which He did to prove their obedience. And in like manner at the present time, God, by the mouth of His Church, prohibits the use of certain meats; and men who aim at perfection, by vow or out of devotion, deny themselves the use of certain pleasant things, to mortify their flesh. I will therefore conceive a resolute determination to use these things with thankfulness and temperance; for if the thing which God has created is good, it is most unreasonable that by my gluttony the use of it should be made evil. In this, then, I will follow the counsel of St. Paul, who says:—" Every creature of God is good, and nothing to be rejected" as though it were evil, " that is received with thanksgiving, for it is sanctified by the word of God and prayer."(22)

2. Secondly, *all* that God created on this day was *good*, although amongst the things that He created were *thorns* and certain *poisonous plants* and herbs. Although these things are hurtful to men, yet they are profitable to other creatures, or for other ends of the universe; and even to man himself they are of use as medicines, when mixed with other things; and if Adam had not sinned, they could never have hurt him; and lastly, they are instruments of the divine justice, to chastise those who abuse other things. This, therefore, suffices to show that they are very good, since God makes use even of things which are very profitable to chastise the wicked and ungrateful; as the water, which cools some, drowns others; and the fire, which warms some, burns others. Hence I am to learn with what great care I ought to make use of these creatures in the service of my Creator, imagining that they all speak to me in those words of Hugo of St. Victor:

(22) 1 Tim. iv. 4.

—"Accipe, redde, fuge. Accipe beneficium, redde debitum, fuge supplicium." "Receive, render, flee. Receive the benefit, render what is due, and fly from the punishment."(23) As if He had said: If thou wilt not serve God for the benefit thou receivest of Him, at least serve Him for the punishment which He may inflict upon thee; for the creature which He created for thy advantage shall be made thy executioner and tormentor. This language I ought to hear and understand when I behold the creatures and intend to use them, and should lift up my eyes to God, from whom they all proceed, and who by them speaks these words to me.

Colloquy.—O supreme good, from whom all that is good proceeds, grant me grace to use Thy good gifts with such goodness and with such gratitude, that I may escape the punishment and obtain the recompense, and may enjoy Thy supreme goodness, world without end. Amen.

***

MEDITATION XXII.

ON THE THINGS WHICH ALMIGHTY GOD DID ON THE FOURTH DAY.

POINT I.

" And God said: *Let there be lights* made in the firmament of heaven, to divide the day and the night, and let them be for signs and for seasons, and for days and years, to shine in the firmament of heaven, and to give light upon the earth. And it was so done. And God made two great lights, a greater light to rule the day, and a lesser light to rule the night, and stars."(1)

(23) Lib. de Arca Morali. cap. iv. tom. ii.
(1) Gen. i. 14. S. Tho. i. p. q. lxx.

1. First, I will consider the greatness of the *benefit* which God bestowed on us in creating the *greater light* of the two, the *sun;* reflecting at the same time on its excellent properties, and on what is to be learned from them to our profit.—i. The first of these properties is, the *great brightness* of this light, which is, as it were, the fountain of light, and the splendour of which is so great, that when it appears in the world, it obscures all the stars, and makes them vanish from its presence as if they did not exist.—ii. The second is its *perpetuity* and *continuance;* for it has never diminished a single jot, nor suffered any disturbance in itself.—iii. The third is the great *size* of the sun, on account of which the Scripture calls it, "Luminare majus," " the greater light;" for it is more than six thousand times larger than the moon, and more than a hundred times larger than the whole earth.—iv. The fourth is its great *power* and *activity* in illuminating the whole world, and communicating light in great abundance in a moment, and without experiencing any resistance, to all bodies that are capable of receiving it; so that it rules as king over the day, of which it is itself the cause, by that swift motion from the east to the west of which the Psalmist speaks.(2) —v. The fifth is, the amazing *heat* of the beams which it darts forth like fire, and the effect of its influences, in causing the propagation and growth of plants and other living things, and in contributing to the life and preservation of all things.—vi. The sixth is, that by its own *motion,* which begun on this fourth day, it causes the difference of the seasons, spring, winter, summer, and autumn, and the different length of the days in different times and places; and also measures the years, making a complete revolution in the time which we call a year. For these ends, therefore, God created the sun, and manifested His omnipotence

<hr>

(2) Psa. xviii. 6.

in producing so beautiful and great a work in an instant, by a mere act of His will. Accordingly, the Wise man calls it "Vas admirabile," "an admirable instrument,"(3) and in an eminent sense " opus excelsi," " the work of the Most High." As often, therefore, as the sun rises, I will give thanks to its Creator, admiring the beauty and perpetuity of this His work, and the regularity that it keeps in its rising and course, according to what David says:—"As a bridegroom coming out of his bride-chamber hath rejoiced as a giant to run the way, his going out is from the end of heaven, and his circuit even to the end thereof."(4)

Colloquy.—O Almighty God. I rejoice in the glory which this beautiful work of Thine brings Thee, and I praise Thee a thousand times for the good which Thou dost us every day by means of it. It is meet, O my Lord, that every time the sun issues forth, I also should rejoice " as a giant, to run" in Thy service the course of that day, beginning from the morning, and persevering in fervour until the evening. Amen.

2. Hence I will ascend to contemplate the sun as a *symbol* and *sign* of the divinity of God, by which He is more clearly known to men than by other works of creation; for which cause the Psalmist says, that God has "set His tabernacle in the sun."(5) In this tabernacle He performs many wonderful works, and there shall they who seek Him find Him, by meditating on the six properties which we have enumerated, and which are found in far greater perfection in the divinity, from whence they proceed.

Colloquy.—O eternal God, " Sun of justice," " light inaccessible,"(6) in whose presence not only the stars, but also the sun itself is obscured; Thou art the fountain

(3) Eccl. xliii. 2.　　　(4) Psa. xviii. 6.　　　(5) Ibid.
(6) Malach. iv. 2. 1 Tim. vi. 16.

of life, a perpetual fountain, which cannot be exhausted; Thou dost illuminate men, especially Thine elect, and together with Thy light, dost give to them vital heat and heavenly influences. Thou art He that ruleth over the sun and the day, over the seasons and years; for it is by Thy will that they are arranged in the order and form which they now have. Let the sun, O my Lord, praise Thee, let the day, the winter and spring, the summer and the autumn, yea, let all things glorify Thee for the glory which Thou displayest in this Thy work. Amen.

Hence, likewise, I will learn to *imitate*, to the utmost of my power, *the properties* of the sun; since it is said of the perfect soul, that she is "electa ut sol," "bright as the sun,"(7) because of the eminent sanctity which she has, and in which she perseveres without any change, shining by good works to the glory of God, and to give light and heat to the souls of her neighbours.

POINT II.

In the second place I will consider the greatness of the benefit which God our Lord bestowed on us, in creating the second "*lesser light*," or the moon, and the excellent properties which she also possesses, and on which it is profitable to reflect.

i. The first property is the *greatness, beauty*, and *grace* which it has, from the light that it receives from the sun; which light, however, it does not receive in order to reserve it to itself, but to illuminate the earth with it, and so "to rule the night,"(8) by dispersing part of the darkness caused by the absence of the sun.—ii. The second is, the *regularity* with which it follows the sun, in such a manner as always to have light on that side which is turned directly towards it, while on the other side, as Ecclesiasti-

(7) Cant. vi. 9.   (8) Psa. cxxxv. 9.

cus says, it "decreases in her perfection...increasing wonderfully in her perfection:"(9) that is to say, its light decreases till it is no longer visible, and then increases again till it is full.—iii. The third is, the great *influence* that it exercises, and the wonderful *effects* that it produces upon the *sea*, and upon *living creatures*, many of which we cannot comprehend or understand, but yet by experience we know them.—iv. The fourth is, that its motion produces various other effects also, and *distinguishes* the different *times* of the year, and especially, as the Wise man says, the *months*, for it continues and is completed in a little more or less than a month. With these considerations I must excite in myself emotions of praise and gratitude to God our Lord, for the creation of so beautiful an object, and for the benefits which other creatures receive from it.—v. But lifting up my thoughts still higher, I will contemplate the moon as a *symbol* and *sign* of *holy souls*, which Almighty God calls "Pulchras ut lunan," "beautiful as the moon." Their beauty and splendour consists in continually beholding the infinite sun of God's divinity, and receiving from Him the light and splendour of His divine grace, and of His gifts and virtues; while they make it their aim, on the one hand, to diminish and decrease in their own estimation, till they attain to a profound knowledge of their own nothingness, and of the darkness in which they are involved of themselves, and on the other hand, to increase in virtues, till they attain to the fulness of grace, and to complete perfection in it.

Colloquy.—O "Sun of justice," on whom the beauty of the moon depends, grant me grace to follow Thee with such fervour, that I may continually receive an increase of Thy grace, together with a more profound knowledge of my own misery. Suffer me not to imi-

(9) Ecclus. xliii. 7, 8.

tate the "fool" that " is changed as the moon,"(10) by *changing* from the *brightness* of virtue to the *darkness* of vice ; but make me constant as the sun in virtue, so that I may change only from *good* to *better*, till I attain the *unchangeable* state of Thy glory, where I shall see Thee and enjoy Thee, world without end. Amén.

POINT III.

In the third place I will consider the great benefit which Almighty God bestowed upon us by creating the *stars*, reflecting on their excellent properties, and wonderful effects.

i. The first of these great properties is, their *multitude*, which is too great for men to reckon like the sands of the sea; and therefore Almighty God makes it His glory that He understands their " number," " and calleth them all by their names." (11)   Yet, though they are so many, and so beautiful, and many of them of extraordinary size, He created them all in one moment, and fixed them in the firmament, where they stand ranged, in admirable order and union, like " *an army*" of soldiers " *set in array*." (12) And so Holy Scripture calls them " the armies on high," because every one steadily keeps its own place and station; and by their mutual order and arrangement, they form remarkable *figures* in the heavens, appointed by their Creator, as He Himself declares to Job. (13)—ii. The second property is, that together with the moon they "*rule*," as David says, " *the night*," and give us light, and serve us as guides for our journey by land and sea; and by their presence greatly beautify and adorn heaven itself when they display themselves in the darkness of the night.—iii. The third property is, that they all and each exercise wonder-

(10) Ecclus. xxvii. 12.   (11) Psa. cxlvi. 4.
(12) Ecclus. xliii. 9.   (13) Job. xxxviii. 31.

ful *influences* upon the *earth*, upon all *living creatures*, and upon *men;* which, although they are of a hidden nature, yet are very beneficial; and therefore we ought to render thanks to Almighty God for them, as well as for those that are manifest, since He ordained them for our good. Of these influences it is said in Ecclesiasticus:—" By the words of the Holy One they shall stand in judgment, and shall never fail in their watches." (14) And the prophet Baruch adds, that when called by Almighty God, they answer very joyfully:—" Here we are; and with cheerfulness they have shined forth to Him that made them." (15) All this ought to be a motive to me to praise God, and, in gratitude for this benefit, to study to imitate their properties here mentioned; for they also are symbols of just souls, especially of such as by word and example teach virtue to others, according to those words of Daniel:—"They that instruct many to justice," shall shine as stars for all eternity." (16)

Colloquy.—I give Thee thanks, O most loving Creator, for the beauty which Thou hast given to so great a number of stars, which Thou hast disposed in heaven in an admirable order, assigning to each its own place, its own splendour, and its own office. Oh how much more admirable will that army of stars be seen to be which Thou hast with Thee in the highest heaven, and which Thou dost also dispose in a like order and arrangement, giving every one his place corresponding to his merits on earth! Grant me grace, dear Lord, I beseech Thee, to become a star in the Church militant, and to keep my place like a faithful soldier, accomplishing my watches without defect, and obeying Thy precepts with delight, so that having shone here to Thy glory, I may obtain an eminent

(14) Ecclus. xliii. 11.   (15) Bar. iii. 35.
(16) Dan. xii. 3.

place in the Church triumphant, and may reign with Thee world without end.   Amen.

POINT IV.

In the fourth place I will consider how God our Lord, having finished this work, "*saw that it was good,*" and took great satisfaction in the perfection of it.   We may notice also that such was the fairness and beauty which Almighty God gave on this fourth day to the sun, the moon, and the stars, that rude and ignorant men thought them to be " gods that rule the world," (17) deeming that there could not be such great goodness and perfection except in God. And this ought to excite us to two strong sentiments.

1. First, of *admiration* of the *omnipotence* and *sovereignty* of this our great God, for He who could create such beautiful works, is, without any doubt, infinitely more beautiful and admirable than they; and, as the Wise man says, if the beauty of the creatures so greatly delights us, much more ought the beauty of the Creator, if we know Him by them.

Colloquy.—O supreme God, " the *first author* of *beauty,*"(18) suffer not men to be so blinded with the splendour of " the sun when" it shines, and of " the moon" in its " brightness," as to " kiss," their " hand with" their " mouth,"(19) in sign of adoration.   Open their eyes, dear Lord, I beseech Thee, to understand that they are Thy workmanship, and the habitation where they are to find Thee, so that they may glorify Thee as God, from whom they all proceed.   Amen.

2. Secondly, of great *love* towards Him, who loved us so much, and created such noble and beautiful objects for our use, and to be, as it were, servants and handmaids to serve us; according to what Moses said when he cautioned the people, " lest perhaps lifting up thy eyes to heaven,

(17) Sap. xiii. 2.   (18) Ibid. xiii. 3.   (19) Job. xxxi. 27.

thou see the sun, and the moon, and all the stars of heaven, and being deceived by error, thou adore and serve them, which the Lord thy God created for the service of all the nations that are under heaven." (20)

Colloquy.—O most omnipotent and most loving God, who will not love Thee with His whole heart for having made such noble works for the service of such mean creatures? For Thou hast created them not only for the service of kings, but for that of base wretches, and, what is more, of most vile sinners. O most high God, who ordainedst that which Thou hast placed in the firmament of heaven for the service of those who live beneath it; grant that I may love Thee so cordially for this benefit, as never to fail in Thy service, world without end. Amen.

POINT V.

Fifthly is to be considered the admirable providence of God our Lord, in the creation of the element of *fire.* Moses, indeed, has made no mention of it, because he speaks only of those corporal things which are *visible,* and this element is not visible in its own sphere; but yet, we may here suitably contemplate the greatness and liberality of the benefit which we receive from that *visible fire* that we enjoy, which bears a wonderful resemblance to the sun.

i. For first, the fire supplies by its *light* the want of the sun and the moon, when they are not visible, and performs the office of the sun for us within our houses and chambers, so that, we come to see by night by the light of the fire, the things that we see by day by the light of the sun.—ii. Secondly, it likewise supplies the distance of the sun in winter time, by its *heat,* and warms those who approach it, dissolving cold and frost, and

(20) Deut. iv. 19.

reviving the body when almost dead with cold.—iii. Thirdly, like the sun, it communicates itself with *liberality* and
readiness to all, *without* any *diminution* of itself, as may be
seen in the light of a candle, which sets light to many
other candles, and imparts its heat to all who approach to
it.—iv. Fourthly, it is an *universal* agent. It effectually
cooks and seasons the meats we eat; it purifies and refines
metals; it dries up humidities; it softens and liquifies
things that are hard, and produces many other wonderful
effects for our benefit, and in order that we should glorify
the Creator of it, and give Him thanks for the providence
with which He has provided a remedy for our necessities.
Let us therefore attribute the works of this fourth day to
His infinite mercy, and say with David:

Colloquy.—" Praise the Lord, for He is good, for
His mercy endureth for ever."(21)   " Who made the
great lights, for His mercy endureth for ever.   The
sun to rule the day, for His mercy endureth for ever.
The moon and the stars to rule the night, for His
mercy endureth for ever."   Who also made the fire
to supply the absence of the sun and moon, and to
shine instead of them in the night, for His mercy endureth for ever.   His mercy endureth for ever, and
will remain with His elect for ever and ever.   Amen.

From this we may likewise elevate our thoughts to consider, how the fire, as well as the sun, is a *symbol* of the
divinity, after the plan that was followed in the Meditations on the coming of the Holy Ghost. We may reflect
further how peculiarly it belongs to our Creator to supply
the defects of His creatures, and to hasten to favour us
with His divine succour, when human succour absents and
hides itself; and again, how liberally He communicates
Himself, like fire, to all those who approach and draw

(21) Psa. cxxxv. 1. et 7.

near to Him, according to that invitation of David:—
"Come ye to Him and be enlightened, and your faces shall not be confounded." (22)

Colloquy.—I give Thee thanks, O uncreated fire, for the twofold fire, material and spiritual, by which Thou revivest our bodies and our souls; inflame my soul, dear Lord, I beseech Thee, with the fire of Thy love, that, like fire, it may mount up to Thy divine essence, and may be joined to Thee in perfect union, through all eternity. Amen.

MEDITATION XXIII.

ON THE THINGS WHICH ALMIGHTY GOD DID ON THE FIFTH DAY.

POINT I.

"God also said, Let the waters *bring forth the creeping creature,* having life, and the fowl that may fly over the earth, under the firmament of heaven." (1) Here is to be considered first, how God our Lord, on this fifth day, was pleased to furnish the sea and rivers with abundance of inhabitants, by creating *fishes,* both many and great, to show His omnipotency and His care in providing for the benefit of men.

1. First, God our Lord ordained that the waters should have their part, and *co-operate* in producing the fishes that were to live in them, in the same manner that the earth had its part in producing plants, for the reason already alleged; and so in virtue of those words, "*let the waters bring forth,*" all the waters of the seas, and of all the rivers, furnished matter, of which Almighty God made fishes, to abide and dwell in them.

(22) Psa. xxxiii. 6.   (1) Gen. i. 20.

2. Secondly, He made them in *immense number*, with a great *variety* of species, forms, and natural properties. Amongst the rest " God created the great whales, and other fishes of extraordinary size, incomparably greater than any of the beasts upon the earth; and to all of them He gave scales and fins, and bodies suitable for swimming, and for moving with great ease and celerity through the spacious sea, and all its waves.

3. Thirdly, " He blessed them, saying, Increase and multiply, and fill the waters of the sea." And, since the blessing of Almighty God is *efficacious*, to bless them, was to give them the property of engendering others like themselves, in great abundance, incomparably greater than that of the birds and beasts upon the earth, according to what David says: " So is this great sea, which stretcheth wide its arms: there are creeping things without number." (2) Yet, though they are so many, God, by means of His providence, supplies them all with suitable food, and that within the same sea, which, like a mother, both produces and sustains them, and bears them, as it were, within her bowels. In the blessing thus bestowed upon the fishes, which was the first of all that God gave, and in the great effects that it produced, we may see the efficacy and the abundance of the blessings which Almighty God bestows upon His creatures, and especially upon men.

4. Fourthly, this multitude of fishes was created by Almighty God for the *benefit* and *use* of man, whom He made, to " have dominion over the fishes of the sea," (3) and endued him with skill and industry, to take them, and subject them " under his feet," not only the little ones, but also the great ones; and since the flood He has given them to man for his sustenance and gratification in eating, and for other beneficial purposes.

(2) Psa. ciii. 25.   (3) Gen. i. 26.

With these considerations I should excite myself to glorify the Creator, admiring not only the omnipotence which He showed in making in a moment, by His mere word, such a multitude and mass of creatures, but also the fatherly providence which He displayed towards us, in filling the seas and rivers with such delicious fishes for our sustenance and pleasure. I may well say with David:

Colloquy.—" How great are Thy works, O Lord! Thou hast made all things in wisdom; the earth is filled with Thy riches. So is this great sea, which stretcheth wide its arms; there are creeping things without number, creatures little and great;" there dwell the dragons and whales which Thou hast made; all swim and sport there, the greater catching the less for their sustenance. Men also by Thy divine providence pass over this sea in their ships, and refresh and delight themselves by catching these and other fishes for food or sport. O my Glory, pour out upon me the abundance of Thy blessing, in order that I may praise Thee and serve Thee for the innumerable bene-fits which Thou givest us through it. Let it be my solace and refreshment to love Thee, my delight to serve Thee, and my exercise to fish in the sea of this world, and catch many souls, which may employ them-selves in Thy holy service, world without end. Amen.

POINT II.

The second shall be to consider how God our Lord, on the same day, furnished the air with a great multitude of *birds*, of different species, which He produced out of the water.

1. Upon this we may notice, first, that in the creation of birds the omnipotence of Almighty God made use of *water*, as the matter, especially that more subtle kind, which is contained in the vapours and clouds of the *air*, in

(4) Psa. ciii. 24.

order that the *air* also might concur in the production of
that which was to be an ornament to it. (5) Thus He
created a multitude of birds, in the different regions of the
world, and in each those which would thrive best there,
according to their nature. To all He gave His blessing
and command to multiply, as He had done to the fishes;
and He furnished all by His providence, with fitting sustenance, some on the earth itself, others while flying in the
air, and others while swimming in the waters; and to
enable them to take their food, He gave them wings,
beaks, claws, and other instruments adapted to their
several needs.

2. I will ponder, secondly, the *greatness* of the benefits
thus bestowed upon us, and the *variety* of the advantages
included in it. For some birds nourish us most deliciously
with their flesh; others enliven us with very sweet songs;
others adorn us with their feathers; others teach us what
we ought to do, by their industry in building their nests,
and nourishing their young ones, and by their foresight in
discerning the change of seasons. God Himself, their
Creator, draws many comparisons from them for the purpose of our instruction; for sometimes He compares Himself to an " eagle enticing her young to fly;" sometimes to
a " hen," gathering " her chickens under her wings;" at
other times He condemns our ignorance by the example
of " the stork," " the turtle," " the swallow,"(6) and "the
kite," which know their times.

3. Finally, all the *works* of birds, with their *propensities*
and *instincts*, are ordained for our gratification and profit.
Some we employ to catch others, letting them loose into
the air, to pursue their prey for us, while we entertain
ourselves with observing their dexterity and swiftness in

(5) S. Aug. Lib. de Gen. ad lit. c. iii. S. Th. i. p. q. lxxi. art. 3.
(6) Deut. xxxii. 11. Matt. xxiii. 37. Jer. viii. 7.

the chase. "The bee," as the Wise man says, "is small among flying things; but her fruit hath the chiefest sweetness." (7) She produces honey for the gratification of men, as well as wax, of which candles are made, and many other very useful things. For all these benefits we ought to give great thanks to our Creator, and benefactor, acknowledging in all birds, both tame and wild, and in their eggs, quills, and feathers, and all that we derive from them, the fatherly providence of Almighty God, who has created so many objects of comfort and pleasure for His children.

Colloquy.—O most sweet and most loving Father, who hast given us tokens of Thy charity, Thy mercy, and Thy great and admirable providence, in the birds which Thou createdst on this day; manifest these attributes towards me most fully by making me solicitous to serve Thee, as Thou wast provident in providing so many different things to delight me. Let the birds be my teachers, that I may learn of them to chant and sing Thy praises early in the morning; help me to gather from them motives of virtue, to make me fly in Thy service, and renounce the superfluous pleasures of the body for that which I shall receive instead of them in my soul. Amen.

POINT III.

The third shall be to consider, how God our Lord, seeing all that He had made on this day, affirmed it to be "*good*," because it was all admirably perfect and suitable for the end for which He had ordained it.

1. In particular we may notice that it was very fitting that the *water* and the *air*, which are nearly akin, and like one another, especially the water of the earth, and the region of the air nearest to it, in which are situated the

(7) Ecclus. xi. 3.

vapours and waters of the clouds, should be peopled on the *same* day. Thus was signified the delight and satisfaction which our Lord takes in rewarding those who are closely united, and aid one another, and in making them alike in favours, as they are alike in charity. But raising my thoughts still higher, I will contemplate what the Church says in the Vesper hymn of the fifth ferial service, "Magnæ Deus potentiæ," &c.

> " Lord of all power, at whose command
>   The waters, from their teeming womb,
> Brought forth the countless tribes of fish,
>   And birds of every note and plume;
> Who didst for natures linked in birth
>   Far different homes of old prepare,
> Sinking the fishes in the sea,
>   Lifting the birds aloft in air."*

By this is intimated that those who are engendered by the water of Baptism, are distributed into two states of life, one *secular*, the other *Religious*. By the fishes are represented those who follow the *active life*, because they remain in "the sea" of this world, and while they employ themselves in works of virtue, mingle with them the affairs and cares of the world; by the *birds* are represented those who choose the *contemplative life*, because, by the wings of contemplation, they fly from that which is earthly to that which is heavenly, and have their conversation above in heaven.

The former have the part of Martha, of whom Christ our Lord said:—" Thou art careful, and art troubled about many things;" (8) they live in the tempestuous and troublesome sea of this world, in which there are many things that molest us, and make us uneasy. The latter, with Mary, Martha's sister, have " chosen *the better part*,"

* Caswall's " Lyra Catholica."   (8) Luc. x. 41.

and rejoice in the quietness that they enjoy; these lift themselves up above the earth, and above themselves, to join themselves in union with God, which is that " *one*" " *necessary*" " *thing*," to which all other things whatever ought to be subservient, as has been said in its proper place.(9) Both the one and the other of these two states of life are good, for God ordained them both, and has sanctified those who follow them with the water of Baptism, and washed them with the water of penance and of tears. Of both, therefore, may be understood what the Scripture says: "God saw that it was good;" but yet, in a different manner, for, as the fishes were made of the waters of the earth, which, in the sea are bitter, even so the exercises of penance and tears of those that live the active life, are accompanied and mingled with grief and bitterness ot heart, for the sins into which they have fallen, and into which they fall through their frailty; but the tears of the contemplatives are sweet and delicate waters, like heavenly vapours, of which the birds were made, for they are tears of love and of devotion, proceeding from desires, and deep sighs, to be united with Almighty God.

2. And though both fishes and birds were made in one day, yet mention is *first* made of the creation of the fishes, which are more imperfect, and afterwards of birds, which have greater perfection in their nature; for it is the manner of our Lord to proceed from the imperfect to the perfect. And thus it is intimated that the active life precedes the contemplative, and that we must first exercise ourselves in deploring our sins with great bitterness before we ascend to the sweetness of contemplation: Lia came before Rachel, and Jacob first espoused Lia, and afterwards Rachel, (10) and thus, from the active life, which is more imperfect, we

(9) Introduc. p. 3. et 5.   (10) Gen. xxix. 16.

ascend to the contemplative, which is the better and more perfect.

3. Finally, God gave His *blessing* both to the fishes and to the birds, and thus imparted to them the property of *increasing* and *multiplying*, by which is signified, that He gives His abundant blessing to the just in both these kinds of life, that they may multiply and bring forth a multitude of good works, which are the fruits of their womb, and may also beget many spiritual children by gaining souls to God. And as every living thing not only engenders its like, but also inclines it to exercise its own virtues and operations, so it is with these spiritual progenies. Again, fishes are more fruitful than birds, and so the active life, like Lia, is more fruitful than Rachel, and begets more spiritual children to Christ than the contemplative. This, however, must be understood of the perfect active life, which likewise gives some part to contemplation, whence it draws what it teaches and preaches to others; but the contemplative life is likewise fruitful, like the birds, and begets children, who, though few, are perfect, like Rachel's. I am to encourage myself to the exercises of these two lives, joining them together in one same day, as God joined together the creation of those two great things, beseeching Him humbly for His grace and assistance to this effect.

Colloquy.—O Creator of all things, who, on this fifth day, didst create the creatures who represent these two lives, for the preservation and sustenance of men; vouchsafe, I humbly beseech Thee, to give every day to my soul the food both of action and of contemplation, to preserve and sustain her life, until by Thy mercy she obtains the eternal, and is enabled to praise and glorify Thee, world without end. Amen.

MEDITATION XXIV.

ON THE THINGS WHICH ALMIGHTY GOD DID ON THE SIXTH DAY.

POINT I.

God said moreover, "Let the earth *bring forth the living creature* in its kind, cattle, and creeping things, and beasts of the earth according to their kinds. And it was so done."(1)

1. First, consider how God our Lord on the sixth day adorned the earth, by creating for it as inhabitants many different kinds of beasts, such as beasts for labour, serpents, and others; a work in which His omnipotence was displayed, by His making in a moment so great a number of beasts in so many distinct regions of the world, by His creating each in the place best adapted for its preservation, and by the fact that the earth obeyed the divine power without resistance, furnishing matter for the formation of them all. By this consideration I may raise in myself those affections which have been before set down. (2)

2. Next I will consider the vast number and variety of beasts which God created, and which the Scripture here reduces to three kinds. Some are called beasts for labour, or, according to their common appellation, domestic beasts, from the help and assistance they give to man; others, "creeping things," to which we give the general name of "serpents;" others the Scripture calls simply "beasts," by which are meant wild or savage beasts. All these kinds He divided into various species, each with its own peculiar and wonderful properties and inclinations; and for each also He provided suitable means of subsistence, and by an

(1) Gen. i. 24.   (2) S. Th. i. p. q. lxxii.

admirable providence furnished them each with the instruments by which they could best procure their food. He also armed them with defensive and offensive weapons, and with very wonderful instincts, with which either to defend themselves against others, or attack them, and so procure what they desire and seek. In all this God glories, when, speaking with Job,(3) He relates in four chapters the wonderful properties which He gave to these beasts, and the providence which He has over all of them; for all which I am to give Him thanks, in the confidence that He who has such providence over beasts, will have much more over men, as we shall hereafter see.

3. I will ponder, thirdly, the great *benefit* which God *conferred* upon us in the creation of these beasts; for some nourish us delicately with their flesh, others clothe us with their wool, and shoe us with their skins, and even the very worms make silk for adorning our persons; others help us in our journeys, and in bearing our burdens, keep our houses, and defend our persons; others serve for our recreation, and by their noble qualities bring us honour, and serve us in time of peace and of war; others teach us their craft and industry, and even the "ant" is for the slothful a mistress, to whom the Holy Ghost sends them, to learn to get rid of their slothfulness.(4) In a word, we derive so many conveniences from these beasts, that we cannot enumerate them; but as we have daily experience of them, we ought also daily to praise Almighty God, and to give innumerable thanks to the Creator, for two motives. First, for the benefits He bestows on those His creatures who know not who is the author of them, for whose ignorance, therefore, I should supply by my knowledge, and return those thanks which they know not how to give. And next for the benefits which He bestows on

(3) Job. xxxviii. et seq.   (4) Prov. vi. 6.

me by means of these beasts, since whatever they have is for my use, and does me greater service than them.

Colloquy.—O most liberal God, who hast given unto us so many means of passing this life commodiously, vouchsafe to assist us with Thy grace, that we may so pass by these goods temporal, that we lose not those that are eternal. Amen.

POINT II.

Next is to be considered, how God our Lord, beholding this work, *saw that it was good*, and approved of these three kinds of creatures which He had made, not only of the domestic and gentle, but also of the serpents, and those that were savage, for the reasons given above, and that although serpents are full of poison, and savage beasts often do great harm to men.

1. In particular, because the divine providence would here show His mercy and His justice.(5)   His mercy, in creating these savage beasts and serpents in such subjection to man, that if he had not sinned, they could never have injured him: His justice, in using them as an instrument for punishing the offender, in order to his correction, and if that fail, then for the chastisement of his sin. Another object in their creation was, that the just might glorify Almighty God when they observed with what care He keeps and defends them, never suffering them to be molested by them, except for their greater good. This is a reflection which is made by the Wise man, where he says:— "The creature serving Thee, the Creator, is made fierce against the unjust for their punishment, and abateth its strength for the benefit of them that trust in Thee."(6)

Colloquy.—O eternal God, by whose providence every creature is "obedient to Thy grace, that nourisheth all,"(7) and obeys Thy precepts in order to

(5) Med. xxi. point 5.   (6) Sap. xvi. 24.   (7) Sap. v. 25.

preserve Thine elect from harm : take me under Thy safeguard and protection, assisting me to serve and obey Thee ; because creatures, being so obedient to Thy will, will not injure me, if I also am in due submission to it.

2. Secondly, to consider how these beasts are called "good" for another reason, because they give us an *occasion of exercising virtues* and avoiding vices, and awaken in us the fear of God, and confidence in His mercy, and by their instincts admonish us of that which we ought to do, an application which Christ our Lord makes when He says to us:—" Be ye therefore wise as serpents."(8) Hence I will learn how to reap profit from the consideration of these creatures in meditation, for they possess some good and profitable qualities which may be imitated, as they are perfect in their kind; although at the same time they have also some imperfection which is to be avoided, since in comparison with men they are imperfect. From the beast of burden I will learn subjection and obedience to God and to the burden of His law, with resignation of all self-judgment, saying with David:—" I am become as a beast before Thee!"(9) but I will avoid its ignorance and brutishness, that the words of the same prophet may not be applied to me:—" Man, when he was in honour, did not understand: he is compared to senseless beasts, and is become like to them."(10)

Colloquy.—O eternal God, suffer not men capable of reason to " become like the horse and the mule, who have no understanding ;"(11) bridle the fury of their passions with the bit and bridle of Thy fear, that, preserving the dignity of men, they may follow the good which Thou hast placed in these beasts, and fly all evil that is in them. Amen.

(8) Matt. x. 16.   (9) Psal. lxxii. 22.   (10) Ps. xlviii. 13.
(11) Ps. xxxi. 9.

POINT III.

The third will be to consider the reason why God our Lord did not bless the beasts of the earth, as He blessed on the fifth day the fishes of the sea and the fowls of the air, saying:—"Increase and multiply;" for doubtless it was not without mystery.

1. Now though one cause of this was, that on the same day, a little after, He gave His blessing to man, and in him virtually to all those other creatures to whom man was allied in corporal and sensitive nature, and in the place of his habitation; yet to rise from this cause to the mystical, our Lord willed that the blessing of these creatures should be, as it were, suspended, in order that we might understand that their blessing or curse, their increase or decrease, depends on the merits or demerits of men, for whose sake God created them; for to reward the just who serve Him faithfully, He promises to bless and multiply the living creatures for the benefit of man, saying to the people of Israel:—" If thou wilt hear the voice of the Lord thy God, to do and keep all His commandments... blessed shall be the fruit of thy womb, and the fruit of thy ground, and the fruit of thy cattle, the droves of thy herds, and the folds of thy sheep:"(12) and on the contrary, to chastise them if they sin, He threatens them with the cursing of their cattle, saying, that they shall be barren, that He will take them from them and destroy them, and that for the same cause He will "send the teeth of beasts upon them with which is no blessing, but a curse for men, in punishment of their iniquities; the fury of creatures that trail upon the ground, and of serpents."(13) That serpents, locusts, lions, and other beasts have in fact been multiplied for this purpose, as appears from the ten

(12) Deut. xxviii. 1, 4.   (13) Deut. xxxii. 24.

plagues of Egypt, and other punishments and inflictions which the Scripture recounts. Hence I will conceive fervent desires of serving a Lord from whom such blessings come, and fear of offending Him, since by offending Him such terrible curses are brought down.

Colloquy.—O most merciful Father, from whom proceed all the blessings both of heaven and earth; grant that the faithful of Thy Church may so faithfully serve Thee, as to merit, like another Jacob,(14) a sufficient blessing on their goods temporal, and a much more plentiful supply of the eternal. Amen.

2. Hence I will go on to ponder how the brutish passions of our flesh are increased and multiplied, in punishment of the rebellion of our will against God; and on the contrary, are lessened in reward of its subjection to and conformity with the divine; a subjection, by reason of which they in their turn become subject to us, and do not disturb our peace; and how these same passions, when reduced to order, increase and multiply by the blessing of God, the affections of the sensitive appetites aiding the will, so as to make the "flesh," the "heart," and the "spirit" rejoice "in the living God,"(15) and go forward happily in His holy service.

Colloquy.—O beloved of my heart, I desire that my soul and my flesh may thirst after Thee in very many ways in Thy service.(16) Pour Thy blessing, I humbly beseech Thee, upon them, that my flesh may multiply affections pleasing to Thee, and that my soul may assist herself by them to serve Thee with greater fervour. Amen.

(14) Gen. xxx. 43.　　　(15) Ps. lxxxiii. 3.　　　(16) Ps. lxii. 2.

MEDITATION XXV.

POINT I.

God said, "*Let us make man to our image and likeness ;* and let him have dominion over the fishes of the sea, and the fowls of the air, and the beasts, and the whole earth, and every creeping creature that moveth upon the earth." (1)

1. First is to be considered, how God our Lord, having made the beasts of the earth, would also make man on the same sixth day, in which there are three remarkable things to be considered. First, that it was not without a mysterious meaning that He would not dedicate one entire day to the creation of man alone, as He did to the making of light. He created him on the same sixth day on which He had created other creatures of the earth, because he was like them in the corporal and sensitive part of nature, and also in order that he might ground himself in true humility, acknowledging his baseness in this respect; for as he was to be exalted to very excellent qualities, it was proper that these should be mingled with some baseness, to prevent him from growing proud; and this rule of mingling lowliness with greatness our Lord always observed, in order that we might ground ourselves in true humility, without which no greatness is secure.

2. Secondly, that God created man *after* other living creatures, because, as in the creation of living things He began with those which were most imperfect, and ascended to the more perfect (for first He made plants, after that

(1) Gen. i. 26.

fishes, next birds, then the beasts of the earth, and lastly man, who is the most perfect), even so He desires His servants to proceed in their works and actions, by continual ascent from less to greater, and by daily increase in the perfection of them, so as to perform them on the second day with more perfection than on the first, and on the third with more perfection than on the second; and thus to mount daily from virtue to virtue, until they come to the height of perfection. And besides, as on each of these six days our Lord either made new things, and each better than what preceded it, or gave a new perfection to those which He had made before; even so He desires that His elect should every day sing to Him new songs of praise and gratitude,(2) and render Him new services with a new fervour, renewing their spirit with new and more intense inward feelings of His greatness and majesty.

Colloquy.—O my soul, since God esteems a " new creature"(3) so highly, endeavour to accomplish every day new works, and attribute them not to thyself, but to Him who created them in thee, through the merits of Jesus Christ, to whom thou owest the glory of them.

3. Thirdly, that Almighty God created man *the last of all* things, and in him finished the works of the creation of these six days, to give us to understand that man was the end of all of them, and an abridged world, in whom all the others were contained, and that the whole building of this visible world, with all its beauties, was designed, that it might be his house and habitation. This, with a most fatherly providence, He first prepared and made ready before He created man, that immediately upon his creation he might recreate his eyes with the beauty of the things which he beheld, and his ears with the music and songs of

<hr>

(2) Ephes. v. 19.   (3) Gal. vi. 15.

the birds which he heard, and his taste with the flavour of the food which was at hand, prepared for him by God Himself, and so of the rest.(4)

Colloquy.— O most loving Father, if before Thou createdst me, Thou didst prepare so many goods in this visible world, where my dwelling is to be for so short a time, how much greater goods hast Thou prepared for me in the invisible world, in which my dwelling is to be eternal; I give Thee all thanks for the one and for the other, and since Thou hast prepared the first to assist me in gaining the second, grant that I may so live in this visible world which Thou hast created for me, that I may afterwards ascend to the invisible world, where I shall enjoy Thee for ever. Amen.

POINT II.

The second shall be to consider the sovereign counsel of the most Holy Trinity in the creation of man, which is implied by those first words, " *Let us make man;*" words in which lie hid many great mysteries which we ought to consider.

1. First, Almighty God did not say of man that which He said of other things, " *Be man made;* let the earth bring forth man," &c., in order to show the excellence of man, whose more noble part, which is the soul, could not be made either of earth, or of water, but only of God alone, the sole Maker of heaven and earth; from which we may understand how we are obliged to love Him above all things, as the only Author of our being, from whom proceeds all our good, and how we ought to serve Him alone, and to crave of Him to perfect us, saying:

Colloquy.—O God of virtues, behold the vineyard

(4) S. Amb. Ep. xxxviii. ad Honorantium.

of my soul, and "perfect the same which Thy right hand hath planted."(5)   Amen.

2. Secondly, He said in the *plural* number, "Let *us* make man to our image," to give some intimation of the mystery of the Holy Trinity, and to show how all the three divine Persons cooperated together in the creation of man in a more especial manner than they did in the creation of other things, in order to communicate to him His image and likeness.   He intended also to signify how the three divine Persons performed this work with mature counsel and deliberation, and as it were exhorting one another to the execution of it; for They had present before Them, and foresaw the issue of the whole affair, and how ungrateful man would become to his Creator, and how he would break His law, and how dear it would cost Him to remedy the evil by the rigour of justice, and how hard it would be to sanctify him, and to make him attain the final end for which He created him.(6)   Notwithstanding these difficulties, the Father said to His Son, and both of them to the Holy Ghost, and all Three together with great resolution: " Let us make man to our image and likeness."

Colloquy.—O most loving and most merciful Creator, what moved Thee to create such a creature, whom you knew would be so ungrateful to Thy goodness? Wherefore gavest Thou being to him, who was to make so evil a use of it?   Why didst Thou create him to Thine image and likeness, who, by his sins, was to defile and efface that image?   It was most easy for Thee to create him, but it cost Thee very dear to redeem him ;   yet, nevertheless, with great resolution Thou didst say, " Let us make man."   O Beloved of my soul, how shall I requite Thee for this so loving a resolve!   My desire is, by Thy help, to make a similar resolve, to overcome manfully every difficulty in

<hr>

(5) Ps. lxxix. 15.   (6) S. Greg. ll. ix. Mor. c. xxvii.

Thy service, since Thou didst so lovingly resolve to create me.

Hence also I will learn, in imitation of my Creator, before I begin any hard or important undertaking, *to deliberate* and ask counsel upon it, reflecting beforehand on what I intend to do, that it may not take me by surprise, nor I have reason to repent my having done it; according to the advice of the Wise man:—" My son, do nothing without counsel, and thou shalt not repent when thou hast done."(7) My principal counsellor, moreover, ought to be one, viz., the Triune God Himself, whose counsels, given us in His law, I ought to follow.

3. Lastly, I will ponder how God our Lord spake these words:—" Let us make," to signify that He created man, as being capable of *reason and friendship*, for familiar converse with Himself; as if He had said: ' Among all the visible things which we have created, there is not any with whom we can familiarly converse; let us therefore make man, who shall be capable of our conversation."

Colloquy.—O eternal Wisdom, whose " delights" in the creation of the world were to create " the children of men,"(8) and to be with them ; since Thou hast made me capable of conversing with Thee, fulfil the end of my creation, and converse with me familiarly. Amen.

POINT III.

The third will be to consider, how Almighty God, Three and One, created man *to His image and likeness*, giving him a *soul*—on which this image is chiefly stamped —like Himself in the highest degree of intellectual being, and in the most excellent perfections of the divinity which can be communicated to creatures.(9)

(7) Ecclus. xxxii. 24.   (8) Prov. viii. 31.
(9) S. Tho. i. p. q. xxiii.

1. These perfections we will reduce to six, and consider in each the excellence of this sovereign benefit.

i. The first excellence of our soul, by which it is the image of God, is, that as God is a *pure spirit*, and consequently *invisible* to the eyes of flesh, and *indivisible* in the place where He is, in every part of which He is whole and entire in a most perfect manner, preserving and giving being, life, and motion to the thing in which He is, according to its capacity; even so our soul is a *pure spirit*, and consequently is *invisible* to our bodily eyes, except as far as concerns the effects which it works in the body, in which it exists entirely and *indivisibly;* for it is wholly in the eyes, ears, hands, and in every part and member, giving to each one its being and its own distinct manner of life and motion, and its own peculiar functions.(10) And therefore, as David says, when Almighty God takes away the "breath" of man, he fails, and his body is turned again into "dust."(11) How great reason, then, has not our spirit, together with all our members, which it animates, to glorify Almighty God, and to become so many tongues to bless His name.

Colloquy.—O infinite Spirit, who createdst sundry spirits both in heaven and earth, to be adored by them "in spirit and in truth,"(12)—for Thou, being a spirit, seekest such adorers,—I adore and glorify Thee for the spirit which Thou hast given unto me, and with the same desire to serve Thee and to "mortify the deeds of the flesh,(13) to the end that my spirit may live to Thee alone, and Thine may dwell in mine everlastingly.   Amen.

ii. The second excellence is, that as God is *immortal,* and although He is in the world, yet does *not depend* on

(10) S. Tho. i. p. q. lxxv. art. 1.
(11) Ps. ciii. 29.   (12) Joan. iv. 23.
(13) Rom. viii. 13.

it, and if the world should cease to be, yet would always remain in Himself;(14) even so our soul is *immortal*, and although it be in this mortal body, its being does *not depend* on it; and when the body dies, and is turned into earth from which it was made, yet the spirit dies not, but continues to exist, and goes to God, who created it, that He may, according to its merits, assign it the place where it is to live.(15)

Colloquy.—O " King of ages, immortal and invisible,"(16) who alone enjoyest immortality by Thine essence, I give Thee thanks for having given unto my soul by participation an immortality depending upon Thy will, without which she would lose her being, and by which she will always keep it. I beseech Thee, when she goeth forth out of this earthly body, even as Thou hast given her the immortality of nature, to give her also the immortality of grace, that, being set free from the never-dying death of hell, she may live a never-dying life in heaven, world without end. Amen.

iii. The third excellence of the soul is, that being one, she has *three noble faculties*, with three most noble kinds of actions:—*understanding*, by which she comprehends things as well bodily as spiritual, and reasons on all the creatures, both of heaven and earth—*memory*, by which she remembers the things she understood, and retains things past as if they were present—*will*, by which she wills, loves, or hates what she knows; and hence it is that she not only has in her the image of the Divinity, but also of the most Holy Trinity. For as the eternal Father, knowing Himself, produces the Word, which is His Son, and these two, loving themselves, produce love, which is the Holy Ghost; even so our soul can, by help of her

(14) Ps. ci. 27.   (15) S. Tho. i. p. q. lxxv. art. 6.   Eccles. xii. 7.
(16) 1 Tim. i. 17.

faculties, behold Almighty God, and by her understanding produce within herself a word and conception like that which is God; and by the will produce another holy love of God, which makes her holy: and in this, as St. Thomas says, consists the principal excellence of our soul, by which she is an image of the most Holy Trinity.(17)

iv. The fourth excellence which springs from the former, is to have free will, like God, so powerful to will and not to will, that which is delightful to it, that it is not possible to force it against its inclination; for neither man nor angel can necessitate it, because it is subject only to its Creator,(18) who has left man "in the hands of his own counsel," and in his own will placed "life and death,"(19) to the end he might choose which of the two he pleased.

Colloquy.—O omnipotent Creator, who gloriest to have some creatures free with the liberty which Thou hast given them; I restore unto Thee, dear Lord, that which Thou hast given me, desiring always to use it, only to will what Thou willest, for my free will will be perfect in proportion to its conformity with Thine.

v. The fifth excellence of the soul, which arises out of both the former, is, that she is *capable of wisdom and knowledge*, of virtue and grace, of blessedness and glory, and of all the natural and supernatural gifts which God can give her in connection with them, and this her capacity is so infinite, that He alone can satisfy it; for so long as it does not see and possess God, it is not possible for it to be fully satisfied. Herein it is in a most glorious manner the image of God, for as God Himself cannot be satisfied with any other thing besides Himself, even so the capacity

(17) S. Tho. i. p. q. xciii. art. 5, 7, et 8.
(18) S. Tho. i. p. q. lxxxiii. et i. 2, p. q. vi. art. 4, et q. ix art. 6.
(19) Ecclus. xv. 14. Deut. xxx. 15.

and desire of the soul cannot be filled but with Almighty God alone.

Colloquy.—O infinite God, since Thou hast given me an infinite capacity, never suffer it to be empty; and because in Thee alone are all good things, fill me with Thyself, for Thou alone canst really fill me.

vi. The sixth excellence is, that as God is supreme Lord of all things, and contains them eminently within Himself, and has power and authority over them, and is the last end to which they are ordained: even so man, principally in respect of his soul, is *superior to all visible and corporal things*, even to the heavens and stars themselves, which, as has already been said, are inferior to man, and minister to his service. For he comprises within him the degrees of all things, of bodies, plants, living creatures, and angels: and, like a little world, contains whatsoever is in this vast world, and rules with great power all things that are in earth, as shall be seen in the fifth point.

2. From these six considerations it follows that to be made after the image of God is a singular excellence, and proper to man alone, amongst all corporal creatures, which are no more than a certain trace or step of the greatness of God and of His Trinity. For this reason I ought to excite my soul, that, knowing and considering her nobility and freedom, she do not degenerate from it, but wholly surrender herself to God, recalling to memory that which Christ our Lord said to those who showed Him a piece of money, and asked Him if it were lawful to pay tribute to Cæsar:—" Whose image and inscription is this? They say to Him, Cæsar's. Then He saith to them, Render, therefore, to Cæsar the things that are Cæsar's, and to God the things that are God's."(20) As if He had said, " Since

(20) Matt. xxii. 20.

by the image of this money which you use you protest that
you are the vassals of Cæsar, render to him that which you
owe in regard of this vassalage, because it belongs to him;
and render likewise to God that which you owe also to
Him."

Colloquy.—O my soul, enter into account and reckoning with thyself, and ask thyself whose this image
is that is within thee; is it peradventure the image of
Cæsar, or of the world and the flesh, or of any other
thing created greater and better than thyself? Acknowledge thine own greatness, for thou art not the
image of any other than of God Himself, who, of His
infinite liberality, created thee to His own image.
Give, therefore, to God that which is God's; acknowledge by this image the service and subjection which
is due to Him, and pay Him the tribute which He has
imposed upon thee. And since thou art the money of
this tribute, on which the image of this king is engraved, yield thyself wholly to His service, for thou
owest thyself all to Him, who gave unto thee all thou
art.

After this manner I may exercise my reason on all the
six mentioned excellencies which constitute this image,
asking myself whose image is thy spirit? If it be the
image of the Spirit of God, give it wholly to God, and
make thyself one spirit with Him. Whose image is thy
soul, with its three faculties? If it be the image of the
most Holy Trinity, give to the Trinity the things that
are the Trinity's, by using them to serve Him, who is
Three and One, world without end, Amen.

POINT IV.

The fourth will be to consider how God our Lord not
only created man after His own image, but also *to His
own likeness,* so that the image was most perfect, and like

the pattern from whence it was taken. (21) Wherefore Almighty God, not contented to have created man to His image, according to nature, after the manner already mentioned, did also create Adam to His own likeness, according to *grace and original justice*, for which reason the Wise man said, that " God made man right:" (22) for the works of God are perfect, and never void of that perfection of which they are capable for the time, conformable to the end for which He created them. And, because Adam, made after the image of God, was capable of His grace and friendship, God would create him with this perfection, beginning to fill this his emptiness and capacity which he had, with supernatural things.

2. Hence in like manner it follows, that the likeness in the being of grace, which God gave to Adam, was *very perfect*, for it did not only sanctify, rectify, and conform his soul to God, but also gave her full dominion and power over all her passions, so that with her free will, she could command the appetites, and produce her acts, with as much duration and intenseness as she pleased, without ever rebelling against reason, or being at war with it, as the flesh is now with the spirit; (23) according to the likeness of God, she had peace in her interior kingdom, so that there was nothing therein which could oppose her free will.

3. Hence also the image and likeness of God, which principally resides in the soul, is likewise *derived to the body*, not only on account of its walking erect, and looking up to heaven, but also on account of its sharing in the immortality which the soul communicates to it, in whose power it was never to die, as indeed man had not died, if he had never sinned. (24)

<hr>

(21) S. Tho. i. p. q. xciii. art. 9.   S. Basil. Ambr. et alii.
   (22) Ecclus. vii. 30.   S. Tho. i p. q. xcv. art. 1.
(23) Gal. v. 17.   (24) S. Tho. i. p. q. lxvii. art. 1.

4. After this manner did Almighty God create Adam and Eve to His image and likeness, and although they alone enjoyed this last supernatural good, inasmuch as they lost it through their own fault, both for themselves and for their children, yet the will of God was to link them together, both in them and in all their posterity, if they had been obedient to His commandments. For this will, therefore, I must render Him many thanks, and reckon amongst my own debts these three benefits which Almighty God gave to our first parents, even as if He had done the same to me, beseeching Him, that since I have lost this likeness, He would vouchsafe to restore it by His holy grace.

Colloquy.—O divine Word, "image of the invisible God,"(25) who camest into the world to repair the losses of man, whom Thou createdst to Thine image, and to restore that likeness in the being of grace, which he lost through his fault both for himself and for all others; behold, dear Lord, I beseech Thee, with the eyes of Thy mercy, my poor soul, acknowledge the image which Thou hast made, although defiled with that which I have done; and since I have taken from it the lustre of grace which Thou gavest it in baptism, restore it to me by penance, blotting out the evil which I have committed, to the end that the image which Thou createdst may recover its splendour. O Father of mercies, who hast predestined Thine elect, that they might be "conformable to the image of Thy Son;"(26) conform me, I humbly beseech Thee, to Him in true sanctity, that I may obtain the perfect likeness of His glory. Amen.(27)

POINT V.

The fifth shall be to consider how God our Lord made man also, that he might "*have dominion* over the fishes

(25) Colos. i. 15.   (26) Rom. viii. 29.   (27) 1 Joan. iii. 2.

of the sea, and the fowls of the air, and the beasts, and the whole earth, and every creeping creature that moveth upon the earth." (28)

1. Here is to be pondered, first, the excellency of man, as made to the image of God, whence it follows that, as God is supreme Lord over all creatures, so also man is like to Him, in being *superior to all the creatures of the earth*, with absolute dominion over them, to make use of them all, and without any wrong or injury, to kill them for his sustenance or recreation. (29)   Wherefore, astonished at the infinite liberality of God towards us, I will say with holy David, " What is man that Thou art mindful of him, or the son of man that Thou visitest him? Thou hast made him a little less than the angels, Thou hast crowned him with glory and honour, and hast set him over the works of Thy hands.   Thou hast subjected all things under his feet, all sheep and oxen; moreover, the beasts also, of the field, the birds of the air, and fishes of the sea, that pass through the paths of the sea. O Lord our God, how admirable is Thy name in all the earth?" (30)   Thou art wonderful, inasmuch as being who Thou art, Thou art yet mindful of a thing so base as man; Thou art also wonderful because Thou hast crowned him with so great honour and glory, as to make him to Thine image and likeness; and Thou art no less wonderful because Thou hast given him power and dominion over the works which Thou hast made with Thy hands. And since Thou hast done me so much good, it is most just that I should preach Thy wonderful name throughout all the earth, with desire that all may honour and worship it.

2. The second, to ponder the providence of God our Lord, as well towards the beasts themselves, as towards men, on this occasion. For, seeing that all the things

(28) Gen. i. 26.   (29) S. Tho. i. p. q. xxxvi.   (30) Ps. viii. 5.

which He had created on the earth were void of reason, and stood in need of some one to govern them, He created man to His own image and likeness, that he might rule over them; *providing* likewise to man himself, thereby, such *solace and delights*, as were needful for him to pass his life, as we see before our eyes, that he who feeds his sheep, and does good to them at the same time, does good to and provides for himself. And hence, Adam being in paradise, our Lord God brought all the fowls and beasts of the earth before him, that he might see them, and impose a name upon each of them,(31) and take possession of his dominion, and that all might acknowledge him after their manner for their lord, serpents and savage beasts subjecting themselves to him, like mild and gentle lambs. And this favour was not done to him alone, but likewise to his posterity; for after He had created Adam and Eve, He said:—"Increase and multiply, and fill the earth, and subdue it, and rule over the fishes of the sea, and the fowls of the air, and all living creatures that move upon the earth:" (32) and by consequence He did this favour also to me, and I should have enjoyed it at this present moment if Adam had not sinned.

3. Notwithstanding the sin of Adam, this mercy and providence of God towards man marvellously shines forth, for, as it appeared by that which is said to Noe, he left him full dominion, use, and command, over all such creatures as might be profitable to him; he likewise rules over the *fishes, serpents, and wild beasts*, inasmuch as with his art and industry, he catches and subjects, not only the little fishes, but also the whales themselves, and takes all sorts of fowls and beasts, how wild and cruel soever they be; and as the apostle St. James says, " For every nature of beasts, and of birds, and of serpents, and of the rest, is tamed, and

(31) Gen. ii. 19.   (32) Gen. i. 28.

hath been tamed, by the nature of man." (33)   Whence I will conceive motives of praise and gratitude to God our Lord for this so great a benefit, showing myself grateful in overruling and taming the brutish appetites of my flesh, which are figured by these four kinds of beasts which God has subjected to us, mortifying the passions of the sensuality of the flesh, figured by the fishes; the passions of pride and of ambition, figured by the fowls; the passions of the covetousness of earthly things, figured by the serpents; and lastly, the passions of anger and revenge, figured by the fierce and savage beasts.

Colloquy.—Omnipotent God, who gavest unto man dominion and industry to tame and subdue four sorts of brutish beasts : give me Thine abundant grace, that I may tame and subdue my natural passions, figured by them.   No mortal man can by himself tame the tongue, because all the four passions conspire together to provoke it, but by Thy grace that is made easy, which otherwise is hard unto us; tame it, dear Lord, I beseech Thee, with Thine Almighty power, so that henceforth it employ itself in no other thing than in singing Thy praises for Thine innumerable benefits, world without end.   Amen.

(33) Jac. iii. 7.

MEDITATION XXVI.

ON THE MANNER HOW ALMIGHTY GOD FORMED THE BODY OF MAN, AND INFUSED
INTO IT A SOUL, AND HOW HE MADE EVE.

POINT I.

" The Lord God formed man of *the slime of the earth,*
and *breathed* into his face *the breath of life,* and man
became a living soul." (1)

1. The first shall be to consider how God our Lord
willed that the making of the body and soul of Adam
should be related apart, and distinctly, and first of the
body which is the less noble, to give us to understand that
the body and soul of man were not like those of other
living creatures, whose bodies and souls were made of
earth, but that the body alone of man was made of earth,
whilst the soul came from without.(2)   And in this faith
we will ground the whole course of our lives, treating the
body as it deserves, and assigning it its place, in such sort,
that it do not put itself before, nor equal with the
soul.   And although some of the holy Fathers affirm that
Almighty God made the body of Adam a little before He
infused the soul, in order that He might the better know
what the body was of itself, and the necessity it had of a
soul, and how great a good came through it; (3) yet it
suffices for our present purpose to imagine it without a
soul, as a dead body is, that in this example I may contemplate how much we owe to Him who gave us a soul
whereby to live.

2. Next I will ponder how Almighty God our Lord, out

(1) Gen. ii 17.   (2) S Tho. i. p. q. xci. art. 1.
(3) Genad, S. Chrys. Tostat. et alii, in ii. Gen. sed contra,   S.
Tho. i. p. q. xci. art. 4, ad 3.

of His high and excellent wisdom, would not create the body of Adam out of nothing, but *of the earth*, and of the dust thereof, mingled with water, as the potter makes clay, and out of clay, vessels, that so man should ground himself in profound humility, seeing and beholding his base original in this point, and should acknowledge the frailty of his nature, and consequently the mortality which comes to him from such a beginning.

i. To repress in me the spirit of pride, I will with this consideration sometimes repeat that saying of Ecclesiasticus:—" Why is earth and ashes proud?" (4)　O proud and presumptuous, wherefore dost thou presume?　Is it for the earth and dust which the wind doth carry away? Humble thyself, therefore, even to the earth, since thou art earth.

ii. At other times to repress the complaints which arise in my heart against the judgments of God, because He gives me not the things which I desire.　I will say with the apostle St. Paul, " O man, who art thou, that repliest against God?　Shall the thing formed say to him that formed it, why hast thou made me thus?　Or hath not the potter power over the clay, of the same lump to make one vessel unto honour, and another unto dishonour?" (5) " Woe to him that gainsayeth his Maker, a sherd of the earthen pots." (6)

Colloquy.—O my soul, submit thyself to thy Creator, since He does no wrong unto thee, if He dispose of thee after His pleasure ; and being just, He will do nothing against thy profit, if thou withdraw not thyself away from His service.

iii. Sometimes to quicken my confidence in God, who made me of clay, I will say that of the prophet Isaias:— " And now, Lord, Thou art our Father, and we are clay:

(4) Ecclus. x. 9.　　(5) Rom. ix. 20.　　(6) Isa. xlv. 9.

and Thou art our maker, and we all are the works of Thy hands:" (7) break not, O Lord, I beseech Thee, the frail vessel which Thou hast made, for Thou madest it, not to break it in Thy rigour, but to employ it entirely in Thy service.　At other times to resign myself with joy into the hands of God, and to glorify Him for all the good there is in me, I will call to mind what He said to the prophet Jeremiah: "Behold, as clay in the hand of the potter, so are you in my hand, O house of Israel." (8)

Colloquy.—O most gentle Creator, I rejoice that I am in Thy blessed hands, for whatsoever shall come from them shall be sweet unto me.　I rejoice that Thou hast placed in "earthen vessels"(9) the treasures of Thy grace, to the end that the glory of them should be Thine, and not our own.

iv. Finally, to fly all sin I will remember that it is sin which breaks and dissolves this work of clay, and converts it into the dust of which it was made, according to the sentence which God our Lord gave against Adam, saying: —That he should return to earth, of which he was taken: " Quia pulvis es, et in pulverem reverteris," "for dust thou art, and into dust thou shalt return."(10)　As if He had said, For this end did I form thee of earth and dust, that thou mightest understand, that unless thou dost fulfil my law, thou shalt again return into that earth and dust of which I made thee; for it is but right that he who esteems not Him who plucked him out of the dirt, fall again into the dirt out of which he was taken.

Colloquy.—O most loving Father, who, with so great and singular providence, formedst my body of the earth : grant me, I beseech Thee, that I may make use of those counsels which Thou gavest unto me

(7) Isa. lxiv. 8.　　　　　(8) Jer. xviii. 6.

(9) 2 Cor. iv. 7.　　　　　(10) Gen. iii. 19.

herein, to the end that when my body shall return into earth, my soul may ascend with Thee to the Kingdom of heaven.   Amen.

POINT II.

Next is to be considered the omnipotence of God in making of a matter so vile and gross, a *thing so precious* as the body of man, reasoning on the excellencies of this work, which may be reduced briefly to four.

1. The first is the *many different parts* and members it has, which were formed of one and the selfsame clay, and even now also are formed of one and the selfsame matter, much more filthy than is the clay, save that now they are made by little and little, and one after another; but then Almighty God made them altogether in a moment, in great perfection, for which I am to give great thanks to Him, wondering at His omnipotence in the words of the prophet David, saying:—"All my bones shall say, Lord, who is like to Thee?"(11)

Colloquy.—O most powerful God, my bones and my flesh, my veins and my sinews, and all the members of my frail body say with a loud voice, " Lord, who is like to Thee" in power ? Who but Thou couldst make in the womb of a woman, a body so full of bones? O my soul, listen attentively to the words of that excellent matron, to her sons, the Machabeans, saying : —" I know not how you were formed in my womb, for I neither give you breath, nor soul, nor life, neither did I frame the members of every one of you ; but the Creator of the world, that formed the nativity of man, and that hath found out the origin of all."(12) "Oh that all my bones were disjointed, and martyred like those of these Machabeans, for His glory and honour who gave them to me.

(11) Ps. xxxiv. 10.   (12) 2 Mach. vii. 22.

2. The second excellence is the *beauty*, greatness, and delicateness of this body, being made of a thing so filthy, gross, and so little as a little piece of clay.   And that which is more to be admired is, that whereas now it is thirty years in attaining to his perfect bigness and beauty, in Adam it had the whole in a moment, Almighty God making him in the state of a perfect man, whereby is to be seen that forth from things very base, He can draw things very high, (13) and that which by course of nature requires the course of many years, He can make in a moment, " For it is easy in the eyes of God on a sudden to make the poor man rich." (14)

3. The third excellence is the noble and *upright figure* which he has, all the other creatures going with their bodies stooping towards the earth; to give us to understand, that, although we were made of earth, yet our end is not anything of the earth, but of heaven, directing thither our eyes and our heart.

Colloquy.—O my soul, blush to go stooping and inclined, with thine affections to the earth, being in a body upright and directed to heaven.   O my Saviour, who didst unloose a daughter of Abraham, who went eighteen years stooping and inclining towards the earth, not being able to look up to heaven; unloose my soul, which Satan has led bound so many years, and has inclined to things earthly, that from henceforth it may aspire and raise up itself to things heavenly.   Amen.

4. The fourth excellence is the *perfection of all things needful to his body* in regard of the soul which informs it; the soul supplying with reason the defects which arise from its delicate complexion: for, although other living creatures excel us in the sharpness and liveliness of sight

(13) Ecclus. xi. 13.   (14) Ecclus. v. 23

and smelling, in the celerity of motion, and are born already clad, and even armed with divers offensive and defensive weapons, yet all this proceeds from the grossness and great earthliness of their complexion and nature, and was not compatible with the delicateness of our constitution. But the soul, with the light of reason and prudence, quickens the senses of the body, and perfects them, clothes and arms the body much better than the beasts; the divine providence having care to supply our want in all these, to the end that men should not want that which is not wanting to beasts. For all these things I am to give thanks to the Creator, who, with such exceeding sweetness, has disposed the frame of my body to be the habitation of my soul, praising Him that He has given me eyes to see, and eye-lids wherewith to shut them, and a head erected on high, with hair to adorn it, and so of all the other members of my body.

POINT III.

The third will be to consider that God our Lord created *of nothing* the soul of the first man, whose creation is expressed in these words: He " breathed into his face the breath of life:" which signify, that the life and soul which God gave to man, proceed not from the earth, whereof the body was formed, but came from without, by the omnipotence of the Creator. (15) For, as the breathing proceeds from man, and is air which issues from the interior part of man by his mouth, even so our soul proceeds from Almighty God, and issues forth from Him, with great love, as it were, drawing it forth from His bowels through His mouth, that is to say, by His power, willing that it so be, there being none at all to resist Him. And in this is discovered the nobility of our soul, and of her likeness

(15) S. Tho. i. p. q. xc. Gen. ii. 7.

with the divine Wisdom, which "came out of the mouth of the most High." (16)

Colloquy.—O my soul, who art the work of God alone, praise and glorify Him who gave thee the being that thou hast with so great love. Thou wentest forth from Almighty God, seek to return again to God, and to enter within His bosom, loving Him with thy whole heart who loves thee.

2. Secondly is to be pondered, that Almighty God calls the soul "spiraculum vitæ," *the breathing spirit*, or respiration, which gives life to the thing into which it enters, to signify that the life of the body consists in this, that God creates and conjoins the soul with it, into which it always breathes, and so preserves it; and for this reason it is said, that He breathed in the face of Adam, where the principal senses of life are, viz., the sight, the hearing, the smelling, tasting, and other interior senses, and certain organs of respiration to preserve life. Whence I will gather, that God, in calling the soul the breath of life, incites me each time I breathe, to remember the Creator who gave me my soul, and the sovereign benefit He did me in giving it, believing that as the life of the body depends on the respiration of the soul, even so the life and being of my soul depends on the inspiration and virtue of Almighty God, for if He preserved it not, it would return into nothing; and, therefore, it is requisite sometimes with every act of inspiration, to make some acts of love, or ot praise and thanksgiving for this benefit, after the manner already declared.(17)

3. Hence I will go on to ponder the *mystery of these words*, for, as the body without the soul wants natural life, so the soul without grace, wants spiritual life; and as Almighty God, breathing into the body of Adam, infused

Ecclus. xxiv. 5.　　　　　(17) Med. xxiii. p. 5.

a soul into him, by which He gave him natural life; so likewise, breathing with the breath of His divine and efficacious inspiration, He infuses into the soul a spirit of grace amd charity, by which He gives it supernatural life; and both these lives did our Lord infuse together into the first man when He created him. And peradventure for this reason the Scripture says in the original tongue, that He breathed into Adam, " Spiraculum vitarum," " the breathing of lives;" because He not only gave him a most excellent soul, whence that vegetative life proceeds, by which it grows like plants, and the sensitive by which it feels, like beasts, and the intellectual, by which it understands, like angels; but He also gave him the Holy Ghost, whence the life of grace and charity proceeds, with the sundry exercises of life that are in it; and in conformity with this, Christ our Lord, by another breathing, gave to His apostles the Holy Ghost, as we have pondered in its due place. (18)

Colloquy.—O eternal Father, who, by the mouth of Thy Son, producest the breathing of the Holy Ghost, by whose presence the souls dead through sin are revived; revive mine with this divine breathing, visiting me often with Thy divine inspirations, to the end I may live the new life of Thy grace, and may persevere in it unto life eternal.   Amen.

POINT IV.

The fourth shall be to consider, that God our Lord, a little after He had created Adam, brought him into the "*paradise of pleasure,*" (19) which He had planted the third day, to be his dwelling; pondering the *tender and devout feelings* which Adam had, when with the know-

(18) Med. ix. p. 5.
(19) Gen. ii. 8.   S. Tho. i. p. q. cil. art. 4.

ledge that God had given him, he knew the benefits which
He had done him.

1. First, *when in that first instant he opened his eyes*,
and saw the beauty of the heavens, with the stars and the
planets, and the goodliness of the earth, with the trees,
plants, birds, and living creatures which were upon it, he
stood amazed with the novelty of such admirable things;
as a man, who from his nativity had been shut up in a
den, should after thirty years issue forth, and see the
things that are in this world, would be ravished out of
himself with admiration to see so many marvels, and
would praise and glorify the Creator of them.

2. What, then, would he feel, *when a little after he
saw himself led* by God *to that paradise* and garden of
delights, which was also given to him for a dwelling and
habitation, with full power to eat of all the fruits of the
innumerable trees which were in it, except one? For he
well understood that this was a new favour without his
merits, no way due to his nature, but only of the mere
grace of the Creator, whose bounty and liberality he
therefore admired, with the beauty of the garden, and
burst forth into new praises for so sovereign a benefit.

3. Scarcely had he made an end of these praises, when
he saw that the same Almighty God, by the ministry of
His angels, *set before him an innumerable multitude* of
fowls, beasts, and serpents, to the end that he should
recreate himself with the sight of so great variety and
beauty of creatures; for if it be so great a contentment
to see an elephant, or some other beast which we had
never seen, what will it be to see so many together, and
to know the quality of each one? And when he saw that
all of them were subject to him, and himself superior of
them all, he wholly converted himself into the praises of

his Creator, for the immense liberality which He had used in his behalf.

4. These considerations I can apply to myself, and lifting up my spirit from things earthly to things heavenly, I will glorify God for the things He has created in this inferior world for my pleasure, beholding them with a new sight, as if they were wholly new to me, and singing new songs of praise for them. Then I will contemplate the tender love by which God our Lord leads and guides me to the celestial paradise, with desire to give it me for a perpetual habitation; pondering the admiration and jubilee of soul, which I shall conceive at the first sight of that new and superior world.

Colloquy.—O God of my soul, now I understand that which Thou sayest by the prophet:—" I will draw them with the cords of Adam, with the bands of love."(20) The cords of Adam were the innumerable benefits of nature and grace, wherewith Thou didst bind and oblige him to love and serve Thee, and with the same dost Thou bind and oblige me, that I likewise may love and serve Thee. The cords of Adam are the heavens with the stars, the sea with the fishes, the air with the birds, and the earth with the plants and living creatures. The cords of Adam is the body which Thou hast given me with the members and senses, and the soul which Thou createdst to Thine own likeness, with all her faculties. The bonds of love are graces, sacraments, inspirations, and paradise itself, which Thou dost promise me. Oh that I did bind myself with most strong love to Him who invented such cords and bands, to the end I might love Him in such sort that I might never break them.

POINT V.

The fifth will be to consider that God our Lord, although

(20) Osee. xi. 4.

He made jointly together both sexes in the birds and beasts of the earth, yet would not create man and woman together, but *first created man*, and *afterwards*, of a rib of his side, *made the woman ;*(21) to give us to understand that man was not created principally to attend to generation, as other living creatures are. For although this work in matrimony is good, and was necessary at that time also for the multiplication of mankind, yet it is a work very base, and common to beasts as well as to men, and therefore He created him alone before the woman, that he might understand that his principal end was to attend to God, to contemplate and love Him, and to exercise with Him alone the works that are proper to angels. Moreover, when He made the woman of a rib of his side, he lay asleep, and rapt in great ecstasies of contemplation; to signify that Matrimony itself ought not to hinder the use of prayer and contemplation, but that men must do as afterwards the apostle said:—" They also who have wives, be as though they had none,"(22) and omit not to attend to holy prayer; and since the world is sufficiently multiplied, it is better for him who has a vocation for it from God, to live single without a wife.

2. Another reason of this was, to *move us to union*, and to love one another, seeing that our Creator, as St. Paul says, " made of one all mankind,"(23) to the end that those who have but one Father in heaven and another on earth, may love together as brethren, according to that which the prophet Malachy said:—" Have we not all one Father? hath not one God created us? why then doth every one of us despise his brother?"(24)

3. Another mystical reason was, to signify that as one man alone was head of mankind in the being of *nature*, of

(21) Gen. ii. 22.

(22) 1 Cor. vii. 29.

(23) Act. xvii. 26.

(24) Mal. ii. 10.

whose rib, when he was asleep, was made Eve; even so *one* new man alone, Christ Jesus, was to be head of all men *in the being of grace*, out of whose side, as He slept the sleep of death upon the cross, blood and water issued forth (the figure of the sacraments), wherewith the Church, His spouse, which is the congregation of all the faithful, is built and preserved. And this reason ought to move them much more to the union of charity, since they have one only Creator and one Father in nature, and one only Father in the being of grace, who is their only Redeemer and healer of all the evils which they incurred by the sin of their first father.

Colloquy.—O most sweet Creator and our Redeemer, who hast spent Thy precious blood to build Thy Church, that she might be to Thee glorious, " not having spot, or wrinkle, or any such thing,"(25) apply Thy redemption and Thy infinite mercy to those whom Thou hast created by Thy sovereign omnipotence, that all may enjoy the same, and that there may be made of them a Church, Thy beautiful " spouse" without " spot,"(26) wherein Thou mayest reign, world without end. Amen.

— — —

MEDITATION XXVII.

ON THE REFLECTION WHICH GOD OUR LORD MADE UPON THE WORKS OF THESE SIX DAYS, DECLARING THAT THEY WERE VERY GOOD; AND ON THE SANCTIFICATION OF THE SEVENTH DAY.

POINT I.

The first shall be to consider how God our Lord, at the end of the sixth day having created all things, saw that they were " *very good.*"(1)

(25) Ephes. v. 27.　　(26) Cant. iv. 7.　　(1) Gen. i. 31.

1. God our Lord three times reflecting upon His works, saw that they were good :—first, on the same day wherein He made them, after He had created them;—secondly, after the creation of every one of them, if in one day He created different things;—and thirdly, at the end of the six days, when He had created all, making a reflection upon all together; and then He not only said that they were good, but very good and perfect, because every one had the goodness which was proper to it in respect of itself, and of the common good of the whole, which was perfect in all things, in number, duration, beauty, and proportion of all the parts, without mixture of evil, in the manner already pondered in the preceding meditations. But I will likewise ponder, that God alone, by reason of His infinite goodness, can (beholding all His works) say that they are very good and perfect, without having in them anything that is evil or imperfect; and this likewise agrees with Christ our Lord, as being both God and Man, of whom it was said:—" He hath done all things well;" (2) and the same, by especial privilege, was also found in the most holy Virgin. But all other men, how holy soever they be according to the ordinary law, on reflecting upon their works, will find some defect or imperfection in some of them, according as St. James says:—" In many things we all offend."(3) Our care ought therefore to be, to approach, as much as is possible for us, to the perfection of Almighty God, procuring all that lies in us, that our works be such that Almighty God, beholding them, may in some sort say that they are " very good."

2. To obtain this perfection, it will help us to make three examens of our works, making a reflection upon them :—

i. The first, at *the end of the day*, reviewing all the

<hr>

(2) Mar. vii. 37.　　　　　　　　　(3) Jac. iii. 2.

actions which we have done therein, weighing if they be conformable to the divine will, so that God may approve them to be good, blotting out by contrition such as are evil, in the manner set down in Meditation xxviii. of the first part.

ii. The second examen, of still greater help to perfection, is to be made *when we finish a work of some importance,* forthwith making a reflection upon it, as our Lord did the third and sixth day, and examining it, without waiting for the end of the day; and if we find that it was wholly good, no due circumstance being wanting to it, we must give thanks for it to Almighty God; and if we find that it was good, but yet intermixed with some imperfections and negligences, we must separate the precious from the vile, and the gold from the dross, consuming with the fire of love and of sorrow all the evil and imperfect in it, with a purpose to do the same work the next time in such a manner that Almighty God, beholding it, may say that it is good. And if we find that the whole was evil, we should be confounded to have employed the day so ill which Almighty God gave us wherein to do well. This examen is to be made at the end of every work and important affair, because, as St. Dorotheus says,(4) we sin often, and forget it immediately, and therefore it is needful frequently and in all hours to seek out, sift, and diligently to search every particular, and to examine ourselves hourly, and even every moment of time, if it be possible, pondering how we have spent it, since, as the Wise man says:—" A just man shall fall seven times;" that is to say, oftentimes, and rises again as many times, without waiting to rise altogether at the end of the day. And as those who are very neat and cleanly, if many times they defile or soil themselves, as many times make themselves clean again, hasten-

(4) Serm. xi.

ing speedily to take away the spot; even so those that are great lovers of cleanliness of soul, cleanse and purify themselves immediately, when they mark in themselves any spot of sin or imperfection, so that Almighty God, beholding their souls, at that moment may say:—" Thou art all fair, O my love, and there is not a spot in thee."(5)

iii. The third examen is, to make a reflection at *the end of the week*, as our Lord Himself did at the end of the work of the six days, comparing one day with another, and observing if I daily seek to adorn my soul with new splendours of virtue, if I go increasing and daily profiting in the perfection of them; if I accomplish entirely my own obligations, and those also for the common good; and out of the profits I shall find I will make one mass, offering them up to God, and giving Him thanks for it, fulfilling that which David says:—" Every day will I bless Thee," (6) for the good Thou hast done me in each of them.   Out of the losses I shall find I will make another mass, to confess them with grief of heart, and to prepare me with this purity for the feast which I am to celebrate on the seventh day, since whosoever desires to increase and grow up in perfection, ought weekly to confess and communicate to obtain it.   This examen and reflection ought to be made at the end of every year, making a general confession of all the faults committed therein; and drawing a comparison of one year with another, I will blush if I see that I have always hitherto walked in a slow and negligent manner, and I will excite myself to go forwards with more fervour. Finally, at the end of my whole life, figured by these six days (if sickness permit it, and I have no other special impediment), it is good to make another examen and confession, to blot out all the evil we have committed; so that the "prince of this world"(7) coming, he find not

(5) Cant. iv. 7.   (6) Ps. cxliv. 2.   (7) Joan. xiv. 30.

then aught in us that is his; and the Prince of heaven coming, He may behold what we have, and approve it for good, and so lead us with Him to everlasting rest, figured by the seventh day.

Colloquy.—O chief good and beginning of all good, whose works were always good, and for such didst approve those which Thou didst on these six days, grant me by Thy grace some part of this goodness, which is proper to Thy divine nature, that in the last examen which I shall make of my life, Thou find nothing of the evil I have committed, but only of the good, which, by Thy grace, I have effected, and for the same to admit me into Thy holy kingdom. Amen.

POINT II.

Consider that God our Lord on the seventh day having finished the work which He made, "*rested the seventh day* from all His work which He had done, and He blessed the seventh day and sanctified it."(8)

1. Ponder first, how God our Lord on the seventh day *ceased* to make any *new* things, not because He wanted omnipotence to do them, if either He would, or it had been expedient for His intent and our profit, but because those already made were sufficient for the perfection of the world which He had designed; and therefore the Scripture says not that God had finished that which He was able to do, but that He had finished the work which He had done, doing it very perfectly, and then rested; not in the creatures, for He had no need of them for His rest and blessedness, but rested, ceasing to work as has been said, and rejoicing in Himself at having accomplished that which He decreed and ordained from all eternity, and which He had now executed with great alacrity. In imitation of this

(8) Gen. ii. 2.

I will endeavour to seek my rest, not in the creature, but in the Creator: for, like Almighty God cannot rest but in Himself; so neither can I find true rest but in Him alone. And although I may rejoice at the works which I do, as the same God, according to the saying of the prophet David, rejoiceth "in His works;"(9) yet this is not to end in the things created, but in Him that created them.

Colloquy.—O my glory and my rest, I rejoice at the eternal rest which Thou hast in Thyself, for Thou neither workest with labour, nor by working losest Thy rest. Grant me, dear Lord, I beseech Thee, that I may place my rest in labouring in Thy service, because without Thee all rest is vain and transitory, and in Thee alone is complete and eternal.

2. I will ponder, secondly, that God our Lord "*blessed the seventh day*, and sanctified it;" and because the blessing of Almighty God is effectual, to bless it was to give to understand, that on that day, although He ceased to create new things, yet He began after another new manner to do good to them, by the benefit of preservation and protection, and the creatures also began to put in execution the benediction they had received, attending to their multiplication; and so the holy Scripture says that God "rested, ab omni opere suo quod creavit, ut faceret,—from all His work which" He "had created and made," to the end that what He had made should increase and multiply in the world; as if He should say, He did not create it that it should be idle, but that everything should do that which belonged to it, to obtain its end. And He likewise created man, to the end that he should work and travail to obtain that sanctity, quiet, and rest which is received in God

(9) Ps. ciii. 31.

alone, and so for him principally He blessed and sanctified the seventh day.

Colloquy.—O eternal God, who createdst me in Christ Thy Son, to the end that I should do good works, and walk by them to Thine eternal beatitude; pour upon me Thine abundant benediction, that even from this hour I may begin to work, and to profit in justice and sanctity, placing my whole rest in giving Thee contentment, world without end.   Amen.

POINT III.

The third will be to consider *the mystery* that is contained in this, that God ceased from His works, and blessed and-sanctified the seventh day.(10)

1. God our Lord gave a ˙precept to the people of Israel, (11) that they should sanctify the seventh day (which to them was the Saturday) in memory and thankfulness of the benefit of the creation of the world, and of the things which He did on those first six days, and in figure of the quiet and rest which the just enjoy, as well in this life by grace as in the other by glory; for which reason Isaias calls it the "Sabbath, delightful, and the holy of the Lord, glorious."(12) To this Sabbath has succeeded now the Sunday, not only in memory and thankfulness for the benefit of the creation of the world, but much more of the redemption and renovation which Christ our Lord made in His Resurrection, and in memory of the quiet which He brings us by His grace, and of that which He hereafter promises us by the glorification of the soul and resurrection of the body.   And consequently *we* have many more reasons to sanctify the Sunday than *they* had to sanctify the Saturday.

To accomplish perfectly this obligation, without all note of ingratitude, four things are to be performed.(13)

(10) S. Tho. 2, 2, q. cxxii. art. 4.   (11) Ex. xx. 10.
(12) Isa. lviii. 13.   (13) S. Tho. 2, 2, q. cvii. art. 1.

i. The first is, *to cease from servile works*, as God ceased from His works, as has been said, to the end that, being freed from them, we may attend with quietness to God; and in like manner we ought to cease from sin, which is a work more servile than the exterior, which servants do, for, as St. John says:—"Whosoever committeth sin is the servant of sin,"(14) which hinders notably from attending to God, and it is the supreme degree of ingratitude to offend the benefactor at that time which Himself assigned for men to give Him thanks for His benefits, profaning by their sin the day which He sanctified with so great magnificence.

ii. The second is, to *attend to God with exercise of prayer* and contemplation, pondering the greatness of the benefits in whose remembrance this festival day was first instituted, meditating them by the points which have already been put down;(15) and by this means is avoided the *second degree* of ingratitude, which is, to forget the Benefactor, and the benefit received from Him.

iii. The third is, *to praise Almighty God vocally*, singing hymns and psalms to Him, in sign of thanksgiving for the benefits we have received. This is frequently used in the church, to the end that thither the faithful should have recourse, and, hearing the song, should move themselves to glorify God, "singing," as St. Paul says, in their "hearts,"(16) and giving thanks to God and the Father of mercies for the benefits we have received, and thus is avoided the *third degree* of ingratitude, which is, not to be grateful even in words for the benefits received.

iv. The fourth is, *to offer sacrifices to God*, to give Him the worship due to Him as our Creator and Sanctifier, and in thanksgiving for the benefits He has bestowed

(14) Joan. viii. 34.   (15) Introduc. p. 6.

(16) Col. iii. 16.

upon us, and to obtain new wherewith to serve Him more. For these three ends is offered to Him, the holy Sacrifice of the Mass (as has been said in its place),(17) at which the faithful ought to assist on all Sundays and festival days, offering the same jointly with the priests, and by their hands; adding also the "sacrifice" of a "contrite and humble heart,"(18) and of justice, exercising divers works of piety and charity; for we cease not from servile works in order to be idle, but to exercise the works which for that day are more agreeable to the Creator, whereby rest and quiet of spirit is obtained.

2. Finally, to animate all of us to this, our Lord would bless and sanctify the seventh day, rewarding those who sanctify the same in the manner just mentioned, bestowing His benediction upon them, and filling them with sanctity; and for this reason the day is called "blessed," for Almighty God appointed it to fill us with celestial benedictions, and when it should be convenient with temporal also, multiplying the temporal goods of those who employ themselves in sanctifying it.

Colloquy.—O most liberal God, I give Thee thanks that Thou hast assigned a time wherein I am to praise Thee for the benefits I have received of Thee, that so I may make myself worthy to receive other new. Deliver me, sweet Lord, I beseech Thee, from ingratitude, which, like a parching wind, consumeth virtues, and drieth up the fountain of Thy mercies.(19) "Turn, O my soul, into Thy rest,"(20) because our Lord hath done good to thee. Let thy rest be to praise Him all the time of this present life, that thou mayest attain to the eternal rest in the other. Amen.

<hr>

(17) 4 par. Med. xv.   (18) Ps. l. 19.
(19) S. August. Solil. c. xviii.   S. Bern. contra vitium ingrat.
(20) Ps. cxiv. 7.

MEDITATION XXVIII.

ON THE BENEFIT OF THE PRESERVATION OF THE WORLD AND THE DEPENDENCE
THAT ALL THINGS HAVE ON GOD, IN THEIR BEING, AND IN THEIR WORKING.

POINT I.

First, to consider how all things which God our Lord created in the beginning of the world, and in the first six days as above mentioned, and all the rest which, by means of them, have been multiplied since their time, *depend, in the preservation of their being on the same Almighty God.*(1)   For preservation is no other thing than a continuation of the work by which God makes any thing; wherefore, as He made all things with three fingers of His hand, which are His goodness, wisdom, and omnipotence, as already has been said, so with the self-same does He sustain them and preserve them; and this Isaias signified, and St. Paul confessed, saying that Almighty God "upholdeth all things by the word of His power."(2)   What thing, therefore, can be more admirable and more glorious than to see the frame of this whole world actually depending on the will and power of God, and that much more than the light of the air depends on the sun? For even as the sun setting, the light wholly ceases to be, so in the same instant wherein God shall please to suspend His action, this whole frame shall turn into nothing, which He can do even in an instant; whence I will deduce divers affections for the ground of my life and perfection.

1. Sometimes I will conceive affections of *confidence* in a God who can do so much, and on whom all depend, overcoming all fear from creatures by this omnipotence of the Creator, like that valorous Machabean who said:—

(1) S. Tho. i. p. q. civ. art. 1.   (2) Isa. xlviii. 6. Heb. i. 3.

"But we trust in the Almighty Lord, who at a beck can utterly destroy both them that come against us, and the whole world."(3)

2. Other times I will conceive affections of *great fear* of His justice, as being joined with such omnipotence, beseeching Him to moderate the same by means of His mercy, saying with Jeremiah:—"Correct me, O Lord, but yet with judgment, and not in Thy fury, lest Thou bring me to nothing,"(4) as my sins have deserved. But much more will I fear to offend a God on whom actually my being depends, and all that I have, as I would tremble to injure a man who held me with his three fingers on the top of some high tower, and in whose will it wholly rested to loose me out of his hand, so to let me fall down head-long.

3. Other times I will conceive affections of *profound humility*, acknowledging this inward dependence which I have on God, in my being, and in all that is necessary to my preservation, joining with humility the affection of charity: for, beholding how this being cannot preserve itself, but by the means of God, I am to humble, and to hold myself for nothing before Him; and considering how Almighty God preserves me, I am to love Him, who does so great a good to me. And by this means humility revives charity, and the knowledge of my own nothing causes great love towards Him, who drew me forth out of it, and always preserves me in the being He gave me.

POINT II.

Secondly, to consider the infinity of this sovereign benefit of preservation, on account of the *innumerable goods* which it comprises, applying them all to myself, as every one may do to himself.

(3) 2 Mach. viii. 18.   (4) Jer. x. 24.

1. First, *all things* which God created in the beginning of the world, and in the first six days, and those which in virtue of them, He has multiplied for so many millions of years, as also those which at this present time are in the world, and are in a maner infinite, also *appertain* in some sort *to this benefit*, some of them helping to give me being, others to preserve the being which I have, our Lord using them for this end. For the heavens, with all their motions, and the angels which move them, with the innumerable influences which they distribute through the whole world, are my benefit, and necessary to preserve me. The elements, and all living creatures which are in them, the whole multitude of fowls, sheep, or fishes, which all this time have proceeded from them, by their succession have caused that this bird should have life, or this lamb, or this fish which I eat, are all benefits to me, since without them I should not enjoy that which now I do enjoy. And the same is to be said of the plants, whence proceeds this apple, this grape, or this wine, which supports me. And if I use any vessel of gold, or of silver, there are contained therein innumerable benefits, by reason of the innumerable things which Almighty God has made, and preserved to the present instant, that I might enjoy and use this vessel, as the influences of heaven which produce the gold, the earth which conceived it in its bowels, the water, rain, or ice, which concurred to it; the men who laboured in seeking and finding the mines, in extracting, purifying, and fashioning it; the instruments of iron and of wood, which they used; and all that which God did to create that iron or wood, until it became an instrument fit for this end, and other innumerable things which concurred to the end, that this vessel might come from the furthest parts of all the world into my power; all these, I say, are the benefits of God, and contained in a thing so

little as that which I now enjoy. The like reasoning I may make on the bit of bread which I eat, on the garment of cloth wherewith I clothe me, on the pen or paper wherewith I write, and so of others; because, every one by itself, although it be no more than one, yet contains infinite more in the manner just said, and consequently for every one I am bound to give thanks to this infinite Benefactor.

Colloquy.—O infinite God, immense benefactor, giver and preserver of all things, what thanks shall I render Thee, even for the least of these goods which Thou hast given me, since therein is contained such an innumerable multitude of benefits? If such a number of creatures concur with Thee their Creator, to preserve me, why shall not I concur with all to glorify Thee? Oh that both I myself and all of them might convert ourselves into tongues to praise and bless Thee for the good which Thou dost me with each of them, so to pay in part the much which I owe Thee for the whole. Amen.

2. I will ponder, secondly, in the same benefit, the infinite charity of Almighty God, which shines in this, that being able by His omnipotence to annihilate whatsoever thing created, yet *never*, as St. Thomas testifies, (5) *did He annihilate any thing*, nor destroy it *totally*, but always as He destroys one, He produces another in its place, and whensoever one is corrupted, another presently is engendered. And although in the time of Noe, the malice of man aspired to that point, that Almighty God said, "it repenteth" me to "have made man," (6) nevertheless He would not annihilate them; so likewise He would not annihilate the devils, nor other great sinners, but as the Wise man says, preserves the lives of many, expecting

(5) 1 p. q. civ. art. 4.   (6) Gen. vi. 6.

them to penance only because He desires to bestow this good upon them, for otherwise they would perish incontinently, for "how could anything endure, unless Thou wouldst? or be preserved, if not called by Thee?" (7)

3. The third shall be to ponder the innumerable benefits which are contained in this preservation; for unknown to me God withholds innumerable things which would hinder the same, and *preserves me from innumerable perils* of fire, water, corrupt air, wild beasts, misfortunes, thieves, sicknesses, and occasions of death. (8)   And forasmuch as there is not any evil which one man suffers, that another may not suffer, by the multitude of evils which I see another man suffer, I may conjecture the multitude from which Almighty God delivers me.   And although these benefits be so many, and so great, yet will He that they be hidden from us, that we may understand that He does not do us good for vain-glory, nor for desire of human praise, but purely and merely for His goodness and mercy; yet for this I will not cease to accomplish my obligation, praising Him for them, although I know not how many they are. (9)

Colloquy.—O sovereign Benefactor of men, I yield Thee as many thanks as possibly I may, for that with the spirit of a father, Thou dost confer on us innumerable benefits, manifest and secret: the manifest to provoke us to esteem them, and to be grateful for the good that we receive by them; and the secret to induce us to conceal the good which we do in Thy service, without seeking our own praises; and with the one and with the other, dost Thou allure us to love Thee as our Father who dost in all things seek the profit of Thy children: grant me sweet Lord, I beseech Thee, that I may serve Thee as a son, per-

(7) Sap. xi. 26.   (8) S. Chrys. lib. i. de Provid.

(9) Med. xxxii. p. 4.

forming my services with the same spirit, wherewith Thou dost impart to me so innumerable benefits. Amen.

POINT III.

1. The third shall be to consider how all things created wholly depend upon God our Lord, not only in the being they have, but also *in the actions which they perform*, in such wise that Almighty God assists them to perform the work, and preserves them all the time that it endures; (10) and if Almighty God should withdraw His concurrence, they could not perform anything, nor use their faculties; and that which with the aid of Almighty God they have begun, with the same aid they are to end, for if it should cease, the work also would forthwith cease.

i. Here is to be pondered, first, the infinite omnipotence of God in assisting and aiding with His *concurrence* so many works, as the creatures of the world perform; the heavens, elements, men, and angels, without failing in any of them, without being weary or fainting, and being no more busied than if He assisted but one alone. For which I will praise and glorify so great a God for such omnipotence, rejoicing at it, and inviting all creatures to praise Him for the concurrence they receive from Him, and for the help they have from Him, in all whatsoever they do.

ii. But applying this to myself, I will next ponder the innumerable benefits which are contained in this concurrence which I enjoy every day, every hour, and every moment; for Almighty God actually co-operates with my *eyes*, that they always see, and with the colours that they display their varieties before them, as means by which they may see: He co-operates with my *ears* that they may

(10) S. Tho. i. p. q. cv. art. 5.

hear, and with the things from which the sound, music, or word, proceeds, which I am to hear; He co-operates with my *mouth and taste*, to eat and relish, and with the meats, that they give me savour; and whilst I sleep, He helps that the meat I have received be digested, and incorporated, and that I take and draw my breath; and with my understanding and my will, He co-operates in all the works which they perform, and generally with all those things which assist me, for as Isaias says:—Thou, Lord, "hast wrought all our works for us;" (11) and Christ our Lord said, "My Father worketh until now; and I work," (12)

Colloquy.—O most Blessed Trinity, who art in all things working with them, I give Thee thanks for the innumerable benefits which Thou impartest to every one, working with them innumerable works : work, sweet Lord, I beseech Thee, always in me that which is pleasing to Thee, that so Thy concurrence may be always profitable to me, and to Thy glory everlastingly, world without end. Amen.

iii. The third shall be to ponder the infallible and *immutable law* which Almighty God has made to concur with His creatures; for though free and concurring of His own will, and because He wills, it is as certain that He will not fail, as if He *could do no other* thing; unless sometimes He miraculously suspend this concurrence, for the greater manifestation of His grace and of His glory; for the good of His elect, (13) as He did when He caused the fire in the furnace of Babylon not to burn the three young children that were there, and in other like miracles. (14) And such is the goodness of this sovereign Creator, that when a man has resolved to sin, and to do him some injury, He

(11) Isa. xxvi. 12.   (12) Joan v. 17.
(13) S. Tho. i. p. q. cv. art. 6.   (14) Dan. iii. 50.

does not suspend or withdraw His concurrence, but contrariwise, preserves man's liberty, and in order not to violate the law which Himself has made, even in regard of that in which he sins, He lends him His concurrence all the time it endures.

Colloquy.—O immense goodness, O infinite liberality of our sovereign Creator! what goodness can be greater than actually to do good to him who actually uses that good to injure his benefactor! O my Beloved, permit not that I abuse Thine omnipotence, to do works whereby to offend Thee; suffer me not to abuse the creatures with whom and with myself Thou concurrest, that they may give me pleasure, and that I may receive pleasure from them; and since in Thee I " live," and " move," and " be,"(15) let all my works be dedicated to Thee, that I may seek in them Thy only glory, world without end. Amen.

2. From hence, finally, I will draw the like affections as in the first point, especially of *humility*, pondering that I have no strength to do anything by myself alone, without the concurrence of God, who, although He preserves the being I have, yet unless He co-operated with me likewise, to work, I should be as a block, and as a thing wholly unprofitable, conformable to that which St. Paul says:— " Not that we are sufficient to think anything of ourselves, as of ourselves, but our sufficiency is from God," (16) on whose will without prejudice of our free liberty, we depend in all our actions, so that we can do nothing, nor can glory of anything as of our own, which we have not received from His holy hand, as the " axe" cannot " boast against him that cutteth with it," (17) attributing the same to itself alone, and not to the workman.

Colloquy.—O my soul, humble thyself into the

(15) Act. xvii. 28.   (16) 2 Cor. iii. 5.   (17) Isa. x. 15.

abyss of this nothing, under the powerful hand of thy God, that He may " exalt" thee " in the time of visitation,"(18) when He shall come to take an account of the works which thou hast done, the concurrence which He gave thee by His co-operation.   O sovereign Judge, who now dost show Thyself so liberal in co-operating with all men to the works which they do by their free will ; begin in me by Thy grace all the works which I do, and finish those I begin ; to the end that at that day of the final reckoning, I may appear without shame before Thee, and may be worthy to be exalted with Thee in the Kingdom of Thy glory. Amen.

MEDITATIONS ON THE PROVIDENCE OF ALMIGHTY GOD.

Although in the preceding meditations we have said many things which touch the divine Providence, inasmuch as it shines in all the works which proceed from the bounty, charity, mercy, wisdom, and omnipotence of God, and in the creation of the world; nevertheless, now we will treat more in particular of that which is proper to the divine Providence in the *government* of His creatures, and especially of men.   Of this we will make certain meditations, in which all those ought to exercise themselves whose aim is to attain to perfection, and whosoever else that desires to pass this life with some profit and consolation, as well for the soul as for the body, for to all this it will profit notably; insomuch that I cannot conceive how he can have in this life contentment and peace, and true solace of heart, who is not well grounded in this variety of the divine Providence; neither do I know how a man can have excessive sorrow or trouble of mind, or desolation that can last long, for any created thing, beside sin, if with a lively faith he profoundly penetrate the secrets of the

<hr>

(18) 1 Pet. v. 6.

divine Providence, as will be seen by that which we shall say concerning it.

MEDITATION XXIX.

ON THE PROVIDENCE OF ALMIGHTY GOD TOWARDS HIS CREATURES, IN WHAT IT CONSISTS, AND THE INNUMERABLE GOODS WHICH PROCEED FROM IT.

POINT I.

In the first place consider *what the divine Providence is*, because hence arises the estimation of it, and the love, confidence, veneration, and subjection which we ought to bear to it. " Providence," as St. Thomas says, " is a cer-tain disposition and order of all the means which God has ap-pointed to attain his ends; and of all the means with which He provides His creatures, that they may obtain the ends for which they were created."(1)

1. Here consider three principal things, gathered out of what has been said in the preceding meditations.(2)

i. The first is, that God our Lord, with His divine understanding illuminated by His divine wisdom, even from His eternity knows and *comprehends all the ends which His creatures can attain* and aspire after, and all the necessary and suitable means which are and can be to attain them. He knows likewise all the impediments that can take place, and the means there are to take away or prevent these impediments, insomuch that God effectually brings to pass what He intends, and the creatures attain their end in the same manner that God will have them. Whereupon it follows, that the providence of God cannot be wanting or be defective, by reason of ignorance, as it happens to the providence of men, of whom the Wise man

(1) 1, p q. civ. art. 1.   (2) Med. iv.

says, that "the thoughts of mortal men are fearful, and our counsels uncertain;" (3) because with our little knowledge and much ignorance, we doubt whether what we thought be true or false, and whether what we foresee will come to be good or evil, secure or dangerous.

ii. The second thing is, that God our Lord, with His divine will, full of infinite goodness and charity, out of all the ends and means, which He knows by His divine wisdom, calls and *chooses those which are most high*, sovereign, and most proportionable to His creatures, according to the nature and capacity of every one. (4) For, first, He would ordain them all to Himself, for His glory, and for the manifestation of His goodness and perfection, which is the highest end He can have, according to that which the Wise man says :—" The Lord hath made all things for Himself." (5) Moreover, to every sort of creature He has assigned his proper end, with means proportionate to obtain it; but above all He would exalt angels and men to the most high and sovereign end that was possible, incomparably greater than that which their nature required, which is, that they should be blessed, as God Himself is, seeing Him clearly, loving Him, and enjoying Him in His glory; and to attain this end, He has provided us with all necessary and suitable means in great abundance; for as His bounty and charity were infinite, He would not be sparing in choosing most sufficient means for so important an end.

iii. The third thing is, that God our Lord by His divine omnipotence, from the beginning of the world, *began to put in execution* the means He had chosen, and by the same prosecutes, and will ever prosecute them, nor can His providence be defective for lack of power, as ours is.

(3) Sap. ix. 14.   (4) S. Tho. i. p. q. ciii. art 1.   (5) Prov. xvi. 4.

Whence it appears, that the providence of God principally rests on these three attributes, on His wisdom, His goodness, and His omnipotence, which are the fountains of the divine benefits, as has been said in the sixteenth meditation.

2. These three considerations I am to apply to the providence which Almighty God has over me, pondering how all my miseries and *my necessities are known to Him,* and the goods which are wanting to me as well of body as of soul. And likewise He knows all the means that there are to deliver me from the evil, and to give me the good, because He is infinitely wise. He can, moreover, apply those means, and put them in execution as Himself wills, because He is almighty. Lastly, because He is singularly good, and a most loving Father, He wills and wishes that I may attain my last end, and desires to give me suitable means to that effect; wherefore I may be most assured that nothing can be wanting to me under such a providence, since neither through ignorance, nor through imbecility, nor yet through malice, any defect can be found therein.

Colloquy.—O my soul, be glad and rejoice to live under so sovereign a providence, " casting all" thy " care" on God, for He has care of Thee.(6) If thine own providence be uncertain, that of thy God will supply its defects ; for with His wisdom He will supply thy ignorance, with His omnipotence thy weakness, and with His goodness thy malice ; have thou, therefore, a care of God, and God will have a care of thee. O God of my soul, let us make this compact most firmly, that Thou have care of me, and that I likewise have a care of Thee : for doubtless I shall have a care of Thee, if Thou with special providence have care of me. Henceforth will I say with great

(6) 1 Pet. v. 7.

joy, "my beloved to me, and I to him," (7) He is careful of my things, and I am likewise careful of His; He will attend to my honour, and my profit, and I will attend to His glory and service for ever and ever. Amen.

POINT II.

Hence I will ascend to consider the infinite and innumerable *goods, which are contained* in the divine providence, to allure myself to love and put my trust in it, making an abridgment of those which afterwards we shall set down more at large.

1. I will ponder, first, how the divine providence is my mother, who gives to me the being I have, and bears me within her bowels; my nurse, because she nourishes and sustains me, and carries me in her arms, like a little babe; (8)—my guide, because she always walks on my right side, and accompanies me in all my ways; (9)—my queen and governess, because she rules and governs me in the whole course of my life; (10)—my mistress and my counsellor, because she teaches me that which I do not know, counsels me in what I doubt, and governs me in what I ought to do, to the end that I err not;—my protector and defender in all my necessities and perils, because she helps me in all of them;—my comforter in afflictions and heaviness, because she gives me for all of them many reasons and causes of consolation;—and, finally, as many offices of charity and mercy as can be imagined, all are found in the providence of God with infinite eminence, exercising the office of a father, a physician, a judge, a pastor, and so of others. Whence I will understand that

(7) Can. ii. 16.

(8) Isa. xlvi. 3.   Osee xi. 3.   (9) Sap. xiv. 3.

(10) Isa. xlviii. 17.

I ought to bear towards the divine providence all the affections of love, confidence, joy, and thanksgiving, which such offices of right deserve, loving it like a son, and having recourse to it as to a mother, keeping company with it, and asking direction, counsel, help, remedy, and consolation.

2. I will ponder, secondly, that the divine providence *is the first fountain of all the goods*, both of body and soul, as well temporal as eternal, which I have received, and hope to receive, and of all those which the other creatures, both of heaven and earth, enjoy at this present time, for which reason St. Dorotheus said, that nothing is done without the providence of Almighty God; " Et ubi providentia, ibi omnino bonum est et omnia ad utilitatem animæ fiunt"—"Where the providence of God is, there absolutely good is, and all things are done for the utility of the soul." (11) Where the providence of God is there good is, and all kind of good;—it is profitable and delightful, because the divine providence is the fountain of virtues, and of the celestial graces which make us just, and of the temporal goods which aid and assist us to pass our life, and of all the delights which proceed from the one and the other. Moreover, by it we are delivered from all contrary evils, or preserved from falling into them, or drawn forth out of them after we have fallen; because in the one and the other God will show His providence, and the divers means He has to manifest it; wherefore it is said of the divine wisdom, that " she showeth herself to them cheerfully in the ways, and meeteth them with all providence;"(12)—taking of them all the care that is possible, and with all the sorts of providence that she can exhibit towards them, to fill them with goods, as we shall presently declare.

<hr>

(11) Serm. xiii.   (12) Sap. vi. 17.

Colloquy.—O supreme Providence, which openest the hand of Almighty God, to fill all creatures with benediction :(13) I adore and glorify thee as a queen and my mother, and beseech thee to do towards me the office of a mother and of a mistress, of my protector and of my comforter, and of an universal helper in all my affairs, for, having thee on my side, I shall have, together with thee, all good, and if thou forsake me, I shall be filled with all evils.

POINT III.

The third will be to consider how the divine providence wholly employs itself in *being careful about creatures*.

1. I will ponder, first, the difference that there is between God and man, because men who govern, and have others under their charge, stand in need to have providence over themselves, and their own things which concern them, which are wont so much to occupy them, that they leave no time to look to all that which is needful to others. But, God our Lord, as St. Thomas says, (14) *has no need of providence over Himself*, nor over the things which appertain to Him, because 'He has all good within Himself, so that nothing can be wanting to Him, nor does He look for ought from any other. All this providence, therefore, He employs in looking to others, that is to say, to the creatures He has created, so to have on whom to manifest His divine providence; which, as it is infinitely perfect, provides with great perfection all that which belongs to His charge, because He would take upon Himself that providence.

2. Hence it is that the divine providence *extends itself to all creatures*, without excluding any, and to all men, without forgetting any, how vile and base soever they be,

(13) Ps. ciii. 28.   (14) 2, p. q. **xxii.** art. 1.

because, as the Wise man says, Almighty God "made the little and the great, and He has equally care of all." (15)

Colloquy.—Wherefore, O my soul, be not dismayed nor discomforted beholding thy littleness, for such as thou art God has made thee, who never excludes out of His providence what He has made by His Almighty power; and He who disdained not to make thee, will not disdain to govern thee.

3. Hence also it follows that the same God is by Himself *the executor of His own providence.* For, although it is true, that by the means of some of the creatures, He provides others, yet He by Himself assists all, in all places, and in all times, because, as already has been said, He is in the whole world, and in all things, by essence, presence, and by power, knowing whatsoever is done, and helping to put it in execution, and providing all with admirable government. And although He leave men in their own liberty, and as the Wise man says, "in the hand of" their "own counsel," (16) to do what they will, yet He ceases not on this account to have providence over them, as also over their free works, directing them, or permitting them for the ends He has ordained them to.

4. Whence, lastly, it follows that *nothing occurs* in this world *casually* or by chance, in respect of God our Lord, although it be very casual in respect of men, because by His infinite wisdom He knows whatsoever shall come to pass, even before it comes, and with His Providence, either ordains or permits it for the supreme end of His government, which is His glory, and the manifestation of His mercy and justice, and of His other divine perfections; (17) moreover, for the good of the just, and of the elect, over whom He is provident, after a most excel-

(15) Sap. vi. 8.   (16) Ecclus. xv. 14.
(17) S. Tho. i. p. q. cxvi. art. 1.

lent manner, converting, as the apostle St. Paul says, all things that they " work together unto good," (18) of such as love Him. From all of which I will conclude, that to enjoy the divine providence, and to enrich myself with the infinite treasures it contains; it will avail very much to think highly of it, attributing all good to it, as to the fountain and beginning whence all proceeds, believing with a lively and most assured faith, that which hitherto has been said of it, and shall be said, after the manner God has revealed and manifested to us by experience. Hence I must conceive great confidence in this providence, together with great and perfect resignation, as shall be said hereafter in the Forty-ninth Meditation. And above all, I will especially love the Father of Providence, who, with so great love provides His creatures, repaying with love and respectful services, the especial care which He has of me, and of all His creatures.

Colloquy.—O most loving and most provident Father, who, with such admirable providence, carest and providest for all Thy creatures, and most of all for those who with faith, inflamed by love, confidently cast themselves into Thy hands; behold I confidently commit myself to it, because in it " my lots are ;"(19) direct my works by Thy holy providence, to the end they may be pleasing to Thine eyes, so that through their means there may befal me the good and happy lot of Thine eternal beatitude. Amen.

(18) Rom. viii. 28.   (19) Ps xxx. 16.

MEDITATION XXX.

ON THE PROVIDENCE OF ALMIGHTY GOD IN THE GOVERNMENT OF THE WORLD,
AND OF MEN.

POINT I.

1. First, to consider as the ground of this meditation the most excellent providence which God our Lord shows *towards men in the creation of the world*, resuming in brief that which has been said in the preceding Meditations. (1)

i. For first, He made the house which men were to inhabit, making it foundations, walls, and coverings, namely, the heaven and the earth, with the elements which are between them both. ii. Next, in the first three days He made divisions and separations, as one that makes different chambers, and halls, for divers inhabitants; and moreover, He planted orchards, and gardens of recreation, and fruits for the sustenance of living creatures; and in the secret coffers of the earth, He laid up treasures of gold and silver, wherewith men might be enriched: He likewise placed lamps, which night and day might give them light. iii. Afterwards He provided inhabitants of the sea, of the air, and of the earth, giving them means and power to multiply, and to perpetuate their species, even so long as the world should last. iv. And lastly, He created man, and appointed him lord over all this house, wealth, and substance, with the revenues of the whole, and with dominion over all, although not absolute, but subject to the divine, with obligation to render an account of the manner he used the creatures and the goods which were delivered

(1) S. Tho. i. p. q. ciii.

to him, as stewards are wont to render accounts to their lords.

2. Pondering all this after the manner already declared, I shall come to see how entire and perfect the providence of Almighty God was in the work of this creation, inasmuch as there is no father of a family, nor any prince who can build a house or palace with so great provision of all that is necessary to his intended ends, as God built the house of the world for ours. Applying this to myself, I will ponder how God our Lord, by His providence, even before I was born, designed me a particular place, house and substance, whereby to live, and how those which my predecessors made with labour, I now enjoy with great quiet. For all which I will render to Him many thanks, endeavouring to imitate His providence, in having the like care of my own soul, so that, before she depart out of this world, I may have gained and provided for her by my works, a house, riches, and other substance in the other; because, He that created me of mere grace, without my own merits in this visible world, will not transfer me to the invisible, save by His grace, together with my merits, which will be by faithfully using the goods which He has given me, in order to make to myself "friends of the mammon of iniquity, that when" I "shall fail, they may receive" me "into everlasting dwellings." (2)

Colloquy.—O most loving Creator, who, with admirable providence, even from the beginning of the world, hast prepared me the goods which I enjoy at this present time; grant me to use them in such manner that when, at the end of the world, Thou shalt require an account, I may render unto Thee a perfect good one. Amen.

(2) Luc. xvi. 9. Med. lii. p. 3.

POINT II.

Secondly, to consider that God our Lord having created the world, He Himself, with His own providence, *took the government* of it under His charge, according to that which is written in Job:—"What other hath He appointed over the earth? Or whom hath He set over the world which He made?" (3) And the Wise man adds:—" Thy providence, O Father," even from the beginning, " governeth it." (4)

1. Here is to be pondered, first, how happy a thing it is for us, that one and the *same should be the Creator and Governor* of the world, and of all of us, because He governs us as His own proper good, and looks on us as the work of His own hands. (5) And because all His works are most perfect, and that He created them to manifest His goodness, for the same cause was it meet that He should govern them, and direct them to their ends, by the means He had given them for the same.

Colloquy.—O most loving God, two titles I have to beseech Thee that Thou protect me, until I attain my final end. The one is, that Thou art my Creator ; the other is, that Thou art my Governor. And although Thou createdst me without my consent, yet Thou wilt govern me without prejudice of my liberty. Govern me, therefore, dear Lord, I beseech Thee, in such a manner that I never resist Thy government, that so I may obtain the end for which Thou createdst me.   Amen.

2. I will ponder, secondly, how well and happy it is for us that the supreme Governor is *only one*, whom all others obey, who by His authority have any part of this government committed to them; for being one, He directs all

(3) Job xxxiv. 13.

(4) Sap. xiv. 3.   (5) S. Tho. i. p. q. liii. art. 1.

creatures to peace and unity, composing the discords and dissensions that are amongst them for the common good of the whole; and therefore all men may be united and conformed one to another, if they accommodate themselves to the government and laws of this only Governor, who is the final end of all;(6) although, to preserve their liberty, He will not force them, but invite them with those delightful and pleasant words which He spoke by the prophet Isaias, saying:—" I am the Lord thy God...Gubernans te in via qua ambulas...that governs thee in the way that thou walkest," and in the life thou livest. " O that thou hadst hearkened to my commandments; thy peace had been as a river, and thy justice as the waves of the sea."(7)

Colloquy.—O Governor of the world, one and supreme, whose government all irrational creatures obey without resistance : since Thou desirest so greatly that we men do obey Thee, give us what Thou commandest, that we may fulfil what Thou desirest, and may obtain the justice and peace which Thou dost promise us.   Amen.

3. Thirdly, to ponder the infinite bounty and liberality of Almighty God, which appears in this, that He governs by Himself *every one*, attending to all that which is needful for him, yet in such sort, that He will not retain to Himself the whole government, *but give a part to His creatures*, communicating to them this honour and dignity to govern others, giving them sufficient faculties for it; and therefore He wills that men be subject to those who in His name govern them, and who " resisteth" them " resisteth" Him, as St. Paul says, because all their " power" is "from God,"(8) who with His infinite providence assists all those who govern in His name, and supplies the defects

(6) S Tho. i. p. q. iii. art. 3.   (7) Isa. xlviii. 17.
(8) Rom. xiii. 2.

of their government, drawing forth from their errors helps for the good of His elect.

Colloquy.—I give Thee thanks, O most wise Governor, for this most singular manner of government which Thou usest, so properly Thine, that it cannot be found in any other; govern, dear Lord, I do beseech Thee, those that govern us, that they may govern us aright; and govern us also who are governed, to the end we may subject ourselves for Thee unto their government, relying upon Thy Providence, who wilt convert all things to our greater profit.   Amen.

POINT III.

1. The third will be to consider the *excellencies* of this marvellous government of God our Lord.

i. It is a *paternal* or fatherly government, and for this reason the Wise man calls our Lord " Father," when he said that His Providence governs all things, and therefore also He governs with great sweetness, disposing, as the Wise man says, "all things sweetly," giving them great inclination to their proper end, to which this government is directed.   And as this benevolent and loving Father saw that man, by reason of his nature, according to the spirit had an inclination to virtue, and according to the flesh suffered some kind of contradiction, He therefore disposed in the beginning, that the flesh should be subject, by original justice, to the end that the inclination of the spirit might prevail; and again, since original sin, He gives to us supernatural virtues, which are powerful inclinations to make the "yoke" of His law exceeding "sweet." (9)

ii. The second excellence is, that this government is to be an *effectual* government, that it be both strong and

(9) Mat. xi. 30.

sweet, according to that which the Wise man says, that wisdom "reacheth from end unto end, mightily, and ordereth all things sweetly,"(10) because all things are under His command, nor can any resist IIis will. (11) This is so potent, that IIe can cause us to will what He wills, and that we find delight in willing it, which is proper to His divine wisdom and omnipotence.

iii. The third excellence is, that this government is *most just;* for being absolute Lord of all, not bound to give an account of what He does, IIe governs with all justice and uprightness, giving to everything what is suitable to its nature; and IIe governs men, promising them rewards, and threatening them with punishments; in which also IIe keeps the law of justice with all, though passing full of fatherly mercy, for IIe threatens as a Father, but with desire that all attain the end of IIis government.

iv. The fourth excellence is, that it is a government *very profitable* to all those who are governed by it, because, as St. Thomas says, the government of Almighty God has three effects in general, in which innumerable others are contained. (12)—One is, "assimilari summo bono," to cause us to resemble the sovereign good, participating in His infinite goodness.—The other is, to preserve us in the good we have received, lest we be deprived of it, or that it be diminished.—The third is, to move us with sweetness and efficacy to the augmentation of this good, and to the perfect possession of it.

2. Pondering these four excellencies of the government of Almighty God, in every one of them I ought to be glad and rejoice, for the infinite goodness, wisdom, justice, and omnipotence of this supreme Governor, and *to hold myself happy to be under His government,* and to give

Him thanks for the way in which He governs me, beseeching Him to assist me, that I never depart from His direction. O my soul, since thou art to be governed, what better Governor, or what better government canst thou desire? Thou having such a Governor, what can be wanting to thee if thou obey Him? "The Lord ruleth me, and I shall want nothing,"(13) for neither shall life be wanting to me, nor health, nor honour, nor contentment, nor temporal good, which may further me to the eternal; and much less shall be wanting to me, virtue, grace, wisdom, and the celestial gifts which shall be needful to attain the eternal. Only that which is nothing shall be wanting to me, namely, sin, if I obey His government; for all that which is for the good of my soul He will give me with great abundance.

Colloquy.—O my Beloved, do Thou rule me, and I shall be well ruled; do Thou govern me, and I shall be well governed; let me not, I beseech Thee, govern myself, nor let the world nor the flesh govern me, nor any other out of Thy government, on whom my whole remedy depends.

3. From these considerations I will learn to *imitate this form of government* over those whom God has committed to my charge, in these four excellencies, which shine in the government of Almighty God; for so much more excellent will the government of man be, by how much it resembles that of God, causing, as St. Peter says, that it be not tyrannical, "not by constraint,"(14) but sweet and fatherly; not remiss, or pusillanimous, but strong and efficacious; not unjust, but just; not principally for the profit of him that governs, but for the profit of the governed, and for the glory of the supreme Governor and Prince of

(13) Ps. xxii. 1.   (14) 1 Pet. v. 2.

the pastors, governors of the world and of the Church, who when He shall come to judgment, will give a crown of eternal glory to those who have governed in this manner.

POINT IV.

The fourth will be to consider another sovereign excellence of the government of Almighty God, which so extends itself from one end to another, as that *it comprehends all the creatures both of heaven and earth*, even from the highest of the Seraphim to the least and most contemptible worm; looking carefully over all those things which appertain to Him as if He had no other thing to do, and consequently governs all men with more solicitude, yea, and each one of them, beholding the very least hair of their heads.(15)　And although they be many, yet He so governs all as if they were but only one, nor has He less care of the innumerable men who are now in the world than of the eight only who were in Noe's ark, or of Adam alone when He was in paradise: for neither does a great number trouble Him, nor the little number discourage Him, since His goodness, which is infinite, extends itself to be careful of all, great and little, many and few. (16)　For, compared to His greatness, all are but little, and compared to His charity very great, and to His infinite wisdom many are as one, and so I may say with St. Augustine:—" O tu bone omnipotens, &c." "O omnipotent Good, who art so careful for every one of us as if Thou wert careful of him alone, and art as careful of all as of every one."(17)

Hence I will gather, that the government of Almighty God *in my behalf has all the excellences* beforementioned;

(15) S. Tho. i. p. q. ciii. art. 5, ex S. Aug. lib. vi. de Civit. et q. lxxxii. art. 2.　Mat. x. 30.

(16) Sap. vi. 8.　　　　　　　　　(17) Lib. iii. Confess. c. xi.

for this government is to me fatherly, sweet, strong, efficacious, just, and profitable, so that I cannot in any reason complain of this government; and therefore not without cause is He put in holy Scripture in the singular number, who governs, as David said:—" The Lord ruleth me:" and by Isaias:—" I am the Lord...that govern thee;"(18) that I may understand that He observes in my behalf the perfection of His government, although it cannot be denied but that the best beloved and the elect He governs with greater providence, for the greater manifestation of His infinite charity. To the end, therefore, to make myself partaker of so especial a government, the three means will help which have been put down at the end of the precedent meditation, believing, hoping, and loving this sovereign Governor.

Colloquy.—I give Thee thanks, O most loving Father, for the especial care which Thou hast of me, as if I alone were in the world, being amongst all others the most miserable. Oh that I could worthily praise Thee for the good Thou dost to all, and that all might likewise praise Thee for the good Thou dost to me, to the end that I and all may enjoy Thee everlastingly. Amen.

MEDITATION XXXI.

ON THE PROVIDENCE OF ALMIGHTY GOD IN THE SUSTENANCE OF CREATURES, ESPECIALLY OF MEN, WITH FOOD, APPAREL, HONOUR, AND TEMPORAL GOODS.

This meditation will be grounded upon the wonderful doctrine which Christ our Lord gave us of the divine providence, declaring by order the words of the sacred text, as follows.

(18) Ps. xxii. 1. Isa. xlviii. 17.

POINT I.

Jesus said to His disciples:—"*Be not solicitous for your life*, what you shall eat, nor for your body, what you shall put on."(1)

1. The first will be to consider *what kind* of solicitude it is which Christ our Lord forbids in these words, pondering four things which may make it sinful.(2)   i. The first, in being solicitous, not for things necessary for our life, or suitable to our estate, but for the superfluous and inordinate hoarding up over covetously the goods of the earth.   ii. The second, in being solicitous before the time and season; taking up those cares which do not appertain to the present time, but to a long time after.   iii. The third, for being inordinate in the intention, or in the order of the things, seeking the temporal before the spiritual, or to their detriment, or by evil means, or for evil ends, or placing in them our final end, rest, and felicity. iv. The fourth, in being excessively anxious, although it be in things necessary, because such anxiety always proceeds from an inordinate affection to the temporal, and is of little faith in the divine providence, as if Almighty God had not care of me, and all depended on me alone.   And for this very reason, anxious solicitude is wont to be sinful, although it be even for spiritual goods, as that of Martha was, when she served Christ with such anxiety, and of certain scrupulous or indiscreet persons, over fearful and pusillanimous in the affair of their salvation.   I will reflect on these four disorders, examining strictly whether I fall into them, that I may drive them from me, lest God say to me, as He said to the covetous rich man who fell into them:—"'Thou fool, this night do they require

(1) Mat. vi. 25.   Luc. xii. 22.
(2) S. Tho. ii. 2, 2, q. lv. art. 6, et 7, et 1, 2, q. cviii. art. 3, ad 5.

thy soul of thee; and whose shall those things be that thou hast provided?"(3) that is to say, what will this thy solicitude avail thee, and the treasures thou hoardest up, if now they take thy soul from thee, for whose sake thou didst gather them. Hence Christ our Lord inferred the doctrine of His providence:—"Ideo dico vobis, nolite soliciti esse"—"Therefore I say to you, be not solicitous for your life, what you shall eat, nor for your body, what you shall put on," nor for anything of this life, since Almighty God has taken into His charge the care of it.

Colloquy.—O my soul, take warning from this covetous rich man, abhorring his inordinate solicitude, if thou wouldst not pass through the punishment of his great poverty. Hear rather the lesson of Thy sovereign master; cast on Him all thy care, and thy anxious solicitude, since He with His providence charges Himself with them.

2. I will likewise ponder the *charity of Christ* our Lord, in forbidding this excessive solicitude for our profit, and to deliver us from the labour linked to it, saying:—"Be not therefore solicitous for to-morrow, for the morrow will be solicitous for itself. Sufficient for the day is the evil thereof."(4) That is to say, do not charge yourselves to-day with travails and cares, which are not needful for to-day, but take to-day those that are necessary for to-day, and to-morrow you shall undertake those of to-morrow; and since you know not what will befal to-morrow, nor whether any to-morrow will be for you, take not to day the superfluous care of that which is to come, and which, peradventure, will be to no purpose; leave this to the divine Providence, which comprehends all times, and each time will provide that which to each one is most expedient.

(3) Luc. xii. 20.   (4) Mat. vi. 34.

3. But for all this Christ our Lord *does not prohibit virtuous solicitude*, which procures things for the present, and prevents those which are to come with moderate care, otherwise called diligence, which comprises other four conditions contrary to those abovementioned, viz., that it should be concerning things necessary or suitable for the body or the soul, in due season, with due intention in the manner of seeking them, and with moderate affection, without trouble or anxiety; and this solicitude is not contrary to the Providence of Almighty God, but an effect, means, or instrument of it, which He uses to obtain His end. Hence the sacred Scripture commends the same to us, saying:—" Walk solicitous with thy God,"(5) and be " careful to keep the unity of the spirit in the bond of peace,"(6) "in carefulness, not slothful,"(7) which destroys good works.

Colloquy.—O eternal God, whose providence is careful without anxiety, and solicitous without perplexity, take from me, I humbly beseech Thee, that solicitude which Thou forbiddest me, and give me that which Thou commandest me, that, imitating the order of Thy peaceable and complete providence, I may be solicitous to serve Thee, as Thou art solicitous of my profit. Let all my cares this day be to have sorrow for the sins which I have committed in times past, and to seek means how to please Thee for the present, and to take care that I sin not for time to come, because all these cares concern this present day, trusting in Thy Providence, that Thou wilt help me with Thy grace to do the same to-morrow.

POINT II.

The second will be to consider the marvellous reason for which Christ our Lord exhorts us to trust in His provi-

(5) Mich. vi. 8.   (6) Ephes. iv. 3.   (7) Rom. xii. 10.

dence, saying:—" Is not the life more than the meat, and the body more than the raiment?"(8)

1. In this sentence three admirable and exceedingly profitable truths are proposed. i. The first, that the *life is better*, and of much more value and estimation, than the *meat*, and the body much more precious than the raiment. Under these two things He comprehends all the riches and precious things of the world, which are ordained to sustain life, to adorn the body, and for our habitation, recreation, and exterior pomp. ii. The second, that God, out of His *mere grace*, without our own merits and our industry, gave us the life and body which we have, and consequently by His disposition we stand in need of meat to preserve life, and of raiment to cover nakedness, since Adam lost the robe of innocency. iii. The third is, that He who gave us that which is more, both *can and will give us that which is less;* and He who created the soul and body, with necessity of some other thing less than themselves for their preservation, evidently declares that He both knows, and can, and will give also that which is less, by which the necessity of that which is better may be relieved; for the same goodness which moved Him to the first, will likewise move Him to the second. Hence Christ our Lord inferred that we ought to lay aside the disordered solicitude of food and raiment, trusting and relying upon the divine providence, who, since He gave us, without any merit, a thing so precious as is soul and body, will also give us necessary food and raiment, which are of much less price.

Colloquy.—O most liberal Creator and most wise master, what thanks shall I give Thee for so sovereign a liberality? And how grateful should I be unto Thee for so sublime a doctrine! Dear Lord, I believe

(8) Mat. vi. 25.

what Thou sayest, and hope for what Thou offerest ; and, relying upon Thy providence, will accomplish all which Thou commandest me, in gratitude for that which Thou dost promise me.

2. From this doctrine of Christ our Lord I am also to gather, that since the soul is more than the meat, and the body more than the raiment, I ought only to take of the one and the other *that which shall be suitable* for soul and body, rejecting all that which may redound to their hurt; for it would be an intolerable error to lose that which is more for that which is less, losing my own soul, or my neighbour's, to gain that which is of little value compared with it; for which reason St. Paul pronounced that memorable sentence, saying:—" Destroy not the work of God for meat,"(9) killing the soul of thy brother, for whom Christ Jesus died.

Colloquy.—O most sweet Redeemer, who saidst : —" What doth it profit a man if he gain the whole world, and suffer the loss of his own soul ?"(10) grant me, I humbly beseech Thee, that I more esteem the good of my soul, than the dominion and possession of the whole world, freely offering myself to lose whatsoever is in the world, that I may not lose my soul. Amen.

3. I will also gather from this admirable doctrine a general rule of *confidence* in the providence of God, assuring myself, that when He gives any great gift to me, He will likewise give that which is less, if it be necessary or suitable to preserve the same; and on this is grounded that which the blessed apostle St. Paul says:—" He that spared not even His own Son, but delivered Him up for us all, how hath He not also with Him given us all things?"(11) For all things are less than the Son, and are ordained and

(9) Rom. xiv. 20.   (10) Mat. xvi. 26.   (11) Rom. viii. 32.

directed for His honour and service : He that offered to us His heaven and His Kingdom, will also give us the necessary means to obtain the same; and He that gives us the state of perfection or of dignity in His holy Church, will likewise give us that which is requisite to comply with this obligation: lastly, He who gives me His own body and blood for meat to sustain the life of my soul, will be careful to give me those other meats which are incomparably less than this, and necessary to sustain the life of the body.

Colloquy.—O most liberal Giver, who, giving us that which is more, dost offer to give us that which is less to preserve the same : since Thou givest me such immense benefits, give me likewise light and perfect understanding to esteem them as I ought, and also grace to serve Thee and love Thee for them, that through this gratitude Thy benefits may always remain in me, world without end.   Amen.

4. I will ponder, lastly, how God our Lord, in saying that He had a provident care of our meat and raiment, likewise says to us that He has the same of our *lands*, *vines*, *olives*, *meadows*, flocks, flax, wool, silk, and of the worms which make it, and of all things which are necessary for this sustentation; and consequently from the same providence proceed rains, snows, winds, and all temporal goods which help thereto, so that all are the benefits of God our Lord, and effects of the care which He has of us; and if we trust in Him and serve Him, He will give us all these, since He gives us that which is more than all these.   In this confidence we are to lay aside all anxious solicitude, which the defect of water, of wind, or of other things brings to us, casting this care upon Almighty God, to whom the same properly belongs, saying:

Colloquy.—O God our Lord, since Thou hast given us a soul and body, standing in need of meat and raiment, vouchsafe to give, I humbly beseech Thee, these temporal goods, that we may with more confidence procure the eternal. Amen.

POINT III.

" Behold *the birds of the air*, for they neither sow, nor do they reap, nor gather into barns; and your heavenly Father feedeth them. Are not you of much more value than they ?"(12)

1. Here is to be pondered, first, the marvellous providence which God our Lord has *over the birds*, providing all with suitable sustenance, not only the great, but the little, and not only the tame, and such as are profitable to men, but also the savage and unprofitable, and which men abhor, such as are ravens, and the like; and so much does He glory of this Providence, that He said to Job:—"Who provideth food for the raven when her young ones cry to God, wandering about because they have no meat?"(13) As if He had said, I am He who with my providence prepare sufficient meat for the raven, though such a devourer, and little profitable in outward appearance; and when she forgets her young ones, I, as Father, sustain them, and hear the cry which they address to me in their necessity. If, therefore, your heavenly Father, says Christ our Lord, feeds the birds, not as their Father, but as their Lord, since they are not capable of being His sons, how much more will He sustain you that are His sons, and esteem you a great deal more than He esteems them? And if your Father hears the croaking of the crows, and takes compassion on their necessity, how much more will He hear your cries, and have compassion on your hunger, which of itself alone shall be a prayer and a cry, to move Him to give you sustenance for its relief ?

(12) Mat. vi. 26. Luc. xii. 7.
(13) Job. xxxviii. 41. Ps. cxlvi. 9.

Colloquy.—O most loving Father, let all the fowls of heaven praise Thee, and all men upon earth, for the providence which Thou hast of their food!   Let the birds with their songs, and men with their words of praise, publish Thy mercies for the care which Thou hast in relieving their miseries.   Amen.

2. Next I will ponder the marvellous *manner in which* the divine providence sustains the birds, which have no care to sow, or reap, nor barns, or garners, where to place their food; but the same Almighty God prepares the meat, of which each one stands in need, and gives them ability and industry to seek it, and bring it to their little ones. " Will the eagle," as the same Lord says, " mount up at thy commandment?......from thence she looketh for the prey, and her eyes behold afar off,"(14) and when she brings it to her young ones, they lick the blood which flows from that meat, and by it are sustained.   The swallows He sustains with flies and gnats, which they gather flying in the air, and with this food become fat, so that, both eating and playing, they enjoy with delight that which the Author of nature has provided for them.   Hence Christ our Lord infers, that we should lay aside excessive solicitude about sowing and reaping, and gathering over-great provisions into barns and garners, and confine ourselves to that moderate care which He Himself prescribes, for, He who provides all this for the birds of the air, will doubtless provide much better for His sons.

Colloquy.—O my soul, henceforth let thy anxious cares for ever cease, because with them thou dost offend the providence of thy heavenly Father, since He who sustains the birds without this solicitude, will also without it much better sustain thee.   O most loving Father, Thy providence shall be my principal sowing

(14) Job. xxxix. 27.

and my reaping, it shall be my barn and my garner, since without it all my anxiety will be in vain, but moderated with it they will be very profitable, for it will supply my defect of carefulness.

3. With the same providence God our Lord provides convenient sustenance for *the fishes of the sea*, and for the beasts of the earth, that there never may be wanting to them great abundance in due season, which caused holy David to say:—" The eyes of all hope in Thee, O Lord, and Thou givest them meat in due season. Thou openest Thy hand, and fillest with blessing every living creature." (15) Thou " givest to beasts their food," and the young lions go forth by night, " ut rapiant et quærant a Deo escam sibi," " seeking their meat from God." (16)

Colloquy.—O most sweet Saviour, who saidst with Thy most holy mouth :—" It is not good to take the bread of the children, and to cast it to the dogs ;"(17) if with so great care Thou givest food to the dogs, with how much greater wilt Thou give it to Thy sons ? If Thou satisfy the hunger of wild beasts, how wilt Thou not satisfy the hunger of men ? " Let the mercies of our Lord give glory to Him, and His wonderful works to the children of men ; for He hath satisfied the empty soul, and the hungry soul with good things."(18) " Who giveth food to all flesh, for His mercy endureth for ever."(19) O my soul, " cast," as David counsels thee, " thy care upon the Lord, and He shall sustain thee,"(20) and will not suffer thee to be tossed from one side to another, for His providence shall be the nurse which nurses thee, the shield which defends thee, the anchor which holds thee, and the crown which shall reward thee, world without end. Amen.

(15) Ps. cxliv. 15

(16) Ps. cxlvi. 9.   Ps. ciii. 21.   Job xxviii. 39.

(17) Mat. xv. 26.   (18) Ps. cvi. 8.

(19) Ps. cxxxv. 25.   (20) Ps. liv. 23.

POINT IV.

"Which of you, by taking thought, *can add to his stature* one cubit?" "If, then, ye be not able to do so much as the least thing, why are you solicitous for the rest?" (21)

1. In this sentence is to be considered how the divine providence has disposed the stature of our body in such a manner that *it is not possible* by any solicitude or great anxiety, *to add aught* to that which God has ordained according to the complexion of every one. Whence Christ our Lord inferred, first, that as the divine providence, secretly by night and by day, causes our bodies to increase, and come to their due stature, while we know not the means by which this is done; so likewise He will provide necessary nourishment, and raiment fit and convenient for them; for having given the greater gift, He will not fail to give also that which is less, in order, if it be necessary, to preserve the greater. And often He bestows these lesser gifts by secret means, of which we are ignorant, that we may more clearly see the great care He has of us, and may learn to trust in His holy providence, and to serve Him with the greater diligence.

2. He infers, secondly, that since our solicitude is not able to add to our body one cubit, nor yet so much as one inch of height, and consequently, it would be vain to pretend a thing which is impossible, so *it is just that we should lay aside all inordinate care* concerning meat and apparel, as if we could procure them by ourselves alone, for this also would be vain solicitude, since without the providence of God we cannot obtain them. For if, as He says, you be not able to do so much as the least thing, for the rest why are you careful? Since without me you can

<hr>

(21) Mat. vi. 27. Luc. xii. 26.

effect nothing, and I undertake the charge to provide with all.

Colloquy.—O heavenly Father, I give Thee thanks that in Thy providence Thou hast not only given me a body, but also the augmentation and perfection of it, and that whether I sleep or watch, or be employed in other things, Thou always hast care of it. I therefore humbly beseech Thee, O Lord, that in the same manner Thou wouldst be careful for the augmentation and spiritual perfection of my soul, which is of much more value than my body; forasmuch as he who "planteth" or "watereth" is nothing, but only Thou "that givest the increase."(22)

3. From the selfsame verity I may also understand *how contented I ought to be* with the stature and propor-tion of the members which are allotted to me, for these also proceed from the divine providence for my profit, and for the glory of Him that gave them to me, who is glorified by little and great, by lean and fat, and every one ought to render Him thanks for the stature which he has received from Him; so that, he that is great in stature, ought not therefore to be vainly puffed up, nor he that is little, to be cast down, since it is most true, which David says:— " Ipse fecit nos, et non ipsi nos," " He hath made us, and not we ourselves," (23) which being so, who may say to Him, " Cur ita facis?" " Why dost thou so?" (24)

Colloquy.—O my Lord, it suffices that Thou hast done it, I am content, and if it were in my own hands to undo what Thou hast done, I would put it wholly into Thine, because nothing can afford me greater assurance than to rely entirely upon Thy government.

(22) 1 Cor. iii. 7.

(23) Ps. xcix. 3.   (24) Job. ix. 12.

POINT V.

" And *for raiment, why are you solicitous?* consider the *lilies* of the field, how they grow: they labour not, neither do they spin. But I say to you, that not even Solomon in all his glory was arrayed as one of these. And if the grass of the field, which is to-day, and to-morrow is cast into the oven, God doth so clothe; how much more you, O ye of little faith?" (25)

1. With regard to this marvellous and divine doctrine, we may consider, first, that the divine providence provides for all living creatures, *raiment conformable* to their nature, for He clothes the fishes with scales, the birds with feathers, the other creatures with wool, or with tough skins, and the trees with hard rinds. But the divine providence went yet farther with respect to man, for, wanting all these things of his own nature, He clothed him marvellously with His grace, and adorned him in the state of innocency, with original justice, that by its virtue he might live, without any corporal vestment, and without either suffering hurt or being ashamed of his nakedness. But after Adam and Eve, by means of their sin had lost this garment, made themselves others of the leaves of trees to cover their nakedness, (26) the divine providence beholding how poorly they were clothed, presently provided them with better, and put upon them garments made from the skins of beasts, either by His own hands, or by the ministry of His angels. Thus He, at the same time, relieved their present necessity, and taught them how to clothe themselves for the future; and above all, made both them and us understand that their offence was not sufficient to make Him entirely withdraw His divine providence from us, nor utterly fail to furnish us with

(25) Mat. vi. 28.   Luc. xii. 27.   (26) Gen. ii. 25.

garments convenient for the state of sinners, as He had before given such as were adapted to the state of the just.

Colloquy.—O most loving and most gentle Father, who will not love Thee for so loving a providence as Thou bearest towards us?   It was no marvel that since Thou clothedst all living creatures, Thou didst likewise clothe man, but that which makes me most to wonder is, that men, having made themselves worse than beasts through sin, yet Thou dost not deprive them of Thy divine providence.   He who had rent the most rich garment of original justice, was worthy. to remain naked everlastingly, with perpetual confusion both of soul and body; but Thy infinite mercy clothed his body with the skins of dead beasts, desiring to clothe his soul with Thy grace by holy penance. Let my soul and body, O Lord, for ever praise Thee for the care which Thou hast to give them convenient clothing, and let both of them wholly employ themselves in Thy holy service; for if Thou hast so great care of sinners who offend Thee, how much greater wilt Thou have of the just who serve Thee?

2. The second point will be to consider how Christ our Lord, in order to prevent excessive solicitude concerning apparel, brings us for an example His providence *in clothing the lilies*, and other flowers of the field; not those which grow in gardens, by the care and industry of men, but those which grow in the open field, which have no need of spinning, as women do to clothe themselves, nor yet of labouring, as men do to gain their garments, but by the only providence of the Creator, are born clothed with such surpassing beauty, that Solomon, in all the height of his glory, was never so gloriously arrayed.   He, therefore, who has so great care to clothe the lilies and grass of the field, which to-day is, and to-morrow withers, and is cast

into the fire, how much greater care will He have of man, whose life is longer, and who was not created for the fire, but to inherit the glory of heaven.

Colloquy.—O my soul, if the princes of the world, although wiser and mightier than the famous Solomon, yet cannot clothe themselves so gloriously as God clothes a little lily, it is much better " to trust in the Lord, than to trust in princes,"(27) since Thou mayest receive of Him that which they all cannot give thee.

3. I will ponder, thirdly, *two causes* why Christ our Lord brought not for an example of this providence the clothing which He gives to fishes, birds, and to brute beasts, but to the lilies, which to-day are, and to-morrow are cast into the fire.   i. The first was to signify the liberality of His providence, in giving us not only necessary clothing, which might have sufficed, although it was rough, and made of the skins of brute beasts, but has provided us also with *costly and shining garments* to adorn our persons with, according to the requirements of our condition; for He has given us velvets, silks, and other precious stuffs, which, yet we are not to use for vanity, but for the glory of Him that gave them.   ii. The second mystical cause was to signify the liberality of His providence in distributing these precious garments, not only to the just, who are elected for the Kingdom of heaven, but likewise to *worldlings*, who are as grass, which to-day flourishes, and to-morrow is cast into the furnace and fire of hell, that so it may appear, that He who is so liberal towards the reprobate, will be much more so towards the elect; for if He clothes with so great glory those who are to be the fuel of everlasting fire, with how much greater glory will He clothe those who are to become citizens of His celestial kingdom?

(27) Ps. cxvii. 8.

Colloquy.—O my glory, I give Thee thanks for the glorious garments which Thou givest to Thy creatures, to show the providence Thou hast over them. With a glad and cheerful mind do I renounce for the love of Thee all garments of temporal glory, desiring that Thou wouldst clothe my soul with the precious garment of Thy grace, and afterwards with that of Thine eternal glory. Amen.

POINT VI.

" *Be not solicitous*, therefore, saying, what shall we eat, or what shall we drink, or wherewith shall we be clothed?" "and be not lifted up on high." " For after all these things do the heathen seek: for your Father knoweth that you have need of all these things." (28)

1. First I will consider the great desire which Christ our Lord had, that His disciples should *lay aside all excessive solicitude* for these temporal things, and trust in God, who has the care of them; and this desire He signified by repeating so often, that we should not be solicitous for meat, or much less drink: and St. Luke adds, that we must not be lifted up on high; in which words our Lord prohibits excessive solicitude for certain things, which belong to His holy providence. i. That we be not anxious of the glory, honour, fame, dignities, offices, or high places of the world. ii. That we exalt not ourselves on account of the goods which God gives us, comparing ourselves with our betters, and preferring ourselves before them. (29) iii. That we aspire not in any matter after that which is above our strength or merit, seeking a higher place or loftier things than our littleness deserves. iv. That we walk not with elevated eyes, curiously beholding the signs of the planets, and of the heavens, as expecting from them the success of our designs. " Nec ea timea-

(28) Mat. vi. 31. Luc. xii 29.   (29) 1 Tim. vi. 17.

mus, quia nec malò possunt facere, nec benè:" " for they can neither do evil nor good." (30)   For the issues of things come not from them, but from the divine providence, in whose charge all things are, and the event of every great thing which we design, whether it is to be determined by the suffrages of men, or by lot, or by the will of kings, for nothing succeeds by chance, but by the providence of God, in whose " hands" our " lots are,"(31) and as the Wise man says, He directs them, and " sicut divisiones aquarum ita cor ejus in manu Domini: quocumque voluerit inclinabit illud," " the heart of the king is in the hand of the Lord, whithersoever He will He shall turn it;" (32) and He it is who principally distributes empires, popedoms, dignities, sees, benefices, and honourable offices of both commonwealths, ecclesiastical and secular.   And, although in these designs there may be mingled ambitions, pride, injustices, and other sin, which the divine providence permits for certain secret ends, yet He directs the success for His own sovereign purposes.   Whence it follows, that it is a very great injury to the divine providence to be solicitous for these things, with excessive anxieties and watchfulness, and to be wholly absorbed in inventing means, to bring our plans to a favourable issue; and a far greater injury is it to practise evil means in opposition to the divine will, for, as we shall presently show in that degree, that these things are convenient for me, the divine providence both can and will bestow them by other lawful means which I may take, or He Himself, without my knowledge may employ.   Hence Christ our Lord likewise said, " be not lifted up on high," that is to say, walk not with solicitude and anxiety, lifting up your eyes after that which is high,

(30) Jer. x. 5.

(31) Ps. xxx. 16.   (32) Prov. xxi. 1.

sighing, groaning, and wandering from one side to another, in search of ways to attain the height to which you aspire.

Colloquy.—O most high God, who dwellest on high, and thence by Thy providence beholdest and providest the things that are here below; I submit myself wholly to Thy divine disposal, and with great confidence will lift up mine eyes on high, where Thou art, hoping thence to obtain what is convenient for me, in order so to live here below on earth, that I may ascend to enjoy Thee above in heaven. Amen.

2. Then will I consider two admirable reasons which Christ our Lord alleged to take away this excessive solicitude.

i. The first reason is, "for all these things do the nations of the world seek;" (33) which is to say, to seek these things with such solicitude, and by such means, is proper to the Gentiles, who deny, as is said in Job, the divine providence, and of worldlings who deny it by their works, or of the imperfect, who by their little confidence in it become anxious like the infidels. (34)

Colloquy.—O sovereign master, whose doctrine the "Gentiles" hold for "foolishness,"(35) and the wise of the world for folly, blaspheming "whatever things they know not,"(36) because they attain not the secrets of Thy most high providence; illuminate them with Thy heavenly light, that they may both know it and worship it; and since I of Thy mercy believe it, grant that my life may so agree with my faith, that I may enjoy the admirable effects which proceed from it. Amen.

ii. The second reason, which is full of consolation, is,— "For your Father knoweth that you need all these things."

(33) Luc. xii. 30.   (34) Job. xxii. 13. Ps. lxxii. 13.
(35) 1 Cor. i. 23.   (36) Judæ Ep. 10.

In these words Christ our Lord declares three divine attributes, on which the confidence we ought to have in His holy providence is to be grounded;—His wisdom, to which all our necessities are most manifest;—His goodness, with which He will relieve them as a Father;—and His omnipotence to apply the remedy, as being a heavenly Father, and the Creator of all. This, therefore, being so, it is most certain that with His fatherly providence He will provide such relief for all as shall be most expedient for us. Whence I will infer a most effectual reason for preserving and maintaining peace, comfort, and consolation in all my undertakings, saying to myself :—

Colloquy.—O my soul, this thing which I desire is convenient for me, or it is not; if it be not convenient for me, because it will be an occasion to me of damage, both in soul and body, I will not have it, and I trust in Almighty God that He will, by His providence, hinder me from obtaining it. But if it be expedient for me, I know assuredly that with the same providence He will give it to me, because He desires my good as being a Father; knows the means of giving it to me as being wise; and can put His gracious purposes in execution, as Almighty. With this consideration, therefore, will I content myself, whatever may happen to me, that what Solomon says may be accomplished in me :—" Whatsoever shall befal the just man, it shall not make him sad,"(37) because he knows that all good proceeds from the providence of his heavenly Father. O most loving Father, henceforth do I desire to serve Thee with great peace, and with great gladness, in dependance upon Thy divine providence, since it suffices .me to believe that Thou knowest my necessities, and that I may securely hope that Thou wilt relieve them.

(37) Prov. xii. 21.

POINT VII.

*Of the providence which God has over those who first seek
the Kingdom of heaven.*

" *Seek ye*, therefore, *first, the Kingdom of God* and His
justice, and all these things shall be added unto you." (38)

1. In this marvellous sentence is declared the order which
we ought to observe in our affairs, in order to make ourselves worthy of God's providential care; and because
every word contains a special mystery, we will ponder
each one apart.

i. The first is "*primum,*" first seek the Kingdom of
God, that is to say, before all things, above all things, and
in the first and chiefest place, making it your first and
principal care to attain to it, and taking it for the last end
of your intentions, so that no other thing are you to
esteem more, or so much as this kingdom, nor to anything
inferior to this great object, as the end of your intentions.
ii. And He says not, "be careful," but "quærite," "*seek*,"
because anxious care, although it be in seeking this Kingdom, is not grateful to Almighty God, as has been said, because it is full of doubts and diffidences of His providence.
iii. The third word is, "regnum Dei,"(39) " *the Kingdom of
God;*" that is to say, the celestial and eternal Kingdom, in
which you will see God and reign with Him everlastingly;
and let this be in the first place, not only because it is for
your own good, but also in order that the same God may
reign in you, and that His Kingdom may be extended
throughout the world, and His name be sanctified by all
people. iv. But you are likewise to seek "Justitiam ejus,"
" *His justice*," i.e., the justice of God, or of His Kingdom,
which makes you just, and comprehends all the virtues
and works which are titles and means to obtain this king-

(38) Mat. vi. 33.   (39) Med. xv. p. 3.

dom, and to gain this crown of justice. And it is not without a mystical signification that Christ our Lord said not, "Seek first the Kingdom of God," and afterwards "His justice," but jointly says that in the first place we should seek both one and the other, because the one cannot be sought without the other, for he who says that he seeks the Kingdom of God, if he does not likewise seek justice and sanctity, deceives himself, for it avails little to desire to go to heaven if fit means be not used to this effect; for as the divine providence will not have us be excessively solicitous and anxious, so neither will He have us be remiss and careless.

Colloquy.—O eternal King, since Thou commandest me to seek Thy Kingdom and Thy justice, prevent me with Thy mercy, and assist me to practise those means whereby I may obtain them.   Amen.

v. The last word is, "*all these things shall be added unto you;*" in which Christ our Lord assures, by way of promise, those who first seek His Kingdom and His justice, that He will have a special care and providence over them, and will provide them all things necessary to enable them to pass their life with much more sweetness than the nations of the world, who seek these things with such anxiety, according to what David says:—" The rich have wanted and have suffered hunger, but they that seek the Lord shall not be deprived of any good;" (40) as if he had said, although those who trust in their riches come to such a pass as to suffer the want of many things, yet those who seek Almighty God, and wholly place their confidence in Him, no kind of good, either spiritual or corporal, shall be wanting to them, supposing it be good for them; and if sometimes they want food or bodily raiment, this shall be for the greater good of their soul.

(40) Ps. xxxiii. 11.

2. Moreover, there is yet another mystery implied in these words: Christ our Lord said not, "*seek in the second place*" these temporal things, for though it be lawful to seek them with moderate care, yet would He not lay us under an obligation to do so, the more to withdraw us from that great solicitude, which easily mingles itself with that which is moderate, so that he who seeks them ought to be, as St. Paul says, as if he sought them not, "and they that use this world as if they used it not," (41) taking away all perturbation and occasion of sin, so that, to seek them in this manner is to seek the justice of the Kingdom of God, since God has commanded us to use convenient means to seek what is necessary to avoid death. Neither did Christ our Lord say, all these things shall be given to you, but shall be "added," whence we may understand that Almighty God does not give these temporal things to the just as a principal recompense of their works, but as an addition, and as things accessory, inasmuch as they are means necessary for the preservation of life. Wherefore, in the day of payment He will no more put these in account than if He had not given them, because He accounts it no honour to Him to repay our services with such base rewards, and for the same reason I am to esteem it great baseness to serve Him in respect of them, or to seek them as the principal recompense of my works. Rather I am generously to seek the glory of this Lord, and of His Kingdom, leaving it to His providence to add such a measure of temporal things as shall please Him, with full resolution to serve Him in whatever manner He may handle me; I shall thus not only not lose things temporal, but if they be convenient for me, shall augment them. for he who serves God shall obtain so much the greater profit, in proportion as he seeks it the less.

(41) 1 Cor. vii. 31.

POINT VIII.

In confirmation of all that has been said, it is to be considered lastly, that so loving is the providence of Almighty God towards His elect, that when human and ordinary means to provide them with food and raiment, and other things necessary for their life are not possible, *He invents extraordinary* and miraculous means, to furnish them with all these things, like as He did with the Israelites during the space of forty years in the desert, giving them miraculously bread from heaven, drawing water out of the rock, and preserving their garments and shoes whole and entire, so that they failed not.(42)

1. But in particular I will ponder *three* miraculous means that the divine providence displayed in relieving Elias.

i. The first was, commanding the crows to "bring him bread and flesh in the morning, and bread and flesh in the evening;" who, though by nature so exceedingly ravenous, yet obeyed the commandment of Almighty God, and took it out of their own mouth to give it to the prophet. In this instance by the crows are signified great sinners, who are wont, by the inspiration of Almighty God, to sustain the just with their substance.

Colloquy.—O most loving Father, who would not obey Thee, leaving for Thy love that which gives him delight, since the very crows obey Thee, leaving that which was delightful to their taste, to give it to Thy friends? Whatever delights me, I will employ, dear Lord, only in Thy service, trusting in Thy providence, that if it should be needful, though men forsake me, the very beasts would serve me.

ii. The second manner was by the means of *a poor widow,* who had no more than a little meal and a little oil left,

(42) Exod. xvi. 35, et xvii. 6.   Deut. xxix. 5.   3 Reg. xvii. 6.

with which God commanded her to sustain Elias, and daily multiplied them miraculously, so that there was sufficient for the prophet, for herself, and for her son,(43) in testimony of the providence with which to sustain His servants, by means of other devout and alms-giving men, multiplying their goods in recompense of the alms which they bestow. For although the divine providence does indeed provide for all, yet with more care does He provide for those whom He takes for instruments of His work, giving to them because they give, and to the end that they may give to His poor.

iii. The third manner was by means of *an angel*, setting him bread and water to eat at such times as he lay asleep, and little thought of any such thing;(44) for the angels are ministers of the divine providence to nourish His elect in time of necessity, when human succour is wanting to them; like as another angel took the prophet Habaccuc by the hair of the head, as he carried food to his reapers, and brought him through the air to the place where Daniel was, in the den of lions, to give him to eat. And so Habacuc said:—" Daniel, servant of God, take the dinner that God has sent thee," and holy Daniel, admiring the infinite charity of Almighty God, said:—" Thou hast remembered me, O God, and hast not forsaken them that love Thee." (45)

Colloquy.—O God of my soul, I give Thee millions of thanks for the memory which Thou hast of Thy servants, protecting and sustaining all who trust in Thy mercy. Thou didst not content Thyself with stopping the mouths of the hungry lions, that they might not eat and devour Thy servant, but also tookest meat from the hungry reapers to give him to eat.

(43) 3 Reg. xvii. 6.   (44) 3 Reg. xix. 6.
(45) Dan. xiv. 37.

Blessed be Thy loving providence, and let all angels and men laud and praise Thee for it; augment in my heart, dear Lord, I beseech Thee, faith and confidence, that, performing with this faith what Thou commandest me, I may find by experience what Thou dost promise me.   Amen.

2. With this doctrine Religious persons ought to live much comforted, who, as Cassian says, leave all things to free themselves from cares and anxieties, casting themselves upon the divine providence, to follow Christ with the greater perfection.(46)

MEDITATION XXXII.

ON THE PROVIDENCE OF ALMIGHTY GOD CONCERNING THE ADVERSE THINGS OF THIS PRESENT LIFE, AND OF ALL EVILS, AS WELL OF PAIN AS OF OFFENCE.

POINT I.

The first point will be to consider that the divine providence comprehends under His government *all the adverse things that happen* in this life, and all the miseries which men suffer in soul and body, disposing and ordaining all the evils which are not sin, and permitting those which are not for very high and secret ends of His government for the good of His creatures, especially of men elected to the Kingdom of heaven. (1)   Hence St. Augustine says, that Almighty God by no means will consent to any kind of evil or defect in His works, but that He is so powerful and so good, " ut benefaceret etiam de malo,"—" that He would draw forth good even from evil;" (2) yea, and from one evil alone many goods: these may be reduced to three kinds.

(46) Collat. xix. c. 5, 6, et 8.
(1) S. Tho. i. p. q. xxii. art. 2, ad 3, et 4; et q. ciii. art. 7.
(2) Enchyr. c. i. tom. 3.

i. The first is, the *manifestation of His goodness* and omnipotence, of His justice and mercy, and of other attributes and perfections which are exercised in these miseries, and shine marvellously in those things which He does to avert or redress them.

ii. The second good is, the *preservation of the universal world*, which is so constituted that it cannot be preserved, except some things be destroyed, in order that others may be engendered or sustained; and hence proceeds the natural enmity of some beasts, fishes, and birds against others, some supplying meat and food to others.

iii. The third good is, the *profit of men themselves*, as well natural as supernatural, because both goods are intermixed with many miseries, and are perfected by them; for virtues exercise their operations in a more excellent manner, about the miseries of the soul and of the body, as well our own as other men's.

iv. Under these three kinds of goods are contained innumerable others, which the divine providence draws forth from our evils, as will be seen in the points ensuing, in which we will notice all the sorts of evils and afflictions which we suffer; yet am I for my comfort always to fix my eyes, not so much upon the evil which I suffer, as upon the good which the divine providence intends to work by its means, rejoicing to have a God so good and powerful, who draws forth good from my evils, and would not suffer any evil, if He could not and did not wish to draw good from it.

Colloquy.—O infinite good, I give Thee thanks for the goodness Thou showest in drawing forth good from our evils, permitting misery, that Thine infinite mercy may shine the more; manifest, dear Lord, I beseech Thee, such a providence towards me, as may entirely avert the evil of sin, and convert into good the evil of pain.   Amen.

POINT II.

1. The second point will be to consider the marvellous providence which Almighty God has touching the afflictions and temptations which come to us by means of the Devil, pondering principally *three* things.

i. God our Lord, in His providence, *gives permission to the Devil to afflict us*, without which leave he could not touch a hair of our garment, nor enter into the swine,(3) vile and unclean beasts though they be; yet evermore God gives this license within certain limits and restrictions, assigning the things in which he is to afflict us, the number of times, the grievousness of them, and how long they are to last, nor can he pass by so much as one only point beyond that which God permits him.

ii. The second thing is, that although the will of the Devil is most perverse, and that he asks license to tempt us in order to destroy us; notwithstanding, the divine providence assents not to his temptations, except for our good, *making use of the Devil's malice for our profit*, and intending by these temptations and afflictions to exercise us in mortification, humility, prayer, and in all the virtues contrary to the intention and drift of the Devil.   For if the Devil designs by temptation to drive me into luxury, Almighty God intends to ground me in perfect chastity; and if by afflictions he seeks to move me to impatience and desperation, Almighty God, by the very same, seeks to fortify me in patience and confidence.

iii. The third thing is, that the divine providence always *adapts the afflictions* and temptations which He resolves to send us to the measure of our strength in nature and in grace; so that, as the apostle says, He " will not suffer you

(3) Mat. viii. 31.

to be tempted above that which you are able,"(4) desiring us to issue from the combat with victory and profit; and for this purpose He provides us with very many admirable means, either by confessors and good advisers, or by the holy angels who resist the devils, or by secret inspirations, favouring and assisting us to attain the end of His providence, unless we ourselves be in fault.(5)

2. From these three considerations I will draw two important grounds of comfort in like afflictions.

i. Not to fix my eyes upon the Devil, who afflicts me, but upon God, who permits it, regarding the affliction as coming from His own most holy hand, since, though able to hinder and divert it, yet IIe does not divert it, and therefore will I say with holy Job:—"If we have received good things at the hand of God, why should we not receive evil?"(6) Our Lord by His providence has given me health, wealth, honour, peace, and gladness, and with the same providence takes it from me, giving leave and permission to the Devil to this effect; it ought, therefore, to be a sufficient ground for me to regard it as good that He has done it, IIis name, then, be blessed for what He has given me, and for what IIe takes from me, world without end. Amen.

ii. To set my eyes not on the evils which the Devil threatens, but on the goods which God intends to do me by their means, trusting in His providence that it will be more powerful to bring to pass what IIe intends, than the Devil to do what he desires. I will therefore turn away my eyes from my own weakness, in order not to be dismayed, and from the fierceness of the Devil, in order not to be affrighted, and will fix them on the omnipotence of God, and on the efficacy of His grace, beseeching Him by His providence to

(4) 1 Cor. x. 13.

(5) Med. xxvii. p. 5.   (6) Job ii. 10.

aid me so effectually, that I may attain the end of His sovereign intentions.

POINT III.

The third point will be to consider the providence of Christ our Lord concerning the *persecutions which come to us by the hands of men*, whether public tyrants or particular enemies, whether feigned friends or false brethren.

1. Here is to be pondered first, that the divine providence *holds the hands of all these our enemies* bound in such a manner, that without His license they cannot take from us the least hair of our head, as Christ our Lord said to His disciples:—" Are not two sparrows sold for a farthing; and not one of them shall fall to the ground without your Father," " and not one of them is forgotten before God." " But the very hairs of your head are all numbered; fear not, therefore, better are you than many sparrows."(7)   In these words Christ our Lord suggests two considerations very full of consolation, touching the divine providence.   i. The first is, that our Heavenly Father has a care of the sparrows, however worthless they may be, nor is forgetful of the least of them all, so that not one of them is entrapped in the snare, nor falls dead upon the earth without His providence.   How much greater care, therefore, will He have of us; of the sparrows He is only the Lord, and not the Father, but of us He is the Father as well as Lord; and the father who is careful of the life and health of his slaves, will have much greater care for his sons, and He that is not forgetful of a contemptible sparrow, will not be unmindful of man, especially if he be His friend, because one man alone is worth more than infinite sparrows; and if the fowler cannot take or kill a little sparrow without the will and permission of God,

(7) Mat. x. 29.   Luc. xii. 6.

much less can any tyrant afflict or kill the just, without the leave and permission of his heavenly Father.

ii. The second reason is, that Almighty God *counts the hairs of our head*, and has a care of them, even as men have of the things which they keep by count, so that none without His leave can take from us so much as one hair of this number. He, therefore, that has so great a care for the hairs of my head, which are the things of least value appertaining to man, and of very little importance, whether there be one more or one less, what greater providence will He have of my health, life, and honour, and of all weighty matters which concern me? And if my enemies cannot take from me even one hair without the permission of my heavenly Father, much less can they take from me my health, my honour, and my life; with this confidence, therefore, ought I to live in great contentment and security, as under the protection of so powerful and so loving a Lord, who says:—" He that toucheth you" in a hair of your head, " toucheth the apple of my eye."(8)

Colloquy.—O my beloved, keep me as men keep the apples of their eyes; put me, I beseech Thee, under Thy wings, as the birds put and cover their little ones under theirs, preserving me from my persecutors, as they keep them from theirs. Amen.

2. Hence I will proceed to consider secondly that the divine providence likewise permits us to be tempted by wicked men on account of the *great advantages which accrue to us from it*, so that He would not give such permission to our enemies, except to make them His instruments for bestowing these advantages upon us, just as He permits tyrants, in order that there may be renowned martyrs. In this two things are very particularly to be

(8) Zac. ii. 8. Psal. xvi. 8.

remarked. i. The first is, to draw from the persecutions that good which is wholly contrary to the evil, which our enemies intend by them; and even sometimes the means which they take to overthrow and cast us down, the same does Almighty God take to exalt us. ii. The second is, to convert the persecution to the good of our enemies themselves, doing them good by the same means which they have taken to do us hurt. Both which things were most apparent in the persecution of Joseph, whom God exalted to be the viceroy of Egypt, by the same means which his brethren took to overthrow him; and by the same means also vouchsafed to relieve them in their necessity, as the same Joseph declared, saying to them:—" You thought evil against me, but God turned that into good, that He might exalt me."(9)   And I came into Egypt not so much by your counsel as by the will of God, who for your good and for the good of many others, sent me into Egypt before you.   From this consideration I will derive comfort when I see myself persecuted, saying with David:—" I was dumb, and opened not my mouth, because Thou," Lord, " hast done it;"(10) and by Thy ordination and permission this affliction has befallen me; since Thou, therefore, hast done it, there is no reason I should complain of it.   And as the same David, when Semei cursed him, said to his servants:—" The Lord hath bid him curse David, and who is he that shall dare say, why hath he so done?...Let him alone, that he may curse as the Lord hath bidden him: Perhaps the Lord may look upon my affliction, and the Lord may render me good for the cursing of this day."(11)   Even so will I say to myself, Think not that this affliction or malediction has befallen thee by chance, for none can say or do hurt against thee without

(9) Gen. l. 20.

(10) Ps. xxxviii. 10.   (11) 2 Reg. xvi. 10.

God's permission; and think not that He gives it for thy detriment, since for this cause it is said that He commands it, that it may be for thy profit. And if He commands it in this manner, who may ask a reason of Him why He commands it? It suffices, O my Lord, if Thou commandest it, to make the command good, for Thy goverment is always just and upright.

POINT IV.

Fourthly is to be considered the Fatherly providence of our Lord, concerning all *corporal adversities*, whether general or particular, whether arising from natural causes alone, or from some malice or negligence of man, as tempests, floods, wars, pestilences, sicknesses, and the pains of the body, with other innumerable miseries and calamities which we suffer, all of which come by the appointment of divine providence, without which not so much as one could befall us; and hence a certain prophet said:—" Shall there be evil in the city which the Lord hath not done?"(12) But in particular I will consider how the divine providence very particularly has decreed all infirmities which happen to me, measuring them according to my strength, as regards the number, quality, intensity, and continuance of them, so that the humour which afflicts the head cannot pass to another part, nor yet increase, or last more hours than God has determined. Similarly the divine providence disposes of the event and success of cures, and of the skill or errors of physicians, so moving them to apply good or evil medicines, and in a fit or unfit season, that none of all these things are done by chance, in respect of our Lord, who avails Himself of them all in order to give effect to His intentions, for as the Wise man says:— " A Deo est omnis medela,"—" All healing is from God," (13) and the success of it, and in His hands are life and

(12) Amos iii. 6.　　　　　(13) Ecclus. xxxviii. 2, et xi. 14.

death, health and infirmity, and in His providence "He will strike and He will cure us," (14) "killeth and maketh alive, He bringeth down to hell, and bringeth back again." (15) Whence I will conclude that in like cases, although I may and ought to apply human means expedient to deliver me from these afflictions, yet my principal confidence ought not to be placed in them, but in God, to whom I am to have recourse by prayers, forasmuch as it is His providence that is to give a prosperous issue to the means which I shall use, or to apply others better.

2. Again, the divine providence disposes or permits these infirmities and afflictions of the body *for the good of the soul*, that she may be purified by them from her sins, overcome passions, exercise virtues, and obtain the perfection of them, because " Virtus in infirmitate perficitur,"— " Power," as the apostle says, " is made perfect in infirmity." (16) Hence regarding infirmity not so much as afflicting my body as proceeding from God, for my great profit, I ought to rejoice with the apostle, saying:— " Gladly, therefore, will I glory in my infirmities, that the power of Christ may dwell in me." And if the flesh refuse such afflictions, I will say to it with fervour of spirit, " The chalice which my Father hath given me shall I not drink of it?" (17) This infirmity and affliction, and the bitterness annexed to this chalice, are prescribed by the providence of my heavenly Father, and consequently are very profitable, and since it is His prescription for me to receive of this chalice, I will drink it, in order to do His will and not to depart from His commandment.

POINT V.

1. The fifth point will be to consider the providence which God our Lord exercises with regard to the miseries *of the soul*, which are of two sorts.

(14) Osee vi. 2.   (15) 1 Reg. ii. 6.
(16) 2 Cor. xii. 9.   (17) Joan. xviii. 11.

i. Some *involuntary*, such as the passions of the rebellious flesh against the spirit, the distractions of the imagination, and other like defects, which result from original sin, and which the providence of God has left not for our damage but for our exercise, and for the great advantages which arise from this war to those who maintain it with valour. And therefore our Lord in His Fatherly providence moderates the fury of these interior temptations, so that they may not overthrow us, and gives us sufficient grace to combat and overcome them.

ii. Other miseries are *voluntary*, proceeding from our own disordered free-will, as sins which are in nowise intended by the divine providence, but come without His order, and contradict the principal end of His government, which is our salvation and His own glory; yet does He permit them in order to leave man in his liberty, and by His infinite goodness and supreme providence draws great good from them. Sometimes He permits them for his sake who commits them, making him by this means more humble and distrustful of himself, more watchful for the time to come, and more fervent in the divine service. At other times He suffers them for the sake of others; for by the cruelty and malice of the wicked He exercises, polishes, and perfects the good, and always draws from them the manifestation of His goodness, either expecting and pardoning with mercy, or chastising severely by His justice; and all, as St. Paul says, He converts to the good of the elect, (18) who by the providence of our Lord draw humility from their own sins, and a warning from other men's; and from the pardon draw love and thankfulness to the divine mercy, and from punishment draw fear and reverence to the divine justice.

(18) Rom. viii. 28.

Colloquy.—O eternal God, whose providence converted the sin of Adam into the good of the whole world, taking from thence occasion to give unto us Thy Son for our Redeemer, convert, by Thy mercy, unto my good that which I, wretch that I am, have done for my evil.   O Redeemer of the world, who redeemest from sins by pardoning them, and by preserving from them : pardon me those I have committed, and preserve me from those I may commit, applying unto me by Thy loving providence the effects of Thy abundant redemption.   Amen.

2. I will ponder, lastly, the innumerable hidden benefits which proceed from the divine providence in all the things before recited, stopping innumerable evils of soul and body, particular and general, which will come to pass in the world, and which in particular would fall upon me, if God of His goodness did not divert them.   For the which, as already has been said, (19) I am to praise Him; and as I ask Him pardon of my "secret" (20) sins, which, though they be secret to me, yet are not secret to Him, and will one day be made manifest, so I am to give Him thanks for His secret benefits, which, though they be secret, yet cease not to be very great, and one day will be manifested to me, and shall make me much ashamed, unless I have been grateful for them.

Colloquy.—I give Thee thanks, O supreme bene.. factor, for the good which Thou dost me, delivering me secretly from the evils which I commit, and into the miseries whereinto I should fall, unless Thou didst hinder them.   Proceed, dear Lord, I beseech Thee, in this sovereign benefit, to the end that by such a providence, my perseverance in Thy grace may be certain, and I obtain a crown of glory.   Amen.

(19) Med. xxviii. p. 2.   (20) Ps. xviii. 13.

MEDITATION XXXIII.

POINT I.

1. The first shall be to consider that the divine providence has taken prayer for an instrument, and a most
principal means to *execute the designs of His government
towards men*, concerning the things aforesaid, and others
hereafter to be spoken of. (1)   For seeing the defaults
which we have of many goods, as well corporal as spiritual,
temporal and eternal, as also the multitude of evils,
whereto we are subject both in soul and body, not having
strength either to obtain the good or to deliver us from
the evil, He ordained that our prayer should serve as a
means both for the one and for the other, promising us
that He would grant us whatsoever we ask of Him, asking
it with the conditions it ought to be asked, and so Christ
our Lord says :—" Petite et accipietis,"—" Ask, and it
shall be given you, for any one that asketh receiveth." (2)
Wherein I will ponder that prayer is a means most effectual, most sweet, and most universal, to obtain all this.
It is most effectual because, as already has been said, (3) it
relies upon the word and promise of Almighty God, which
cannot fail, because He is most absolutely faithful in accomplishing what He says, and most powerful to perform
what He promises.   It is most sweet, for there is nothing
more sweet and more easy than to ask that which is wanting to me of Him that loves me, and commands me to ask

(1) S. Tho. 2. 2, q. xxxviii. art. 2, et 1; p. q. xxiii. art. 8.
(2) Mat. vii. 7.   Luc. xi. 10.   (3) Med. xviii. et xix. par. iv.

it of Him, and desires to give me what I ask more than I myself desire to receive it. It is most universal, because it is of force to purchase all the goods that are convenient for me, and to deliver me from all evils that are hurtful to me.

2. It is also a means of the divine providence for the *execution of the works which proceed from the divine attributes* and perfections, which already have been mentioned. For it is a means whereby the goodness of Almighty God communicates itself to us; His charity loves us, His mercy remedies us, His justice rewards us, and His omnipotency executes that which His wisdom has designed; and if it be needful He will alter and change the order of natural things; for prayer obtains that the divine omnipotency give sight to the blind, life to the dead, makes the heavens to obey, and alters one thing into another.

3. Finally, prayer is a means of the divine providence, *to adorn and perfect the creatures which He made* in the beginning of the world for the profit of man. For by the means of prayer He makes the earth fruitful, sends water from heaven, multiplies cattle, and beasts that are profitable, destroys the destructive, tames wild beasts, takes away plagues, purifies the air, and performs many other things proper to the omnipotence of God, who by this means communicates after such a manner as is possible for Him, even His power itself, to those which have no power at all, nor can do anything without Him.

Colloquy.—O Almighty and most powerful God, I give Thee thanks for the omnipotence which Thou hast imparted unto prayer, to obtain of Thy bounty and mercy that which Thy supreme providence has disposed. Make me attached, dear Lord, I beseech Thee, to this holy exercise, because I am well assured that if I remove not from me fervent prayer, Thou wilt never remove from me Thine abundant mercy.

POINT II.

1. The second shall be to consider that the divine providence *grants us* with great liberality what we ask of Him, *if it be profitable;* and with great charity denies us if it be hurtful, willing that prayer be a means unto us profitable, not damageable. This verity Christ our Lord declares to His disciples by this parable, saying:—" What man is there among you, of whom, if his son shall ask bread, will he reach him a stone? Or if he shall ask him fish, will he reach him a serpent? If you, then, being evil, know how to give good gifts to your children," " how much more will your Father in heaven, give the good Spirit to them that ask Him?" (4) In which parable Christ our Lord instructs us, that like as a father, when his son asks him something to eat, does not give unto him a stone, because it is merely unprofitable, nor yet a serpent, or a scorpion, because it is detrimental; even so, likewise, when I ask of our Lord, health, wealth, honour, pleasure, or any other temporal thing, if His Majesty see that it will not be for the profit, but to the prejudice of my soul, He does not give it me, because He loves me as a Father, and with the love of a Father, will not give unto His son that which shall be a stone of scandal unto him whereon to fall, or a serpent, which may poison him with malice, or a scorpion, which may bite his conscience with any sin, and to deny me this is to hear my prayer; for it is reason, when I ask any such like thing, that it be under this condition, viz., for my profit, and not for my hurt.

2. And after the same manner, as a father, when his

(4) Mat. vii. 9.　Luc. xi. 13.

son asks him to eat, gives him that which is necessary and convenient for him, as bread, eggs, and fish, even so our Lord will give unto us what we shall ask Him, not only what is necessary as bread, but what is *decent and convenient*, as eggs and fish. For if you, says He, being of your own nature, inclined to evil, have this good inclination to give unto your sons the goods which yourselves have received of God, how much more shall your heavenly Father, who of His own nature is good, and has an inclination to do good unto all, give His goods to those that ask Him, especially His good Spirit, viz., the spirit wherewith we are good, and which disposes us to receive the Holy Ghost, from whom all goodness proceeds, and with whom all things come that are for our profit.

Colloquy.—I give Thee thanks, O most loving Father, for the providence which Thou hast in denying me what is detrimental, and granting me what is profitable, and I give Thee thanks, as well for the one as for the other, since both the one and the other proceeds from Thine equal love; grant me, dear Lord, I beseech Thee, that I may always ask Thee what is grateful unto Thee, that Thou mayest always give me what I shall ask Thee for Thy glory, and for my own profit and utility. Amen.

3. I am also to ponder the infinite liberality of this sovereign providence which manifests itself, in *not dismissing empty the humble prayer* of His children, when by ignorance they ask Him ought which is *hurtful* to them, for in such manner does He deny them, that instead thereof He gives them some other thing more profitable unto them; like as when St. Paul craved three times of Almighty God, that He would take from him the "sting of the flesh," although He denied him that, yet He gave him a thing much better instead thereof, which was

His grace, to the end that the prick should not endamage, but profit him, pricking him to seek his salvation. For which cause St. Bernard said, "Let no man despise his prayer, since God Himself does not despise it; and before it issues forth of our mouth, has it written in His book."(5) And undoubtedly one of the two we may expect, either that He will give us that which we ask, or that which shall be more profitable to us.

Colloquy.— O God of my soul, I will not hold my prayer in little account, since Thou dost hold it in so great; and although it be of little worth as proceeding from me, yet it is of great worth as relying on Thee, in whom I trust that it shall never depart empty forth of Thy presence, but that Thou wilt either give me what I ask Thee, or that which worthily I ought to ask Thee.

POINT III.

1. The third shall be to consider the providence which God our Lord has in giving that which is demanded *in due time and season*, when it is more convenient for His own glory, and for our good, without anticipating or procrastinating the time; and for this cause peradventure did the same Lord say,—" In an acceptable time I have heard thee."(6) And holy men, who already knew somewhat of these times, demanded of God remedy of their necessities, as David did: " In tempore opportuno," " in a seasonable time." (7) And when they see themselves pressed, they beseech Almighty God, that the time wherein they pray, may be this convenient time wherein to be heard, as the same David said, " My prayer is to Thee, O Lord, for the time of Thy good pleasure, O God: in the multitude of Thy mercy, hear me in the truth of Thy salvation."(8) Hence

(5) Ser. v. in Quadrag.   (6) Isa. xlix. 8. 2 Cor. vi. 2.
(7) Ps. xxxi. 6.   (8) Ps. lxviii. 14.

it is, that when it is convenient, Almighty God will presently grant that which is asked, yea, He presently gives, if it be craved as is convenient, and if there be no impediment to receive it. And this does principally succeed unto us, when we ask Him pardon of our sins, for the obtaining of which all times are very convenient, and in these cases is accomplished that which Isaias says:—"Then shalt thou call, and the Lord shall hear; thou shalt cry and He will say, Here I am:" (9) and yet further adds, "Before they call, I will hear; as they are yet speaking, I will hear."(10) But at other times, although He hear and understand our petitions, and determine to grant what we require, yet does He defer the execution until another time more convenient, or because there is some other who craves the contrary, for another just respect; like as it succeeded to Daniel himself, who besought of God the liberty of his people, whom, though He heard immediately, yet He deferred the answer for one-and-twenty days, because another angel had demanded the contrary, for the good of the Persians, who held them captive:(11) or else defers it, because there is on our part some impediment of sin, ingratitude, or sloth, in asking it, or remissness in desiring it. And with this delay takes away the difficulty and augments the desire, and we are made worthy to receive that which we demand, and thus the whole is ordained for our profit.

Colloquy.—Thy paternal providence, O my Father, be ever praised, as well for the times Thou grantest what I demand Thee, as for the times Thou deferrest to grant it me; for I am assured, O my Lord, that if Thou delay to hear me, yet wilt Thou not be long; because although Thou stay contrary to my desire, yet

(9) Isa. lviii. 9.   (10) Isa. lxv. 24.   (11) Dan. x. 13.

Thou wilt not stay otherwise than will conform to what my necessity requires.(12)

2. I will ponder, secondly, the liberality of this our Lord, even then, when by His providence He delays to grant us that which we demand, because, if we persevere asking, *He will recompense that delay*, by granting us much more than what we asked. Of this point Christ our Lord advises us in the parable of the man, who went at midnight to the house of his friend, to desire that he would lend him three loaves, who, although he refused him the first time, yet he persevered in calling at his gate, until his friend opened unto him, as overcome by his importunity, and gave him not only three loaves, but also as many as he stood in need of, and those not lent, but freely given him. (13) In the same manner those who repair to the gates of Almighty God, who is our true friend, in every time and hour we repair unto Him, have their prayer heard, because Almighty God never sleeps; and although sometimes He returns distasteful answers, as He did to the Cananean woman, (14) in order to prove our faith and perseverance, yet if we persevere faithfully, He afterwards grants us much more than we demanded of Him. For He gives unto us the three loaves of faith hope, and charity, and all the other virtues necessary and convenient for our perfection; He likewise gives us those three daily loaves, the corporal, which sustains the body, the spiritual that of grace; and that of the most holy Sacrament, which sustains the soul.

Colloquy.—O my soul, repair confidently to the gates of Almighty God, who is Thy true friend; knock with instancy and perseverance, for He is not wearied of the importunate, but of the lukewarm; and if He sometimes seem to sleep, it is because He delights to

(12) Hab. ii. 3.　　(13) Luc. xi. 5.　　(14) Mat. xv. 26.

hear thee knock with greater fervour, to give thee what thou askest more abundantly."(15)

POINT IV.

The fourth shall be to consider how the divine providence, in this manner of prayer, extends itself *to all the men* that are in the world, without excluding any, because that general sentence of Christ our Lord speaks to all that say:—"Ask, and it shall be given you, seek, and you shall find, knock, and it shall be opened to you. For every one that asketh, receiveth; and he that seeketh, findeth; and to him that knocketh, it shall be opened." (16) In which promise marvellously shines the immense liberality and omnipotence of our great God; for having in the world innumerable men, charged with innumerable desires, and oppressed with innumerable necessities, all repairing innumerable times to His gates for remedy, He attends all, and hears the petitions of all, as if there were but one alone who asked of Him, nor is ever wearied or troubled that so many ask of Him, and so many things, and one contrary to another, and with so great importunity, but is delighted that they do ask of Him. Which delight He manifests by the repetition of these three words, which in a manner signify the same. Ask—seek—knock : as if He said, behold how much I desire that you ask of me, ask me, ask me, ask me. (17)

Colloquy.—O immense charity ! O infinite liberality! What does it import Thee, O my God, that men ask ought of Thee, that with so great desire Thou exhortest them to ask of Thee ? The princes of the world are wearied, and take it ill that anything is asked of them, and Thou because Thou art not asked. They give not entrance into their presence, unless to

(15) Ephes. iii. 20.   (16) Mat. viii. 7.   Luc. xi. 19.
(17) S. Aug. l. i. Retract. cap. 19.

the primates and nobles of the realm; Thou admittest the most vile and most despised of the world; they oftentimes either will not or cannot give that which is asked of them; Thou always wilt give that which is convenient, because Thou art good, and always canst give, because Thou art almighty; and since all enjoy Thine abundant liberality, let all praise and glorify Thee for the same.　Amen.

2. The second shall be to consider the desire which our Lord had, *that we should ask of Him with great fervour and affection,* so that our fervour and affection in asking, be like to that He has, that we ask Him: and for this, cause, by the often repetition of these selfsame words, ask, knock, and seek, He teaches us to ask with instancy and fervour, as if He should say, ask with faith and constancy, seek with great diligence, and knock with great perseverance, and cease not to ask until you obtain what you ask, because "we ought always to pray, and not to faint." (18)

3. The third shall be to ponder, that not only the just, *but sinners* also enjoy this providence, and are heard in their prayers, so that they ask things that are good, for a good end, and in a good manner, persevering and removing the impediments which hinder to receive what they ask, for otherwise the apostle will say unto them:—" You ask, and receive not, because you ask amiss." (19)　And Christ our Lord will say unto them that which He said unto the sons of Zebedee:—" You know not what you ask." (20)

Colloquy.—O most merciful God, who, with great delight dost " the will of them that fear" Thee, and " wilt hear their prayer;"(21) grant me that I may always do Thy holy will, so that I also may be worthy

(18)Luc. xviii. 1.
(19) Jac. iv. 3.　　(20) Mat. xx. 22.　　(21) Ps. cxliv. 19.

that Thou do mine, inasmuch as it is conformable to Thine.(22) O my soul, endeavour that thy heart do not reprehend thee of any sin, that thy confidence may increase, and thou be worthy to be heard; turn not away thy ears "from hearing the law" (23) of Almighty God, and the cry of the poor, lest Almighty God shut His to hear thy prayer.

4. I will ponder, lastly, the sweetness of the divine providence in applying this means, for not contenting Himself to exhort all generally, that they should pray, and prescribing the manner how to pray, as has been said, He does the same to every one in particular, by His secret inspirations, inspiring us what we are to ask, imprinting the desire and fervour of asking, and the reasons and titles we have to allege to obtain the same, according to that which the apostle St. Paul says:—"We know not what we should pray for as we ought, but the Spirit Himself asketh for us with unspeakable groanings." (24) And when we pray after this manner, it is a sign that God will grant us what we ask Him, for from the desire He has to grant it, proceeds the inspiration which suggests that we ask it. Therefore, the divine providence, as St. Gregory says, to bring to pass what it intends, uses as a means this of perfect prayer. (25)

Colloquy.—O divine Spirit, whose providence doth govern me, I give Thee thanks for the great care which Thou hast of me, that I do not fail in holy prayer. If I know not what I ought to ask, Thou dost teach me; if I forget, Thou dost put me in mind; if I grow slack, Thou dost excite; if I faint, Thou dost cherish me; if I would desist, Thou dost make me to persevere, asking, seeking, and knocking, until I receive and find what I intend. O most loving Father,

(22) 1 Joan. iii. 22. (23) Prov. xxviii. 9; et xxi. 18.
(24) Rom. viii. 26. (25) Lib. i. Dial. c. 8.

manifest always towards me this sovereign providence, giving me such a spirit in time of prayer, that I may call Thee Father, and may obtain of Thee what is convenient for me to become Thy perfect son, world without end.   Amen.

MEDITATION XXXIV.

ON THE PROVIDENCE OF ALMIGHTY GOD IN GIVING US ANGELS, TO GUARD US: AND THE GREAT GOODS CONTAINED IN THIS BENEFIT.

POINT I.

The first shall be to consider, how the divine providence ordained *that all men should have angels that might keep them*, and lead them in the way of eternal salvation, pondering the *motives* which induced God our Lord hereunto.

1. The first was, *to show the great love He bears to men*, and the great estimation and desire He has of their salvation, since He ordained that the angels, as St. Paul says, should be His " ministering spirits"(1) in this work, sending them from heaven to solicit the same, so that not only all the creatures of heaven and earth should serve man, but also those which are above heaven, and are greater than he in their nature, should occupy themselves in assisting him.   And for this cause Christ our Lord said:—"See that you despise not one of these little ones; for I say to you, that their angels in heaven always see the face of my Father, who is in heaven."(2)

Colloquy.—I give Thee thanks, O eternal Father, for this love and estimation which Thou hast of us, giving us for guardians the most familiar of Thy house. Now I do not, like David, wonder that " Thou hast subjected all things under" my " feet," making me " a

(1) Heb. i. 14.   '(2) Mat. xviii. 10.

little less" than " the angels,"(3) since Thou givest me the same angels, that they may serve me for the love of Thee; let me serve Thee, O my Lord, as they serve Thee in gratefulness for the good which, by Thee, they do to me.   Amen.

2. The second motive was, *because the divine providence saw our great imbecility*, and the great necessities and perils in which we live; and notwithstanding that He could by Himself alone have succoured us, yet would He make use of the angels for this effect, entrusting us to their care; hence holy David says:—" There shall no evil come to thee, nor shall the scourge come near thy dwelling, for He hath given His angels charge of thee, to keep thee in all thy ways: in their hands they shall bear thee up, lest perhaps thou dash thy foot against a stone.''(4) In which words David insinuates three singular favours. i. The first, that Almighty God has *committed the care of me*, not to one angel, but *to angels;* giving us to under stand that many have the care of me, as we shall see immediately.   ii. The second, that *they keep me*, " in omnibus viis," in all my ways and steps, in what part of the world soever I be and walk, by sea or by land, in all the affairs which I treat, and in all the works which I perform.   iii. The third, that *they bear me up* in the palms of their hands, that I do not stumble, preserving me from the occasions into which I may stumble and be in danger of falling, their hands serving me like a bed, wherein they carry me, protect me, lift me up from the earth, and defend me against the injuries of the air and the stumbling stones of the earth.

Colloquy.—O most loving and most delightful providence of our heavenly Father!   What thanks can I give Thee for the care Thou hast to remedy by such

(3) Ps. viii. 8.   (4) Ps. xc 10,12

means my great imbecility!　Oh that I had such a care to serve Thee, as Thy angels have to guard me! Oh that in all my paths and paces I might obey them faithfully, that I might be in all things pleasing to Thee!　Oh that I suffered myself to be always borne up in their hands, that Thou mightest never dismiss me from Thine!　O most blessed angels, have, I beseech you, a continual care of me, that neither evil approach me, nor chastisement overthrow me, nor I cease to serve Him faithfully, who never ceases to defend me.　Amen.

3. The third motive was, because Christ our Lord, seeing that the evil angels who had been cast from heaven were to persecute men with great rage and envy, provided, in His loving providence, that the good angels who remained in heaven should come *to defend them against the devils*, that man might have invisible spirits to defend him against the invisible enemies who molest him.(5)　And therefore in the state of innocence itself, as there was a devil who tempted our first parents, so was there an angel who guarded them and protected them; and if Eve had hearkened to the inspirations of the good angel, she would never have believed the words of the Devil.　And for the same cause did the divine providence ordain this, that so we might be defended against other enemies, who, although visible, yet are hidden and in secret, and therefore it was needful that we should likewise have some secret friend, who might discern them, and defend us against them. From all this I will gather a great confidence and courage against the devils, and against all other secret enemies, since I have on my side holy angels, much more powerful than they all.

Colloquy.—O my soul, if God opened thine eyes as He did Eliseus's servant,(6) to see how many more and

(5) S. Tho. i. p. q. cxiii. art. 4, ad. 2.　　　(6) 4 Reg. vi. 16.

better those are who fight for thee than against thee, thou wouldst doubtless conceive great courage in thy combat, and great confidence to overcome; praise and glorify, therefore, the providence of thy supreme captain, who has given thee so many and such valiant defenders against so many and so powerful enemies. Amen.

POINT II.

This sovereign providence extends itself to all the men that are in the world after a wonderful manner. Not only the predestinate, but the reprobate also, have angels to guard them; not only the just, but also sinners; not only Christians, but also Pagans and all kinds of infidels, without excluding any, no, not so much as the wicked Antichrist; (7) for as God desires "all men to be saved,"(8) so does He provide this means of salvation for all; and that none may attribute the same to his own merits, angels are assigned to all, even from the time that the soul is created and united with the body, or from the instant of their nativity.

1. But that which is more to be admired is, that one angel alone being sufficient to watch over men, who live in the same city, or in the same kingdom, yet for all this the divine providence would that *one angel should employ himself in the custody of each single man,* in what part and place of the world soever he were, and that he should serve this man alone as a perpetual assistant and companion all the days of his life, and never forsake him totally, although he were much rebellious to him.

Colloquy.—O most loving Father, what thanks shall I give Thee for so sovereign a benefit as Thou dost to men, commanding the angels, Thy beloved friends, that they should be helpers of Thine enemies? From

(7) S. Tho. i. p. q. cxiii. art. 4.   (8) 1 Tim. ii. 4.

my mother's womb was I born the child of wrath, and ever since Thou hast given charge of me to him who is a vessel of mercy, that he might labour to make me like himself.   I will serve Thee, O my Lord, as he serves Thee, that I may come to enjoy Thee as he enjoys Thee.   Amen.

· Hence I will conceive a great love and *estimation of my neighbour*, how vile and contemptible soever he be, since being so vile yet Almighty God gives him an angel, wholly dedicated to his custody, and for this cause Christ our Lord said:—" See that you despise not one of these little ones," since how little soever he seems to be, yet has he an angel very great and very powerful who protects him. And if I durst not murmur against a man who is absent before some great friend of his, nor yet injure him in the presence of him who is his helper or powerful protector, reason requires that I be not so bold as to do this, considering that my neighbour has an angel for his helper and protector, who is powerful to ask justice and vengeance of Almighty God against me, and to execute the same upon me without resistance.

2. The divine providence was not content to give to every one his angel guardian from the last choir of the lowest hierarchy, but *would also appoint Archangels and Principalities to govern and defend kings and princes*, and their kingdoms and cities, as also the universal Church, and the metropolitans thereof, Religions and provinces, monasteries and their prelates, and persons placed in dignity, that by means of this heavenly spirit they might execute the decrees of the divine government with greater sweetness; whence it follows that I have not one angel alone to guard me, but that the Archangel, or Principality, also aids me, who guards the kingdom and city in which I live, and he that defends the Church universal

and particular in which I abide, and the Religion and monastery in which I dwell, and that also who by reason of my dignity and state is assigned to me. Moreover, the Angels of the second hierarchy, the Virtues or Powers, which have power to repress the devils, likewise help me in temptation, and so sweet is the divine providence, that for the respect of man He has assigned angels, who attend to the preservation of corruptible things, that they never fail, and that man be not deprived of the goods which he receives from them, nor frustrated of the end for which God created them.

All this ought to be a motive to me of new praises, rejoicing in the love which Almighty God shows to us in so loving a providence, provoking my angel guardian, the Archangel, Principality, and Power, under whose government I remain, to give thanks in my behalf, and for the good which He does to infidels, who know Him not, nor are thankful to Him.

POINT III.

Consider *the delight and contentment with which the angels repair to this office of our custody,* without standing upon their own greatness and nobility, nor upon our littleness and vileness, pondering the *causes* of this contentment, and applying the same to ourselves to imitate them.

1. The first and principal cause is, that *God has so commanded them,* and this suffices; for as they love Him, so they desire very inwardly to accomplish everything which He commands, nor hold they aught for vile and base that is commanded by Almighty God, whom to serve is to reign, and therefore with as great contentment did the Angel Raphael, being " one of the seven" principal spirits " which stand before the Lord God," (9) serve Tobias in

(9) Tob. xii. 15.

his journey and in his lodgings, as if he had governed some great kingdom, or moved the starry heaven; for he considered not so much the thing commanded as Him who commanded the same; and as much contentment in his office does an angel take, who keeps a slave, as he that keeps an emperor or pope.

Colloquy.—O angels of God, "mighty in strength" (10) to perform that which is commanded, and to hear His word, fulfilling with promptitude whatsoever He wills; bless Him for this good affection which He has given to you, and beseech Him to assist me, that I may imitate you, glorying to obey and accomplish whatsoever it shall please Him to command me. Amen.

2. The second cause is, *the great charity and love which they bear towards men,* as it were to their neighbours, for seeing that Almighty God loves them, they cannot but love them also; and seeing that God loved them so much, as to make Himself Man for the love of them, they also take delight in loving us so much, as to make themselves servants for our sakes. For this cause St. John willing to adore one of them for his exceeding excellency, the angel would not consent to it, saying:—" See thou do it not; I am thy fellow servant and of thy brethren, who have the testimony of Jesus." (11) As if he had said, I glory not so much to be an angel as to be the servant of Jesus Christ, whose servants thou thyself and thy brethren are, and for whom I delight to serve as a servant, and not to be adored as a lord. And so far does this love proceed, that they not only love the servants of Almighty God, but even His very enemies, desiring to do good to them, in order to convert them into friends, and for this cause do they keep them with great contentment.

(10) Ps. cii. 20.   (11) Apoc. xix. 10, et xxii. 9.

3. From these two causes proceeds a third, namely, *the great desire they have to fill the seats of heaven*, which their companions have left empty; they use great diligence in procuring our salvation, so to lead us thither with them. Whence it is, that "over one sinner doing penance" they rejoice and make feasts in heaven; (12) and if they were capable of sorrow "the angels of peace" would "weep bitterly" (13) over the fall of the just, because nothing can move them to tears unless it be this. And for the same reason are they sorrowful after the manner aforesaid for our coldness, and rejoice for our fervour, and desire that we increase in all virtue, and, even above that which they themselves have; for so far are they from being envious, that our guardian angels rather rejoice that men be placed in heaven in a seat more high than the Cherubim and Seraphim themselves.

Colloquy.—Wherefore, O my soul, acknowledge the inflamed charity of these sovereign spirits, and strive to imitate the same without envy, sorrowing for those that sin, and rejoicing in those who become just, and joining in those who have attained to a greater height than thine. And since thy angel places his contentment in thy profit, do thou nothing that may offend him, nor omit to do the thing which may be grateful to him, ministering matter of joy to him, who with so great delight procures thy profit.

POINT IV.

1. The fourth shall be to consider the *providence and care which our guardian angels bear towards us*, and the great *spiritual good* which by their means comes to us. Pondering first the *cause* of this their great and special providence, which Christ our Lord touched when He said: —"For I say to you that their angels in heaven always

(12) Luc. xv. 10.   (13) Isa. xxxiii. 7.

see the face of my Father, who is in heaven." For it is from this sight they derive those three properties necessary for perfect providence, which we have already touched, that is to say, wisdom, goodness, and power, to know what they are to do in our behalf, to will the same with exceeding love, and to execute it with great ability. And when the will of God is not apparent to them, every one does what he judges most convenient for the good of him who is under his charge, although it be contrary to that which another intends; like as it happened to the angels guardians of the Jews and Persians; (14) yet when God reveals to them His holy will, and the disposition of His providence, presently they all agree to execute the same. (15) And in this faith I ought very firmly to root myself, calling to mind what Ecclesiasticus says:—"Say not before the angel, there is no providence, lest God be angry at thy words, and destroy all the works of thy hands;"(16) that is to say, consider thou art before thy angel, and say not in his presence that neither God nor he has any providence, for this may be cause why thou reap no profit thereby, but the chastisement which thy blasphemy of right deserves.

2. Hence I will ascend to ponder *the wonderful effects* of this providence of the angels in spiritual things, reducing them to three hierarchial acts, which St. Dionysius terms— " to purge, to illuminate, and to perfect,"(17) which acts the superior hierarchy exercises towards the middle, and the middle towards the interior, and these towards men, though sometimes extraordinarily, they also which are of the supreme hierarchy exercise those acts towards men.

i. According to which, therefore, the angels first *purify us from errors and sins,* helping us to issue out of them.

(14) Dan. x. 13.   (15) S. Tho. i. p. q. cxiii. art. 8.
(16) Ecclus. v. 5.   (17) Cap. iv. Col. Hier.

inspiring us to the exercises of the purgative way, like the Seraphim who, with a hot coal, purified the lips of the prophet Isaiah, saying:—" Behold this hath touched thy lips, and thy iniquities shall be taken away, and thy sins shall be cleansed."(18)

ii. They also *enlighten us*, illuminating our souls with verities, and adorning them with virtues, because with their interior illustrations they discover to us that which we know not, and draw us to perform that to which we are bound, and by this means we profit in the way which we call " illuminative."   At other times they inspire us to repair to the masters, who can instruct us and assist us, as it chanced to Cornelius, after the manner already declared (19).

iii. Thirdly, the angels *perfect us in all virtue*, and in the exercises of union with Almighty God, and so have a special care of our exercises of prayer, meditation, and contemplation, by means of which the effects aforesaid are obtained, and, as David says, " prevent"(20) us, soliciting us to pray, and accompanying us when we pray, quieting us in it, and helping us with fervour.   And, as St. John says in his Apocalypse, having ended our prayers, they represent them to Almighty God, and negotiate the despatch of them ;(21) wherefore, when I shall feel any sudden desire to fall to pray, I may presume that my angel invites me to pray, and it is but just that I obey; and when I pray, it ought to be done as David did it, " in the sight of the angels,"(22) praising God, adoring in His holy Temple, and confessing His holy name, taking them as witnesses, not to think in their presence what I would be ashamed to think in the presence of men, for otherwise they will not offer my prayers to Almighty God.

(18) Isa. vi. 7.   (19) Act. x. 5.   (20) Ps. lxxxvii. 14.
    (21) Apoc. viii. 3.   (22) Ps. cxxxvii. 1.

Colloquy.—O sovereign prince, who hast care to guard and protect me, purge me from vices, enlighten me with virtues, and perfect me with the union of charity; move me to pray, accompany me when I pray, and inflame my prayer with the fire of fervour, that it may ascend by thy hand to the presence of my Creator, and from thence may depart with the good despatch which I desire, uniting me with Him, world without end. Amen.

iv. Finally, from this providence it proceeds that the angels with particular care assist us to *remove the impediments of our salvation*, and, as it was revealed to St. John in his Apocalypse, fight most valorously for us against the devils, and assist in our battles and temptations to defend us.(23) And if we will avail ourselves of their valour and counsel, the victory will for certain be ours, and the Devil will remain overcome. And with the same valour they defend us from other enemies, for which cause David said that " the angel of the Lord shall encamp round about them that fear Him,"(24) and delivers them from all their tribulations, bringing with him whole armies of celestial soldiers, to receive them in the midst of them, and defend them from their enemies, as it happened to Eliseus.(25)

Colloquy.—I give you thanks, O most blessed spirits, for the care with which you hasten to my defence, since it is a thing most certain that you will not be less vigilant to defend me than the devils are to persecute me, nor will your charity be less solicitous for my good than their malice for my evil. And since that they like roaring lions(26) go about, encompassing me on all sides to devour me, come, I beseech you, like valiant lions, environing me also to defend

(23) Joan. xii. 7.

(24) Ps. xxxiii. 8.

(25) 4 Reg. vi. 17.

(26) 1 Pet. v. 8.

me, since it will be your honour, if by your help I bear away the victory.

POINT V.

1. The first shall be to consider the providence of the angels towards us, as *concerning corporal goods*, in order to the spiritual of our salvation; in regard of which they attend to our life, health, honour, substance, food, raiment, and other things necessary for our preservation, conformably to our estate; they also have a care of the estate itself, which it behoves us to hold, conformed to the disposition of the divine providence. They likewise assist us in sicknesses, sadnesses, perils, and the miseries which we suffer, either delivering us from them or moderating them, or comforting us, or inspiring those who can deliver and comfort us, and make intercession before Almighty God for us, without omitting to do all that which appertains to their office with great love and solicitude, after the manner that the angel Raphael did towards Tobias, whom he delivered from the fish, which would have devoured him, and animated him to take him, with whose flesh he made meat to sustain them all their journey;(27) of his heart they made use to drive away the devil Asmodeus, who sought to strangle him; and of his gall they made a medicine with which to heal his blind father; he recovered the money he went for, espoused him to a rich and honourable wife, filled him with temporal goods, gave him admirable counsels, both before and after his marriage, until he left him rich, contented, and prosperous in the house of his father. And that which this holy angel did visibly to Tobias, he does invisibly to all; for which cause I also may say to mine that which Tobias said to him:— "If I should give myself to be thy servant, I shall not make a worthy return for thy care."(28)

(27) Tob. vi. 4, et 6.   (28) Tob. ix. 2.

Colloquy.—O my most blessed angel, although I should deliver myself to be thy servant, yet should I not be worthy of thy loving providence; behold, therefore, here, how I deliver myself to be thy slave, go forward, therefore, with that which thou hast begun, taking a care of my soul and body, until thou place me in the house of my celestial Father, rich and blessed for evermore. Amen.

2. Hence I will ascend to ponder *what I ought to do towards my good angel* in thankfulness of the care which he has of me.

i. For first, it is reason to *have a frequent memory of him*, beholding him present, as a witness of my life, very wary to do nothing alone in the secret and hidden part of my house, or lodging, which may offend the eyes of so good a friend. And, as the apostle St. Paul says, that "therefore ought the woman to have power over her head,"(29) that is to say, ought to cover her head in the church, "because of the angels;" even so I will procure to be chaste, modest, temperate, and very composed in all my actions, public and private, out of respect of him who stands by my side, and will have frequent and familiar conversation with him. For as he performs towards me the office of a master, counsellor, governor, defender, friend, and companion, so it is reason there be correspondence of my part, speaking familiarly to him, sometimes as to a master, asking him light against my ignorance;—sometimes as a counsellor, asking him counsel in my doubts;—sometimes as to a defender, asking him favour in my perils;—sometimes as to a friend, asking him comfort in my calamities. Sometimes I will give him thanks for the favours he has done me; at other times I will rejoice for the goods he possesses; at other times I will praise Almighty God for the gifts

(29) 1 Cor. xi. 10.

He has given him.   And because sometimes he departs from me, and ascends to heaven, although he behold me from thence, and have a particular care of me, yet will I call upon him that he come to me, and stand by my side; and he is so loving, that he will do it, and will even give me interior testimonies of his presence by rejoicings, which my heart will feel by means thereof.(30)

ii. But above all, I will endeavour to *gain him for my friend at the hour of my death ;* for as he is an executor of the means of our predestination, which depends upon our perseverance, until a good and happy death, so there he uses greater diligence, that he may save me, as that of the Devil is greater to damn me.   And he who in life has served and obeyed him, will find him much more propitious and favourable to him in his death, not leaving him so much as a moment, until he bring him, like the soul of Lazarus, unto the bosom and repose of glory.   For all this it will be good to do him every day some kind of service, or to offer unto him some special prayers, saying:

Colloquy.—Hail, holy angel of Almighty God, most noble prince, my keeper and my loving master, all hail !   I rejoice that God has created thee with such excellent greatness, and sanctified thee with His grace, in which thou hast persevered until thou hast obtained glory.   I give thanks to Almighty God for the favours He has done thee ; and to thee, for the good thou hast done to me, and for the love and delight with which thou keepest me.   I commend to thee my body and my soul, my memory, my understanding, my appetites, and all my senses, that thou mayest keep me, direct, defend, and govern me, and mayest likewise purify, enlighten, and perfect me in such manner that being filled by thee with all good, I may persevere

(30) S. Tho. i. p. q. 113, art. 6, ad. 3.

always in grace, until together with thee I may see and enjoy Almighty God in His glory.   Amen.

- - -

MEDITATION XXXV.

ON THE PROVIDENCE OF ALMIGHTY GOD IN THE REPARATION OF THE WORLD BY THE INCARNATION OF CHRIST OUR LORD, AND OF HIS MARVELLOUS GOVERNMENT.

POINT I.

The first shall be to consider the most excellent *providence* which God our Lord had of *the salvation of men, lost by the sin of Adam*, comparing it with that which He had of Adam himself, and of his posterity, in the state of innocence.

1. For first, Almighty God *created Adam in grace and original justice, as head of all mankind*, with that condition, that if he persevered in His service, all his posterity should be born with the same grace, in which they should easily persevere all their life.(1)   For Almighty God took from them those three great impediments which now we suffer,—that is to say, the rebellion of the flesh against the spirit and of the passions against reason, the miseries of the mortal body, which oppress and weigh down the poor soul, and the persecutions and contradictions of the wicked, which disturb and trouble the good; for if at that time there had been any one evil, immediately God would have separated him from the rest.   And although He left them a tempter, which was the Devil, yet it was easy to overcome him, because he could not tempt at that time, as he can do now, altering the humours, nor awaking the passions or imaginations, but only proposing outwardly what

(1) S. Tho. i. p. q. lix. art. 1 et 2, et q. c. art. 1.

he intended, so to deceive them;(2) whose deceit, therefore, was most easy to be discerned, if they had made use of the knowledge and grace which God had given them. By all which is to be seen, the great desire which our Lord had, that Adam and his posterity should persevere in grace, and should obtain the crown of glory. And therefore I am to render many thanks to Him, since although I do not enjoy this providence at this present, yet His will was, that all the sons of Adam should enjoy the same.

2. Our Lord, seeing that by the sin of Adam the designs of His providence were disappointed for the salvation of men in that state, yet *did not for all this utterly forsake them, as they deserved*, but determined to use another means of providence to remedy them, much more excellent than the former; for His goodness is so great, that He had not suffered that Adam should sin with the loss of all mankind, unless He both could and would draw forth of this sin other goods exceedingly greater, manifesting His infinite charity in the love of His enemies, which until that time He had not done. For the goods which in the beginning of the world He did for angels and for men, although they had not merited the same, yet had they not demerited them, seeing that then they were not, and consequently were neither friends nor foes. But Adam sinning, although God deprived him of original justice, yet He left him the lordship of this visible world, and the sun, which was wont to rise only upon the good, began now also to rise upon the wicked, and the rain, which only fell before upon the just, fell also now upon sinners, and Almighty God began to be bountiful towards the ungrateful, to do good to those who served Him ill, and to pardon His enemies, that, being converted, they might again become His friends.

(2) Ibid. 2. 2. q. clxv.

3. To this end, out of His infinite mercy,—as has been pondered in the beginning of the second part,—of many means which He had, He chose the most glorious which His divine wisdom could invent, His omnipotency put in execution, or His goodness could will; so disposing, that of the posterity of Adam and Eve *there should be born another Man, which should also be God,* by whose merits the sin of Adam should be forgiven, and the damages repaired which had proceeded from the same. So that God would not only have a providence over such men as were lost, but also Himself would be He that should execute this providence, and that after an unspeakable manner, making Himself Man for their sakes. And He that was their governor and *invisible* head, would make Himself their governor and *visible* head, uniting human nature with His divine Person, honouring them infinitely more than before sin, and redressing the same with infinite means of His grace and mercy.

Colloquy.—" O happy sin, which deservedst to have such and so great a Redeemer!"(3)   O happy prevarication, which art repaired with so admirable a providence!   O celestial Father, to what farther pass may Thy providence come, than to give Thy Son for the remedy of Thy slave!   O most blessed Son of God, what could Thy wisdom more do than to clothe itself with mortal flesh, to quicken by Thy grace the flesh that was dead through sin!   O most Holy Spirit, what greater sign couldst Thou give of infinite charity than to give infinite gifts to him who is infinitely unworthy of them!   O most blessed Trinity, since Thou wouldst repair us according to the image of Jesus Christ, true God and true man, show to me Thy loving providence, repairing the image of my nature, defiled with

(3) Ecclus. ex. S. Greg.

sin, according to the lively similitude of Thy glory. Amen.

POINT II.

Hence I will ascend to consider in particular, that as the second Adam, Jesus Christ, infinitely exceeds the first, even so *the goods which come to us by means of the second, infinitely exceed those which should have come to us by the first*, if he had not sinned.

i. For, first, although the sons of Adam had been born in grace, yet those who are engendered by Christ in holy Baptism, *receive greater grace ;* for that Almighty God should have given to infants of His liberality, but this He gives to the same for His infinite merits, who gained the same by His Passion and death.

ii. Secondly, although the sons of Adam in that state had no conflict with their passions, and now the children of Christ have, yet the divine providence has so disposed the same, *that their victory may be the greater*, by how much the combat is the sharper, and that their work should be the more meritorious, by how much the difficulties they overcame were greater, our Redeemer assisting with more abundant grace those who are weaker.

iii. Thirdly, although the sons of Adam would not have died, nor endured those corporal miseries which now the sons of Christ suffer, yet the same Lord *so honours them, in clothing Himself with them*, that it is a great happiness to have them, because He converts them all into matter and exercise of heroic virtues, whose excellent acts should have ceased in that other state, for there should have been no occasions of poverty and patience, nor of martyrd m and the love of enemies, nor of resignation in a thing so dearly beloved as is health and life.

iv. Finally, the greatness of this mercy infinitely surpasses the greatness of the misery which the sin of Adam caused, since, as the apostle says, *the fault had not so great force as had the gift*, nor yet could Adam bring us so much hurt, but that Christ could bring us greater profit,(4) pardoning us the sin which we inherit by him, and those other sins which we afterwards commit of our own will, and doing to us so many favours after we had been so prodigal of so many goods, that those who had been in that state might in many things envy the excellencies, sacraments, and sacrifices which we have in this by the merits of our Redeemer.

Colloquy.—O most sweet Redeemer, I give Thee as many thanks as I possibly can for the fatherly providence which Thou hast of us, supplying the felicity of the state of innocency with the abundance of Thy divine grace, which Thou givest to us. Dear Lord, I had rather live with Thee in the state of war, than without Thee in the state of peace, for peace without Thee is lost in one day, and war, with Thy grace, will obtain an everlasting peace.

POINT III.

1. The third shall be to consider the sovereign providence which shines *in the government of Christ our Lord*, together with the *properties* and marvellous effects of it, reducing them to four, described by St. Paul, when he says of Christ our Lord:—" Who of God is made unto us, wisdom, and justice, and sanctification, and redemption." (5)

i. He " is made unto us *wisdom*," because He is the wise governor, " in whom are hid all the treasures of wisdom and knowledge"(6) of Almighty God, with which He governs without error, with great efficacy and with great

(4) Rom. v. 15.   (5) 1 Cor. i. 30.
(6) Colos. ii. 3.

sweetness, and knows the inclinations of all, and offers to every one grace and succour powerful to overcome evil and to follow good with perfection; and His government tends to this, to make us wise, not with worldly and earthly wisdom, but with divine, communicating the same in great abundance to His servants.(7) For which cause Isaias said, that in the time of His government the earth should "be filled with the knowledge of the Lord,"(8) and that all His children should be instructed of our Lord, who jointly should be our governor and master, teaching us the necessary truths for our salvation, and governing us accordingly, that we may obtain the same.

Colloquy.—O most wise governor, who, being the wisdom of the angels in heaven, madest Thyself the wisdom of men on earth, setting before them Thine own life and doctrine, Thine examples and words; direct me, I beseech Thee, with this Thy wisdom, that I lose not the end which Thou intendest by Thy providence. Amen.

ii. Christ our Lord is "unto us" "*justice*,"(9) because He is a most just governor, and is by excellency called "just," in whom no injustice can be found, and always justifies His works with the will of His eternal Father, and consequently His government is always with justice and equity, without the injury of any, or accepting of persons, not wresting justice for human respects, but giving to every one what he deserves, rewarding the good and chastising the wicked, as the universal judge of all, although His desire is more so to govern, that He may reward with a crown of justice than chastise with the zeal of vengeance. And hence it is that His government is ordained to justify men with true justice, making them before Almighty God just

<hr>

(7) Jac. i. 5.   (8) Isa. xi. 9, et liv. 13.
(9) Isa. xlv. 8, et passim.

and clean from all sin, and replenishing them with that peace which accompanies justice, for which cause David said:—" In His days there shall spring up justice and abundance of peace;"(10) and those who shall suffer themselves to be governed by Him shall obtain, as Isaias says, a flood of peace and a sea of justice.(11)

Colloquy.—O most just governor, Thou shalt be my justice, because Thou dost justify me with Thy grace, which Thou of justice hast merited for me, and helpest me to merit by justice the crown of glory ; Thy works are my justice, because they merit the pardon of my offences ; they are the satisfaction of the pains which I am indebted for them ; they are the title for which my prayers are to be heard ; and lastly, are my right to obtain the Kingdom of heaven. Dear Lord, I humbly beseech Thee, in virtue thereof, to assist me to imitate them, that I also may be just in my works, as Thou wast just in Thine.   Amen.

iii. Christ our Lord is "unto us" "*sanctification*," because He is a most holy governor, and the "Saint of saints." (12) in whom are the treasures of holiness, of whose " fulness we all have received,"(13) not only justice, which cleanses from sin, but also holiness; that is to say, great augmentation of graces, virtues, and celestial gifts, with great stability to persevere in them.   And to this end His holy government goes accompanied with holy laws, holy counsels, and holy examples, and therefore He says to all: —" You shall be holy, for I am holy," and " Be ye therefore perfect, as also your heavenly Father is perfect."(14)

Colloquy.—O most holy governor, be Thou my sanctification, sanctifying me " in truth"(15) with Thy

(10) Ps. lxxi. 7.

(11) Isa. xlviii. 18.   (12) Dan. ix. 24.   (13) Joan. i. 16.
  (14) 1 Pet. i. 16. Mat. v. 48.   (15) Joan. xvii. 19.

most evident verities, since Thou didst sanctify Thyself
for me, offering Thyself to death to fill me with them.

iv. Christ our Lord is "unto us" "*redemption*," because
He is a most powerful governor, to deliver us from the
servitude of the Devil, of sin, of the flesh, and of her passions, from the world and from its tyrannies, placing us in
the liberty of spirit proper to the sons of God.(16)   And
to this His government is directed, because He is also the
Redeemer of the world, redeeming those He governs, and
governing those whom He redeems, that they may attain
the end of their redemption, which is the perfect "adoption of sons"(17) of God, exempt from all misery, with the
inheritance of glory.

Colloquy.—O most loving governor, I give Thee
thanks that Thou art my "redemption," delivering
my soul from hell, my spirit from the slavery of the
flesh, my flesh from the miseries it suffers, and in time
wilt also free it from death and corruption : apply to
me, dear Lord, I beseech Thee, the fruit of Thine
abundant redemption, that, redeemed by Thy grace, I
may for ever enjoy Thee in Thy glory.   Amen.

2. These four excellencies of Christ our Lord, after the
manner they have been set down, *I am always to carry in
my memory,* saying oftentimes to Him with great affection, "Most sweet Jesus, be "unto me wisdom, justice,
sanctification, and redemption," applying to me effectually
that which Thou art to all, with so great sufficiency.

(The other points which touch this benefit are set down
largely in the meditations of the second, third, and fourth
Parts, besides many other things which have been handled
in this Part, in the meditations of the goodness, charity,
and mercy of Almighty God.)

(16) Rom. vi. 18.   (17) Rom. viii. 15.

MEDITATION XXXVI.

ON THE PROVIDENCE OF ALMIGHTY GOD IN THE FOUNDATION OF HIS CHURCH,
WITH ALL NECESSARY MEANS FOR OUR SALVATION, AND
THE EXCELLENCE OF THESE BENEFITS.

This meditation we will ground upon the saying of the
Wiseman, that "Wisdom hath built herself a house, she
hath hewn her out seven pillars. She hath slain her vic-
tims, mingled her wine, and set forth her table. She hath
sent her maids to invite to the tower, and to the walls of
the city," and in her name says to them, "Come, eat ye
my bread, and drink the wine which I have mingled for
you." (1)

POINT I.

1. The first shall be to consider that God our Lord, by
His infinite wisdom, *built a "house" for Himself in the
midst of this world, "which is the Church of the living
God,"* (2) providing her with admirable providence, of all
things necessary for the salvation of all those which should
live within her, viz., that they might be delivered from
the two greatest miseries which may possibly be in this
life and in the other, which are sin and hell, and might
obtain two felicities contrary to them, which are grace and
glory.

2. The greatness of this providence may be pondered
by *the greatness of the end* for which this house and Church
is ordained, which is *the glory of the same God,* and of
Jesus Christ our Redeemer, that so it might be His house
of recreation here in earth, and His special habitation,
wherein He might inhabit and converse with the sons of

(1) Prov. ix. 15.   (2) 1 Tim. iii. 15.

men, as also that the same men might be saved, and obtain life eternal; and since the end is as high as high may be, so likewise ought the means to be, and the providence of Almighty God, in disposing them for such an end; for if the providence which He has over man is so great and admirable, as has been said, concerning the natural of his body and his temporal life, how much more great and admirable will that be which He has of him concerning the supernatural of his soul, and of life eternal? And He that furnished him with so many means to preserve the life of the body, which to-day is, and to-morrow perishes, how much more will He provide him of most apt means, to gain and preserve the spiritual life of the soul, which is never to perish? Out of doubt, by as much as the spirit surpasses the flesh, and eternal temporal, so much does the one providence surpass the other; and as St. Paul says,—" hath God care of oxen," that He commands in his law,—" Thou shalt not muzzle the mouth of the ox that treadeth out the corn?" (3) giving to understand, that although Almighty God have indeed care of oxen, yet all is in order to men, of whom He has so great care, that this other is as if it were not. And even so all the care which God our Lord has of the body, and of the corporal and temporal life, and the means which He has given us by His providence to preserve the same, is in order to the soul, and to life eternal, in comparison of which care this other is very little. And for this cause the Wise man says, that the divine Wisdom has care of her elect, " et in omni providentia occurrat," and " meeteth them with all providence."(4) For which I am to give many thanks to our Lord, confessing my own unworthiness, and the greatness of this benefit, saying that which Tobias said to

(3) 1 Cor. ix. 9.   (4) Sap. vi. 17.

the angel:—"If I should give myself to be thy servant, I shall not make a worthy return for thy care." (5)

Colloquy.—O most loving Father, although I should deliver myself to Thee for Thy slave, yet shall I not be worthy of Thy providence. I offer myself to Thee to be Thy perpetual servant, since with Thy providence Thou dost govern me, not as a servant, but as a son.

POINT II.

Secondly are to be considered *the admirable means* which the divine providence has placed in His Church for *our salvation*, reducing them to *seven*, like to seven most strong and beautiful pillars of this house.

i. The first is true *faith*, and knowledge of the true God, and of the Mediator and Redeemer, which He has given to us, which is His Son Jesus Christ; (6) the knowledge of whom is the beginning and foundation of life eternal, because, without this faith "it is impossible," as St. Paul says, "to please God," and without the name of this our Lord there is no salvation under heaven. (7)

ii. The second means is, a most pure and *most holy law*, in which are contained all the commandments of things that are necessary to obtain life eternal, and all the counsels which may help us to purchase the same with security and perfection.

iii. The third is a most observant *religion*, with sacrifices and exterior ceremonies, ordained for the honour and worship of the true God. And although the ancient Church had a temple with many sacrifices, yet now our Church has many temples, with one sole Sacrifice, which is infinitely more worth than all those others, because in her is offered the same body and blood of our Redeemer, under the species of bread and wine.

(5) Tob. ix. 3.   (6) Joan. xvii. 3.   (7) Heb. xi. 6.   Act. iv. 12.

iv. The fourth means is, *seven* most excellent *sacraments*, ordained for the remedy and medicine of our sins, amongst which one is, a table of the best bread, and of the best wine, which God could possibly set before us for our sustenance; and all the seven are like seven exterior pillars, upon which the greatness and stability of this house rely.

v. The fifth is *seven* true and solid *virtues, faith, hope*, and *charity, prudence, justice, fortitude*, and *temperance*. And seven gifts of the Holy Ghost, which are as seven interior pillars, on which depend the sanctity and beauty of this spiritual building, with admirable exercises of virtuous works, in order towards God, towards one's neighbour, and towards oneself.

vi. The sixth is, assured and most excellent *promises of life eternal*, and of the incomparable rewards, which both in this life and in the other are given to the truly virtuous that live in this house, together with terrible threatenings of hell, and horrible chastisements, both in this life and in the other, inflicted upon those who live out of her, or live not in her as they ought.

vii. The seventh means is the *Sacred Scripture*, in which are revealed all those things hitherto said, and is like some delightful table of bread and wine, for the sustenance of holy souls, who, by faith and the verities which are written in it by the revelation of God, sustain, comfort, and encourage themselves until they attain the eternal life contained in them, according to the words of the apostle, saying:—" For what things soever were written, were written for our learning, that, through patience, and the comfort of the Scriptures, we may have hope." (8)

Pondering these seven means which the divine provi-

(8) Rom. xv. 4.

dence has ordained for our salvation in the house of His Church, and beholding myself within the same, as an inhabitant, who may enjoy them all to save me, I will glorify this our Lord, for so sovereign a favour, as He has vouchsafed me, saying:—

Colloquy.—Seven thousand times, dear Lord, let the angels of heaven praise Thee for the seven means which Thou hast given me here on earth for my salvation ; and since by Thy grace Thou hast made me an inhabitant of this house, grant me to enjoy her goods, living in such manner, that I may come to be an inhabitant of the house which Thou hast in heaven. Amen.

POINT III.

1. The third shall be to consider how this Church and House of the living God is *but one* in the whole world, in which all those may save themselves who shall make use of her means, and out of her all infallibly shall perish. In the same manner, that as in the time of the flood, there was no more than *one* ark, and all those which were out of her perished, and those which entered into her were saved, (9) even so, now there is no more than *one Church*, one faith, one religion, one law, the same sacraments and Sacrifice, one sacred Scripture, and one means of our salvation; (10) like as there is no more than one God, one Creator, and Sanctifier—one last end of all—and one Mediator of all. The head, therefore, being but one, the mystical body ought to be no more but one, which is the congregation of the faithful, who believe and profess the seven things aforesaid, and all infidels, in what other law and sect soever they live, will be condemned everlastingly.

2. Hence also it is, that like as the ark of Noe *had but one door*, even so, to enter into the house of Holy Church,

(9) Gen. vi. 14. Gen. vii. 23. 1 Pet. iii. 20.　　(10) Ephes. iv. 5.

there is *one only door*, which is Christ our Lord, and His faith, which we profess in holy baptism, according to that which the same Lord says:—"I am the door. By me if any man enter, he shall be saved." (11) And, "he that believeth, and is baptized, shall be saved: but he that believeth not shall be condemned." (12) Out of which consideration I may better understand the greatness of the benefit which God has done me by bringing me into this ark, leaving out of it innumerable infidels, who perish in the flood of infidelity;—and amongst Christians them-selves many infants do not obtain this happy lot, either because they die in their mother's wombs, or, after they are born, die without having applied unto them the sacra-ment of Baptism. And they not having demerited the same no more than I, nor I merited the same no more than they, yet would the divine providence deliver me from these perils, and that I should receive the benefit of Bap-tism, myself not knowing what I did receive, but Al-mighty God, of pure grace, making me His son, before I knew how to call Him Father. (13)

Colloquy.—O most loving Father, what thanks shall I give Thee for this so great a benefit; for before I knew to choose good and to reject evil, Thou tookest sin from me, and didst justify me with Thy grace, that I might "know how to refuse the evil, and to choose good;"(14) I knew not yet how to speak, when Thy fortitude destroyed in me the strength of Damascus, which is the Devil, casting him out of the possession which he had taken from the day of my conception; keep me, therefore, dear Lord, I do beseech Thee, in Thy Church militant, fighting therein in such manner that I may come to enjoy Thee in the triumphant, world without end. Amen.

(11) Joan. x. 9.   (12) Mar. xvi. 16.
(13) Isa. viii. 4.   (14) Isa. vii. 15.

MEDITATION XXXVII.

Concerning the sovereign *benefit of vocation* six things
are to be pondered.—i. Wherein it *consists.*—ii. *What goods*
it brings with it from heaven.—iii. By *what means* it is
effected.—iv. *To what persons* it extends itself.—v. *How*
long it lasts.—vi. And the *titles which bind us* to hearken
to the same.

POINT I.

1. The first shall be to consider that vocation is *an inspi-*
ration or illustration of the Holy Ghost. with which He
touches the heart of the sinner, and of His mere grace, without man's merits, prevents him, excites and helps to convert him, and to obtain the grace of justification.(1) Without this vocation he cannot by his own forces either enter
into the Church or go out of sin; for which cause Christ our
Lord said:—" No man can come to me unless the Father
who hath sent me draw him;"(2) and as Lazarus, when he
was dead in the sepulchre, had remained dead until he
had been converted into dust, if the voice of Christ had
not called him, saying:—" Lazarus, come forth;" (3) even
so I for ever should remain dead in my sins, if the voice
of divine inspiration did not call me, and help me to issue
out of them.

2. Hence it is that the divine vocation and inspiration
is the only instrument of the Holy Ghost, for all the means
of our sanctification. For it brings us from heaven the
gift of faith, without which it is impossible to please God,
and the virtue of hope, by which salvation enters, (4) and

(1) Trid. Sess. vi. Cap. 5.   (2) Joan. vi. 44.
(3) Joan. xi. 44.   (4) Rom. viii. 24.

the spirit of fear, which begins to cast forth sin, (5) and of sorrow and contrition, which break the heart for having committed the same, and the fire of charity, which consumes the rust of our offences, and the splendour of divine grace, which purifies and cleanses us from them. She is the seed by which we are engendered in the being of the sons of God by holy Baptism, which if we lose she is the seed to recover the same by holy Penance. And this benefit is bestowed upon us without any merits of ours, according to that which St. Paul says:—"God who hath called us by His holy calling, not according to our works, but according to His own purpose and grace, which was given us in Christ Jesus." (6)

Colloquy.—O eternal God, I give Thee thanks for this immense liberality of Thy loving providence, by which Thou sendest us from heaven " every best gift and every perfect gift, descending from the Father of lights."(7) If Thou hadst not called me, I had never arisen again from death; and if Thy inspiration had not prevented me without my deserts, I should long since have been punished as I deserved. And since by Thy only mercy Thou hast called me, I beseech Thee by the same to help me, that I may worthily answer to Thy holy vocation. Amen.

POINT II.

1. The second shall be to consider *those apt and wonderful means by which Christ our Lord brings to pass the vocation of men.* Some He calls by the means of preachers or confessors, or by discourse and conversation with devout persons;—others by the reading of good books, or seeing in others good examples;—some He draws by adversities and calamities, and others by prosperities and benefits; (8)

(5) Ecclus. i. 27.   (6) 2 Tim. i. 9.   (7) Jac. i. 17.
(8) S. Greg. Hom. xxxvi. in Evang. S. Greg. Naz. in sua vita.

some He calls by ordinary ways, suffering things to take their ordinary course, by success of which He takes occasion to convert them;—others He calls by extraordinary and miraculous means, using His omnipotency to recall them, for the force of love is incredible when it is conjoined with power; and because God loves men infinitely love moves His omnipotency to call and draw them to His service, as St. Augustine says, "miris modis," "after wondrous manners." (9) Of all which there are most evident examples in holy scripture, especially in the Gospel, as it appears in the vocations and parables, which have been meditated to this effect in the third and fifth parts. And applying this to myself, I will ponder the sovereign benefit which Almighty God has done to me, that having fallen into many grievous sins He has called me to penance by a thousand ways, sometimes hedging in my ways with thorns and repulses of adversity, that so I should return to Him; at other times drawing me with "the bands of love," (10) and with the chains of benefits, that He might wholly oblige me to His service;—at other times with sudden inspirations, bringing to my memory death, judgment, hell, heaven, and other innumerable motives, with which He ministers continual matter to my heart, that it open to Him. And notwithstanding that, oftentimes I have shut the gate against Him, and at other times, after I have admitted Him, have cast Him out of my possession, yet He has remained at the gate to return to call me, until I returned to open to Him, that so He might give me His grace and friendship. (11)

Colloquy.—O most loving Father, what thanks may I give Thee for this especial care which Thou hast of me! Blessed be Thy mercy, which so hast solicited

---

' (9) S. Aug. contra duas Epist. Pelag. c. 19.
(10) Osee xi. 4.   (11) Apoc. iii. 20. Cant. v. 2.

Thy providence, by which I beseech Thee to prosecute what Thou hast begun, to the end that I may attain life eternal. Amen.

2. *There is not any man in the whole world whom Almighty God does not call by one means or other;* for all the infidels of what sect soever they be, or in what place or corner soever of the world they live, all are under His holy providence. And as the sun of justice, Jesus Christ, arose for all, and the rain of His doctrine descended from heaven on all, and built the house of His Church for all, and placed the sacraments that are in her—even so He calls all, and by the dictates of natural light moves them to fly evil, and to follow good, and by His especial illustration "enlighteneth every man that cometh into the world" (12) with the use of reason, with desire that he receive His divine grace, and afterwards enter into His glory,—as He showed to St. Peter in the vision of the sheet, which descended from heaven, (13) as has been declared in the fifth part; and because many do not acknowledge this benefit, I am to glorify Him for them to whom He does it, saying:—

Colloquy.—O eternal Wisdom, who "preachest abroad, and utterest Thy voice in the streets,"(14) and corners of the world, calling to all passengers, that they come to Thy house to enjoy Thy banquets; I give Thee thanks for Thy sovereign providence with which Thou callest them, alledging to them so evident reasons, that they understand them, and so effectual as to move them to enter; oh that all obeyed Thee, that, entering into Thy school, all might obtain life eternal, world without end. Amen.

3. I will ponder, thirdly, that this providence *lasts towards all men, during the whole time of their life,* without

<hr>

(12) Joan. i. 9.　　　(13) Act. x. 11.　　　(14) Prov. i. 20.

forsaking any totally, or denying him the necessary means
of his salvation, but like a good father of a family, goes
forth to call every one into His vineyard, (15) and if at
the first he resist His vocation, He goes forth at another
time in his youth, and in his old age, and when he is
drawing near to death, and in every hour and moment
that he hears His calling He admits him into His friendship.
And although to those that are hardened in their sins He
is wont to deny those special favours, which are accustomed to molify their hearts, and for this cause is said to
have forsaken them, yet He never denies them sufficient
vocation and necessary means for their justification.

4. Hence I will take counsel *not to distrust of the salvation of any sinner*, how evil otherwise soever he be, and
much less of mine own, how much discouraged soever I
be, because both I myself, and all others, are under the
divine providence, who has us under His charge and protection, and he who to-day is rebellious, to-morrow will be
called with as great force as was the good thief, that
whether from the cross, or from the bed, he may go to
paradise.   Nevertheless, I must not grow careless, leaving
all to the divine providence, because if I take not care to
remove the impediments of the divine vocation, perhaps I
shall find myself deceived, although God will not be
deceived, because He ever attains the principal end of H's
glory, either justifying me if I consent, or chastising me if
I resist.

Colloquy.—O most loving Father, whose providence
has two arms of government,—one of mercy, to do
good to those who submit themselves to it,—and another of justice, to chastise those that are rebellious ;
put under my head the left hand of Thy justice, and
embrace me with the right hand of Thy mercy, sus-

(15) Mat. xx. 1.

taining me with the fear of Thy chastisements, that I resist Thee not, and encouraging me with the hope of Thy gifts, that I may obey Thee and subject myself to Thy government, world without end. Amen.

POINT III.

1. Of all that which has been said I will conclude the *divers motives and titles which oblige me* speedily to hear the divine vocation, when Almighty God calls me to give over sin, and all slothfulness, reducing them to *six*.

i. The first, for the *infinite greatness of the Lord that calls* me to serve Him, not because He has any need of me, but because I stand in need of Him, and for the desire He has to do me this good, because He is good, and because in Him concur all the reasons which may oblige me to hear His voice, since there is nothing more consonant to reason than that the creature should hear the voice of his Creator, the vassal of his king, the slave of his lord, the son of his father, the sick of his physician, the disciple of his master, and the captive of his redeemer.

ii. The second respect is, *the baseness of him that is called*, to whom a great honour is done, in that Almighty God vouchsafes to call him, and to make use of him, he deserving to be forsaken, and to be abandoned into the abyss of his own miseries.

iii. The third respect is, the infinite *misery of sin*, from which God desires to deliver us, drawing us out of a state far worse than hell itself, as touching the pain thereof, as has been said in its place.

iv. The fourth is, the infinite *greatness of the goods* to which Almighty God calls me, since He invites me to receive the life of grace, the beauty of virtues, peace which surpasses all understanding, the gifts and joys of the Holy Ghost, and the Holy Ghost Himself, the giver of the same gifts, with pledges that He will afterwards call me to enjoy the goods eternal of His glory. (16)

v. The fifth is, in respect of the *sweet manner with which He calls me*, using so many interior and exterior means, with which to mollify my heart, and to induce me to hear Him, as if that imported Him which imports me.

vi. The sixth is, for the most *grievous damages*, which may befal me, *if I resist the divine vocation;* since if I make myself deaf unto His calling, my condemnation will be certain, like those of the invited, who would not come to the supper, to whom He said, that they should never afterwards taste of it.(17)

2. In these six things is discovered likewise the greatness of this benefit; and those which are motives to hear the divine vocation, are also motives to glorify Almighty God for the favour He has vouchsafed me in calling me, and aiding me to hear Him.

Colloquy.—O eternal God, I give Thee thanks for this sovereign benefit, which for so many respects, is, as it were, infinite. Blessed be Thy providence whence it flows, and blessed be Thine omnipotence by which Thou performest so great works. Call, dear Lord, I beseech Thee, with Thy holy vocation, all men whom Thou hast created, that all may enter into the city of Thy Church, and may aspire to attain to the top of Christian perfection, and afterwards to that of Thine eternal glory. Amen.

(16) Par. v. Med. 22.·   (17) Par. iii. Med. 56. Luc. xiv. 24.

MEDITATION XXXVIII.

ON THE PROVIDENCE OF ALMIGHTY GOD IN THE INSTITUTION OF SEVEN SACRA-
MENTS FOR THE JUSTIFICATION AND SALVATION OF MEN.

The excellence of this sovereign providence an angel showed to the prophet Zacharias, in the figure of a great "candlestick, all of gold,"(1) which represented the Universal Church, upon which there was a great lamp, which was a figure of Christ our Lord, head of the Church; and round about it were seven other lesser, which represented the multitude of the faithful; and to feed them, there was adjoined seven vessels of gold, after the manner of seven pipes, full of oil, which represent the seven sacraments, which are as vessels, in which are contained the oil of divine grace for two ends,—that is to say, to heal us of all kinds of sins and spiritual infirmities,—and to fortify us and perfect us in all kinds of graces and virtues; so that we be like resplendent and burning lamps before Almighty God, in the middle of His Church, by the merits of Jesus Christ our Lord, of whose two natures, human and divine, united together in one Person, proceeds the oil of grace which the sacraments have, and to signify this more manifestly, the seven vessels were fastened with two olive branches, which held the greater lamp; all which shall be considered in the ensuing points.

POINT I.

1. Consider *the particular ends for which* the Divine Providence ordained these seven sacraments in the house of His holy Church, discoursing briefly through every one of them.(2)

(1) Zach. iv. 2.
(2) S. Tho. iii. p. q. lxv. art. 1.

i. *Baptism* is like a vessel of celestial oil, with which to heal the wound of original sin; and moreover engenders us in a new being of grace, and to live a new life in Christ our Lord, in testimony of which the baptized are anointed with oil, that they may be like Christ, which is as much as to say, " *anointed.*"

ii. *Confirmation* is ordained to cure our imbecility, and to fortify the new soldiers of Jesus Christ in the faith and grace they have received, anointing them with chrism, composed of oil and balsam, in sign that they are to fight courageously against the enemies of their King and of His law, giving a sweet odour of sanctity to themselves.

iii. The sacrament of the *Eucharist* is ordained against the perverse inclination of self-love, which consumes the life of the spirit, and contains within it the same Christ, who is the physician and the medicine, and anoints us with the oil of devotion and of spiritual gladness, to preserve and perfect the life of the spirit.

iv. The sacrament of *Penance* is ordained to heal the deadly wounds of our actual sins, and to repair the life of grace we have lost by them, anointing us like the merciful Samaritan with wine and oil, that so our wounds may be perfectly healed.

v. The Sacrament of *Extreme Unction* is a vessel of oil to anoint the sick, with which to cure the relics of sin, to fortify the sick, to fight against the Devil in the battle of death, and to dispose one to enter into eternal life.

vi. The sacrament of *Holy Orders* anoints with this divine oil the priests and ministers of the Church, against the aversion and small inclination which men have to things that are common, giving them grace and authority to offer the sacrifice of the precious body and blood of Christ our Lord, for the sins of the living and of the dead; and to minister the other sacraments and necessary remedies for our salvation.

vii. The sacrament of *Matrimony* is a medicine of the feeble, wherewith to cure fleshly concupiscences; so that the married, united in charity, without detriment of their souls, may engender children, who may receive these sacraments, and may multiply the Church militant, and afterwards the triumphant.

2. Pondering this so high and sovereign a disposition, I will glorify Almighty God for the care which He has to provide us with so many remedies, so easy and sweet, and so proportionate to the end unto which they are ordained, saying:—

Colloquy.—O infinite Wisdom, who reachest "from end to end mightily, and orderest all things sweetly," (3) I give Thee thanks for the seven sacraments which Thou hast instituted in Thy Church, with which Thou hast favoured me, even from the beginning of my life until the ending of it, directing it with sweetness and efficacy, that I may finally attain the life eternal. Amen.

POINT II.

1. The second shall be to consider the *excellency of these seven sacraments*, as touching their *efficacy*, because they are not as the sacraments of the ancient law, which were vessels empty of what they signified; but are *full of the oil of grace, which they represent*, causing the same in those who receive them worthily;(4) so that when he who baptizes says,—" I baptize thee in the name of the Father, and of the Son, and of the Holy Ghost;"—in virtue of this sacrament the soul remains washed from original sin, and whatsoever other it had before. And the priest saying,

(3) Sap. viii. 1.   (4) S. Tho. i. p. q. lxii. art. 3, et 6.

"I absolve thee of thy sins," the sinner remains, freed of them, receiving the grace of justification.(5)

2. Moreover these sacraments *make contrite a man before only attrite;* for the sinner, receiving them with an imperfect sorrow, which is called attrition, in virtue of them, receives grace, the sacrament supplying the defect of contrition, which is perfect sorrow. Yea, and he that communicates only with attrition, thinking that he is in the grace of God, receives the same by means of the sacrament, and remains justified.(6)

3. Finally, all the sacraments *confer grace,* "*ex opere operato,*" as divines term it; for besides that grace which every just person may merit by his own acts, he receives other degrees of grace in virtue of the sacrament. All which the Divine Providence so disposed, partly the more to facilitate our salvation, the sacrament supplying the defect of our slender disposition; for many more would be damned than are if perfect contrition were of necessity to receive a sacrament; partly also to enrich us by such means with more abundance of grace and glory, supplying by this means the want of our merits, which are very few. Hence is to be seen how happy we are who live in the law of grace, rejoicing in so loving and efficacious a Providence; and what great reason I have to animate myself, often to frequent the sacraments of confession and communion, which may be frequented as often as I will.

Colloquy.—O my soul, run with great joy to the "fountains of thy Saviour,"(7) to draw the waters of celestial graces, with which thou mayest wash thee from thy sins, and mayest replenish thy desires, until there be made within thee "a fountain of" living "water,"(8) which may spring up, and draw thee with it to life eternal. Amen.

(5) Trid. Sess. vii. Can. 6.

(6) Ibid. Can. 8.

(7) Isa. xii. 3.

(8) Joan. iv. 14.

POINT III.

Consider that the Divine Providence offers these seven sacraments to all men, *in that degree and condition in which they are necessary* or convenient for them, for their salvation and perfection.

1. For first, *to all unbelieving sinners* He offers the sacrament of *Baptism*, and to all *believing* sinners, that of *Penance*, without excluding any. And for this cause the prophet calls them "fountains, open to the house of David,"(9) which is the Church, for the ablution of the sinner. And He invites all to confirmation, and to the food of the Holy Eucharist. And to all the sick in danger of death he offers Extreme Unction. And to the divine Providence it appertains that there want not some to receive the sacrament of Orders. that so there may be sufficient ministers in the Church; and therefore, though I myself receive not this sacrament, yet is it not therefore unprofitable to me, since others receive it, at whose hands I am to receive the other sacraments.

2. These sacraments are vessels, not of brittle glass, which is easily broken, but of most rich and massy gold, which *will endure to the end of the world*, and the oil and grace which they contain will never fail, although they be given to innumerable men, because the fountain whence they receive their virtue and celestial liquor is Jesus Christ our Lord, whose merits are infinite, and can by no means be exhausted. And as the oil of that poor widow, by the word of Elias, never ceased to increase and flow, so long as there were empty vessels in which to receive it, and flowed with so great abundance, that it sufficed to pay her debts, and moreover to preserve her life,(10) even so the oil of divine grace will never cease to flow from these

(9) Zach. xiii. 1.   (10) 4 Reg. iv.

sacraments, as long as there shall be men remaining to receive them, to pay the debts of their sins, and to attain and preserve the life of grace.

3. And in one and the selfsame man, when he shall receive those sacraments, which may be iterated, they go perpetually flowing, *and augmenting grace*, as long as his life shall last, and the vessel of his soul be capable and well-disposed to receive that augmentation.

Colloquy.—I give Thee thanks, O most merciful Redeemer, for the providence which Thou hast over my poor soul, charged and laden with so many hindrances, providing her so many rich vessels of oil with which to pay them, with so great abundance, that there remains over and above, to live richly in holy virtues. Grant me to receive them in such a manner that I may obtain by means of them life eternal. Amen.

(Of Baptism and Penance we make no special mention in these meditations, because those are sufficient which have been made in the third and fourth part.)

MEDITATIONS ON THE SOVEREIGN BENEFIT OF THE MOST HOLY SACRAMENT OF THE ALTAR.

Presupposing the meditations of the most holy Sacrament of the Altar, which have been put down in the fourth part, amongst the mysteries of the supper, I will consider here some others of the same, inasmuch as it is a principal means of the Divine Providence for our salvation and perfection, and inasmuch as it is a sum or memorial of the excellencies of Almighty God and of His benefits, to the end that as well the priests as those who communicate frequently, may, without weariness, with this variety of meditations, prepare themselves to perform the same with profit.

MEDITATION XXXIX.

OF THE SINGULAR PROVIDENCE OF GOD OUR LORD IN
THE INSTITUTION OF THE MOST HOLY SACRAMENT OF THE ALTAR, FOR THE
SUSTENANCE OF OUR SOULS.

POINT I.

Consider the singular excellency of the Divine Providence, sustaining our souls with this sovereign Sacrament, *comparing it with that which Adam had in the state of innocence,* for whose sustenance God made many trees in the garden of Paradise, and amongst them the tree of life, whose fruit, if it were eaten now and then, sufficed to preserve life for ever. (1) In the same manner the Divine Providence, although He has placed in the paradise of His Church many meats for the sustenance of our souls, yet above all has He ordained this Divine Sacrament as the tree of life, because it is the true bread of life eternal, and infinitely exceeds that other tree. For first, that was earthly, and made of earth,—this is heavenly, and came from heaven.(2)—That gave life to their bodies, this to the soul.—That preserved the life of the living, this after the manner that has been said, gives life even to the dead. —Hence it is that this Sacrament may be much better compared to the tree of life which was in the celestial paradise, whereof St. John says:—that it brought forth twelve fruits, "yielding its fruits, every month"(3) his own, either of different kinds to delight with their variety, or one and the same coming forth twelve times a year to recreate with his novelty; and the leaves of that tree were the health of nations. For even so this Divine Sacrament,

---

(1) Gen. ii. 9. S. Tho. i. p. q. xcvii. art. 4.   (2) Joan vi. 35.
(3) Apoc. xxii. 2.

in which is contained that Lord who said,—"I am the way, and the truth, and the life,"(4) brings twelve fruits, producing in our souls all the variety of virtues, and moving her to the exercise of the twelve fruits which St. Paul calls the fruits of the Holy Ghost, namely,—" Charity, joy, peace, patience, benignity, goodness, longanimity, mildness, faith, modesty, continency, chastity,"(5) which this divine Sacrament renews every time it is duly received, and its leaves which are the words which are written thereon are powerful to give perfect health, because of them the same Lord said,—" The words that I have spoken to you, are spirit and life." (6)

Colloquy.—O most loving Father, I give Thee thanks for this generous providence which Thou hast of us, planting such a tree in the midst of Thy Church as brings forth to us eternal life ; grant me that I may vanquish my sins and passions, that so I may taste of the fruit " of this tree of life,"(7) which Thou hast promised to him that shall overcome.   Amen.

POINT II.

Consider the excellence of this providence, *comparing it with that which our Lord took in sustaining the people of Israel with Manna*, which in four excellent properties that it had, was a figure of this divine Sacrament which has the same, but with infinite advantage.(8)

i. " Manna" was *the bread of heaven*, and of angels, by whose ministry it was made in the region of the air, and as a little "dew" in the likeness of " coriander seed," fell upon the earth, and the people "gathering it ground it in

<hr>

(4) Joan xiv. 6.
(5) Gal. v. 22. S. Tho. i. 2, q. lxx. art. 3.
(6) Joan. vi. 64, Med. L.   (7) Apoc. ii. 7.
(8) S. Tho. 3, p. q. lxxiii. art. 6.

a mill, or beat it in a mortar," and "made cakes of" it,(9) and baked it in the fire, and so ate it. But this divine bread came from the highest heaven, made by the work, not of angels, but of the Holy Ghost, to whom is appropriated the Incarnation of the divine Word, who, like dew, descended to the earth and joined Himself with the littleness of our humanity, was ground with corporal labours, kneaded with the water of interior afflictions, and baked with the fire of torments, and of loving affections, and in this manner was made our meat, covered with the accidents of bread and wine, changing that pain which He had imposed upon us, when He said,—" In the sweat of thy face shalt thou eat thy bread,"(10) because with His own afflictions and bloody sweat, He has gained the bread which we now eat with so little labour.

Colloquy.—O most loving Father, I give Thee thanks for that Thou hast given to Thy children such excellent bread, the bread in very deed of angels, with which they are sustained, though after another manner than men are ; bread by excellence true, in comparison of which that which Thou gavest to the Hebrews was no more than figurative bread, and since Thou hast prepared the same at Thy so great expenses, that I might eat it, I, by Thine assistance, will prepare myself to receive the same, grinding my heart with sorrow for my sins, and my body with penances, kneading and uniting my powers with the lively water of Thy grace, and baking it with the burning fire of Thy charity.

ii. Manna was *medicinal bread*, preserving from sickness, so that all the time that the Israelites ate the same, " there was not," as David says, "among their tribes, one that was feeble;"(11) although many perished by sudden

(9) Exod. xvi. 15. Num. xi. 8. Ps. lxxvii. 24. Sap. xvi. x.
(10) Gen. iii. 19.   (11) Ps. civ. 37.

death in chastisement of their sins, and afterwards all came
to die at the last of old age; but this divine Sacrament heals
the sickness of the soul, preserves from the death of many
sins, and from eternal death, which we incur by the
means of them, and in its time also will deliver our body
itself from death, according to that saying of our Saviour,
—" He that eateth my flesh and drinketh my blood hath
everlasting life, and I will raise him up at the last day."
(12)

Colloquy.—O most powerful Saviour, our physician
and our medicine, how admirably has Thy providence
been, destroying death which we incurred by one
meat, with the life which Thou givest us by the means
of this other!　Suffer not, dear Lord, I beseech Thee,
that men eat the same with so little reverence, that
they die or become sick,(13) converting by their sin
into poison that which Thou institutedst by Thy mercy
for their remedy.

iii. As manna had only one natural taste, but to the just
had all kinds of tastes, *tasting to every one as himself would ;*
even so this divine meat, although it have only one natural
taste of the species of bread and wine,—yet to the just *has
all spiritual tastes which every one can desire* according to
his own necessity, because it contains within it the fountain
of all savour and sweetness, which, says the Book of Wisdom, " thou hast shewed to thy children complying with
the will of each one, so that it turned to that which each
one would."(14)　To him that receives the same, with
desire of obedience or patience, it gives the savour of these
virtues, and makes them sweet that he may take contentment in them; and to those who communicate worthily,
it gives the taste and sweetness of spirit which contains in

(12) Joan. vi. 55.　　　(13) 1 Cor. xi. 30.　　　(14) Sap. xvi. 21.

itself, with eminence, the taste of those things which give contentment to the flesh.

Colloquy.—O most sweet providence! O fountain of all sweetness, whence to me so great a good as that Thou shouldst serve my will! Oh that I could always employ myself in serving Thy will, fulfilling it willingly on earth, as the angels fulfil the same in heaven. Amen.

iv. "*Every one gathered a measure of Manna, which was assigned great or little, and this sufficed* for his sustenance, he remaining as full who gathered a little, as he who gathered much."(15)   Even so, here what measure soever every one receives of this divine Sacrament, it suffices him for his entire spiritual sustentation, for Christ is wholly in the great host, and in the little, and in every particle of it, and he receives as much, who receives the half of a host, as he does who receives the whole, and one receives as much as a thousand, and a thousand no more than one, because all receive the one and the same Christ, most sufficient to fill all.   And for the same reason he receives as much who receives the host alone, and he who receives both host and chalice, because the whole Christ, with His flesh and blood, is under the forms of bread, and is like-wise wholly under the forms of wine.

Colloquy.—O bread of life, extreme of little, and extreme of great!   For what thing can be more little than a little crumb of this divine bread?   And what thing can be more great than God and Man con-tained in it?   O supreme bread, make me little and make me great; little in mine own eyes, and great in Thine.   And since Thou alone art sufficient for mil-lions of souls, satisfy the desire of my soul, that hence-

<hr>

(15) Exod. xvi. 18. Med. xvii. p. 3.

forth I may be wholly Thine, world without end. Amen.

POINT III.

Consider how the divine Providence has ordained *that we cooperate with Him in seeking* and tasting this divine bread after the manner that He commanded the Israelites, that early in the morning they should gather manna, before the rising of the sun, for "after the sun grew hot, it melted,"(16) in punishment of the negligence of such as were slothful, that all may understand, as the Wise man says, that it behoves to "prevent the sun,"(17) to receive the benediction of Almighty God, and to bless Him for it. In which He admonishes us that we arise in the morning with great fervour and diligence for three causes:—

i. The first, to *mediate the greatness of this divine Sacrament*, and to gather the manna of most sweet devotion, which is collected from the consideration of it, before that the sun of earthly occupations and temptations, which, as the day approaches, distract us, and dries our spirit.

ii. The second, to *praise and glorify Almighty God with a mind very grateful* for this benefit, assisting at the Sacrifice which is celebrated for this end, and observing a perpetual memory of it. For if God our Lord desired that such a memory should be kept of the manna with which He sustained the Hebrew people only forty years, that for this cause He commanded a vessel full of it to be kept in the ark of the testament,(18) how much more will He that we keep a perpetual memory with great gratitude for this divine meat with which He has sustained the Christian people more than a thousand and five hundred years, and will sustain them with it to the end of the world.

(16) Exod. xvi. 21.　　　(17) Sap. xvi. 28.　　　(18) Exod. xvi. 32.

iii. We are especially to rise early on the day of sacred communion *to dispose ourselves diligently for it,* taking this employment for the first and principal of that day, remembering that which the Scripture says, that gathering manna every day, the sixth they doubled their measure, because on the Sabbath day there was none to be found, (19) and they suffered much hunger who had been negligent to gather on the sixth day: even so, if in the six days of this life, I gather not the fruit of this divine Sacrament, in the Sabbath of the other life, I shall not find it, and shall suffer perpetual hunger, nor will there be for me any Sabbath of rest, but of eternal torment. Wherefore, O my soul, the more thou approachest to the end of thy life, so much the more prepare thyself to gather a double measure, with which thou mayest obtain eternal satiety. For the good execution of the three things aforesaid, the ensuing meditations will much help.

MEDITATION XL.

ON THE MOST BLESSED SACRAMENT, INASMUCH
AS IT IS A SUM AND MEMORIAL OF THE EXCELLENCIES AND WONDROUS
WORKS OF GOD FOR THE GOOD OF MEN.

This meditation shall be grounded upon that verse of the Psalm of David,—" *He has made a remembrance of His wonderful works, being a merciful and gracious Lord, He hath given food to them that fear Him.*"(1) These wonders we will reduce to *seven or eight heads,* that they may be meditated on the seven days of the week.

POINT I.

This holy Sacrament *is a memorial of the stupendous*

(19) Exod. xvi. 21.　　　　　(1) Ps. cx. 4.

marvels of the Divinity and Trinity, which are contained in it.

For first, in it is *the Person of the Divine Word,* united with the sacred humanity, in whom, as St. Paul says, "dwelleth all the fulness of the Godhead, corporally,"(2) and, consequently, the most Holy Trinity is with Him, for it is impossible to separate one Person from the other, because all Three are One and the same God, and all the works which the Son does in this divine Sacrament, the Father, and the Holy Ghost, likewise do, although all in a special manner are attributed to the Son, inasmuch as His Person alone sustains the flesh and blood which there is given us for food.

Hence it is that in this Sacrament are likewise all the *perfections and attributes of Almighty God,* since, as the same apostle says, in Christ Jesus "are hid all the treasures of wisdom and knowledge,"(3) and, furthermore, those of His bounty and charity, which shine most admirably in this work,—His wisdom in having invented such a means, that God should make Himself the meat and drink of men;—His bounty in communicating Himself after this manner unto the faithful;—His charity in uniting, and incorporating Himself with His friends, not denying Himself to His very enemies;—His mercy, in giving Himself for meat to the hungry, and drink to the thirsty, and that Himself comes in Person to visit and cure those that are sick;—His liberality, in giving us of mere grace, whatsoever He has,—and His omnipotence, in working so many miracles for the performance of all this. In every one of these divine perfections, I may make a great pause, reducing to memory that which, to this purpose, has been said of them in the preceding meditations, and in some of the fourth Part,(4) gathering from all great admiration for

(2) Coloss. ii. 9.   (3) Coloss. ii. 3.
(4) Med. viii. xi. xiii. part iv. Med. xi.

the great esteem which Almighty God makes of us, saying with David,—"O Lord, our Lord, how admirable is Thy name in the whole earth!"(5) Thou wast admirable in the creation of man, more admirable in his reparation, and no less admirable in his sustenance, making a sum of Thy wonders, to sustain him who is as a sum of all Thy works.

POINT II.

This divine Sacrament *is a memorial of the wonder of the omnipotence of Almighty God,* who works many and very great wonders, invisible to the eyes of the body, but admirable and stupendous to the eyes of the soul, which beholds them with the light of faith.

1. The first miracle is, that Almighty God *dissolves by His word that union and natural connection* which the *accidents* of bread and wine *have with their substance,* destroying the substance, and preserving the accidents without their subject, because, although I perceive with my senses the colour, taste, and savor of bread and wine, yet really the substance of bread and wine is not there, but of the flesh and blood of Jesus Christ, into which it is converted miraculously.

Colloquy.—O Divine Word, "more piercing than a two-edged sword,"(6) since with one only word Thou so dividest the connexion of the accidents from their substance, divide likewise my soul from my spirit, that living in this natural and exterior life, which the senses perceive, I may not live the interior life which I was wont, but that Thou mayest live in me, so that I may say with Thine apostle:—"I live now, not I; but Christ liveth in me."(7)

2. The second miracle is to convert so *small a substance* of bread and wine *into so perfect and great a body* as that

---

(5) Ps. viii. 2.   (6) Heb. iv. 12.   (7) Gal. ii. 20.

of Christ; so that, under the accidents which remain, the body of Christ remains with all His integrity and glory, which He has in heaven. There is His most sacred head, with those divine eyes, which rob the heart of His beholders, and with their look "scattereth away all evil."(8) There are His most blessed feet and hands, with the marks of His wounds, which the nails made, and His side, with the wound which the lance pierced, and the heart, inflamed with the fire of love, which moved Him to receive them, and the whole body, with the dowries of brilliancy and beauty, which far surpass the sun, the moon, and the stars. What, therefore, can be a greater wonder, than for Almighty God to make in an instant a conversion, and change so extraordinary of a thing so little into another so great, of a thing so vile into another so precious, only for the sustenace of man!

Colloquy.—O my glory, vouchsafe to change me into another man, that I may faithfully serve Thee for this change which Thou hast made in favour of me. If Thou givest me all that Thou art for to sustain me, I will give Thee all that I am for to serve Thee; my body with my senses, my heart and whatsoever I have I will employ in obeying Thee, since Thou hast employed Thyself wholly in the nourishment of me.

3. The third stupendous miracle is, that the whole body of Christ is in the Sacrament, *after the manner of a spirit indivisibly,* so that the whole is in the whole host, and the whole in every part thereof; whence it arises, that although the host be divided, yet Christ our Lord is not divided, but the whole remains entire in every little part of it. And hence also it is that the life which Christ lives in the Blessed Sacrament is not a life of the flesh,

(8) Prov. x. 8.

but as it were, a life of the spirit; for although He there has feet, yet He walks not, and although He has hands, yet He touches not, and although He has a tongue, yet He speaks not, but only uses spiritual faculties proper to the spirit.

Colloquy.—O my beloved, what thanks may I give Thee to have moulded Thy Divine flesh after so miraculous a manner, that, remaining true flesh, it has the properties of a spirit! Oh who may give to me that living in flesh, I work " not according to the flesh,"(9) but according to the spirit, only practising the works of the spirit, and mortifying those which are proper to the flesh! Oh that I could preserve entire and without division my heart and the interior of my soul, although the exterior occupation of the body be divided into many parts! Work, O my God, these marvels in me, since for my sake Thou workest them in Thee. Amen.

4. The fourth miracle is, that Christ our Lord remaining in the empyreal heaven, occupying the place which His sovereign excellency deserves *without ceasing to be there, descends into the Blessed Sacrament,* and is at the same time in different places of the world, wheresoever the same is consecrated without excepting any place, and attends with such vigilance to the consecration of every priest, that he saying,—" This is my body:" in the same instant Christ causes those words to be most true, and performs all the miracles before mentioned.

Colloquy.—O sovereign omnipotence of our Lord Jesus, who dost so employ Thyself for the profit of men, as to offer to put Thy body in every place of the earth, wheresoever theirs can be ; what shall I give Thee, dear Lord, for so admirable a benefit, but dedi-

(9) 2 Cor. x. 3. Rom. viii. 1.

cate myself entirely in all times and places to Thy holy service. Amen.

POINT III.

This divine Sacrament is a *memorial of the offices which Christ our Lord exercised* towards men whilst He lived in the world, renewing them every one in this most holy Sacrament towards every man in particular. Wherefore, going through every one of these offices, I will ponder three particular things,—i. The *manner how* Christ our Lord *exercised* the same on earth.—ii. The manner how He exercises the same in the Blessed Sacrament.—iii. And the great necessity that I have, that He exercises this office towards me, approaching to the holy communion with this spirit and desire conformably to my necessity.

1. Christ our Lord living in mortal flesh, *performed towards us the office of a physician*, giving sight to the blind, health to the sick, and life to the dead,—and this not with corporal medicines, but with His only word, or with the touch of His hand, or of His garment; and in the same manner healed the infirmities of the soul with the infinite virtue, which went forth of Him for the good of all. He put Himself in this Blessed Sacrament to be the medicine and physician of every one of us, even to the ending of the world;·for with the touch of His body and His blood, by means of the sacramental species, He heals the spiritual infirmities of him that receives Him, cures his wounds, represses his cupidities, and gives him perfect health of spirit, and sometimes, if it be convenient, He gives also health of body. Then will I behold myself in the extreme necessity I have of this sovereign physician, as being sick of so grievous and dangerous sicknesses, all which I will deepen, and recount them to Him particularly, as those that are sick are wont to do, beseeching Him to cure them

with His divine presence, since for the same end He visits me.

Colloquy.—O celestial physician, who comest from heaven to visit the sick who live on earth; it will redound to Thy great glory, if Thou cure one so miserably sick as is myself; heal me, therefore, dear Lord, I beseech Thee, of all my infirmities, that being sound and safe, I may wholly employ myself in praising and serving Thee for the good which Thou dost me in delivering me from them. Amen.

2. After the same manner I may likewise consider that Christ our Lord *performed in this mortal life the office of a master*, after the manner that has been pondered in the twelfth meditation of the third part, and in this same manner He performs that office in this Sacrament, towards him who receives it; for whilst He is in this little world of man, He also is " the light of " this " world," (10) and illuminates it interiorly, teaching within the heart the verities which are written in the holy Gospel, and beholding the necessity which I have of this divine master, I will say to Him with great affection:—

Colloquy.—O sovereign master, who comest from heaven to teach me the way of perfection, repel my ignorance, and enlighten my darkness, that my soul, by means of Thy presence, may be full of Thy verities and virtues. Amen.

3. Christ our Lord *performed the office of a Saviour* and of a *Redeemer*, drawing out of the power and tyranny of the Devil the bodies of many that were possessed, and the souls of many sinners, giving His life and His blood, with terrible torments and contempts, in price of this redemption. And after the same manner performed the office of

(10) Joan. ix. 6.

pastor of His flock, fulfilling all that which belonged to the charge of a good shepherd, even to the giving of His life for His sheep. And the same office He does in this divine Sacrament, for He comes principally to apply to us the fruit of His abundant redemption, delivering us from the tyranny of the Devil, from the slavery of the flesh, and of its passions, and from the bondage of our vices. He also performs the office of a pastor, being so careful of every soul, as if there were but that one alone, feeding her with His own body and His blood; so that the sheep not only eats at the pastor's table, as the prophet Nathan said to David, but eats of the very flesh of her own pastor, contrary to the pastors of the earth, which eat of the flesh of their sheep. Then, beholding myself, I will ponder the servitude and slavery in which I live, and the great perils to which I am exposed, to perish for hunger and feebleness, and of falling into the hands of the infernal wolves, and with this feeling I will cry to my Redeemer and my pastor, that He vouchsafe to favour me, saying:—

Colloquy.—O most merciful Redeemer and sovereign pastor, " save me from the lion's mouth,"(11) and since " Thou hast prepared a table for me against them that afflict me,"(12) so feed and fortify me with the same, that I may here obtain the victory, and hereafter may enjoy that table which Thou hast prepared for me in Thy glory. Amen.

After this manner may other offices be considered, which Christ our Lord performed on earth, of advocate, comforter, protector, and universal Father of all.

POINT IV.

This divine Sacrament *is a memorial of the most noble virtues* which Jesus Christ our Lord *exercised on earth*, the

(11) Ps. xxi. 22.   (12) Ps. xxii. 5.

which He likewise exercises here; so that, as He came into the world, to give us an example of His life, and to set before us a pattern of virtues, which all of us ought to imitate—even so in this Sacrament He also comes to give us daily new examples of the same virtues, especially of those which are most necessary for our salvation and perfection.

i. The first is *humility*, covering His infinite greatness and splendour, under a figure and veil so vile as is that of bread and wine, whence it comes that many contemn Him, and treat Him as pure bread and pure wine.

ii. The second is prompt and punctual *obedience* to the priest who consecrates the same, presently obeying, so soon as he has pronounced the words, although he be evil, and speaks them with an ill intention, and for an evil end; and that in whatsoever place and hour he shall speak them, without any reply or delay.

iii. The third is admirable *patience* and *meekness* in the injuries which are done to Him, as well by heretics and infidels as by sinners which receive Him, being in sin, or by the carelessness of slothful priests; none of all these things being able to cause Him to cease to be in the host, all the time that the sacramental forms endure.

iv. The fourth is the *charity* and *mercy* with which He comes into the Sacrament to exercise all the works of mercy towards all men, both great and little, without any exception of persons, respecting nothing more than the good of every soul that receives Him, giving Himself wholly to every one, in testimony that He died for every one.

v. The fifth is *perseverance*, as well in remaining in the host and chalice, until the sacramental forms be consumed, as also in accomplishing all that has been said until the ending of the world, no sins or sinners hindering Him from accomplishing what He promised.

In every one of these five virtues most excellent considerations may be made, like as they were in the Fourth Part, (14) and in the preceding meditations. But when I am to come to the holy communion, I am to ask them of our Lord, fixing the eyes of faith on the signs of the wounds which He has there in His glorified body, and saying to Him:

Colloquy.—O most sweet Jesus, since Thou vouchsafest to come to my poor habitation with Thy five wounds, by them I beseech Thee to bestow upon me these five virtues. By the two wounds of Thy sacred feet I crave humility and meekness; by the two wounds of Thy holy hands I beg obedience and perseverance; and by the wound of Thy blessed side, vouchsafe to fill me with Thy burning charity; that, loving Thee and obeying Thee perseveringly, I may obtain the crown of glory. Amen.

POINT V.

The fifth shall be to consider how this sovereign Sacrament, inasmuch as it is *a sign of a sacred thing, has some special privilege above the other sacraments,* which is to be a sign and sum of three of the greatest benefits which God ever did, or ever will do in the behalf of men—one *past,* which is the benefit of redemption,—another present, which is the benefit of sanctification,—and another to come, which is that of *glorification;* all which it represents after a most singular manner, Christ Himself being present in the Sacrament that signifies it, as appears by that antiphon which the Church sings,—" O sacrum convivium," &c., " O sacred banquet in which Christ is received, the memory of His Passion is renewed, the mind is filled with

(14) Med. xi. xiii. xvi.

grace, and a pledge of future glory is given to us." Of these three things will I discourse in the ensuing meditations, to which we will reduce all that which remains to be spoken of this venerable Sacrament.

MEDITATION XLI.

ON THE MOST HOLY SACRAMENT OF THE ALTAR, AS IT IS A MEMORY OF THE PASSION OF CHRIST OUR LORD.

Our Redeemer desiring that in His Church there should remain a perpetual memory of His Passion and death, and of the excellent benefit which He did us in it, instituted for this effect this sacred banquet, in which He daily gives us to eat, and to drink His body and blood, under the forms of bread and wine. (1)

POINT I.

Concerning this verity of our holy faith, first are to be considered *the causes wherefore* Christ our Lord would that the sign and memory of His Passion and death, which had been so ignominious and so painful, should be a banquet full of sweetness and of pleasure, since it might seem that it would have been more to the purpose that the sign and memory of it should have been some sacrament, in which we should shed our blood, as in the circumcision, or that we should have eaten some bitter thing, as bitter lettuces were eaten with the Paschal lamb, and drink some little vinegar in memory of the gall and vinegar which He drank. But none of all this would our loving Lord permit, but that the memory should be only in the species of bread and wine, and yet not in bread made of barley, such

(1) Luc. xxii. 19. 1 Cor. xi. 24.

as Himself sometimes ate, but in bread made of wheat; and not in sour wine, but in most sweet and incorrupt.

The principal causes of which were four, all full of wonderful sweetness.

i. *To discover to us His infinite goodness*, and the charity and love He bears to us as a Father, choosing to Himself the things that are painful, and giving unto us those that are delightful, in memory of His pains, and to apply to us the fruit and profit which proceeds from them. For it is the property of fathers to take to themselves that which is painful, and to give to their children that which is sweet and delightful; and this spirit He will that all His children have towards their brethren and their neighbours.

ii. That by this *we might see with what pleasure He suffered the labours of His Passion*, inasmuch as they were beneficial to us, and for our good, and therefore would that the memory of them should be in **a** thing of pleasure and sweetness, and a banquet of great rejoicing, that so we might with more contentment remember the same, and give Him thanks for them. For as the day of His Passion was to Him a day of espousals, and wedding with the Church His spouse, so the memory of it ought to be in a banquet of joy, as is accustomed in wedding banquets.

iii. That we might *see the sweetness of His law*, of which Himself had said, that " His yoke was sweet and His burden light;" (2) for all His sacraments were most sweet, and this especially above all the rest, as having flowed out of His side, wounded with the wound of a cruel lance.

iv. *To oblige us hereby to imitate the bitter and ignominious things of His holy Passion*, for by how much He showed Himself more liberal, in willing that the memory of it should be in a banquet full of such unspeakable sweetness, so much more does He oblige us by the law of gratitude

(2) Matt. xi. 29.

that we commemorate the same by embracing things full of bitterness, namely, penance, fasting, mortification, humiliation, and whatsoever is conformable to Christ crucified and despised, saying with the prophet Jeremiah:—" I will be mindful and remember, and my soul shall languish within me," (3) consuming with mortification whatsoever has separated me from Thy holy service, and cheerfully embracing the pains which Thou hast endured for the love of me.

Colloquy.—O beloved of my heart, what shall I be able to do for Thee in recompense of so singular a benefit, and of so excessive love, as Thou in this hast showed to me? If I behold Thee as a Father, Thou art most amiable, if as a Redeemer, Thou art most delectable, if as a lawgiver, Thou art most sweet and most desirable, and on all sides dost " crown me with mercy" and with innumerable works which proceed thence. I desire, for the love of Thee, to crown myself with the crown of innumerable thorns, repaying with innumerable labours Thine innumerable torments, all full of innumerable mercies.

POINT II.

Consider the *causes why* Christ our Lord *would leave Himself really and truly in this holy Sacrament*, to be a memory of His Passion, since to this purpose only bread and wine had been sufficient, as pure water suffices in holy Baptism, which likewise is a figure of His death and burial. (4)

i. The first cause was, to *discover to us the great estimation which He made of His Passion*, that Himself would be the memorial of it, to oblige us to have a most high estimation and continual memory of this benefit, thanking Him exceedingly, since Himself will be the awaker of our

<hr>

(3) Thren. iii. 20.   (4) Rom. vi. 4.

memory against our forgetfulness, and the enkindler of gratitude against our ingratitude.

ii. The second cause was, the *more to discover to us His infinite charity*, and the immense desire which He had to suffer for our sakes, for every time that Mass is celebrated, as Christ makes a representation of His death and Passion, so He is ready for the love of us to suffer and die really and truly, if it were needful for our advantage; but because this is not necessary nor convenient, He is delighted to suffer and die at the least in the representation of His death and Passion; and as He is called in the Apocalypse "the Lamb which was slain from the beginning of the world," (5) because He died in the figures of the beasts which were slain in memory of Him, even so may we call Him the Lamb which dies to the end of the world, since in the same manner does He Himself die in this representation of His death, which shall endure to the end of the world. And with this He obliges us that we ourselves really and truly procure to support part of His Passion and death, as well for the love of Him as for the good of our brethren, saying with St. Paul:—"Always bearing about in our body the mortification of Jesus, that the life also of Jesus may be made manifest in our bodies," (6) for whose sake "we are put to death all the day long," (7) and are esteemed and handled as sheep appointed for the slaughter, and " I die daily by your glory brethren." (8)

iii. The third cause was, *to supply by this His real presence, the defect of the gratitude of men*, not only for the benefit of redemption, but for other benefits which they have received of Almighty God, which being infinite no pure creature can be sufficiently grateful for them, and therefore Himself would, in this Sacrament, in His own

(5) Apoc. xiii. 8.   S. Tho. 3, p. q. lxxxiii. art. 3.
(6) 2 Cor. iv. 10.   (7) Rom. viii. 36.   (8) 1 Cor. xv. 31.

person, be He who should return thanks in our behalf for all these benefits.   And as the Apostle St. Paul says, that " the Spirit Himself asketh for us with unspeakable groanings;" (9) so we may say that Christ our Lord, in this divine Sacrament, renders thanks for these benefits with ineffable affections, moving us to exercise the same affections with great efficacy and virtue, whence it comes that this Sacrament is called " Eucharistia," that is to say, " Thanksgiving."

Colloquy.—O God of love, what is this that Thou doest!   O infinite benefactor, what is this that Thou ordainest!   If to thank Thee for the benefits received, Thou dost me another new benefit as great as all the rest, with what shall I thank Thee for this new benefit!   Let Thyself, Lord, praise Thyself, both for this and for all the other, and let this benefit itself praise Thee for itself, and for all the other, since " Thy work is praise and magnificence,"(10) giving Thyself for meat to those that fear Thee ; and since I cannot give Thee anything for the great favours and benefits which Thou hast done me, " I will take the chalice of salvation, and I will call upon the name of the Lord."(11)

POINT III.

Consider the *causes why* Christ our Lord would *leave Himself under the forms of bread and wine*, to be a memory of His Passion, which, doubtless, have some similitude with the same.

1. The first was to signify, that like *as Christ* in this Sacrament joins Himself with bread, made of many grains of wheat, ground and bruised, and with wine made of the grains of grapes, *pressed and strained*, even so in His Passion *was His most sacred body tormented and bruised with whips, thorns, and nails*, and was also ground with most

(9) Rom. viii. 26.   (10) Ps. cx. 3.   (11) Ps. cxv. 13.

grievous ignominies, and pressed even to the drawing forth of all His blood, and He was left wholly exhausted as the grape in the wine-press. (12) For which cause, by the presence of these forms of bread and wine, He will that we remember the pains and ignominies which they represent; and as we eat the bread and drink the wine, so that we eat, drink, and incorporate within us the intolerable pains of His death and Passion. And especially we ought to bruise and grind our heart with contrition for our sins, and to chastise our flesh with penances, and to take pleasure to be despised in imitation of Him.

2. But this charity of our benign Lord passed yet further, because in Baptism he that is baptized represents, as St. Paul says, (13) the death and burial of Jesus Christ, when he is drowned under the waters, as Christ was drowned under the waves of His tribulations and afflictions, and placed in His sepulchre under a great stone. But in this Sacrament *Christ Himself represents His death and burial* when He is eaten, and as it were torn with the teeth, and when He is transported into the stomach He is a memory of Himself torn with the teeth of His persecutors, delivered to earth and placed in a sepulchre. And at all those things our Lord Himself assists, that the same may be done with reverence and spirit, communicating the fruits of His Passion and death to him that receives Him.

Colloquy.—O my soul, remember when Thou dost communicate, that thou art made the sepulchre of Jesus Christ, receiving Him within thee truly alive in Himself, but dead in representation. See that thy " sepulchre" be " glorious"(14) now, and " hewed out in a rock ;"(15) that thou mayest understand that thou thyself oughtest to be glorious by virtues, new by renovation of spirit, and grounded in the imitation

(12) Isa. lxiii. 2.   (13) Rom. vi. 8.   (14) Isa. xi. 10.
(15) Mat. xxvii. 60.   Part 4, Med. lv. p. 3.

of that living rock, which is Jesus Christ.   O most sweet Christ, sanctify, I beseech Thee, this sepulchre, into which Thou enterest at this present, that so long as Thou shalt remain in it, it may be made Thy worthy dwelling ; and as in Thine own sepulchre, there was never any placed but Thyself, so in this there enter not for time to come anything that may displease Thee, nor any creature which may profane it, preserving it always new and pure for Thy glory everlastingly.   Amen.

(In the thirteenth Meditation of the fourth part there are other considerations to this purpose, what it signifies to consecrate, by itself and apart, the body and blood of Christ our Lord, in different species of bread and wine.)

MEDITATION XLII.

ON THE MOST HOLY SACRAMENT AS IT IS A CAUSE OF THE GRACE AND SANCTIFICATION WHICH IS GIVEN AT THE PRESENT: AND OF THE WONDROUS UNION WITH CHRIST OUR LORD.

POINT I.

Christ our Lord having decreed to ordain seven sacraments, which should be seven sensible signs of grace, and seven instruments to apply to us the fruit of His Passion, which is our sanctification, determined that one of them should *not be a pure creature*, as pure water, or pure oil, or balsam, or pure bread and wine, *but Christ Himself, true God and true Man*, would really and truly join Himself with the creature, and hide Himself miraculously under the accidents of bread and wine, so that Himself might give us grace, and apply to us the fruit of His Passion, manifesting in this the infinite charity and love which He bears to us, and how much He esteems our sanctification.

and the daily augmentation and perfection of it, which may be pondered by some examples:—

1. Because our loving Jesus is not like a physician who ordains a medicine, and charges the keeper of the sick that he apply it to him, himself not touching the sick, for Christ *Himself is the physician*, and the *medicine*, and *He who* invisibly *applies* the same, entering into us in form of meat, and giving us grace to heal our disease.

2. He is not like the rich and powerful man, who gives the price to redeem the captive, and commands his servant that he go and redeem him, but *Himself is the Redeemer*, and the *price* of our redemption, and *He who applies* to us *this price* of His blood, and by Himself imparts to us the perfect liberty of grace, and of the adoption of the sons of God.

3. He is not like a mother, who having brought forth her son with pain and sorrow, afterwards commits it to some other nurse, that she nourish it with her milk, but *Himself*, who begot us with pains on the cross, *will nourish us like a loving mother*, with *His own body and His blood.*

4. He is not as a king, who invites his subjects to a banquet, and commands his servants that they serve at the table, but *Himself will be He* who both *invites us*, is *the banquet*, and *He who serves* us at the table, giving Himself to us in meat and drink. And all the priests are His ministers to this effect, yet Himself really and truly assists in all, being united with the forms of bread and wine.

Colloquy.—O most merciful physician! O most liberal Redeemer! O most pious king! O most loving mother! What shall I do in the service of Thee, in recompense of the much which Thou hast done for the profit of me! How shall I not love Him who so much loves me! How shall I not highly esteem the grace of my sanctification, since the sanctifier Himself comes in person to impart it to me! How shall I not greatly hunger after so sovereign a banquet, since God Himself who invites me, is the meat itself, which I am to eat, to receive life by the eating of it! I give Thee thanks, O most loving Father, for this so sovereign a benefit, and suffer not, I beseech Thee, that I' be sparing in thankfulness, therefore, nor slothful in making my profit of it.   Amen.

POINT II.

Consider *the gifts* which Christ our Lord bestows upon the soul, when He enters into her by the means of the Sacrament.

1. For with His entrance, " mens impletur gratia," " *the mind is filled with grace*," and charity, and with all the supernatural virtues, and with the seven gifts of the Holy Ghost, with great augmentation and perfection, much greater than in all the other sacraments, because there is here the fountain itself of all graces, and the giver of them. For as when a king gives an alms by the hands of his alms-giver, he permits him to give but a little, but when himself gives an alms with his own hand, the same ought to be a great gift, and beseeming a king;—even so in this Sacrament, as Christ Himself does by Himself give the gift of grace and of virtues, so He gives it most copiously, and like an alms that is given by the hand of God, accomplishing that which David says, that " He crowneth" us " with mercy" (1) and great works, which proceed thence, filling our desires with great good things.   And therefore I may imagine that when He enters by my mouth, He says to me that of the psalm:—" Open thy mouth wide and I will fill it;" (2) dilate and enlarge the bosom of thy soul, and the desires of thy heart, because I come with purpose to fill and replenish them.

(1) Ps. cii. 4.   (2) Ps. lxxx. 11.

Colloquy.—O my soul, hear the voice of Thy beloved, and since He will be liberal in communicating His gifts to thee, be not thou sparing in preparing thyself to receive them; enlarge thy heart with hope, dilate it with charity, and adorn it with fervent acts of devotion, that when thy beloved shall enter there, He may fill it with His gifts, and replenish it with His abundant benediction.   Amen.

2. Then will I ponder the spiritual banquet which Christ makes within the soul, *communicating to it, at His very entrance, spiritual refection*, which is the grace proper to this Sacrament, which may be understood after the manner that St. Gregory says, (3) that the virtues and gifts of the Holy Ghost, figured by the three daughters and seven sons of Job, make a very solemn banquet to the soul, with the exercise of their actions, Christ our Lord moving them with His presence to exercise these acts with exceeding joy. He makes us also a banquet by the means of charity, moving it to exercise the acts of the love of God, of spiritual joy, of the zeal of His glory, and of a vehement desire of joining her with her beloved. He moves the virtue of religion to exercise acts of reverence, praise, and gratitude, with a thousand affections of prayer and devotion. He moves the gift of wisdom that it may bring forth deep feelings of Almighty God, with admiration of His excellencies, with great faith and light of His verities, and with great taste and sweetness of His perfections, and in this manner it moves faith, hope, humility, and obedience, with the other virtues and gifts of the Holy Ghost, whose acts are refection, sustentation, and spiritual satiety of the soul.

3. Hence I will conceive an *inward desire of inviting Him* as He invites me, saying—" I will sup with Him, and

<hr>

(3) Lib. i. mor. c. 25.

He with me," (4) animating myself to exercise these acts with my free will, assisted and seconded by His grace, although it be somewhat dry and sluggish, because Christ our Lord is much delighted with this meat, and to sup with us within our hearts. And for this cause the Holy Ghost bids, that if we sit down " to eat with a prince," we " consider diligently what is set before" (5) us to eat — sciens quod talia te oportet preparare,— "knowing that thou must prepare the like for him to eat." (6)

Colloquy.—O sovereign prince, vouchsafe to enter into this poor habitation to sup with me, but bring with Thee the supper Thou delightest to eat; I on my part offer myself to prepare the same, endeavouring with all my ability to do that which may give to Thee contentment in it.   Amen.

POINT III.

Christ our Lord particularly instituted this divine Sacrament, to unite Himself with us with the union of charity during the whole time of this present life, which is the greatest benefit that here He bestows upon His elect.   This is signified when He said, " He that eateth my flesh and drinketh my blood, abideth in me and I in him," (7)—that is to say, is in me by charity, as he that loves is in the thing that is loved; and I am in him by grace, imparting to him the goods that proceed thence, and this is not only whilst this sensible meat abides in the body, but permanently; for although the sacramental forms be consumed, and that Christ as man remains no longer with us, yet He remains with us as He is God, and we with Him, with the love of mutual friendship, He loving

(4) Apoc. iii. 20.   (5) Prov. xxiii. 1.
(6) S. Aug. tract xlvii. et 84, in Joan.   S. Ambr. i. offi. c. 13.
(7) Joan. vi. 56.

us and we loving Him, doing that which St. John said—
" God is charity, and he that abideth in charity abideth in
God, and God in him." (8)   For Christ our Lord, as He
is God is charity itself by essence, and from Him proceeds
by means of this Sacrament participated charity, and therefore he who receives Him, remains united with Him by
charity, and so is in Almighty God, as in his house of
refuge, and God is in him as in His temple and house of
recreation.

Colloquy.—O my soul, how dost thou not go out of
thyself, considering the greatness of this benefit, and
the efficacy of the charity which Jesus Christ gives to
thee in this Sacrament? If Christ be charity, what
thing is better? If he that be in charity be in Christ,
what thing is securer? If Christ be with him, what
thing more delectable? If thou obtain all this in this
holy banquet, what thing is more amiable? O banquet
of infinite charity, in which the same charity itself,
covered under the species of bread and wine, enters
within me, to convert me into Him!   O my beloved,
convert me wholly into Thee, that I may always love
Thee, praise Thee, and glorify Thee, world without
end.   Amen.

2. In this consideration I am to pause, pondering the
three things which have been put down.—i. That He who
invites me in the Sacrament is *Almighty God*, who is charity
itself, and moved with this charity, ordains this sovereign
and stupendous banquet.—ii. The *meat* which here is proposed, is principally the *same charity* which is God, and
He enters within me and sits in the midst of my heart, as
Solomon the beloved of our Lord sat in the midst of his portable throne,(9) attracting with His presence the daughters
of His Jerusalem, which are the devout souls.—iii. And

(8) 1 Joan. iv. 17.   (9) Cant. iii. 10.

finally that *the end* and fruit of this divine banquet *is the union of charity,* Almighty God remaining in me as in His portable throne and place of rest, and in Him as in my protector and place of refuge.

POINT IV.

Consider the *excellency of this sovereign union* by the similitude which Christ our Lord declared when He said,— " As I live by the Father, so he that eateth me, the same also shall live by me."(10)

1. In these words Christ our Lord proposed the greatest similitudes which He could deliver to this end; which consists in this, that as the Son of God by eternal generation receives of His Father the being and life of God, and all the perfections, virtues, and works of God, so that the Son by this generation is one God with His Father, lives in Him, and by Him is wise, good, holy, infinite, and wholly as powerful as the Father is, and has with Him the same desire, will, and work in all things—so likewise he that worthily receives Christ in this Sacrament, in virtue of this meat, receives by participation the being and life of Christ, His perfections and virtues, and is made conformable to Jesus Christ in thinking, willing, and working the same which Christ did, so that he becomes one spirit with Him, and may say that of St. Paul:—" I live, now not I, but Christ liveth in me;" (11) and " to me to live is Christ," (12) because I live in Him, by Him, and for Him.

Colloquy.—O most sweet Jesus, since Thou hast so great a desire that I be made one thing with Thee, as Thou art with Thy Father ; enter into my soul by means of this Sacrament, and work in it the union which thereby Thou hast promised to me, that Thou

(10) Joan. vi. 58.   (11) Gal. ii. 10.   (12) Phil. i. 21.

mayest be glorified thereby, world without end. Amen.

2. In this consideration I am to ponder these words,—"he that shall eat me, shall live" "*propter me*," "*for me*." Which words comprehend all the kinds of causes, giving to understand that He will be the most perfect cause of all the living works that he does who eats Him. For by His inspiration He will be at the beginning of them, moving him to do them; He will be the final end, to whose glory they are ordained—the pattern and example who is to be imitated in doing them,—and lastly the matter of the words, thoughts, and affections which he shall have, so that he always lives "propter Christum," "for Christ," as he that knows no other thing "but Jesus Christ and Him crucified,"(13) or will love or speak of other things than of Christ, or ought but for Christ and by Christ; after this manner Christ will be our life, which He communicates to us in the most holy Holy Sacrament, and for this cause is called by excellency, "panis vivus," the "living bread," (14) because by Him we live the life of God, and the life of Christ united with Him, as He lived the same life with His Father.

Colloquy.—O bread of life, quicken me with Thy celestial and divine life, that henceforth I may no more live in myself, but in Thee, and that I may not live the life of man, but of God Himself, united with Him, world without end. Amen.

POINT V.

The first shall be to consider the wonderful *effects of this union* by some similitudes.

1. The first is *of the bread and wine* in which this banquet is celebrated. For even as meat uniting itself with

(13) 1 Cor. ii. 2.   (14) Joan. vi. 51.

the body imparts to it its proper qualities, whence it proceeds that gross meats engender gross humours, and delicate meats delicate and wholesome humours; even so Christ our Lord, entering into us and uniting Himself with our souls, communicates unto us His properties and celestial qualities, His charity, humility, obedience, patience, and other virtues, so that we remain in such wise renewed after the image of this new man, and of this celestial Adam, that it may be said of us, such as " is the second man from heaven heavenly, such also are they that are heavenly," (15) and such as Christ is, such are they that eat Him.   And although it be true that He communicates all virtues, yet especially He gives to every one that virtue of which he stands most in need, desires most, and most intends by that meat, like as Manna, although it had all kinds of savours, yet was it answerable to the will and taste of every one of the just, as has before been pondered.

2. After this manner I may also consider, how in *this Sacrament is that Lord who said :—" I am the vine,* you the branches, he that abideth in me, and I in him, the same beareth much fruit," (16) to accomplish which He enters into us, and like sap, places Himself in the midst of our heart, and unites to Himself the branch of our soul with all her powers, and gives them virtue that they may bud forth most sweet fruits of benediction, viz., devout cogitations, fervent affections, holy words, and perfect works, nor is He alone the vine, but also the labourer and husbandman who cuts off the superfluous branches that they may bring forth fruit.   For entering into a man, He inspires into him what is to be cut off and to be mortified, and helps him to it that he may preserve union, and may receive more abundant fruit of it.

Colloquy.—O my soul, since thou knowest that the

<hr>

(15) 1 Cor. xv. 47.   (16) Joan. xv. 5.

branch cut off from the vine cannot bring forth fruit, nor serve for ought but to be cast into the fire, engraft Thyself with this sovereign vine, which is Jesus Christ, receive Him into thy bowels, and cut off whatsoever thing may separate thee from Him, that, freed from the fire of hell, thou mayest always burn in the fire of love.   Amen.

3. In this Sacrament is *that Lord whom the glorious apostle St. James calls,* " *insitum verbum,*" " *the engrafted word* which is able to save your souls:"(17) " for by means of the Incarnation He engrafted and united Himself with our humanity, like as a fruitful tree is engrafted in a stock of a barren tree, and by the same wrought works more than human, the selfsame Lord by means of the communion of this Sacrament comes to enter into my soul, and engrafts Himself in it by grace; and I being of my own nature a barren stock, which brings forth no other than sour fruits of sin, He, engrafting Himself in me, causes me to bring forth sweet and divine fruits, not as of myself, but as of Him, after the manner that the stock of a bitter almond tree, being engrafted, produces sweet fruits.

Colloquy.—O my beloved, most sweet tree brought from heaven for the health of the world, now I content not myself only to say as did the spouse :—" I sat down under His shadow whom I desired, and His fruit was sweet to my palate ;"(18) but I further desire that Thou enter within me, and that Thou make me one thing with Thee, that, in virtue of Thee, I may bring forth most sweet fruits like Thine, which may remain to life everlasting.   Amen.

POINT VI.

Lastly, upon all which has been said, I will ascend to ponder how Christ our Lord instituted this Sacra-

(17) Jac. i. 21.   (18) Cant. ii. 3.

ment, *under the accidents of bread and wine,* rather than of other more precious and rare food, to signify how frequently the same was to be received,—by what persons,—with what disposition,—and the union and effects which it works in them.

1. First, by this means He declared the *inward desire which He has every day to make us this banquet,* and that we *every day* prepare ourselves to be partakers of it. For the kings of the earth hold it for a greatness, not only that their banquets be very sumptuous, but also rare, twice or thrice in every year; but the King of heaven holds it for greatness that His banquet be very sumptuous, and also every day during our whole life; and so instituted the same in the form of bread and wine, which is our daily food; that we may understand that as the body, although it have no precept given it of preserving life, yet by necessity and delight is drawn daily to eat bread, and to drink wine, wherewith to sustain it—even so the soul, although there were no commandment to communicate, yet ought to do the same frequently, for the necessity it has to preserve the spiritual life, and for the delight that there is in this divine food, and to give contentment to Him who invites us to it with so great a love, and *out of the great desire He has to give it us, commands us that we daily ask of Him* "*this daily bread.*" And the more to allure us to it, He likewise threatens us, that unless we "eat His flesh, and drink His blood," we "shall not have life in us,"(19) neither the life of grace, nor the life of eternal glory.

Colloquy.—O most loving Father, make me worthy daily to eat this daily bread; and since Thou wilt that I receive the same so frequently, assist me with so much grace that I may reap fruit thereby. Amen.

(19) Joan. vi. 39.

2. Moreover, as bread and wine are the ordinary sustenance of all sorts of persons, rich and poor, great and little; even so Christ our Lord will *that this Sacrament be the sustenance of all the faithful, of what state or condition soever they be*, high or low; because He invites all, as appears in the parable of the king who made " a great supper, and invited" all persons, even those that were "lame" and blind,"(20) and took it ill that many excused themselves, as we have considered in the meditation on this parable.(21)

3. Christ our Lord joined Himself with the forms of bread and wine, which are made *of many grains of wheat, and of grapes, united together*, to signify, that by this Sacrament, He does not join Himself spiritually, save only with souls *united by charity*, both with themselves and with their neighbours. So that as the grains of wheat, or of the vine, cannot be consecrated until they be made bread and wine with the aforesaid union—so likewise, although Christ our Lord enter by Sacramental communion into a man, yet will He not unite Himself with him spiritually, if he be divided and disunited for lack of charity, and dispose not himself duly to take away its impediments, which we shall obtain, if, like wheat, we grind ourselves by contrition and penance, and like grapes, suffer ourselves to be trod on by all, by true humility and subjection for the love of God. Hence results great fortitude to all the works of a spiritual life, with great alacrity of mind. For as " bread," as David says, " strengthens man's heart, and wine cheers the heart of man,"(22)—and although they be our ordinary meat, yet cause not any loathsomeness, or dislike, but are as salt, which seasons other meats—even so this bread and wine of heaven comforts and recreates the spirit, and

(20) Luc. xiv. 21.　　　(21) Med. iv. 13. iii.　　　(22) Ps. ciii. 15.

although it be eaten every day, yet causes it not loathsomeness if it be eaten worthily, but rather provokes a new desire and appetite to eat the same another time, because it contains in it " the sweetness of every taste," (23) not earthly like the Manna, which cau-ed loathing to the children of Israel, but celestial, which recreates the angels of heaven.(24)

Colloquy.—O beloved of my soul, who by so many ways and means provokest me to enjoy this sovereign banquet, suffer not that I excuse myself by the inordinate love of earthly goods, nor approach to it without the " wedding garment"(25) of holy charity ; but strip my heart, I beseech Thee, of all earthly love, and clothe it with divine, that I may assist with love at this banquet of love, and may attain by means of it the perfection of love, uniting myself with Thee by perfect charity.   Amen.

MEDITATION XLIII.

ON THE MOST HOLY SACRAMENT OF THE ALTAR, AS IT IS A SIGN AND PLEDGE OF THE GLORY WHICH WE EXPECT.

GOD our Lord, desiring to give us some *sign and pledge of the glory which He promised us*, for our consolation, and for the security of our confidence, instituted this most holy Sacrament, in which concur all things that may be desired for this end, which will be seen in these ensuing points.

POINT I.

This most holy Sacrament *is a sign and pledge of the glory promised to us, because it includes in it the most pre-*

(23) Sap. xvi. 20.   (24) Num. xxi. 5.   (25) Matt. xxii. 12.

cious thing, and best beloved, which Almighty God has, whose value is infinite, and which is worth as much as the same glory which He promises to us,—as amongst men, to assure the payment of some debt, or the accomplishment of some word which has been given, or of some promise which has been made, they give in pledge and guage some jewel or other thing much esteemed and beloved, and which is of so great price, that it exceeds, or is equal to that which afterwards is to be given.

This may be considered by going through the three divine Persons, who give this pledge, and by that which the pledge itself is.

1. First, *the eternal Father* could not give us a pledge more precious and more beloved *than His Son Himself,* who is as good as Himself, as kings and princes, to assure peace or truces, or some great debt, are wont to give in pledge or gauge their eldest son.   And since in this Sacrament He gives us His Only begotten Son Jesus for the pledge of glory, He has given us the greatest thing He could, not only in pledge of it, but of all other things, which He has promised us, with so great security on His part, as if they were already given us, according to that which St. Paul says,—" He that spared not even His own Son, but delivered Him up for us all, how hath He not also with Him, given us all things?"(1)   As if He should say, He that gives me His Son for my Redeemer, and gave Him to me for my sustenance and for my food, how shall He not also give me. His grace and His glory, and all things else which He has promised me.   So certain am I that He will give me them, as much as lies on His part, as if He had already given me them, because in this gift the others are included which He is to give to me.

(1) Rom. viii. 32.

Colloquy.—I give Thee thanks, O most loving Father, for such a pledge as Thou dost give me of my salvation and perfection. I beseech Thee, O my God, that it which is so certain on Thy part do not fail on mine, assisting me, that I may make my profit of the pledge which Thou hast given me, to obtain that which Thou dost promise me. Amen.

2. Secondly, *the same Son of God* our Saviour could not give us a greater pledge *than Himself*, covered in this Blessed Sacrament, in whom are contained all the titles and rights we have for our salvation, as he that promises some great inheritance, and gives for a pledge the privilege or writing, on which it is grounded. For our Lord, who is here, is our elder brother, (2) the heir of the eternal Father, and inheritor of heaven, who made Himself man, as St. Paul says, (3) to save those who were predestinated to glory, by whose means they are to obtain the end of their predestination, and who, by the price of His precious blood purchased us heaven, and opened us its gates, that we might enter into it, by the means which for this effect He offers to us. If, therefore, all this be here included, what greater pledge can He give us for the security of heaven, which He has gained for us, and promised to us?

3. Finally, *the Father and the Son* cannot give to us a greater invisible pledge of His glory than *the Holy Ghost Himself*, of whom St. Paul says, that He is " the pledge of our inheritance;" (4) which pledge, as the same apostle says, Christ gives "in our hearts" (5) for the security of all His promises, and for this end came He into the world, and comes also in this most holy Sacrament. Wherefore, we here receive two pledges of glory, the greatest that can

(2) Heb. ii. 11. Col. i. 15.   (3) Rom. viii. 29.
(4) Ephes. i. 14.   (5) 2 Cor. i. 22.

possibly be,—one visible, which is the Blessed Sacrament,
in which is contained Jesus Christ, true God and true
Man,—and another invisible, which is the Holy Ghost,
who gives Himself to us by the same Sacrament.

Colloquy.—O most blessed Trinity, I give Thee
innumerable thanks for such pledges as Thou givest
me of Thy sovereign promise.   It is evident to be
seen, O my Lord, that Thou wilt be a good paymaster,
since it grieves Thee not to give to me so many and
so good pledges for my security.   Rejoice, O my soul,
in such pledges, be glad with the hope which, is
grounded in them, endeavour to glorify and serve
Him who delivers them to thee, that thou mayest
come to possess the glory promised to thee.   Amen.

POINT II.

This most holy Sacrament is a pledge of the glory promised us, in being *a most effectual and powerful means to
obtain the same*, since there cannot be a more certain
pledge for obtaining any end than that which is the most
effectual *means* of obtaining it.

1. That which is most necessary to obtain glory effectually, is *pardon of sins past, preservation from those to come,
and a nourishment of the grace received*, with perseverance
in it until death.   In all these this excellent sacrament is
most eminent, by reason of the presence of Christ our
Lord; for although the sacrament of Baptism, or of
Penance, pardons sins, yet this greatly confirms the pardon, the selfsame King who pardons us, admitting us to
His table in sign He has forgiven us.   It also preserves us
from sins, because it bridles the passions of the flesh,
gives fortitude against the temptations of the Devil, and
prevents us against all the perils of the world.   Moreover,
it sustains the life of grace, as meat sustains the life of the
body, which it performs with so great efficacy, that it may

preserve the augmentation of grace which it has given, even to life eternal; all which is grounded upon the promise of Christ our Lord, saying:—" This is the bread that came down from heaven." " I am the living bread which came down from heaven. If any man eat of this bread he shall live for ever. He that eateth my flesh, and drinketh my blood, hath life everlasting, and I will raise him up in the last day." (6)   In which words Christ our Lord assures us that this divine bread, as already has been noted, with His celestial virtue, will deliver us from all that is contrary to eternal life, because it delivers us from the first death, which is of sin, and from the second of the soul, which is damnation; (7) and in due time will deliver us from the death of the body, in the Resurrection. Moreover, He grants us all that which is eternal life, because He gives us the life of grace, and preserves it to the end; and afterwards will give us the life of glory, which the soul will enjoy; and at the end of the world, that glorious life which the body likewise is to enjoy. Of all this we have pledges in this Blessed Sacrament, because it contains virtue for all these, and gives force to him who receives it often, and with due reverence.

Colloquy.—O tree of life, placed in the midst of the Paradise of God,(8) in sign of the pledges of immortality and of life eternal, give me to eat of Thy most sweet fruit, which may preserve my soul from all kind of death, and may give to it all kind of life. O my soul, if thou desire eternal life, feed with spirit on this divine food, which is the pledge and cause of it. O my body, if thou desire to rise again to the life of blessedness, feed on this precious body, which is an assured pledge of thy resurrection, and of that glorious life which is promised to thee.

(6) Joan. vi. 59.   (7) Apoc. ii. 11.
(8) Apoc. xxii. 2.

2. But the excellency of this pledge passes yet further, in that with its presence it causes in us *somewhat which is a part of eternal life*, as its root and fountain, with which it is to remain for ever, and it is impossible that life eternal can be denied to him who has the same, namely, the union with Jesus Christ our Lord, by means of His grace, and of the virtue of the Holy Ghost, who is the " fountain of water springing up into life everlasting;" (9) and, as St. Thomas notes, (10) is not only a pledge of our inheritance, but also an earnest, because a pledge is only given until the payment be made, and then ceases, but an earnest penny is given for ever,—even so the Blessed Sacrament of the Altar, and the gifts of faith and of hope are no more than a pledge of glory, which lasts for the time of this present life, but the union with Jesus Christ, which is made in this Sacrament, and the union of the Holy Ghost, which is given us by charity, is an earnest " reward," (11) and will endure and last for all eternity, unless we lose it through our own default, because charity never fails, and the Holy Ghost remains with us for ever and ever. (12)

Colloquy.—O most sweet spouse of just souls, who, for an earnest, givest to them Thine own self, joining them with Thee in the union of charity, although my soul be not worthy of this sovereign greatness, yet exclude her not from the same, for Thine infinite mercy, I beseech Thee.   Amen.

POINT III.

This Sacrament is a pledge of glory, in that it is a most excellent banquet, *in which Almighty God gives us to eat and drink the same which He gives us in His glory* but yet disguised and accommodated according to our state, namely, the state of wayfarers hidden under a veil of obscurity.

(9) Joan. iv. 14.   (10) Lect. v. in Ephes. i. 14.
   (11) 1 Cor. iii. 8.   (12) Joan. xiv. 16.

1. Christ our Lord, according to that which He promised to His apostles, has in heaven all the Blessed sitting with Him at His table, to whom He makes a solemn banquet, in which the meat that is set before them is His own divinity and humanity, which they see clearly, and fill with it all their desires, and are inebriated with the wine of beatifying love, drinking of the abundant river of His celestial delights.   In this banquet the same Lord, as St. Luke says, girds Himself, and making them to "sit down," " ministers to them," (13) for Himself gives them this reward of justice.   But He girds Himself because He is so infinite that none can comprehend Him, nor behold Him unless girded, and accommodated to His merits.   Hence I will descend to ponder that this infinite God, who makes this banquet above in heaven, mindful of His children whom He has on earth, girds Himself much more to invite them, *putting Himself wholly with His divinity and humanity under these forms of bread and wine*, being so little and so confined, that there with the eyes of faith we may behold Him present, and receiving Him within us, may fill our desires as much as here they may be filled, and may also inebriate us with the wine of His love, and give us to taste the sweetness of His delights, giving us all this as pledges, in hope of that which He will hereafter give us in full possession; for which I will render Him infinite thanks, with very inward desires to gird, mortify, and constrain myself to serve Him, since He girds Himself so much to favour me.

Colloquy.—O my beloved, if Thou, being in heaven descendest to gird Thyself on earth in favour of me, what great thing is it that I, to ascend from earth to heaven, gird myself for Thy holy service; quicken, O Lord, my faith, that I may be so delighted with the

<hr>

(13) Luc. xii. 37.

banquet which Thou makest me in this life, that I may come to enjoy that which Thou promisest me in the other.   Amen.

2. With this spirit I will excite myself *to procure a celestial life, so to be worthy of this banquet,* in which is given to me the same which is given in heaven, since for this cause Christ our Lord, in the prayer of the "Pater noster," first commands us to say,—"Thy will be done on earth as it is in heaven," and then bids that we should ask this daily, and "supersubstantial bread," (14) signifying that he who will eat it worthily must aspire to the purity which is in heaven, accomplishing here all that which God commands as it is accomplished there.

3. Finally, hence I will gather that this Sacrament being a pledge of glory, and the beginning of the banquet which is made in heaven, is *the "viaticum," "the voyage food,"* *to pass from this life to the other,* which is to be received in that perilous passage with great faith and confidence, since as Elias, in the strength of the bread which the angel gave him, walked to the mountain of God, Horeb, (15) even so I, in the strength of this divine bread, shall make my journey securely, even to the mountain of bliss and glory. And to the end that I may receive it then with profit, it behoves me to accustom myself every time I communicate to dispose myself with the same spirit as if I took it for my last voyage, imagining how perhaps that communion will be the last of all my life, following in this the counsel of the Wise man, saying:—"When thou shalt sit to eat with a prince at his table...put a knife in thy throat," (16) that is to say, so eat this bread as if the knife were now in thy throat, and that thou were at the point to die; and for this cause Christ our Lord instituted this Sacra-

(14) Mat. vi. 11.   (15) 3 Reg. xix. 8.

(16) Prov. xxiii. 1.

ment the night before His death, to signify, as has been said in its place, that this meat fortifies the soul to suffer and die, and to pass from this life to the eternal.

Colloquy.—O most sweet Redeemer, who, at Thy departure out of this world, saidst to Thine apostles :—" I will come again, and will take you to myself, that where I am you also may be;"(17) come, I beseech Thee, to visit my soul with the grace and presence of Thy venerable sacrament, and in virtue of it bring me where Thou art, that I may there see what I here believe, possess what I hope, and enjoy Thy Divine presence, world without end.   Amen.

MEDITATION XLIV.

BY APPLICATION OF THE SENSES OF THE SOUL TO THE MOST BLESSED SACRAMENT.

This manner of prayer, by application of the senses, which has been declared in the second Part, is very profitable concerning the Blessed Sacrament, in which closing the five senses of the body we revive those of the soul, somewhat of which St. Bonaventure touched in his treatise on the seven journeys to eternity,(1) as has been said in the second chapter of the Introduction of this book.   But here we will consider it after another manner, more easy for all.

POINT I.

The first shall be to *see with the interior eye of the soul,* illuminated by holy faith, all that which *is the object of this sight* concerning this Blessed Sacrament, drawing forth divers affections conformable to that which has been seen.

(17) Joan. xiv. 3.   (1) Itin. vi. dist. 6.

1. I will behold the *quantity, the colour, and the figure of the bread and wine* separated from their substance, which Almighty God, by His omnipotency, destroys, to put in their place the body and blood of Christ, and actuating this faith I will captivate my understanding that it believe the same, renouncing the judgment which proceeds from the senses, and confessing that God can do, by His omnipotency, more than our short reason can conceive. And so I will say I believe, that although I see the colour of bread, and perceive the smell and savour of bread, yet that the substance of bread is not there, because faith says it, and God has so revealed it.

2. Then will I behold with the same sight *the majesty of Jesus Christ,* as entire and as glorious as it is in heaven. I will behold His sacred head with the crown of glory— His divine face with beams of immense splendour—His hands, feet, and side, with the most beautiful marks of the wounds which are in them, and His whole body, incomparably more beautiful than all the sons of men; and afterwards ascending higher, beholding Him as He is God, "the brightness" of the "glory" of the Father, "and the figure of His substance," (2) and of such infinite beauty that He makes blessed all those who clearly see Him. And beholding Him in this manner sometimes I will produce acts of reverence and humility, abasing my eyes and shrinking in myself in the presence of such a majesty.—At other times I will produce affections of joy and of gladness, to see Him so beautiful and resplendent, and so near to me.— At other times I will burst forth into affections of praise and thanksgiving for having placed Himself there, with all His glory and His majesty.

3. Thirdly, I will behold the *conjunction of that exterior bread with the majesty of Jesus Christ,* admiring to see con-

(2) Heb. i. 3.

joined two extremes so greatly different, one so little and so base as are the accidents of bread and wine, and the other so great and high as is God and man, covering the greatness of His splendour with the veil of so base a creature, provoking myself to the imitation of such a manner of humility.

Colloquy.—O my beloved, who remainest in this visible sacrament after an invisible manner, let me behold Thee by faith, and reverence Thy greatness, as if I saw Thee evidently, since Thou art the same in the Sacrament and in heaven, and as worthy to be reverenced and loved in the baseness of the one as in the highness of the other.

POINT II.

The second is, to hear with *the hearing* of the soul that which Christ our Lord *says to me* in the Sacrament, imagining that thence He speaks to my heart, and says to me sundry things which are to my purpose.

1. Sometimes I will imagine that *He invites me to eat Him*, saying to me that of the Wise man:—" Come, eat my bread, and drink the wine, which I have mingled for you. Forsake childishness and live, and walk by the ways of prudence;" (3) that is to say, come and receive me in this Sacrament, but lay aside first the childishness of this life, because I am the meat of the great, and of such which live warily and prudently. And in this manner also I may imagine that He says to me that of the Canticles:—" Eat, O friends, and drink, and be inebriated, my dearly beloved." (4) And that of the prophet Isaiah:—" All you that thirst come to the waters...Hearken diligently to me, and eat that which is good, and your soul shall be delighted in fatness." (5) Hence I will conceive desires to receive Him, obeying His voice, and saying to Him:—

(3) Prov. ix. 5.   (4) Cant. v. 1.   (5) Isa. lv. 1.

Colloquy.—Whence is this to me, O Lord, that Thou invitest me to Thy table? Behold I approach to it because Thou commandest me, speak to me, I beseech Thee, whilst I eat, that my heart may be melted in Thy love.

2. At other times I will imagine that He *exhorts me from thence to imitate Him,* saying to me:—" Learn of me, for I am meek and humble of heart, and you shall find rest to your souls;" (6) learn humility of me to conceal yourselves, and to invite with charity one another.

3. At other times I will behold Him compassed about with holy angels, who say to me:—" Ecce sponsus venit, exite obviam ei," " *Behold the bridegroom cometh, go ye forth to meet Him*" (7) with burning lamps, namely, with affections greatly inflamed, to unite yourselves with Him in perpetual charity.

4. Finally, after I have received this divine Sacrament, I will say that of Samuel:—" *Speak, Lord, for Thy servant heareth ;*" (8) and I will diligently attend to the inspirations which shall be suggested to me to hear, and I will obey them with readiness, saying with David:—" I will hear what the Lord speaketh" in me, who is within me, because I know full well that " He will speak" words of " peace" (9) and of eternal life.

POINT III.

1. The third is with *the smell* of the soul, to feel the smell and *fragrancy of Christ* our Lord in this holy Sacrament, who, in the Sacrifice of the Mass, offers Himself to His Father in an host and sacrifice in the odour of sweetness. Oh how well smells this Sacrifice to the eternal Father, appeasing with it His anger against us! Oh how

<table>
<tr><td>(6) Mat. xi. 29.</td><td>(7) Mat. xxv. 5.</td></tr>
<tr><td>(8) 1 Reg. iii. 9.</td><td>(9) Ps. lxxxiv. 9.</td></tr>
</table>

powerful is the smell of it to dissipate and annihilate the evil odour of all sinners, and of all the sins that are in the world!

Colloquy.—O sovereign Father, since the most sweet smell of this Sacrifice is so agreeable to Thee, pardon me by the same my grievous sins, and pacify the anger which Thou hast conceived against me for them. Amen.

2. I will likewise smell the savour of *the virtues* of this holy Sacrament. For, like as amber, balm, and other odoriferous things comfort with their fragrancy not only those that touch them, but others also, though they be somewhat separate and remote;—even so the odour of this Sacrament not only comforts him that receives it, but also him that beholds it, adores it, and desires to receive it. And as the same Lord says that "wheresoever the body shall be, there also shall the eagles be gathered together," (10)—that is, attracted by the smell, to eat and to sustain them with the flesh; even so souls, like eagles, fly in prayer and contemplation, perceiving this most sweet odour of the body of Christ, go where it is to eat the same, and to sustain them with His most precious flesh.

Colloquy.—O most fragrant flesh of Jesus Christ, comfort me with the odour of Thy virtues, make me to smell the fragrance of Thy charity, and draw me after Thee, in the odour of Thine ointments, that I may join me with Thee in the union of perfect love. Amen.

POINT IV.

1. The fourth is with *the taste* of the soul, to taste first *the great delight* with which Christ our Lord remains in this holy Sacrament and in every Host, although it be

(10) Matt. xxiv. 28.

placed in some base and vile place, and the great delight He has to see Himself devoutly received. Other meats being dead—though they give delight to him that eats them—yet feel no delight in being eaten; but this meat, because it is living bread, feels exceeding delight in that it is eaten, and more desires to be eaten of men than they desire to eat.

Colloquy.—O bread of life, I give Thee thanks for the delight which Thou hast in becoming our meat and our sustenance; purify, dear Lord, I beseech Thee, the taste of my soul, that it may receive Thy most sweet taste, so that I may delight to receive Thee with the same delight with which Thou delightest to be received. Amen.

2. Then will I taste the *sweetness of Christ* in this Blessed Sacrament, beholding how He communicates to those who receive Him worthily a certain taste of the divinity, much more sweet and delectable than was the Manna; because it has the savour of all spiritual meats and the relish of all virtues, and that which so greatly sweetens, that it sweetens all the bitternesses that are in this life and in the exercise of mortification, and of all other virtuous works; and I will imagine that of the psalm to be said to me,—" O taste and see by experience that the Lord is sweet." (11)

Colloquy.—O most sweet Jesus, how sweet art Thou to those that love Thee, and with love come to receive Thee! O fountain of sweetness, who givest Thyself to be tasted in great abundance by the pipes of these two sacramental forms; fill my soul with Thy sovereign sweetness, that I may reject all earthly sweetness. Amen.

POINT V.

1. The fifth is with the interior *touching*, to touch spiri-

(11) Ps. xxxiii. 9.

tually, and in due time corporally also, this Blessed Sacrament, by whose touching virtue goes forth to heal, to revive, to rejoice, and to perfect all those who touch the same duly, as in former times virtue went out of the vestments of Christ to heal fluxes of blood and the infirmities of those that touched them.(12)

2. At other times I will imagine when I approach with my lips to the consecrated Host, that with great reverence and trembling *I give a kiss to Christ our Lord*, and receive one most lovingly from His most sacred and sweet mouth, saying that of the Canticles:—" Let Him kiss me with the kiss of His mouth," for His "breasts are better than wine, smelling sweetly of the best ointments." (13)

Colloquy.—O most sweet Saviour, give me the kiss of peace, pacifying me with Thine eternal Father. O sacramental forms of bread and wine, since you are as the breasts of my beloved, full of the milk of celestial delights, and much more precious than the wine of earthly pleasures, touch me and fill me with your milk, that all flesh may be distasteful to me. Amen.

3. At other times I will quicken my faith to believe and to see by it the sacred wounds of Christ our Lord, touching with my spirit *His, feet, His hands, and His sacred side*, like him who approaches to drink the water and blood which issues thence, and touching them with a lively faith, I will cry out with St. Thomas, saying;—" Dominus meus et Deus meus," " My Lord and my God." (14)

Colloquy.—O God of my soul, wound my heart with the dart of Thy charity, by the wounds which Thou receivedst in Thy sacred body. Satisfy the thirst of my soul with the water and blood which issued forth of Thy sacred side. Wash me, purify

<hr>

(12) Mat. ix. 25. Marc. v. 30. Med. lii.   (13) Cant. i. 1.
(14) Joan. xx. 28.

me, inflame me, and perfect me therewith, and give me leave, in spirit, to enter into these glorious wounds. And since Thou with them dwellest within me, I with all my soul desire to dwell within them, and within Thee, uniting myself with Thee by the union of love, until I be made one with Thee in eternal glory. Amen.

MEDITATION XLV.

OR THE FEAST, AND SOLEMNITY OF THE BLESSED SACRAMENT, AND TO ACCOMPLISH WITH SPIRIT THE PROCESSIONS AND THE OCTAVES OF THIS DAY.

POINT I.

1. Christ our Lord in this Sacrament *comes into our earth to renew what He did* when He lived therein. Then He walked throughout all the streets and markets of Judea and Galilee, and through the synagogues and particular houses, and in the Temple of Jerusalem itself, and as St. Peter said, He "went about doing good and healing all that were oppressed by the Devil, for God was with Him," (1) not only by grace, but also by unity of Person; and the good which He did was in all kinds exercising the divers offices which we have before related, so that whithersoever He went He left steps of His divinity and omnipotency, and of His immense charity and mercy.

2. After this manner I will imagine that Christ our Lord now walks in this Sacrament, *through the temples, market-places, and streets of Christendom*, doing good to all those who with a lively faith approach to Him, confessing, adoring, and praising Him with all their heart. For now also this most holy Sacrament goes throughout, doing good, and healing all that are oppressed of the Devil, because

(1) **Act. x. 39.**

God is within the same, and therefore communicates to them all kind of goods, with celestial splendours of His light and inspirations of His divine Spirit, teaching them as a master, curing them as a physician, pardoning them as a Saviour, and feeding them as a pastor, with His own most precious body and blood. And although He performs all this more liberally towards those that receive Him, yet He likewise gives some part of it to those who, with a lively faith, behold, adore, and glorify Him.

3. And with this spirit *am I to accompany Him* in processions, as I would have accompanied Him when He lived in this mortal flesh, if then I had had that faith which now I have, and as the devout people accompanied and went after our Saviour, so to enjoy His most sweet company.

Colloquy.—O my beloved, I give Thee thanks for having of purpose so left Thyself with us, that although Thou hast Thy habitation in heaven, filling their streets with joy, yet wilt Thou also be on our earth, filling our market places and our streets with Thy mercy. And since Thou art so powerful under this veil, as Thou art above in heaven, and as Thou wert before on earth, come to this poor habitation of my soul, walk through all her powers and senses, doing good to them all, that they may all serve and glorify Thee, world without end. Amen.

POINT II.

1. Christ our Lord *desires now again to renew spiritually the entrance which He made into Jerusalem* on the day of palms; for then He entered into Jerusalem meek and humble, sitting upon an ass, a great multitude of people going forth to receive Him, and all leading Him in procession with great pomp. Some spread their garments on the ground, that He might walk upon them; others cut down boughs of trees to strew in the way; and others carried

palms in their hands, and all cried out, saying:—"Blessed is He that cometh in the name of our Lord; Hosanna in the highest."(2)   This so solemn an entry Christ our Lord made to show on His part with what delight of mind He conversed amongst them, although they persecuted and ill-treated Him; as also that His disciples and the devout people should manifest the faith, the love, and devotion which they bore to Him, and for other causes which we have pondered in the third part.(3)

2. In the selfsame manner will *He now be borne in the most Blessed Sacrament through the market-places and streets of the Church* with great pomp and majesty.   He goes in that host meek and humble, hid and covered under that veil and light cloud of the accidents of bread; but yet all the faithful and princes of the Church hold it for an honour to accompany Him, adorning the streets with boughs and with rich hangings, carrying torches and lights, accompanied with singers and songs of gladness, celebrating His coming into the world with the greatest pomp and exterior honour which here on earth can be given to Him.   Of all which I am to be glad and rejoice; for if I rejoice for the honour which on the day of palms they did to this our Lord, the conclusion of which ended in ignominy, how much more ought I to rejoice for the honour that all now exhibit to Him, being directed to His greater glory.

3. Christ our Lord so disposed this solemn pomp, *to declare to us how willingly He remains with us,* and that He is neither wearied nor disgusted, although there are many causes that He should be so, by reason of the ill entertainment which many sinners give Him, who communicate unworthily, or celebrate Mass unbecomingly.   And although reason require that I be sorry for the injury which is done to Him, yet will I praise Him, because, notwith-

(2) Mat. xxi. 9.   Joan. xii. 13.　　　　　(3) iv. Med. iii.

standing this, He is not wearied to remain with sinners, that so He may do good to the just.

4. Hence I will conceive a great desire *that all of us celebrate with spirit these devout processions* in such manner that Christ our Lord be delighted with the honour which we exhibit to Him; for He is not satisfied with the exterior, if it be void and empty of the interior.

Colloquy.—O my beloved, I wish that all of us spread our garments upon the ground, laying all that we have before Thy feet, to the end that Thou dispose of them as it pleases Thee. Oh that all prostrated themselves upon the earth with profound humility, suffering themselves to be humbled and trod upon by all, that so Thou mightest be exalted and glorified of all! Oh that all of us accompanied Thee with palms in our hands, obtaining glorious victories over our enemies, the glory of which we might wholly attribute to Thee! Oh that all with great spirit might praise and glorify Thee for the victories which Thou gainest every day by means of this divine Sacrament, desiring that the whole world might be made partaker of them! O my soul, praise and glorify this our Lord when thou accompaniest Him, or assist in His presence, conjoining the song of the Seraphim with the song of the Hebrews, saying with great spirit:—" Holy, Holy, Holy, Lord God of Sabaoth! heaven and earth are full of Thy glory. Hosanna in the highest! blessed is He that cometh in the name of our Lord! Hosanna in the highest."(4) Amen.

POINT III.

1. The eternal Father desires with these honourable processions *to recompense on earth the dishonourable and sorrowful stations,* which His Son, Jesus Christ our Lord made the night and day of His Passion, through the market-

(4) In præfat. Missa.

places and streets of Jerusalem. He then went from the garden of Gethsemane to the house of Annas and Caiphas, led bound, with torches and lanterns, with lances and swords, and with a great clamour and shouting of the soldiers, triumphing over their prisoner with derision;—and another day with the like ignominy they led Him from house to house, and from one tribunal to another, until He went to the mount of Calvary, with the cross upon His shoulders, the criers sounding forth whatever might cause Him ignominy:—and finally, was placed on the dreadful throne of the cross, between two thieves, where He was blasphemed and scorned with most notorious ignominy and cruelty.

2. In reward of these journeys the eternal Father will *that His Son be honoured on earth with these processions*, all bearing lights and torches in their hands, in token that He is the true light which enlightens the whole world, and the faithful soldiers of His Church accompanying Him, singing a thousand songs of musical praises, the priests bearing Him upon their shoulders, and placing Him on thrones of great majesty, where all bow their knees before Him, and adore Him as their God and their Redeemer, commanding all that they do the same, much better than king Assuerus commanded Mardochius to be honoured, leading Him with great pomp through all the streets of the city, the king's chief favourites crying out:—"Thus shall He be honoured whom the king hath a mind to honour."(5)

Colloquy.—O eternal Father, I give Thee thanks for the honour which Thou wilt have exhibited to Thine Only-begotten Son here on earth, in recompense of the dishonour which He received there. O most sweet Redeemer, I rejoice for the honour which this

(5) Esther vi. 9.

day Thy faithful servants do to Thee, since Thou hast worthily deserved the same for the dishonour which Thou sufferedst for them. I bow my knee before this throne on which Thou art placed in this Blessed Sacrament, and do cast my crown and whatsoever I have before Thy holy feet, saying with those ancients in the Apocalypse:—" Thou art worthy, O Lord our God, to receive glory, and honour, and power, because Thou hast created all things, and for Thy will they were, and have been created."(6)

3. Hence I will gather *how faithful Almighty God is in rewarding those in this life that serve Him*, exalting them in the same things in which they were humbled. And if I honour Christ in this holy Sacrament, He will likewise honour me, and if I treat Him irreverently, I also shall be dishonoured. To which purpose it will help to recal to my mind the history of the Ark of the Old Testament, which David bore in procession, with a great company of priests and Levites, and of all the people, with excellent music of divers instruments, David himself dancing before the Ark with great fervour of spirit.(7) And although Michol, his wife, despised him in her heart, yet was he not sorry for what he had done, but purposed to humble himself, and to abase himself before Almighty God. On the other hand, Oza, who with temerity and little respect touched the Ark, was struck dead upon a sudden for that fact; to signify that if I touch with little reverence this Divine Sacrament, I shall be chastised as Oza was, and my chastisement will be so much the more terrible, as I ought to bear greater reverence to Him that deserves it, much more than did the Ark; but if I honour it as David did, singing and leaping in my heart with jubilees of joy and affections of love, humbling and abasing myself in His

(6) Apoc. iv. 11.   (7) 2 Reg. vi. 14.

blessed presence, without making any account of the sayings of men, He will honour me here on earth, and much more hereafter above in heaven.

Colloquy.—O my glory, I desire no greater honour than to honour Thee, for Thy honour is my honour, and that Thou be honoured of all, I take for an honour to myself; and if Thou please to honour Thyself with my dishonours, this also will I hold for a very high honour, that so I may glorify Thee, who art worthy of infinite honour and glory, world without end. Amen.

POINT IV.

1. Christ our Lord will *that some feast be made to Him here below on earth, as there is above in heaven*, that by this means benedictions may descend from heaven to earth. Thus our Lord is in heaven compassed about with angels and saints, who continually make a feast to Him;—some, like the "four-and-twenty ancients,"(8) cast their crowns before His feet, saying that He alone is worthy of honour and glory;—others like to the four beasts, saying: —" Holy, holy, holy, Lord God Almighty, who was, and who is, and who is to come."(9) Others offer to Him " golden vials, full of odours, which are the prayers of saints;"(10) and every one after his manner glorifies Him, and presents Him canticles of thanksgiving and of praise, so that through the ways and streets of that celestial Jerusalem is always heard, "Alleluia,"(11) which is a voice of joy and gladness, giving of thanks, of joy, and everlasting jubilee.(12)

2. Notwithstanding this, Christ our Lord *delights to descend to our village in this most holy Sacrament*, and will that after our manner we place Him in His throne, and

(8) Apoc. iv. 10.   (9) Apoc. iv. 8.   (10) Apoc. v. 8.
(11) Tob. xiii. 22.   (12) Isa. li. 3.

make a feast to Him, although it be after a simple manner, imitating so far as we may His celestial courtiers, intending herein not His own profit, but wholly ours, that, discovering the love we bear Him, He may take occasion to honour us, and to bestow great goods upon us; and therefore, imitating the Blessed in heaven, I am to honour Him principally with three kinds of affection.—i. The first of *humility*, like those elders, despoiling myself of whatsoever I have, and confessing that it is not mine, but His, giving to Him the glory of all.—ii. The second affection is, to be of *a lively faith* of His excellency, and of the office for which He comes, and is to come to judge us, praising Him as the holy beasts for His sanctity and omnipotence, for His eternity and immutability, and because He now comes to me to save me as a Father, who afterwards will come to crown me as a judge.—iii. The third affection shall be of *oblation*, presenting to Him the vial of my heart, gilded with the most fine gold of charity, full of the odour of fervent prayers, mingled with the mortifications of self, dissolving myself in the fire of love, to smell most sweetly to this our Lord, to whom I am to make a feast in the best manner that I may, admiring that a Lord, who is so greatly feasted in heaven, deigns to delight in the feast which is made Him here on earth; like to a king, who, having seen the feasts which are made to him in his court, should likewise take delight in that which is made to him in a village. I will also persuade myself that as Christ our Lord, for the new services that are done to Him in heaven, gives them new accidental joys, even so will He reward the services which the just do to Him in these feasts here on earth with new graces and increase of virtues.

Colloquy.—O sovereign King, I wish that I could make of earth a heaven, sanctifying Thy name,(13)

(13) Mat. vi. 10.

and fulfilling Thy will in this vale of tears, as the blessed spirits do in their paradise of delights! I should be assured that if I could do so, this valley of tears should become to me a valley of comforts, and the paradise of delights should become a valley of tears, converting my weeping into joy, and filling me with gladness. O my King let Thy kingdom come to me, and since Thou art with me in this Sacrament, quicken my faith and inflame my charity, that I may know Thee and love Thee, so that Thou mayest reign in me, and I truly rejoice in Thee, reigning with Thee in the kingdom of Thy Father, world without end, Amen.

MEDITATION XLVI.

ON THE FATHERLY PROVIDENCE OF ALMIGHTY GOD
IN DISTRIBUTING STATES AND OFFICES, GIVING TO EVERY ONE THAT WHICH
IS MOST CONVENIENT FOR HIS SALVATION.

POINT I.

1. God our Lord is our Father by excellency,(1) and performs this office towards us infinitely better than all the fathers of the earth, since in comparison of Him none other merits this name; whence it follows that He not only creates and begets us in the being of nature and of grace, and after we have been engendered, preserves and sustains us in the one and in the other, by means and manners very admirable, as has been said; but also His fatherly providence *has a care to place us in such a state and office as is convenient for our salvation*, inspiring, moving, and alluring every one to that which is fittest for him to this end. For some He moves to the state of matrimony, others to the state of continency or Religion, and others He chooses for the

(1) Mat. xxiii. 9.

state of prelacy. For as in a natural body there are "many members,"(2) having different offices, even so will He that there be in this mystical body of the Church, as well as in the civil commonwealth; and by His providence ordains that some shall be as heads to govern others;—others as eyes to shine in virtue and doctrine;—others as hands to exercise the works of the active life;—others as the breast and heart, who hide themselves in the secret of the contemplative and unitive life;—others as feet, who employ themselves in base and humble offices. And as our Lord knows the complexions, wits, and talents of every one, so with His providence He induces them to that state and office which best agrees to their nature, unless a man will withdraw himself from the direction of the divine government, and choose a state and office after his fancy, for evil ends and by evil means.

2. From this verity well pondered I am to draw *great gratitude towards our Lord for this fatherly providence which He has of us* with two reflections.—i. That if I have not as yet made choice of a state of life, *I am to have recourse to God,* and to ask the same seriously of Him, using lawful means, which do not derogate from His divine providence, who will give to me that state and office which is convenient to me, by such means, if I put my trust herein; and if these which I make choice of be not sufficient, He knows how to apply others, which shall bring to pass what He intends: of which there are admirable examples in Holy Scripture, such as are the marriage of Isaac with Rebecca, of Tobias with Sara, by means of the angel Raphael, the election of Joseph for viceroy of Egypt, and that of David for king of Israel.

ii. But *if I have taken a state* already by the disposition of the divine providence, *I ought to remain much contented*

(2) 2 Cor. xii. 12.

with it, trusting to obtain eternal life by such means, since for this end our Lord called me to this state. And if the state or office be base, I will not blush for this, nor hold myself as disgraced; nor contrariwise, if the office be high, I will not puff myself up, or become proud, but, as the apostle says:—" Let every man abide in the same calling in which he was called,"(3) whether a bondman or free, whether great or little, living in the great with humility, and in the little with confidence; for it is better to be the feet of the Church, and to obtain heaven, than, being the head of it, to go down to hell.

Colloquy.—Wherefore, O my soul, rejoice in thy God, in whose hands thy lots are,(4) and what state soever He shall give thee, receive it with gladness; for the lot of the state and office which He has designed thee in this life is directed by His providence, that thou mayest obtain the lot of the Blessed in the other. Amen.

POINT II.

1. Consider *the sweetness of the divine providence in the distribution of states and offices*, which shines in a thing so proper to God, that there is no prince or monarch who can perform the same. Because as He is universal governor of all the world, and glories much to govern "from end to end mightily, and to order all things sweetly,"(5) He dis·tributes to men inclinations to divers states and offices with so admirable sweetness, that there is no office, how heavy and base soever it be, to which some man has not a very vehement inclination, without inclining themselves to other things: and although they be sons of the same fathers, and brethren of the same womb, as Esau and Jacob were, yet are they wont to be born with different and repugnant inclinations. For as the potter of one and

(3) 1 Cor. vii. 20.   (4) Ps. xxx. 16.   (5) Sap. i. 8.

the same mass makes vessels of different figures, and applied to different uses, and of one and the same seminal matter are made divers members of the same body for different offices: even so the divine wisdom and omnipotency, out of the mass of mankind produces divers men, applied with divers inclinations to divers offices. For which cause I am to glorify Him, beholding how all these inclinations redound to my profit, as that there are men who take delight to defend me in war, to govern me in peace, others to till the ground, others making garments, and others doing other things of which I stand in need; for, as St. Paul says,—" If all the body were the eye, where would be the hearing? If the whole were hearing, where would be the smelling?"(6) If all were tongues, who could work? And if all were hands, who could speak? As the offices of all the members are for the good of every one, so the divers states and offices of men, and their inclinations thereunto, are for my profit, and therefore, as a benefit to me, they are to serve me for a motive to glorify Almighty God, who by His providence distributes them after this manner amongst men. And according to this, I am diligently to observe the good inclination which God has given me, and to make my profit of it, embracing with contentment that state and office which He has given me conformable to it, giving Him thanks for the sweetness with which He governs me, not willing to draw me violently to any state in which I should live, as striving against the stream, especially in that which is to be perpetual, or for long continuance of my life.

Colloquy.—O most loving Father, I give Thee thanks for the sweetness with which Thou vouchsafest to govern man, making the burden pleasant to some

(6) 1 Cor. xii. 17.

which is painful to others, to the end that " every one may bear his own"(7) with greater facility, and all may help one another with gladness and willingness. Grant, dear Lord, that I may bear my own with such contentment that I may profit my neighbours, as I desire that they profit and help me. Amen.

2. In the same sweetness of the divine providence, *when there is wanting in us a natural inclination to the state and office* which He desires to impose upon us, *He gives us liberally a supernatural inclination* by the means of divine inspirations and illustrations, which are wont to discover to us so many reasons concerning the utility and conveniency of that state and office; that although it be hard and difficult, yet they make it easy and delightful. And so we see by experience, that many, by this touch of Almighty God, have a vehement inclination to leave the world, and to embrace a Religious state, or some troublesome and humble office, with greater delight than others embrace other states and offices of much more sweetness and facility for the flesh, because the grace of God supplies abundantly that which is wanting to nature. And if sometimes our Lord does not give this inclination and sensible delectation in the election of this state, yet at the least He gives so effectual reasons, as convince the understanding, and cause it to judge that it is convenient to take it, which the will accepts with great resolution, overcoming all repugnancy of nature with the superior light of the spirit.

Colloquy.—O God of my soul, I wholly cast myself into Thy hands, wholly trusting in Thy divine providence, that Thou wilt give me pleasure and comfort in bearing the burden which Thou shalt please to impose upon me. And if the flesh feel not those contentments

(7) Gal. vi. 5.

which it desires, it suffices me that my spirit feel them, reputing this for its proper pleasure to embrace and fulfil that which is Thine.   This shall be my only inclination to accomplish in all things Thy holy will, world without end.   Amen.

POINT III.

1. Consider the *efficacy of the divine providence*, in providing sufficient *helps to comply with that state and office* which by His disposition is elected, for He commands none that which is impossible, nor desires to lay a greater burden upon any man than he is able to bear according to the forces he has, and the talent of grace which God has given him.   And therefore to the married, to undergo the burden of their state, He gives a special grace by the sacrament of Marriage; and to priests, to bear the burden of their office, He gives them the Holy Ghost by the sacrament of Orders; and to all Religious He gives grace, according to the strictness of that Religion which every one professes; and to prelates and governors He gives spirit sufficient for their government, and the more heavy and difficult it is, so much more abundant is the spirit which He gives them.   Whence it was, that when Almighty God took from Moses part of the government of the people, He said to him:—I will take of thy spirit, and will deliver it to the seventy ancients, " that they may bear with thee the burden of the people, and thou mayest not be burdened alone:"(8) as if He had said, " I gave thee sufficient grace to bear all this burden, but since thou givest part of it to others, I will give to these part of that assistance which I gave alone to thee, that they may bear that part of the burden imposed upon them."   Whence it proceeds, that it is as easy for me, by the providence of

(8) Num. xi. 17.

God, to bear the double burden as the single, because He will give me double forces to bear the double, and so with great fervour I may say to our Lord that of the psalm:—"Prove me, O Lord, and try me; burn my reins and my heart,"(9) impose upon me the burden of offices and labours as Thou shalt please, "because Thy mercy is before mine eyes, and I am well pleased in Thy truth," whereby I am assured that Thou wilt augment my forces if Thou augmentest my labours.

2. Of all that has been said I am to conclude, that *it is a perilous thing to undertake a state contrary to the will of God*, and by prohibited and unlawful means. For this is to cut the thread of the means which the divine providence disposed for my salvation, and therefore upon my account will all the errors be put which shall happen to me in that state; and I deserve that God do not give me assistance to support the burden which I undertake of my own will contrary to His, and therefore that will befal to me which Christ our Lord said:—"Every plant which my heavenly Father hath not planted shall be rooted up;"(10) but notwithstanding this, if the error be already committed, and cannot be remedied, by reason the state is perpetual, or for some other cause, yet I am not to despair of the divine mercy, for His charity is so great, that when any one goes out of the way by which, according to His Fatherly providence, He decreed to guide him, He both knows how, and can reduce him by another way to that from which he departed, drawing good forth of evil, and forth of errors that which is right, upon condition that there be repentance for the fact, as the prodigal son returned confidently to cast himself into His hands who never forsakes those who have recourse to them.

(9) Ps. xxv. 2.   (10) Mat. xiii. 30.

Touching the admonitions to make election of a state, somewhat has been said in the seventh and eighth Meditation of the third Part.

MEDITATION XLVII.

ON THE PROVIDENCE OF ALMIGHTY GOD, IN THE INSTITUTION OF A RELIGIOUS STATE, WITH THE VARIETY OF INSTITUTIONS, AND OF THE VOCATION OF SOME TO IT.

POINT I.

1. The divine providence has ordained that in the Church *there should be houses and families of Religious*, dedicated to His divine service, for very high and sovereign ends, of which the principal are the following:—(1)

i. The first is, that *Religion should be the school of Christian perfection*, which consists in perfect charity and union with Almighty God and our neighbours, giving the farewell to all things which withdraw from it, that the precept of charity may be fulfilled with the greatest perfection that can possibly be. Wherefore, Religion is the house of charity, "the generation of them that seek"(2) God, the dwelling of those who live in union, and the congregation of the sons of wisdom, whose nation and condition is obedience and love.

ii. Whence it is that *Religion is likewise the school of imitation of God and of Christ*, in which the Religious study to imitate the virtues and examples of God, procuring to be perfect, as their heavenly Father is perfect, and likewise imitate the same Christ, keeping not only His precepts, but His counsels, after the manner that Himself kept them.

(1) S. Tho. ii. 2, q. clxxxvi.   (2) Ps. xxiii. 6, et cxxxii. 1.

iii. The third end was, that *Religion might be a house of refuge*, to which the faithful might retire, flying from the perils of the world, and the more assure their salvation by the means which therein are most powerful, fly all sins, and the occasions of them, and to obtain virtues, with perseverance in them to death; so that by the means of Religion is accomplished that which David desired, when he said to our Lord:—" Be Thou unto me for a God, a protector, and a house of refuge to save me."(3)

iv. The fourth end is, that Religion *might be a house of recreation for God our Lord in the midst of the earth*, and His " Paradise of pleasure,"(4) because as His " delights " are " to be with the children of men,"(5) His divine providence so disposed, that there should be a particular house of some special friends and favourites, with whom He might converse and delight Himself, dedicating themselves to converse familiarly with Him; so that Religion is a house of prayer, "a cellar" of celestial "wine,"(6) a place of retreat for the celestial King, into which He brings His beloved friends, and discovers His secrets to them.

v. The fifth end is, that Religion *might be as the candlestick of the Church*, and as a city placed upon a high mountain, to give light to other faithful, as well the light of doctrine as of exemplary life, which might confirm the truth and purity of Christian religion, and exhort all to follow the same, and to glorify our Father who is in heaven, that being fulfilled in Religious persons which St. Paul said:—" That you may be blameless, and sincere children of God, without reproof in the midst of a crooked and perverse generation, among whom you shine as lights n the world."(7)

(3) Ps. xxx. 3.   (4) Gen. ii. 8.   (5) Prov. viii. 3ı.
   (6) Cant. ii. 4.   (7) Ephes. ii. 15.

vi. The sixth end was, that Religion *might be a place deputed to gain many merits* and great augmentation of virtues, so that men might ascend to very high degrees of glory in the company of the most exalted angels that are there, because the life they lead is more angelical than human.

2. With the consideration of these six ends, if I be Religious, I am to procure these six affections and desires, which are like to the six wings of the Seraphim which Isaias saw,(8) that is to say, the perfect love of God and of our neighbour; a desire to imitate the perfection of God and of Christ our Lord; to fly the occasions of sins and imperfections, to assure the most that I may my own salvation; to converse familiarly with our Lord; to live as an example to the edification of my neighbours; and to grow in virtues, to the attaining of great increase of glory.

With these wings will I fly to accomplish the obligation of my state, confiding in the divine providence, that with His spirit He will assist and further my flight.

Colloquy.—O Father of mercies, since Thou hast called me to a state so high, and for so noble and excellent ends, I most humbly beseech Thee that my life be not base and abject, but that the sublimity of my life be consonant to the sublimity of my calling, that I may with both obtain the sublimity of Thy glory.   Amen.

These six ends are to serve for rules to know the vocations of men to the state of Religion, for those which are the vocations of God evermore depend in part upon the motives before recited.

POINT II.

The divine providence ordained that there should be great variety of Religion, and divers institutions and rules,

(8) Isa. vi. 2.

to obtain with more sweetness the ends aforesaid, of which three principal causes are these.

i. First, as perfect charity has divers acts, in order to the glory and worship of God and to the advantage of our neighbour, exercising towards them divers works of mercy, as well corporal as spiritual, and one Religion alone cannot be eminent in all of them together, the divine wisdom ordained *that there should be divers institutions of Religious,* and that some should excel in contemplation and unitive love of Almighty God,—others in things pertaining to the divine worship,—others in penance, and rigorous affliction of the flesh,—others in spiritual works of mercy towards their neighbours, teaching, preaching, and administering to them the holy sacraments,—others in corporal works of mercy, serving the sick, redeeming captives, or defending the Church against their enemies. And after this manner, in all Religious jointly together, all the works of charity shine with singular excellency, the one excelling in that in which the others do not excel. For which cause Religion is as the house of divine wisdom, "hewn out of seven pillars,"(9) which are the seven institutions before recited, adorned with divers works of most effectual means to obtain her ends, as are frequentation of sacraments, examination of conscience, direction of spiritual masters, silence, convenient inclosure, and others the like.

ii. Because Christ our Redeemer is a pattern of infinite perfection in all kinds of virtues, so that *one Religion cannot excel and shine with eminency in imitating all His virtues* by reason of our great imbecility for so great an enterprise, therefore the divine Providence invented divers Religious institutions that some might imitate Him with excellency in holy poverty,—others in obedience,— others in zeal of souls,—others in humility and humble

(9) Prov. ix. 1.

exercises, each Religion giving example of these virtues to the other, and to the whole Church, which, for this cause, is like a queen and the spouse of Jesus Christ, clothed as David says, "in gilded clothing surrounded with variety,"(10) like her beloved spouse, whose divine steps she endeavours to imitate. According, therefore, to this, if I be Religious, I am to consider what the principal thing is in which my Religion most excels, as well as in imitation of Christ our Lord, as in the works of charity, of which I have made election for His love, and to endeavour to excel in them, yet not neglecting others, so that that may be said of me for this my singular diligence, which the Church applies to each of the saints:—" There was not found the like to him in glory, who kept the law of the Most High."(11).

iii. Because God our Lord *knows the inclinations and complexions of many men to be very divers*, and because it was very difficult for all to accommodate themselves to one kind of way to perfection, His divine providence decreed that there should be divers manners, that every one might find some one to his contentment, and accommodated to his inclination and his power, and by this way might more ensure his own salvation, and more increase in all virtue. For some are inclined to solitude, and it is hurtful to them to converse with men,—others are, on the other hand, inclined to deal with men, and solitude is detrimental to them. Some have a strong complexion and are inclined to undergo great asperities,—others are more feeble, and cannot endure so great austerities. To the end, therefore, that all might be perfect, our loving Lord would that there should be ways appropriated to all, and of His paternal providence, He inclines and directs every one to that way which is most convenient for him.

(10) Ps. xliv. 10.   (11) Ecclus. xliv. 20.

Colloquy.—O infinite wisdom, who dost all things "mightily," and orderest all things "sweetly,"(12) I give Thee thanks for having built within Thy Church a house of religion, with great variety of institutions, which, like "pillars," support it, and, as a table full of delightful meats and ordinances, accommodated to the appetite and necessity of its dwellers; and since Thy high providence has vouchsafed to join me to one of these pillars, bind me strongly to it, that, persevering in Thy service conformably to my state, I may come to be "a pillar in the Temple"(13) of Thy glory. Amen.

POINT III.

Consider *the care which the divine Providence has in calling people to the state of Religion,* and to every several order of it, pondering the *most remarkable things* that are in this vocation.

1. The first, that *none can undertake this sovereign state,* nor enter into Religion as he ought, *unless he be called of God* with an especial vocation to it, for chastity, obedience, and religious poverty, do so far exceed our feeble nature, that none can by himself, have so much power as to promise them to himself or to be able to keep them. For this cause, Christ our Lord speaking of chastity, said: —"All men take not this word," sed quibus datum est, "but they to whom it is given;"(14) and even so none can come to Jesus Christ imitating His perfection, unless His heavenly Father "draw him,"(15) calling him by His inspirations, and aiding him in order to his coming.

2. Because the state of Religion is not necessary to enter into heaven, therefore God our Lord *calls not all men to undertake it,* but only those whom Himself will,—and this

(12) Sap. viii. 1.   (13) Apoc. iii, 12.   (14) Mat. xix. 11.
(15) Joan. vi. 44.

not for their merits, but of mere grace and mercy; and so oftentimes leaves those in the world who are very good, and calls others who are not so in order to amend them, and because He will do this good to them according to that which He said to His apostles,—"You have not chosen me, but I have chosen you," and have placed you in the state in which you are, to the end that you go throughout the world "and bring forth fruit, and your fruit should remain."(16)

Colloquy.—I give Thee thanks, O sovereign master, that Thou hast chosen me to be Thy disciple in the school of perfection, leaving many others which deserved better to enter into it.   I could never have chosen this state unless Thy mercy had formerly prevented me to this effect; and since Thou hast now vouchsafed to choose me, I beseech Thee to assist me to bring forth fruits which may abide to life everlasting.   Amen.

3. Those who are called of God to this state *ought promptly to answer to this calling*, because the benefit and favour which He does them in it is exceedingly great, and to resist it were great discourtesy and ingratitude, and an occasion of most grievous falls.   For it may be that our Lord, in His eternal wisdom, foresaw that this state was to be the means of their salvation, which, if they reject, He will say to them as He did to those which were invited, who would not come to His banquet, namely, " none of those men that were invited shall taste of my supper;" (17) and that which He said to another who deferred to follow Him;—" No man putting his hand to the plough, and looking back, is fit for the Kingdom of God."(18)   Wherefore with great care I am to consider

(16) Joan. xv. 16.

(17) Luc. xiv. 24.   (18) Luc. ix. 62.

if I be one of those who are called, for if I consent to it, it is a sign that I am one of the elected, and if I resist, I may rightly fear that I am one of the rejected.

4. The divine providence, with an especial vocation, *calls every one to that Religion which is most convenient for him;* in which are to be observed at once *two things—* for God, inasmuch as He is the *universal* governor of all Religions, provides to all, such persons as are careful to preserve them; and as He is the *particular* governor of every man, He inspires every one of those whom He thus calls to that Religion which will most help him for his salvation and entire perfection. Wherefore, to resist this vocation is a grievous error, for he may most easily obtain his end with great sweetness in that Religion to which he is truly called, and perhaps will not do it in another, or will not persevere in it because he wants sufficiency for the same, as has been said in the former meditation. Upon this consideration I will give great thanks to our Lord for the singular care which He has of all Religious, confiding in His divine providence that He will preserve them for His glory. Every one may likewise trust that God has called him to that Religion which is most convenient for him, encouraging himself to persevere with augmentation of virtues, in the place in which of His goodness He has placed him until He shall see him clearly in His holy Sion. Amen.(19)

(19) Ps. lxxxiii. 8.

MEDITATION XLVIII.

ON THE GOODS WHICH A RELIGIOUS STATE CONTAINS, AND THE EXCELLENCE OF THIS BENEFIT.

To ponder the greatness of this benefit, we are to cast our eyes upon *the calamities of the world out of which* Almighty God draws him that is Religious, and upon *the excellencies of the state in which He* places him, as also upon *the rewards which* both in this life and the other *He promises* to him.

POINT I.

1. Within this visible world, which both is good, and is the workmanship of Almighty God, *there is another world founded in malice*, whose prince is the Devil, and whose employment, as St. John says, " is the concupiscence of the flesh, and the concupiscence of the eyes, and the pride of life."(1)   Wherefore this world is a congregation of men, wholly given over to the inordinate love of carnal delights, of riches, and of impertinent and vain honours, whence proceed the thorns of sins and perplexities, which prick worldly men and choke the seed of divine inspirations, who afterwards become the fuel of eternal fire.(2) This wicked world has two parts.—i. The one is *out of the Church*, which is the congregation of unbelievers, who, as they want faith, easily fall into innumerable vices and make no stay until they precipitate themselves into the bottom of hell.—ii. Another part is *within the same Church* which is the congregation of sinners, who possess or seek inordinate delights, riches, and dignities, with the loss of charity, and with the danger of their salvation.   For

(1) 1 Joan. ii. 16.   (2) Luc. viii. 14.

being led by this love they resist the divine vocation, as those three resisted who were called to the supper, and were for ever excluded from it.(3)   In the midst of this world live the just secular men who lawfully possess these things, yet are in great peril by reason of the occasions which arise from the temporal goods which they possess, and of the evil example of worldly men with whom they live, and for the calumniations and molestations which they receive of those who covet the same which they possess.   For which cause Christ our Lord, speaking of a certain rich man who was just, but resisted this vocation to be made more perfect, said,—" It is easier for a camel to pass through the eye of a needle, than for a rich man to enter into the Kingdom of heaven."(4)   Out of this so dangerous and perilous a world, God our Lord of His infinite mercy draws those that are Religious, placing them in a state exempt from these riches, delights, and vain liberties, to the end that they may live free from the sins and perils which they bring with them.   Wherefore so many benefits do I receive of our Lord in holy Religion as are the vices and perplexities which I see those to suffer who live out of the same, for which I am to give Him continual thanks saying :—

Colloquy.—O most sweet Jesus, whence so great a good to me, that Thou sayest to my heart, as Thou didst to Abraham :—" Go forth out of thy country, and from thy kindred, and out of thy father's house, and come into the land which I will show thee."(5)   I give Thee as great thanks as I possibly can that Thou hast brought me forth of Ur of the Chaldeans,—the fire of the Chaldeans, to the end that I should not perish in the fire of my covetousness ; and since Thou hast removed me far from this fire, suffer me not again

(3) Luc. xiv. 24.   (4) Mat. xix. 24.   (5) Gen. xii. 1.

to draw near the same, but inflame me with the fire of charity, that all covetousness may be utterly extinguished in me.

2. I will ponder yet further the disposition of the divine Providence in this case, because when many are so addicted to the things which they possess in the world with danger of perishing, unless by means of the loving inspirations with which they are called, they voluntarily relinquish them, He *is wont after a manner to inforce them that they forsake them*, suffering them to fall into afflictions, infirmities, and temptations, and sometimes into grievous sins, that seeing evidently their own peril, they may endeavour to fly the same, as the angels, seeing that Lot lingered to go forth from Sodom(6) out of the affection he bore to the things he had in it, took him by the hand and led him out by force, in order that he should not be burnt with the fire which fell there.

Colloquy.—O most loving Father, what thanks shall I give to Thee that Thou hast compelled me to enter into Thy house,(7) to fly the fire which burns the world. Keep me, I beseech Thee, within the same, although it be by force of afflictions, that, freed from the fires that threaten me, I may obtain the rewards which attend me. Amen.

POINT II.

1. The state of Religion contains within itself with great excellency *three kinds of good.*—i. The first is *becoming good*, which embraces all sorts of virtues as well moral as theological, together with the gifts of the Holy Ghost.— ii. The second is *delectable good*, which comprehends "the peace of God which surpasses all understanding," (8) and the joy of the Holy Ghost, together with all the delights

(6) Gen. xix. 16.   (7) Luc. xiv. 23.   (8) Phil. iv. 7.

which spring from the works of virtue.—iii. The third is *profitable good*, which contains the convenient means to preserve and augment the life of the soul, and to obtain the life everlasting, as also those which help to pass this temporal life of the body with profit and utility of the spirit; all this is found most eminently in holy Religion, so that there may be said of it that which the Wise man says of divine wisdom;—"All good things came to me together with her, and by her means I have obtained innumerable riches......and I knew not that she was the mother of them all." (9)   For even so it is, that Religion is the true mother of all virtues in their perfection, for she it is who nurses and sustains them with the milk of her doctrine, makes them to grow by those means which she prescribes to exercise their acts, encloses them in the vestment of vows within her house, to the end that they wander not forth of the same, and lifts them up to so great heights that they contend with that of angels, because, as St. Basil says,—"Religion is no other thing than a certain passage from the manner of leading a human life to that which the saints live in heaven;"(10) and by the similitude of that which passes in heaven, the life may be known which the Religious profess on earth.   For even here they take especial possession of the Kingdom of God, which is "justice, peace, and joy in the Holy Ghost," (11) "who with particular assistance is the Father of all these kinds of goods of which Religion is the mother, and with which He fills those that are His children.

Colloquy.—O most loving Father, I give Thee thanks that Thou hast brought me to live in the house of sanctity, making me a son of her who is the mother of all virtues, that so I may nourish myself in them.

(9) Sap. vii. 11.   (10) Reg. ex fusis et de Const. mon. c. 19.
(11) Rom. xiv. 17.

O my soul, hear the counsels of thy mother, who says:
—" My son, keep my words, and lay up my precepts
with thee...and thou shalt live,"(12) not the life that
thou wast wont, but another, more than human, a life
holy, happy, peaceable, celestial, and divine. Begin
to exercise by and bye that which she commands thee,
and thou shalt prove by experience what she promises
thee.

2. In every one of these three kinds of goods I may
reflect, particularly pondering that Religion is mother of
charity, of contemplation, temperance, &c., and of the
delights and fruits which proceed thence, as will be seen
in the examples of the points ensuing.

POINT III.

To ponder yet further the inestimable riches of this
state, is to be considered the discourse between St. Peter
and Christ our Lord, which the Evangelists recount by
these words:—" Then Peter answering said to Him,
Behold we have left all things and have followed Thee;
what therefore shall we have? And Jesus said to them,
Amen I say to you, that you who have followed me in the
regeneration, when the Son of man shall sit on the seat of
His majesty, *you also shall sit on twelve seats, judging the
twelve tribes of Israel. And every one that hath left house, or
brethren, or sisters, or father, or mother, or wife, or children, or
lands for my name's sake, shall receive an hundred fold, and
shall possess life everlasting.*"(13) In this demand of Peter
and answer of Christ, is to be pondered that Religion is an
admirable covenant between Almighty God and man, in
which—i., man offers himself to do the most that he may
for Almighty God—and ii., God again offers most excellent
favours and rewards in recompense to man.

(12) Prov. vii. 1, et vi. 20.
(13) Mat. xix. 27. Luc. xviii. 28.

1.—ON THAT WHICH THE RELIGIOUS DOES FOR GOD.

Consider first *that which the Religious does for God*, reducing the same to *the two things* here expressed by St. Peter.

i. The first is to *leave all things which may be left for His sake*; for with the vow of *poverty* he renounces the dominion of all the temporal goods which he possesses, and his right to them, and even his will to assert them, so that if the world were his, yet would he leave it, contenting himself with that which is only necessary to pass his life, and this also with dependance upon the will of his superior. With the vow of *chastity* he renounces all the pleasures of the flesh, not only the unlawful, but even the lawful, of matrimony itself, renouncing all right of having wife, children, or family; and further, to preserve this purity of flesh, offers himself to mortify the same with penance, and with the shutting up and custody of the senses. (14)—With the vow of *obedience* he renounces his own liberty, offering himself to deny his own judgment and his own will, to perform the will of Almighty God and of His prelates, who in the name and place of God rule and govern him. And the better to accomplish all this, he rids himself, and quite forsakes his own father, mother, brethren, friends, and kinsfolks, and his own country, so denying them all, as if he had never known them, and is prepared to lose both health and life when the law of charity and obedience exact it. Whence it follows that the Religious offers up to Almighty God both himself and all his substance, as a perfect holocaust, giving Him, as St. Gregory says, all he has, knows, and is able. (15)

Colloquy.—O sweet Jesus, what great thing do I in offering myself such a holocaust to Thy service,

(14) S. Bas. reg. 8, ex fusis.   _   (15) Hom. xii. in Ezech.

since Thou offeredst another much greater of Thine own self for my advantage. Thou renouncedst all things in this life to remedy me; reason, therefore, will that I renounce them all to serve Thee.

ii. The second thing is *to follow Christ our Lord*, every one imitating according to his ability the most resplendent virtues which shined in Him, and the counsels of perfection which He taught us, beholding Him as an example of his life, conversing with Him familiarly in holy prayer, "following this Lamb whithersoever He goeth," (16) never turning their eyes from Him, or alienating themselves from His holy company. And in order that it may appear how much these two things comprehend, of those things which a Religious person offers to God, I may apply to those that are Religious that which St. Paul says of the ancient Saints; (17) for with a noble faith like Abraham's, they go forth out of their land, and from the house of their own father, and live as pilgrims, expecting an eternal city whose founder is Almighty God;—and, like the same Abraham, offer in holocaust their only begotten son Isaac, sacrificing by the vow of obedience their own will, that so they may fulfil the divine, trusting that God can raise it again to a better life than it had before;—and like Moses they deny the pedigree and nobility of the world, choosing rather to be afflicted with the just than to enjoy the delights of sinners, reputing the reproach of Jesus Christ far more precious riches than the treasures of Egypt, making no account what men say, because they behold as present the invisible God. With this faith they go out of the tyranny of Pharaoh, who is the Devil, and pass on dry foot the Red Sea, breaking down the walls of difficulties which stop the entrance into the land of everlasting pro-

(16) Apoc. xiv. 4.   (17) Heb. xi. 8.

mise, quench the fire of their covetousness, become strong in their infirmities, wax hard in battles and temptations, clothe themselves with coarse skins and sharp haircloths, suffer hunger, and thirst, seek solitude, dwell in caves, and lead so excellent a life that they follow the steps of their captain Jesus, of whom the world is not worthy. When I shall have accomplished these two things, as St. Peter did in virtue of faith and confidence in the grace and omnipotency of our Blessed Saviour, I may say to Him:—" Quid ergo erit mihi," " what therefore shall I have ?"

Colloquy.—O most sweet Saviour, I intend not to serve Thee principally for reward ; for it is a sufficient reward to serve Thee because Thou art who Thou art ; but to encourage my weak heart, tell me, I beseech Thee, what I shall have in reward of that which I do for the love of Thee.

2.—ON THAT WHICH ALMIGHTY GOD DOES FOR THE RELIGIOUS.

Then will I ponder *what Almighty God does for the Religious*, reducing them to those *three things* which Christ promised to St. Peter in the same order which He spoke them.

i. The first is, that He *will give him in the day of judgment a most excellent place and throne*, for the place which he left in this present world and undertook in Religion; (18) so that when other men shall appear before the tribunal of Jesus Christ, such as are Religious will be set with the apostles in the thrones of glory after the manner of great judges, and that with singular joy and honour for having imitated the judge Himself in poverty, chastity, obedience, and in the other virtues to which He counselled us in His gospel, because He greatly' inclines to glorify (19) those

(18) S. Aug. Beda et alij.   (19) 1 Reg. ii. 30.

who glorify Him, and to exalt those who humble themselves to honour Him. (20)

ii. The second promise is, *to give him for what he leaves
" a hundred fold in this life;"* and this payment sometimes
is made in the selfsame money, for as Cassian says, (21)
and as experience teaches, leaving one house or inheritance,
one father, brother, friend, or faithful servant, he shall
find all the houses, rents, and alms of Religion, and many
hundreds of persons who perform towards him the office
of father, brother, and friend, and serve him with more
fidelity than secular did; and for the honour which he
left in the world, he will receive without seeking it, an
hundredfold.   Moreover, the especial providence of
Almighty God, is to be reputed a hundred thousand times
more than all I leave; for in that I leave them for His
love, He takes upon Him to give me whatsoever shall be
fitting for me after the manner that has been said, like as
the apostles experienced, to whom our Saviour said:—
"When I sent you without purse, and scrip, and shoes,
did you want anything? But they said, nothing." (22)
At other times the payment is made in other money much
more precious, giving us instead of the things we leave, so
great consolation to have left them, that it exceeds a
hundred times that which we took in possessing them.
For the delights of the spirit exceed incomparably those of
the flesh, and the perfect Religious is more delighted in
dishonour and poverty than the ambitious in honour and
plenty.(23) And the more to assure us of this, our Saviour
said by St. Mark, that He would give us a hundred times
as much with persecutions." (24)

Colloquy.—O most loving Father, what thanks

(20) Mat. xxiii. 12.   *(21) Coll. ult. cap. ult.
(22) Med. xxxi.   Luc. xxii. 35.
(23) S. Basil de Const. mon. cap. vii.   (24) Mar. x. 30.

shall I give Thee for having brought me into Thy house, since, in truth "one day" is much more worth in it than "thousands"(25) are out of it; and I had rather be despised in it, than to live much honoured in the palaces of the world, for there is no greater honour nor delight than to live under Thy protection. What can I, O my Lord, forsake for Thee, for which Thou renderest not an hundred fold? If I leave my father, Thou Thyself becomest my Father;—if I renounce my inheritance, Thou Thyself art my inheritance; and if I forsake all things, Thou Thyself art all things to me. O celestial bank! O divine exchange! Take me, O Lord, as Thine, since so liberally Thou gavest Thyself to be mine. Amen.

iii. The third promise is of "*life everlasting*," adding to that which He promises to all the faithful, an especial providence of leading them to this life, by means so secure, that they will obtain the same with more facility and with greater advantage. For which cause the saints say that perseverance in Religion is a sign of predestination, because in reward of renouncing their own judgment, and the government of themselves, God Himself governs them with an especial care, to the end that they may obtain His blessed recompense. (26)

Colloquy.—O my soul, rejoice that God has chosen thee for this blessed state; let thy call be to thee a heaven, living in it with that purity with which the angels live in heaven; for if Thou perseverest faithfully in it to death, thou shalt be translated thence to heaven, where thou shalt reign with Christ, world without end. Amen.

<hr>

(25) Ps. xxxviii. 11.

(26) S. Ber. ad Fratres de mônte Dei. S. Laur. Justin. de perfect. Monast. convers. cap. vii.

MEDITATION XLIX.

ON THE MOST SPECIAL PROVIDENCE WHICH ALMIGHTY GOD HAS OF THE PRE-
DESTINATE CONCERNING THEIR GOOD DEATH AND PERSEVERANCE IN
GRACE, AND ON THE EXCELLENCE OF THE BENEFIT OF PREDESTINATION.

The most sovereign benefit which Almighty God bestows upon us in this life is, to dispose by His providence in such a manner of our things, *that we may die a blessed death in His grace and amity,* in which consists our salvation, and therefore in it are comprehended all the benefits which are proper to the predestinate, of whom the apostle says:— God hath "predestinated" many " to be made conformable to the image of His Son...And whom He predestinated them He also called ..And whom He called, them He also justified...And whom He justified, them He also glorified." (1) In which words He declares three singular benefits of the predestinate.—i. The first is, to *call them* before their death, and so to justify them effectually.—ii. The second is, to *justify* them in such manner that they persevere in justice to their death.—iii. Whereupon follows the third, which is to *glorify* them with the reward of eternal glory. And the providence which Almighty God has concerning all this we call Predestination, (2) whose causes, effects, and signs, we will ponder according to our purpose, for our comfort and advantage.

POINT I.

1. The first shall be to consider the most particular providence which God our Lord has *to call and justify certain sinners before their death,* because He has predestinated them for the Kingdom of heaven. This so singular voca-

(1) Rom. viii. 29.   (2) S. Tho. i. p. q. xxxiii.

tion consists in calling them in such time and opportunity, with such frequency and efficacy of inspirations, and with such interior and exterior touches, that at last they consent to the divine calling, and obtain the grace of justification, as it succeeded to the good thief upon the cross; (3) and sometimes He uses extraordinary means, and in a manner miraculous, as experience teaches us every day, of which somewhat has been said in the thirty-seventh meditation.

2. Then I will consider the special providence which God our Lord *has of the death of the just who are predestinated, that they may persevere in grace, and die in the same.*

.i. For first He prevents them with special favours, to the end that they be not overcome by temptations, and preserves them from many which might cast them down.

ii. Moreover, He ordains that kind of death which is most convenient for their salvation, whether it be with many pains or without them, or by little and little, or on a sudden, " lest wickedness should alter their understanding," (4) or seeing themselves ready to die they should be troubled and afflicted. Again, some He leads through great fears, that they come not to vanish away, nor to perish with pride; others through great delights and consolations, that they be not dismayed, nor come to perish through despair; to others He does singular favours in reward of their singular service. (5)

iii. Finally, by marvellous and secret means He grants to them the great gift of perseverance, of which Christ our Lord said:—" He that shall persevere unto the end shall be saved." (6)   And because this gift comes not unto us for our merits, we are to ask it, and to beseech the saints

<table>
<tr><td>(3) Luc. xxiii 42.</td><td>(4) Sap. iv. 11.</td></tr>
<tr><td>(5) Trid. cess. vi. can. 26.</td><td>(6) Mat. x. 22.</td></tr>
</table>

to crave it for us by fervent prayers, since they also are a means of predestination.(7)

Colloquy.—O eternal God, whose works are perfect, since Thou hast begun in me the work of my salvation, finish it most perfectly, giving me the gift of perseverance, by which I may obtain a crown. O celestial saints, to whom our Lord granted this so sovereign gift, negotiate the same in my behalf, beseeching Him to have such a providence of my death, that it may be the beginning of my eternal life. Amen.

POINT II.

1. Consider *the causes whence proceed this sovereign benefit*, that we may have confidence to obtain it.

i. The first is, the infinite *goodness and mercy of God*, who seeing all men of their own nature to be very mutable, and that by reason of their liberty and frailty it was most easy for them to fall and perish, in resisting the means of His general providence would, " according to the purpose of His will," (8) have another much more special of some in *particular*, in whom without their merits He would manifest, as the apostle says, " the riches of His glory," and for this cause calls them " the vessels of mercy," (9) which He prepared to glory.

ii. The second cause is, *the infinite merits of Christ our Lord*, for which the eternal Father would assure to Him a certain family of elect, which should be conformed to His own image, " that He might be the first-born amongst many brethren," (10) like with respect to the being of grace and of glory, as they were in the being of nature. And hence it is that although these predestinate be but few in comparison of those who perish by their own de-

(7) S. Tho. i. 2. q. cix. art. 10, et q. cxliv. art. 9.
(8) Ephes. i. 5.   (9) Rom. ix. 23.   (10) Rom. viii. 29.

fault, and reject conformity with Jesus Christ, yet absolutely, as St. John says, (11) they are very many, and as it were innumerable, because so it was convenient for the greatness of the mercy of Almighty God, for the dignity of our Saviour, and for the efficacy of His merits.

2. From these two fountains I will draw *great affections of joy* for this election, which Almighty God makes of so many predestinate, trusting that I myself shall be one of them, since upon such pledges my salvation depends, if only as being called to Christianity, I labour, as St. Peter says, " by good works" to " make sure" my " calling and election," (12) since on the part of God sufficient aid will never be wanting to me to obtain perseverance and a blessed death, although His majesty will that all this be concealed from me, that I become not remiss nor slack in His holy service.

Colloquy.—Wherefore, O my soul, trouble not thyself with excessive anxieties, but cast thyself confidently into the hands of so loving a Father, and of so merciful a Redeemer, confiding that they will finish in thee with perfection the work they have begun by His grace, and since His pleasure is that both thy predestination and thy perseverance should be hidden from thee, praise Him, therefore, and cease to search into the same, because it is not fit that man should desire and will to know that which God has not a will to reveal; but search, as the Wise man says, " the things that God hath commanded thee"(13) to accomplish, and so thou shalt come with the predestinate to enjoy the reward of them.

POINT III.

There are many *signs and conjectures to know those that are predestinate*, which we ought to obtain, as well for our

(11) Joan. xvii. 9.   (12) 2 Pet. i. 10.   (13) Ecclus. iii. 22.

consolation as for our encouragement, since as our Saviour said, there can be no greater motive of joy than that our "names are written in heaven." (14)

These signs are,—gladly to hear the word of God, to obey His secret inspirations and counsels, especially to leave all things for the love of Him, to frequent the sacraments and the exercises of holy prayer, to be very devout to the Blessed Virgin, and greatly inclined to the works of mercy; and the continual fear of Almighty God. and of His judgment, is also a sign of predestination, for God imprints this fear in our hearts that it may be the keeper of our vineyard. Finally, by means of these works "the Spirit Himself," as St. Paul says, and as St. Bernard explicates, "gives testimony to our spirit that we are the sons of God, and if sons, joint heirs also with Christ." (15)

Colloquy.—O eternal King and sovereign pastor, whose sheep are known in that they hear Thy voice, and follow Thy life, grant me that I may hear what Thou sayest, and accomplish what Thou commandest, that I may have the pledge to be a sheep of Thine elected flock, and that at the day of judgment Thou mayest place me upon Thy right hand, leading me with Thee to the Kingdom of Thy glory.   Amen.

To take away the anxious solicitude of our perseverance and predestination, it will help to ponder that which has been said in the thirty-first meditation, and to assure the same in such manner as it may here be assured, the meditation ensuing will greatly further.

(14) Luc. x. 20.   (15) Rom. viii. 16. Serm ii. de Oct. Pas.

MEDITATION L.

ON HUMILITY AND RESIGNATION WHICH DISPOSE TO GATHER THE COPIOUS FRUITS OF THE DIVINE PROVIDENCE.

1. Humility which disposes us to receive the favour of the divine providence is not only that which appertains to those who have been sinners, and is grounded in the knowledge of our sins, of which we have treated in the first Part, but that humility which appertains to those who are very holy, and even to the soul itself of Christ our Lord, *which is grounded on the knowledge of the nothing which we have of ourselves,* (1) which has been treated in the meditations of the sixth Part, in which have been pondered *four principal points.*

i. *All the being of my body and soul,* with all my members, and my faculties, and with the ornaments added thereto, as well natural as supernatural, *is not mine but God's,* who gave them to me, and unless He had given them to me, I had always remained in the abyss of nothing, as we have pondered in the second and seventeenth Meditations.

ii. After I have received all this being, yet *I cannot preserve the same,* so that if God did not preserve it actually, it would immediately return to nothing, as has been said in the twenty-eighth meditation.

iii. *The use of all my faculties, powers, and senses, and all my works so depend on Almighty God,* that without His actual concurrence I could do nothing, no, not so much as to think a thought, as was there considered.

iv. Although I have received much, yet *all is nothing*

(1) S. Tho. ii. 2, q. cxci. art. 1, ad. 4.

in comparison of Almighty God, and of His virtues and perfections, as was said in the sixth meditation.

2. Of myself *I am a fountain of all that which is merely nothing, and even less than nothing*, namely, of sin, as has been pondered in the fourth meditation of the first Part.

All this will be seen gathered together in the ensuing meditation, grounded upon the similitude which Christ our Lord used frequently, saying:—" Amen I say to you, unless you be converted, and become as little children, you shall not enter into the Kingdom of heaven. Whosoever, therefore, shall humble himself as this little child, he is the greater in the Kingdom of heaven.' " Suffer children to come unto me, and forbid them not, for of such is the kingdom of God." (2)

POINT I.

1. Consider the *heroic humility proposed to us in this comparison*, and the *fruits* of the divine providence which are gathered thereby, for which cause I will place myself in the presence of God, like a little child, whose properties are these ensuing:—

i. The first, that if it be unclean, it *cannot cleanse itself*, unless another make it clean.—ii. The second, if it fall to the ground, it *cannot rise*, unless another lift it up.—iii. The third, if he be set upon his feet, he *cannot stand* unless he be held, nor walk a step unless he be led.—iv. The fourth, if he be hungry or thirst, he *can neither eat nor drink*, unless it be given him.—v. The fifth, if he be cold, or that any wrong or peril of enemies approach him, he *cannot deliver himself* unless another deliver him, nor defend himself unless another defend him.—vi. The sixth, for the consummation of his miseries, *he neithe:*

(2) Mat. xviii. 3. Luc. xviii. 16.

knows how, nor can ask what he wants, nor so much as knows it, that he may ask it.

These are the miseries of an infant, for which he has no other remedy than the piety and love of his mother, and the motherly providence which she has of her son.

2. In this manner am I to imagine myself in the sight of God, applying to myself the six properties before specified.

i. That my weakness is so great that I can sin of my own free will, and defile myself with many offences; but after I have sinned, *I cannot of myself alone wash myself,* nor cleanse myself from them unless Almighty God wash and cleanse me: wherefore I may with David worthily say:—" Wash me yet more from my iniquity, and cleanse me from my sin." (3)

ii. The second that with the weight of my depraved inclinations, and of this corruptible body which weighs it down, I easily fall to the ground, and lie prostrate on it with inordinate affections to earthly things, because I am the son of earthly Adam; but being once fallen *I cannot rise by myself alone,* unless God give me His hand, and help me up; for otherwise I should soever lie, prostrate, like the house of Israel, of which a certain holy prophet says:—" The house of Israel is fallen, and it shall rise no more." (4)

iii. If God of His mercy lifts me up, and sets me on foot, giving me some virtue or spirit of devotion, *I cannot sustain myself,* nor preserve that which He has given me, nor make so much as one step unless Himself help me therein, wherefore I ought always to stand in fear of falling, according to that of the apostle St. Paul:—" He that thinketh himself to stand, let him take heed lest he fall." (5)

(3) Ps. l. 4.   (4) Amos v. 2.   (5) 1 Cor. x. 12.

iv. If I suffer hunger and thirst of spiritual meats, as are the sacraments, the word of God, and the works of justice, *I cannot seek them by myself alone*, nor so eat them that they may turn to my profit, unless God help me in all this; and if I have a desire to amend myself, I cannot accomplish this my desire, if Almighty God Himself who gave me the same, does not give me grace also to perform it.

v. I am so beset with the temptations and dangers of the Devil, the world, and the flesh, that *it is impossible for me to deliver myself from them* by my own forces, unless God deliver me, nor have I weapons with which to defend me, unless God give them to me; I should even always be cold by sins and tepidities if God did not heat me with the fire of His love, and contrariwise, I should·be enkindled with the fire of self-love, if God did not refresh me with the lively water of His grace.

vi. Finally, so great is my misery, that *what I should pray as I ought, I know not*, unless the Spirit of God Himself teaches me, nor can I know my perils and necessities if Almighty God does not discover to me the grievousness of them. This is the misery which I have of myself, whence it follows that to make myself a child, is not to be ignorant of these things, nor to be actually fallen into these miseries, but to acknowledge myself to be subject to fall into them, whence, as from the root, perfection springs, for the apostle St. Paul says:— "Brethren, do not become children in sense, but in malice be children, and in sense be perfect." (6)

3. After that I have pondered these miseries, which I have of myself, I am to lift up my eyes to consider that the infinite charity and paternal providence of God hastens with speed to remedy all, and that with much more care than

(6) 1 Cor. xiv. 20.

mothers run to remedy the necessities of their little children, because it is possible that mothers sometimes forget their children, but as the same Lord says, He will never forget those that are His. (7)   Wherefore, with His providence He hastens to wash me, being defiled, to raise me from the earth, being fallen, to sustain me standing, to feed me with convenient food, being hungry, to defend me from my enemies, being oppugned, and to teach me to pray in such manner, that on the part of His providence, remedy shall never be wanting to me, but be much more ready than if the same were in my own free liberty. And, therefore, with the affection of humility and diffidence of myself, to see myself as feeble as a child, I am to conjoin the affection of love and confidence in God, seeing the care which He has to procure me remedy, to the end that the consideration of my own infancy and weakness does not make me pusillanimous, but rather encourage me the more. For as a mother has greater providence and care of her tenderest child, who cannot care for itself, nor help itself, than of her elder son, who is more able,—even so God our Lord has a more favourable and especial providence of the humble, who hold themselves for children in their own eyes, than of those who presume themselves, and hold themselves for very great; and so He says by the prophet Isaias:—
" As one whom the mother 'caresses, so will I comfort you; you shall be carried at the breasts, and upon the knees they shall caress you." (8)   O happy that just man who makes himself a child by humility, and therefore will enjoy so admirable and fatherly a providence!   O blessed humility, by which the divine providence produces so abundant fruits!

Colloquy.—O most merciful Father, the more I acknowledge my miseries, the more do I love Thee for

(7) Isa. xlix. 15.   (8) Isa. lxvi. 13.

the care which Thou hast to deliver me from them. And since I came forth of Thine omnipotency, as a child in necessity of Thy continual assistance, vouchsafe to give it me by Thy paternal providence, to the end that I never desist to praise Thee, since " out of the mouth of babes and of sucklings" proceed the praises which please Thee, and will for ever please Thee, world without end.   Amen.

POINT II.

1. Consider the *humble resignation proposed in this comparison,* and *the fruits* which are gathered by it from the divine providence.

A child naturally is careless of all things needful to him, leaving them to the care and providence of his mother. For he has no care of the milk which is to be given him, whether it be good or evil, nor weighs whether he be wrapped in fine or coarser linen, or in mantles of silk, or grosser cloth, because he is contented with every thing, he notes not whether he dwell in sumptuous palaces, and be laid in soft and precious cradles, or whether he dwell in a poor cottage, and be laid in a sorry manger; he is not puffed up with the honour which is done him, because he is the son of a king, nor is afflicted that he is contemned, because he is the son of some poor slave.   Finally, being careless of himself, such is his condition, as is that of his father and mother, and such his education as is the providence of those who be careful of him, and nurse him.

2. In this manner am I to study to *make myself a child before God our Lord,* doing that by virtue which the child does by nature, casting from me all anxious cares, and placing them in God, " for He has care" of (9) me, and He it is who nourishes me, as a child who is His own son, providing me food, raiment, honour, and the rest, which

(9) 1 Pet. v. 7.   Ps. liv. 23.

before have been related.   For which cause I am to rejoice for the good lot that has befallen me, in having such a Father, and such a mother, as God Himself is, whose providence and care towards me infinitely exceeds that which all kings and princes, fathers and mothers of the world, can possibly have of their children.   For if it be true which the apostle says:—" If any man have not care of his own, and especially of those of his house, he has denied the faith, and is worse than an infidel;"(10) how is it possible that God our Lord, who has given His word to have care of us, and cannot possibly deny Himself, or be unfaithful in His promise, that He, I say, cease to have a special care of those that are His, and in His charge, and especially of His children, who are in His house, and have no other protection than His, because they are as children.   Of which thing that is a most sweet testimony which our Lord said to the prophet Jonas:—" Shall not I spare Nineveh, that great city, in which there are more than a hundred and twenty thousand men that know not how to distinguish between their right hand and their left?"(11)   As if He had said, although the men that are in Nineveh should not move me to compassion, yet it would suffice to move me to pity to behold in it a hundred and twenty thousand innocent children, which set not by prosperities signified by the right hand, nor by adversities signified by the left, because, like little children, they are quite careless of all this, of whom notwithstanding I will not be careless, because I am their Father.

Colloquy.—O most loving Father, I give Thee as many thanks as I possibly can for the paternal providence which Thou hast of those who, with humility and resignation cast themselves into Thy hands. Suffer not, dear Lord, I beseech Thee, that I fall into

(10) 1 Tim. v. 8.   (11) Jonas, iv. 11.

the ignorance of Ephraim, " to whom Thou was like a foster-father."(12) carrying them in Thine arms, and they knew not that Thou curedst them, nor the remedy of their miseries which Thou gavest them. Let me know myself, and know Thee, that my own misery may make me to trust in Thy infinite mercy. Amen.

POINT III.

Consider *five other favours and particular privileges of the little and humble*, which are insinuated in the afore-said sentence of Jesus Christ.

i. The first is, that for their littleness *they will find entrance into the Kingdom of heaven*, so that those who do not become as little ones shall not enter into it, and consequently will lose the means and the end of the fatherly providence of God, without ever enjoying the same.

ii. The second is, that *they will become great in the same Kingdom*, according to the measure that here they made themselves little; for the more humble they shall be, so much more holy shall they be in this life, and more abundantly rewarded in the other; for which cause St. Basil says, that increase in humility is the increase in all virtue, and by how much humility is the deeper, by so much virtue is the higher.(13)

iii. The third is, that *he who receives one of these little ones in the name of Christ, receives Christ Himself* ;(14) for, being united with them by love, what good soever is done to them, He takes it as done to Himself. And if Christ our Lord so much desire, that all receive these little ones, and that they treat them as His own Person, with what delight will Himself receive them under His protection into His house, into His kingdom, and into heaven

(12) Osee, xi. 3.

(13) Serm. Abdic. Verum.   (14) Mat. xviii. 5.

itself. For this Lord always glories Himself to do that which He teaches others, and that His example always goes before His doctrine.

iv. The fourth is, that *whoso shall scandalize one of these little ones*, giving them occasion to fall into sin, *shall be chastised most terribly*, and "it were better for him that a millstone should be hanged about his neck, and that he should be drowned in the depth of the sea,"(15) than that he should be a stone of scandal to little ones; for as He accounts as done to Himself the good which is done to them, so He reputes Himself injured when they are injured or offended.

v. The fifth is, that *they have angels for their keepers, who behold the face of their celestial Father;* for although all men have their guardian angels, as has already been declared, yet the humble especially enjoy this providence, as well on the part of Almighty God, as on the part of the angels themselves, who with more particular care run to the succour of these little ones, because they better know their necessity, and they are more subject to their angel governor, and more grateful to him for the good they receive of him. In confirmation of which the Scripture recounts, that when Agar "wandered in the wilderness," and "the water in her bottle was spent, she cast the boy" Ismael "under one of the trees that were there, and she went her way" that she might not see the child dying. "And God heard the voice of the boy: and an angel of God called to Agar from heaven, saying: What art thou doing, Agar? Fear not; for God hath heard the voice of the boy from the place wherein he is. Arise, take up the boy...for I will make him a great nation."(16) The mother and the son, therefore, suffering a like necessity, the Scripture says not that Almighty God heard the voice of

(15) Mat. xviii. 6.   (16) Gen. xxi. 15.

the mother, but of the child, neither came the angel for respect of the mother, but of the little child, and for his sake provided water for her, that by this event may be seen the loving care which God and His angels have over little ones, whose necessities and tears are voices which cause them to have a tender feeling. And when their father and mother leave them, and cast them from them, God receives them, and sends His angels who may have a care of them.(17)

Colloquy.—O happy littleness, that art so familiar with Almighty God, and with His angels: thou art the gate of heaven, the measure of the greatness and perfection thereof; upon thee God opens His liberal hands, and fills thee with His abundant benediction; (18) for thy sake He loves him who receives thee, and abhors him who repels thee. Him that loves thee He beholds very near, to assist him and exalt him; and him that abhors thee He beholds "afar off,"(19) to humble and to chastise him. Thou holding thy peace, thy necessity cries out, and thy groanings ascend to the tribunal of Almighty God, whence angels are sent to succour thee. Oh who may give to me that I may love Thee and embrace Thee with my whole heart, to imitate Him who made Himself a little one for my sake? O most sweet Jesus, who so greatly lovedst most pure littleness of spirit, that for it Thou likewise tookest the littleness of body, making Thyself little for the love of us, giving us an example to make ourselves little by humility; vouchsafe to grant me that I may make myself little in imitation of Thee, that being made partaker of the littleness which Thou choosest in this life, I may come to participate of the greatness which Thou hast in the other life, world without end. Amen.

(17) Ps. xxvi. 10.   (18) Ps. cxliv. 16.   (19) Ps. cxxxvii. 6.

MEDITATIONS ON THE LAST AND SOVEREIGN BENEFIT OF CELESTIAL GLORY.

With the meditations of the celestial glory I will make an end of this book, because it is the last end of our life, and of all the other divine benefits, which are means ordained by the divine providence to obtain the same, amongst the which one most effectual is, to beseech our Lord to give to us the most clear eyes of faith, to behold and contemplate the same, after the manner that He gave them to St. John, when He said: " I, John, saw the holy city, the new Jerusalem, coming down out of heaven from God, prepared as a bride adorned for her husband. And I heard a great voice from the throne, saying:—" Behold the tabernacle of God with men."(1)

Colloquy.—O eternal God, who causest to descend from heaven the celestial Jerusalem, giving knowledge of it to us who live on earth, enlighten the eyes of my soul, that I may know the excellency of this city, the great sanctity, the vision of peace, the unheard-of news, the wondrous ornament of it, and the ineffable espousal which it has with thee. Oh that the voice of Thine inspiration might sound in mine ears, which might say unto me, Behold the tabernacle of God with men, discovering unto me the beauty of this habitation, and the union which Thou hast with the happy inhabitants thereof! O most sweet spouse of souls, show me Thy face, because it is fair, speak unto me with Thy voice, because it is sweet, and discover unto me the goods which Thou dost promise me, that I may animate myself to procure them, that at the last, to the glory of Thy name, I may obtain them. Amen.

(1) Apoc. xxi. 2, 3.

MEDITATION LI.

ON THE CELESTIAL GLORY, AS CONCERNING THE PLACE AND SOCIETY OF THE BLESSED.

POINT I.

Consider in general *what glory is,*—what paradise and beatitude, which, as divines affirm, is a certain *perfect state, in which all goods are conjoined together.*(2)—Or it is a state eternal, secure, immutable, and free from all evils both of sin and pain which can be feared, and full of all goods of nature and grace which can be desired;—and therefore he is blessed, as St. Augustine says, who has all things he will, and will have no evil thing.

1. This may be easily pondered if I reflect upon all the evils which I have, or which I imagine may befal me; and upon all the goods both of body and soul which I may reasonably desire, rejecting the imperfections of this state, in which we live, and in their place putting *these four excellencies.*

i. The first is *eternity,* because it is to endure as long as God Himself shall endure, of whose " Kingdom there shall be no end."(3)   ii. The second is *security,* which shall likewise be eternal, for the saints know that there cannot be any sin for which God will take away or change the decree which He has made, never to exclude them out of heaven.   iii. The third is *immutability,* because essential glory will never suffer detriment, nor will the joy of the Blessed ever be diminished, but be augmented at the least by new accidental glories, which will make the same much

(2) S. Tho. i. 2, q. iii. et sequent. et q. lxxxii. addit. lib. 23, de Tr. in c. iv. et 5.

(3) Luc. i. 33.

more amiable.—iv. The fourth is *fulness without loathing,* so that the immutability shall be without irksomeness, and the rest without weariness of joy, with a continual novelty in the delight of it, as great as the first day the same began.

2. These properties shall be considered in every point; for the present I may ponder them in general, comparing this blessed state with the present state of this mortal life, to which, how prosperous soever it be, yet many goods are wanting, and it is intermixed with many evils, and is a state temporal, mutable, unquiet, full of tediousness and fastidiousness, which caused Christ our Lord to say to His disciples:—" Lay not up to yourselves treasures on the earth, where the rust and moth consume, and where thieves break through and steal. But lay up to yourselves treasures in heaven,"(4) where none of these things are to be feared. In which words He puts down the difference betwixt the treasures of the earth and those of heaven; that earthly treasures are corruptible, and indeed perish, for one of these three causes,—i. either because they are consumed by using, as meats are; or ii. because even out of themselves something arises which destroys them, as garments which are eaten by the moths, which proceed from them; or iii. because some exterior cause takes them from us, as thieves, and such as by deceit or calumny retain to themselves the things that belong to us. Hence proceeds that he who places his heart upon these treasures is subject to a thousand incumbrances and anxieties. But the celestial treasures are in every respect incorruptible and eternal, because they are not worn or consumed by use, but with the same integrity with which they first began, they endure for all eternity; there cannot be bred in them any "moth" of sin which can consume them, and

(4) Mat. vi. 19. Luc. xii. 33.

the vessels in which they are put up, although they are frail and brittle of their own nature,·yet they are so fortified by the divine omnipotence, that they can by no means be broken, nor can they be robbed by violence, nor by deceit, because these thieves and deceivers cannot enter into heaven, as St. John says.(5)   And although the treasures of grace and virtues incur these dangers in this life, yet is there this difference between these three trea·· sures;— that the temporal may be destroyed, and lost against our wills;—the spiritual treasures of grace and virtue, not unless ourselves consent unto it through sin, but not against our will; lastly, those of glory can in no-wise be lost, nor is it possible to will to want them.

Colloquy.—O my soul, if thou desirest true treasures, despise the first with a lively faith, procure the second with great diligence, that thou mayest enjoy the third with great security. O blessed state, which is enriched with such treasures ! O divine wisdom, who art an " infinite treasure to men, which they that use become the friends of God,"(6) give me part of the treasure of thy grace, that I may obtain the infinite treasures of thy glory. Amen.

POINT II.

1. Descending to the particulars of glory, before all things is to be considered the *excellency and beauty of the empyreal heaven*, and of that superior world which Almighty God created for the habitation of His elect, which is free from all the evils and defects which are in this inferior world, and which is called a valley of tears, because it is full of innumerable things which continually provoke us to weep, from all which heaven is exempt, in which, as St. John says, there will not be so much as one only tear,

(5) Apoc. xxii. 27.   (6) Sap. vii. 14.

because there will be no occasion of tears; (7) but it has together all the goods which are in this visible world freed of their imperfections, and in a much better manner. Wherefore, when St. John says, that the streets of it are of "gold, like a clear glass," and the walls thereof as "jasper stone," the foundations and gates thereof of "precious stones" (8) of inestimable value; all this is as a picture, because there are not in this world things more precious to which to compare those that are in heaven, in comparison of which all that is on earth is as a picture; for as the apostle St. Paul says:—"Eye hath not seen, nor ear heard, neither hath it entered into the heart of man, what things God hath prepared for them that love Him,"(9) which exceed incomparably all things that are perceived by our senses, and by the reasoning proceeding from them.

2. But coming in particular to that which touches the empyreal heaven, there are *four excellencies of that place.*

i. The first is, that it is most *clear,* so that there never is in it darkness nor night, but a continual and everlasting day, with a certain pleasing, divine, and celestial light, because Almighty God Himself is the light thereof, and illuminates it with a brightness worthy of God, and the Lamb, which is Christ our Lord, with the splendour of His sacred humanity, enlightens it and replenishes it with gladness.

ii. The second is, that the place is most *temperate,* without the variety of weathers, which here molest us; for there are no winters nor summers, autumns, heats, drynesses, nor damps, but an uniform temperature, and so divine, that it neither wearies nor brings any irksomeness. And so it is a place most quiet and most healthsome, because no tempests can come thither, no earthquakes, no

(7) Apoc. vii. 17, et xxi. 4.　　　　(8) Ibid. xviii.
(9) 1 Cor. ii. 9.　Isa. lxiv. 4.

thunders, no lightnings, no plagues, nor corrupt airs, nor the maledictions of this miserable earth, because it is a land of most complete benediction,—"a land" truly and properly "of the living," whither not so much as the shadow of death can approach.

iii. The third is, it is a place very *secure, durable, and eternal*, without fear or dread that ever it can have an end, or can be ruined, nor can anything enter into it which may disturb or disquiet it, or hurt the integrity of it so that those who inhabit there shall have perpetual quiet, serenity, and perfect sweetness.

iv. Finally, it is a place most *beautiful fair, and delightful*, incomparably more than all the delightful and pleasant places of this world, much more even than the earthly paradise, which yet was called the Paradise of delights, for it is a place designed, not for good and evil, nor for pilgrims and voyagers, but only for the good, and to be the reward of the elect, who have travailed faithfully in the service of their King. For since Almighty God has put so many goods in this visible world, which is a place common to men and beasts, to the just and to sinners, what goods, what delights, and what riches, has He put in that place common to men and angels, but proper only to the just.

Colloquy.—O right happy and blessed place! O Paradise of ineffable delights, and worthy dwelling of our God! "How lovely are Thy tabernacles, O Lord God of hosts! My soul longeth and fainteth for the courts of the Lord!"(10) Oh when shall I come to inhabit thee, and to enjoy so great a beauty! Shut yourselves, O mine eyes, and do not behold what is on earth, because all is vile in respect of that which you shall see in heaven.

(10) Ps. lxxxiii. 2.

POINT III.

1. Consider the *beauty and excellency of the citizens* of that sovereign city in whose company I hope to live everlastingly.

i. The number of them is *without number*, yet so that being innumerable all know and converse with one another with such familiarity as if they were but few, which is a matter of great joy. Of the angels alone Daniel says:—" Thousand of thousands ministered to Him, and ten thousand hundred thousands stood before Him;" (11) and of men St. John says :—" After this I saw a great multitude which no man could number;" (12) for though it be true that the number of the blessed is but little in comparison of the damned, for which cause Christ our Lord said:—" Broad is the way that leadeth to destruction," and " narrow is the gate, and strait is the way, that leadeth to life, and few there are that find it;" (13) yet speaking absolutely they are many who are saved, and therefore the same Lord says:—" In my Father's house there are many mansions;" (14) with the first moving us to fear, and with the second to hope to obtain the place where so many are to dwell.

ii. Secondly, the *quality* of these citizens is *most glorious*, because all are most noble, most holy, most wise, most prudent, most affable, and most eminent in all things, which can be desired in condition, complexion, civility, discretion, and in all virtue, because there cannot enter there neither devil, nor sin, nor person which is " defiled" so much as with the savour of sin, nor of other imperfection. All are lilies without thorns, grain without straw, and wheat without cockle; because the thorns, straw, and cockle remain out of heaven to be the fuel of the fire of

(11) Dan. vii. 10.   (12) Apoc. vii. 9.
(13) Mat. vii. 13.   (14) Joan. xiv. 2.

hell. If, therefore, I take so great delight to converse with a wise, discreet, and holy man, what contentment shall I take to treat with so many, and so excellent in wisdom, discretion, and sanctity.

iii. Thirdly, *the order, together with the variety* which they have, is very admirable, for all are not alike equal in the things of which we have spoken, but like "as star differs from star in glory," (15) even so they *have great diversity in their beauty and celestial brightness*, but yet with great agreement and order in their degrees. There are three Hierarchies, and nine choirs of Angels, Archangels, Principalities, Virtues, Powers, Dominations, Thrones, Cherubim and Seraphim, all greatly different in nature, and in the gifts of wisdom and grace, with unspeakable beauty. And amongst them there are men intermixed in their choirs, and some above all of them, because they far excel them in sanctity; for there are choirs of Patriarchs and Prophets, of Apostles and Evangelists, of Martyrs and Confessors, of Bishops and Doctors, of Priests and Religious, of Virgins and Widows, and of other states, all agreeing in singular peace and concord, so that we may say of them that of the Canticles:—"What shalt thou see in the Sulamitess but the company of camps?" (16)

Colloquy.—O peaceable city, spouse of the peaceable Solomon, what other thing is there in thee than choirs of saints, who sing with gladness, and were strong and valiant warriors, and therefore now enjoy the peace which they have gained by their victory? Oh that I could fight as these valiant soldiers have fought, that I may be worthy always to live in so sweet a society. Amen.

Hence will I conceive a desire of *serving God with the greatest excellency and perfection that I possibly can*, be-

(15) 1 Cor. xv. 41. (16) Cant. vii. 6.

cause if I can attain to the choir of Seraphim I ought not to content myself with an inferior place, but to buy, as the same Lord says:—"gold, fire-tried," that I may "be made rich," (17) to love with great purity and fervour Him who is worthy of infinite love.

iv. Above all, *the union and concord* of such a multitude with such variety is very eminent, which union is most strict and most amiable, for all love one another with a most ardent love in Almighty God, with great conformity of wills, without any opposition, strifes, ambitions, or envies. For the greater love the lesser very tenderly, and desire to impart to them all the good that ever they can; the lesser love the greater most intensely, and rejoice for the good in which they excel. The good of one is the good of all, and the good of all is the good of every one, for every one holds the good of another for his own, and joys in it as if it were his, because of the eminence of charity that is amongst them. All eat at the same table of divinity, and drink of one celestial cup; they all have the same exercises, serving the same God with the same spirit, because God is in all, and is all things to all, uniting them all amongst themselves, and with Himself.(18)

Colloquy.—O blessed society, in which neither the multitude confounds, nor excellency breeds pride, nor variety troubles, nor inequality causes dissension, or cools love! O my soul, if this sweet society be so pleasing to thee, endeavour henceforth to imitate the virtues thou seest in it. Follow their obedience, fulfilling the divine will here on earth, as they fulfil the same in heaven. Imitate their brotherly union and charity, loving all thy neighbours as thy brethren, and preserving peace with all of them. Be subject to

(17) Apoc. iii. 18.　　　　　　(18) 1 Cor. xv. 28.

the greater, honour the lesser, rejoice in the good of all, and so thou wilt imitate in life those whom thou desirest to imitate in glory.

2. These are the principal fruits which I am to gather from this point, craving of our Lord to grant them to me for the merits of these most noble citizens of whom I am likewise to request the same, saying:—

Colloquy.—O blessed saints, who were in the same perils in which I am, but enjoy now that tranquillity which I desire, assist me with your prayers to the end that I may imitate your virtues, and may come to have part in your crowns, rejoicing in your blessed company, world without end.   Amen.

MEDITATION LII.

ON THE ESSENTIAL GLORY OF THE SOUL, AND OF THE BODY AND ITS SENSES.

POINT I.

Consider the greatness of *glory which properly appertains to the soul* and makes it entirely blessed, which is so great, that as St. Thomas says, Almighty God could not give to it a greater blessedness since it contains in it the same God,(1) and therefore this glory consists in this, that the whole soul be as it were deified, full of God, and made a god by mutual participation, Almighty God so uniting Himself to it as fire is wont to penetrate iron, communicating to it His light and splendour, His heat and other properties which it has, so that the iron seems to be fire.

1. Hence it comes to pass that the soul is filled and replenished with all the good it desires, conformable to

(1) S. Tho. q. xcii. addit. 1, p. q. xxv. art. 6, ad 3.

that which David says,—" I shall be satisfied when Thy glory shall appear;"(2) this may be pondered reflecting upon *the three spiritual faculties* of the soul.

i. The *memory will enter into the powers of our Lord*, and be ingulfed in the abyss of His divinity, that it may " be mindful of " His " justice alone,"(3) for it will be full of Almighty God, having Him always present, and will not be able to forget Him, nor to divert itself to any other thing.   It has in mind continually the benefits it received, receives, and hopes to receive, with exceeding joy, never forgetting that which causes it so great contentment,— nor remembering any thing which might cause it pain, for if it remember the labours and perils of this life, and the sins it committed, of all this it draws forth joy and gladness, and motives of continual praises of Almighty God, giving Him continually thanks for the benefits which He has done it, does it, and will do without end, fulfilling that which David says,—" They shall publish the memory of the abundance of Thy sweetness, and shall rejoice in Thy justices,"(4) remembering how just and faithful Thou hast been to them, performing all which Thou hast promised them.

ii. *The understanding will be full of God, with the clear sight of His Divinity and Trinity.* There will He, not as " through a glass, in a dark manner," but " face to face"(5) see God wholly, the Father, the Son, and the Holy Ghost, and will know how the Father begets the Son, and how they two produce the Holy Ghost, and how the Three are One God, infinite, eternal, immense, and incomprehensible. He will see all His divine perfections, His infinite bounty, wisdom, charity, omnipotency, and providence. He will see the sovereign mysteries of the Incarnation of the Son of God,

(2) Ps. xvi. 15.   (3) Ps. lxx. 16.
(4) Ps. cxliv. 7.   (5) 1 Cor. xiii.

of His sacred humanity, and the marvellous works which God has wrought, both of nature and grace, so that all ignorance, errors, doubts, and opinions, which here he had, will utterly cease.—Faith will cease, because he will *see* what he believed.—Hope will cease, because he will *possess* what he hoped ;(6) and in particular he will see clearly the secret judgments of Almighty God, concerning the government of men which here vexed and afflicted him, and more particularly see the immense secrets of the paternal providence, with which Almighty God governed him and directed him in his salvation, that at the last it might take effect. He will know the perils from which He delivered him, and the hidden benefits which He did him, giving him herewith a motive and occasion of most singular joy. Finally there will be filled the insatiable desire that men have to know, seeing Almighty God, in whom all things are, and thus they will attain, after an ineffable manner, to that which the serpent said in Paradise, namely,—to become like Gods, that know both "good and evil,"(7) greatly rejoicing for the good, and having no part at all in the evil.

iii. *They will* likewise be full of God, *united to His divinity with an union of love*, which will be perpetual, continual, internal, and admirable, in all the manners, and with all the titles that can be of holy love: because all have place in Almighty God, being seen clearly and distinctly, whom the will loves as a father, as a friend, as a spouse, as an infinite benefactor, sovereign good, first beginning and last end. And from this love flows a continual, perpetual, and copious "torrent" of ineffable "pleasure," (8) of which he will drink, and will be made drunk, and will be ingulfed within the infinite joys of his Lord. (9)   Whence it is that the soul will

(6) Rom. viii. 24.

(7) Gen. iii. 5.

(8) Ps. xxxv. 9.

(9) Mat. xxv. 21.

be full of all virtues, exercising the acts of them with singular delight. For with obedience she will obey God with great alacrity:—with humility she will wholly render herself to Him with loving submission:—with religion she will give to Him, with great reverence, due worship and adoration, and gratitude, with continual thanksgiving, with jubilees, canticles, and everlasting alleluias; for there will be no passions, nor contradictions, nor any thing which may hinder or make distasteful the variety of these delights, which will be so divine that none can know them unless they prove them, because they are like to the "hidden manna," (10) whose savour is not discovered unless it be tasted.

2. Finally, to understand at once the greatness and the fulness of this glory, I will ponder this reason which comprehends all the rest. That which makes Almighty God blessed, and fills Him and gives Him infinite joy, will suffice proportionably to do the like in me; (11) since, therefore, God, since He has been God, and throughout all eternity is blessed, and is full and joyful, without any weariness, with the only beholding and loving Himself, not having necessity of any other thing out of Himself; so I likewise shall be blessed, and shall be full and joyful, with the only sight of Almighty God, shall love Him, and enjoy Him, without necessity of any other thing out of Him, and without any fastidiousness or weariness in this work, but a certain eternal novelty, and an eternity always new, always seeing Almighty God, and desiring always to see Him without ceasing.

Colloquy.—O my glory, when shall I see Thee with so great clearness, that Thou wilt fill the desires of my heart? When shall I have such cleanness of soul that I may behold Thy divine face? Oh that I

(10) Apoc. ii. 17.   (11) S. Tho. i. p. q. xxvi. 1.

had never done anything which had displeased Thy divine goodness, and hindered me from so blessed a sight. Take to Thee, dear Lord, I beseech Thee, all my powers, and employ them even from this present in that which they are for ever to do. Let my mind be always busied in beholding Thee, my understanding in knowing Thee, my will in loving Thee, my tongue in blessing Thee, and my senses and my members in obeying Thee, all rejoicing in Thee, of Thee, and for Thee, world without end. Amen.

Of that which has been said I am to understand that the exercise of *mental prayer*, which is a work of the three faculties of the soul, as already has been said, is a description of glory in which consists the blessedness of this life, which they call " begun," which is a resemblance of that which our soul will have in heaven. For which cause blessed St. Bernard well said, that to a Religious man, his cell is a heaven, (12) because the exercises which are done in heaven, are likewise done in his cell, where God is known and beloved, where the Religious enjoys God, and loves and praises Him with his whole heart; for this reason the angels themselves rejoice in cells, as they do in heaven, because they behold in them the work of prayer, which is a work performed by angels, and in the same manner to every one addicted to prayer, his oratory will be his heaven if he pray as he ought.(13)

POINT II.

1. Consider the excellency of the glory of the blessed *body*, with *its four dowries*, reflecting upon each one of them. (14)

i. The first dowry is *charity*, with admirable beauty, for then will every just man " shine as the sun in the

(12) Ad fratres de monte Dei.   (13) S. Joan. Clym. græ. xxviii.
     (14) 1 Cor. xv. 42.   S. Tho. q. lxxxii. addit.

Kingdom of" his " Father," (15) like the body of Christ
our Lord, although he who is most blessed, will shine
with greatest splendour, but the body of Christ above all
will have perfect integrity in all parts with great proportion, and with an admirable colour and figure, without
any deformity, spot, or wrinkle, (16) or such like thing to
obscure its splendour. And if it received in this life any
blow or wound for Christ, and that the sign of it remain
in the body, it will be like a brooch of most precious
pearls, which will make it much more beautiful. And
besides the exterior beauty, the interior beauty of the
same body will be visible, and most pleasant, because it
will become transparent, discovering all the harmony of
the bones, veins, and arteries, with unspeakable splendour
of the whole; and for this cause is it compared to resplendent gold, and to glass or crystal, which is transparent.(17)

ii. The second dowry is *immortal impassibility*, or impassible immortality, because they will never suffer more,
neither hunger nor thirst, nor sorrow, nor sickness, nor
fear of death, (18) for though they be in the midst of fire,
yet will it not burn them, and although they go through
rivers and seas, yet will they not so much as once be wet.
They will always have such a freshness as will never
whither, such a health as cannot impair or decay, and
eternal impassibility with singular joy, so that their
" heart" and their " flesh" (19) will rejoice in the living
God, of whom they will receive a life so joyful and so
blessed.

iii. The third dowry is *agility* or celerity, by which the
soul will have so much dominion over the body, that it

(15) Mat. xiii. 43.   (16) Ephes. v. 27.
(17) S. Greg. lib. xxvii. mor. cap. 27. S. Tho. q lxxxv. addit. art. 1.
(18) Apoc. vii. 16. Isa. xlix. 10.   (19) Ps. lxxxiii. 3.

may move it from one place to another without repose, weariness, or painful delay, but with great quickness and velocity, "running to and fro like as sparks" (20) of lightning through the empyreal heaven at their own pleasure, sometimes to the throne of Christ our Lord, now to the throne of His Mother or of other saints.

iv. The fourth dowry is *subtilty* or spirituality, because it will not be subject to the works of the vegetative life any more than if it were a spirit, and so will pass the whole life without meat or drink, without sleep, and without other works which are common to beasts; and therefore our Saviour said, that in the resurrection they should "neither marry nor be married," (21) but should be as the angels in heaven, being like in this to pure spirits. It will likewise have subtilty to be able in the virtue of Almighty God to penetrate the heavens and any other body whatsoever, without any manner of impediment, as Christ after His Resurrection entered into the supping chamber, "the doors being shut," (22) and went out of the sepulchre, penetrating the stone with which it was closed, whereby He showed how delicate and subtle His glorified body was. (23)

2. These are the four dowries of a glorified body, with the consideration of which I will encourage myself willingly to suffer the miseries and labours of this life, reputing it for happiness to suffer them, since they will be so well rewarded.

Colloquy.—O blessed ignominies, whose end is so great beauty! O happy pains, which cause the body to be so impassible! O happy labours, which are rewarded with so great solace! Oh how well did the

(20) Sap. iii. 7.   (21) Mat. xxii. 30.
(22) Joan. xx. 26.
(23) Mat. xxviii. 2. S. Tho. Lect. vi. in 4, ad. Cor. xv.

apostle St. Paul say, that " the sufferings of this time are not worthy to be compared with the glory to come, that should be revealed in us."(24)   Animate thyself, O my soul, to bear in thy body "the mortification of Jesus,"(25) because my body so humbled will be conformed to His glorified; receive in thy flesh His sorrows and torments, since the glory is so great which thou art to receive for them.

POINT III.

The third will be to consider the glory and delectation of *the five corporal senses*, reflecting upon every one.(26)

i. The sight will receive exceeding delight, beholding the beauty of so innumerable glorious bodies, with the variety there will be in them, of faces and of most delightful figures.   But above all others it will be delighted with the sight of the sacred humanity of Christ our Lord and of His resplendent wounds, whose sight will be so glorious, that holy Job in the midst of his sores and pains comforted himself with the hope of this sight, saying;—" I know that my Redeemer liveth, and in the last day I shall rise out of the earth.   And I shall be clothed again with my skin, and in my flesh I shall see my God.   Whom I myself shall see, and my eyes shall behold, and not another: this my hope is laid up in my bosom." (27)

ii. The *hearing* will be delighted to hear the sweet words which the Blessed will speak one to another, full of wisdom, of discretion, and of sanctity, and the praises of Almighty God, which they will pronounce with their tongues, as is said in the Apocalypse of the " four living creatures:"—" They rest not day and night, saying; Holy, holy, holy, Lord God almighty;" (28) and David says:—

<hr>

(24) Rom. viii. 18.   (25) 2 Cor. iv. 10.
(26) Doctores in 4. Sent. dist. 49.   (27) Job. xix. 25.
(28) Apoc. iv. 8.

"The saints shall rejoice in glory." The high praises of God shall be in their mouth." (29) The hearing will be likewise recreated with celestial music, and with new songs invented by the wisdom of Almighty God, to recreate the ears of those who delighted in this life to hear His words that they might believe them, and His precepts to fulfil them.

iii. The *smelling* will be recreated with the most sweet odour which the glorified bodies will cast forth, especially that of Christ our Lord, which of Himself said:—"Wheresoever the body shall be, there shall the eagles also be gathered together." (30) O what fragrancy and variety of odours will the divine piety invent to recreate that flesh which here gave of itself the "odour of" a holy "life." (31)

iv. The *taste* will have a fulness and celestial satiety, without any fastidiousness, our Lord communicating to it without meats, the sweetness which it might receive by the meats themselves, after another manner much more delicious and sublime. For if manna being but one sort of meat, contained in an excellent manner the delight and taste of all sorts of meats, (32) to solace the just, God doubtless knows how to give such a taste, as may contain with eminency all tastes to delight and solace the Blessed in heaven.

v. Finally, the sense of *touching* which is diffused throughout the body will be filled with delights most pure and holy, so that all the Blessed will be as drowned in the river of the delights of our Lord. Oh how well rewarded there will all the senses be for the mortifications which they sustained in this life, since David says;—"According to the multitude of my sorrows in my heart, Thy comforts

(29) Ps. cxlix. 5.   (30) Mat. xxiv. 28.
(31) 2 Cor. ii. 16.   (32) Sap. xvi. 20.

have given joy to my soul." (33) O my body encourage thyself to suffer for Christ, that thy senses may be partakers of the joy which His feel : rejoice in those things which are said to thee, that thou art to go into the house of our Lord," (34) and although thy feet walk upon the earth, yet fix them with desire upon the palaces of heaven and on the celestial Jerusalem.

Colloquy.—O Jerusalem our mother, who, after the manner of a city which is built of " the living stones" (35) of thy citizens, united with unspeakable peace betwixt themselves, receive my heart even from this present, and admit me in spirit to enter into thee, to the end that in time thou admit me also to enter with soul and body. O infinite God, Father of our Lord Jesus Christ, who, " according to Thy great mercy," hast " regenerated us"(36) in the being of grace, and hast given us a lively hope of obtaining an inheritance incorruptible, and incontaminate, and that cannot fade, preserved in the heavens, and kept by a lively faith in Thine elect, to reveal it to them in the latter days : regenerate me, for Thy mercy's sake, in the being of Thy Son, preserving always in me Thy holy grace, that I may obtain this sovereign inheritance of Thy glory. Amen.

MEDITATION LIII.

ON THE CELESTIAL GLORY AS IT COMPREHENDS THE REWARDS OF THE EIGHT BEATITUDES.

The greatness of celestial glory, Christ our Lord declared in the sermon made on the mountain, by the seven rewards which He promised in the acts of heroic virtue, which He named beatitudes, of which we have treated in

(33) Ps. xciii. 19.   (34) Ps. cxxi. 1.
(35) 1 Pet. ii. 5.   (36) Ibid. i. 3.

the eleventh meditation of the third Part; presupposing, therefore, that which there has been said, we will meditate *these seven rewards* as they are found in the celestial glory.

POINT I.

Consider this glory to be *that Kingdom of heaven* which Christ our Lord promised *to " the poor of spirit,"* and to those that "suffer persecution for justice sake," which is nothing else than the *clear vision of Almighty God* and the possession of His infinite riches, with sanctity, "justice, peace and joy in the Holy Ghost," (1) which the Saints have in the empyreal heaven. In which each of these things are with great excellency; for the vision or sight of God is without mixture of obscurity; those riches, without defect or poverty,—the sanctity, without any kind of malice; the justice without any injury or partiality; the peace without anything that may cause discord; and the joy without any sign of sorrow or sadness.—This kingdom is within every one, (2) and every one possesses it entirely without dependance on another. For although there had been but one blessed alone, yet should he have had his kingdom entire, notwithstanding he receives no little joy from the sweet company of the rest of the Blessed. Hence it is, that all the inhabitants of heaven receive this Kingdom for their own, in such a manner that they are true kings, and rejoice greatly in their kingly dignity, and reign together with the supreme King of kings, who is God; for which cause the triumphant Church is called Regina, "a queen," who stands on the right hand of her spouse " in gilded clothing, surrounded with variety"(3) of gifts and virtues, as it becomes the spouse of so sovereign a king. What thing then can there be more glorious than to possess such a kingdom, and to be a king in the com-

(1) Rom. xiv. 17.   (2) Luc. xvii. 21.   (3) Ps. xliv. 11.

pany of so many other noble kings, the least of whom is incomparably greater than all the kings of the whole earth. (4)

Colloquy.—O King of kings, and Lord of lords, I give Thee thanks that Thou givest Thy servants, in recompense of every little service, a kingdom so surpassingly excellent. O infinite Kingdom and immense heaven, straitened and comprised within the heart of the just, and purchased by the works of justice! If all the goods of this life "shall be added"(5) to him who seeks this kingdom, how infinite will thy goods be which shall be given for principal payment to him who is worthy to obtain the same! O happy those who humble and impoverish themselves by their own will, or are humbled and persecuted for justice sake, seeing they will be rewarded with such a kingdom! Dear Lord, let Thy "kingdom come"(6) to me, and let it enter into me, that I may enter into it, and may enjoy Thee everlastingly. Amen.

POINT II.

Ponder how the celestial glory is *the blessed possession of that earth which is promised to the meek,* and so far exceeds this which we tread upon, as the starry heaven exceeds this in greatness, beauty, and splendour; for this earth is the earth of those which are to die, and the sepulchre of those who die in it, whom it converts into dust. It is a valley of tears,(7) a banishment from our country, and a place full of all misery, because it is a land of malediction, dry and barren, through the fault of his first inhabitant. But the land which is here promised is a region of the living, where none can die, and where all change an earthly life with a celestial. It is a valley of delights, in

(4) Mat. xi. 11.   (5) Mat. vi. 33.

(6) Mat. vi. 10.   (7) Ps. lxii. 3, 4. xxi. xli. 4.

which flow the milk and honey of divine consolations, without sighs or tears, or any occasions of them. It is a land of benediction and watered with miraculous fertility, because, as St. John says, it is continually watered with the "river of water of life," (8) like crystal which proceeds from the throne of Almighty God and of the Lamb; and on both sides of the river there are many trees of life, which bring forth fruit twelve times a year, and their leaves are the health of all nations.

Colloquy.—O most blessed land, from whence perpetually flows living water, and the clear vision of the divinity of God, and of the humanity of the Lamb Christ Jesus, whose inhabitants are as trees of life, which are always moistened and bedewed with the water of this divine river, in virtue of which they produce innumerable fruits of new joys, and of new delights. O happy trees, whose leaves give health to the nations that live on earth, for by the testimonies we hear of them, and the protection we receive from them, we hope to live with them in heaven. Oh! who may give to me the possession of this happy land! O my soul, love the meekness of the Lamb Jesus, that He may give in possession to thee this supreme land, where the goats cannot enter, which will be placed at the day of judgment upon His left hand, but "sheep alone," which will be upon "His right hand." (9) Amen.

POINT III.

The third shall be to consider, that the celestial glory is *a comfort* which is promised *to those that mourn;* in which is to be pondered who He is that comforts—with what things—in what manner—and for how long time.

1. *He that comforts,* is He who by excellence is called

(8) Apoc. xxii. 1.　　　　　(9) Mat. xxv. 33.

Paraclitus, (10) Comforter, " et Deus totius consolationis," and " the God of all comfort; " (11) and from whom proceeds all whatsoever can comfort us, and in heaven performs this with great eminence, for there are innumerable things which comfort with great excellence.

2. There comforts the *clear vision of Almighty God*, and of the humanity of Christ our Lord, the presence of His glorious Mother, the company of the Hierarchies of Angels, the sweet conversation with the choirs of Patriarchs and Prophets, Apostles and Martyrs, and other Saints of that happy celestial court, each one is a comforter of another, inasmuch as the goods of all comfort every one. The security of the place likewise comforts, the eternity of the state and the tranquillity of conscience, which far surpasses all understanding.

3. But who shall express the *manner* of the comfort? For Almighty God does not comfort there by pardoning sins, and by moderating sadness, but *banishing thence for ever the one and the other*, with a perpetual music of praise and thanksgiving, and of " a perpetual Alleluia,"(12) with which to cheer and recreate the heart.

4. And all this comfort will be eternal without cessation or interruption, because all are within the joy of their Lord, and none shall take from them the joy which He hath given them. (13)

Colloquy.—O blessed life, where comfort is as eternal as the life itself, and the life as eternal as the comfort is !   Oh happy he who mourns in this mortal life, since he will receive such comfort in the immortal ! O " God of hope,"(14) replenish me with joy and comfort in believing the magnificence of Thy glory, to

(10) Joan. xiv. 26.   (11) 2 Cor. i. 3.
(12) Isa. li. 3. Tob. xi . 22.
(13) Mat. xxv. 21. Joan xvi. 22.   (14) Rom. xv. 13.

the end that I may suffer the sorrows and torments of this life, with assured hope of the eternal comforts which Thou wilt give me in the other. Amen.

POINT IV.

The celestial glory is the *fulness* which is promised *to those that hunger and thirst after justice;* which fulness is an abundance of all good things, which men may reasonably desire. Where is to be pondered, that the earth is a place of perpetual thirst and hunger; for some hunger for the meats and delights of the flesh; others after the riches, honours and dignities of the world; others thirst after sciences and curiosity of the senses; and others thirst after virtues and celestial graces; nor can any one be fully satisfied in this life, because temporal goods cannot fill our desire, but spiritual goods are given in weight and measure, so that there always remains a desire to increase in them, for which cause the divine wisdom says,—" They that eat me, shall yet hunger; and they that drink me, shall yet thirst." (15) But heaven is a place of complete fulness, for as the prophet David says,—We shall all be filled with the sight and apparition of the glory of God, which so enriches and exalts the Blessed, that it excludes all desire of the riches and excellencies of this world, because all these things compared with the sight of Almighty God, are miseries and basenesses. This vision fills the desire men have to know; for seeing God, all things are seen which can be desired. It likewise fills the desire of virtues, because it brings complete and final perfection to them all, and all this will endure for all eternity, yet will it never cause irksomeness, but every day will be tasted as new as in the first beginning. Finally, there will be fulfilled that which is written:—" He will cast death down headlong

(15) Ecclus. xxiv. 29.

for ever, and the Lord God shall wipe away tears from every face;" (16) and that of the Apocalypse:—" They shall no more hunger nor thirst, neither shall the sun fall upon them, nor any heat, because the lamb which is in the throne shall rule them, and shall bring them to the fountains of living water, (17) and shall wipe away all waters from their eyes."

Colloquy.—O my soul, hunger and thirst after this glory, since this alone is sufficient to give to thee complete fulness. Hunger and thirst likewise after justice, without which thou canst not attain the excellency of it.

POINT V.

The celestial glory is the fulness of " mercy " which is promised to " the merciful," pondering three places which there are for three divers sorts of men, that is to say, hell, heaven, and the earth, which is in the midst betwixt them both, the which, as St. Paul says, is as it were "a great house," wherein " there are not only vessels of gold and of silver, but also of wood and of earth, and some indeed unto honour, but some unto dishonour," (18) some are vessels of wrath deputed to destruction, in punishment of their sins, and others are vessels of mercy, deputed for life, in reward of their good works grounded upon divine grace. From this middle place come inhabitants to both these two extremes. Hell is a place deputed for vessels of wrath and contumely, in whom Almighty God shows His supreme wrath and vengeance on His enemies, chastising them with that supreme chastisement which His rigorous judgment has denounced against them. But heaven is deputed for the vessels of honour and mercy, on whom

<hr>

(16) Isa. **xxv.** 8. Apoc. vii. 16.
(17) Isa. xlix. 10.   (18) 2 Tim. ii. 20. Rom. ix. 21.

Almighty God manifests the supreme mercy which He desires to exhibit to the just by His infinite mercy and charity, rewarding in them the works of His grace, with the sovereign recompense of His glory. Heaven therefore is a house or parlour, full of most beautiful vessels of gold and silver, amongst which there is not any of wood or earth, which neither can be broken if it be knocked, or can be corrupted with rust or consumed with fire. All there are vessels of honour and of glory, and none of contumely or of infamy,—all are likewise vessels of mercy, because from all eternity Almighty God chose them by His mercy, and crowns them with infinite mercies, as David says, replenishing their "desires with good things," and renewing their "youth like the eagle's, without fear or danger to become old again." (19) Hence I will infer that the celestial glory, although it be the "crown of justice," (20) yet as this is founded in grace, so much more is the crown of infinite mercy, which the vessels of mercy obtained, because they were merciful.

Colloquy.—Wherefore, O my soul, since thou livest betwixt heaven and hell, endeavour to be "a vessel of gold,"(21) by charity, and a vessel of silver by purity; purify thyself from sins and passions, and so thou shalt become a vessel of sanctification, in which Almighty God will now lay up the treasures of His grace, and afterwards those of His everlasting glory. Amen.

(Concerning this point, those things may be perused which are set down in the meditations of the charity and mercy of Almighty God.)

POINT VI.

The celestial glory is the clear vision of Almighty God,

(19) Ps. cii. 4. (20) 2 Tim. iv. 8.
(21) 2 Tim. ii. 20.

which is promised to " the clean of heart," in which con-sists our essential beatitude.

As fathers give dowries to their daughters when they marry, and bestow upon them rich gifts with which to adorn them, and the spouse himself the same day that he leads his spouse to his house, delivers to her rich jewels;—even so the Eternal Father to every soul which is espoused to His Son on the day which she enters into the house of heaven, where this spiritual marriage is fully perfected, gives her three most rich dowries of glory, answering to the three theological virtues which she had in this life, with which she is adorned and beautified, and her beatitude is made complete.

i. In reward of *faith* is given to her a most excellent light of glory with which she clearly sees Almighty God and all the mysteries which she believed in this life, not any one being hid from her, fulfilling that which David said:—" In Thy light we shall see light;" (22) and " they shall walk, O Lord, in the light of Thy countenance, and in Thy name they shall rejoice all the day, for Thou art the glory of their strength." (23)   O how sweet is this light, and how delightful to the eyes to see the sun of justice replenish me with this divine light, that I may see thee in Thy glory and splendour.   Amen.

ii. In recompense of *hope* is given the second dowry which is called comprehension, namely, to have always present and as in propriety and *possession of whatsoever in this life was either hoped or desired.*   For there she has present her God and her Father, her spouse, her final end, and all her good, and enjoys the same as a thing which she has in her own power, and which she embraces with great security of never losing it, or never being separated from it, because she has now so run that she comprehends;

(22) Ps. xxxv. 10.   (23) Ps. lxxxviii. 17.

and in that first entrance of heaven, she says:—" I have found Him whom my soul loveth, I will hold Him and I will not let Him go." (24)

iii. In reward of *charity* is given the third dowry of glory, which is called *fruition, or love, which is to love the sovereign good which he sees*, and to rejoice in the convenience and goodness which it has with that joy and ineffable pleasure which arises to see herself united to Him whom she so greatly loved, loving as she is loved, and mutually rejoicing in this love, and so she says:—" My beloved to me, and I to Him." (25)

Colloquy.—O my soul, love cleanness of heart, quickening within thee these three virtues, that God may give to thee His three glorious dowries. O Father of lights, give me, I beseech Thee, the light of Thy glory, that I may see that which I believe with the light of faith. O divine Word, spouse of souls, give Thyself to me, that I may possess with security what I desire with hope. O most Holy Spirit, show me Thy goodness, that I may enjoy with fulness that which I love with charity. Amen.

POINT VII.

The celestial glory is *a perfect adoption of the sons of God*, which is promised *to the peacemakers*. For as Christ our Lord was twice declared to be the Son of God, first in His Baptism, and next in His Transfiguration, the Holy Ghost descending upon Him in form of a dove or of a cloud, and the voice of the Father sounding, which said:—" This is my beloved Son;" (26) even so the just is declared and published of God for His adoptive son, two several times.—The first is in this mortal life, when He calls and justifies him by the sacraments, and exalts him

(24) Cant. iii. 4. (25) Cant. ii 16.
(26) Mat. iii. 17; xvii. 5. Luc. ix. 35.

with such gifts and graces as discover the dignity of the
Son of God, as has been declared in the meditation of the
baptism of Christ.(27)　But this adoption of sons is yet imperfect, because it is in danger to be lost through our offence;
for which respect even those that were very holy who
received the first fruits of the Spirit, groaned within themselves, " waiting for the adoption of the sons of God," (28)
namely, the perfection and accomplishment of the first
adoption by another much more perfect, signified by the
Transfiguration of Christ, which is communicated to a soul
the same day that she enters into glory, and takes possession of the inheritance due to sons, with right to receive
in the end of the world a body glorified with the four
dowries of glory already recited,(29) and then will Almighty
God discover the dignity of those that are His sons, for, as
St. John says:—" We are now the sons of God, and it
hath not yet appeared what we shall be. We know that
when He shall appear, we shall be like to Him, because we
shall see Him as He is." (30)

Colloquy.—O most loving Father, I give Thee
thanks for the sovereign inheritance which Thou dost
give to Thy beloved sons, although here Thou hold
them somewhat in humility, and hardly treated, because Thou chastisest " every son" whom Thou receivest,(31) thereby to honour and exalt him, and to
constitute him heir of Thy Kingdom. Oh that I might
glory in the hope of this perfect filiation, living like
the son of such a Father here on earth, that He may
glorify and crown me with His glory, in the Kingdom
of heaven. Amen.

(27) Med. iii. p 3.

(28) Rom. viii. 23.　　　　(29) Med. xxi. xxii. p. 3.
(30) 1 Joan. iii. 2.　　　　(31) Prov. iii. 12.　Heb. xii. 6.

MEDITATION LIV.

ON CELESTIAL GLORY AS COMPREHENDING THE SEVEN REWARDS PROMISED IN THE APOCALYPSE BY CHRIST TO THOSE WHO OVERCOME.

The greatness of the celestial glory Christ our Lord likewise declared in the Apocalypse, by *seven other kinds of rewards* which He promises *to those that overcome*, that is to say, to those that overcome the Devil and his temptations, the flesh and her passions, the world and his vain honours, tyrants and their persecutions, and lastly, to those who overcome themselves, and their own will and inordinate appetites, mortifying them with perseverance to death. In which promise goes always proportioned the reward and crown, with the manner of the combat in which the victory was gained, as will be seen in the points ensuing.

POINT I.

Glory is the reward which Christ our Lord promises to those who persevere in their first fervour, or by penance return to the same, saying:—" To him that overcometh I will give *to eat of the tree of life*, which is in the Paradise of my God." (1)   In which words are to be pondered, i.— *which tree* of life this is,—ii. in *what Paradise* it is,—iii. *what it is to eat it*, and—iv., *to whom* it is given to be eaten.

i. This *tree* of life *is God Himself*, with all His excellencies and perfections; the fruits are the works which proceed *from* Him, or which remain *within* Him, as is the generation of the eternal Word by knowledge, and the production of the Holy Ghost by love;—all which are out

(1) Apoc. ii. 7.

of Him, as is the creation and government of the world, the sanctification and glorification of His elect. And He calls Himself the tree of life, because He always lives in Himself, and is infinite "life" itself, and the "fountain of life," (2) as well of the life of nature and grace as of glory and life eternal.

Colloquy.—O most blessed Trinity, I rejoice that Thou art a tree of life, from whom proceed so precious leaves; preserve in me, if it be convenient, the life of nature, augment in me the life of grace, and give me afterwards the life of glory. Amen.

ii. The *Paradise* in which this tree is planted is *the empyreal heaven,* where it produces in great abundance the delights which are proper to Almighty God, which they enjoy who eat of it.

iii. Eating is made by means of the *clear vision of the divinity, and of the humanity of Christ our Lord,* in knowing of whom consists life eternal; (3) and such is the efficacy of this meat that it converts into trees of life all those that eat the same, for the great similitude they have with their God. For which cause the same St. John, in the end of his Apocalypse, calls the Blessed "the tree of life on both sides of the river, bearing twelve fruits, yielding its fruit every month;" (4) because they live perpetually, and bud forth new and most savoury affections and tastes, with which they preserve continually without weariness their happy life.

iv. This is that celestial glory masked under the name of so glorious meat, which Christ our Lord promises to *those that overcome,* and unless I overcome I cannot receive it.

(2) Joan. i. 4. Ps. xxxv. 10.
(3) Joan. xvii. 3.   (4) Apoc. xxii. 2.

Colloquy.—Take, therefore, O my soul, the counsel of thy Redeemer, and if " thou hast left thy first charity," be mindful, therefore, from whence thou art fallen ; and do penance and do the first works,"(5) that thou mayest recover the same, and overcome thy own slothfulness ; live like a tree planted by the courses of the waters of grace, to the end that thou mayest eat the fruits of this tree of life, world without end. Amen.

POINT II.

Glory is the second reward which Christ our Lord promised to those *who are faithful in all temptations and persecutions unto death,* saying:—" Be thou faithful unto death, and I will give thee *the crown of life.*" (6)

1. *They who in this life are overcome by the Devil* and his ministers, and either for fear or slothfulness sink under sin, although they escape for a little time the first death, which is the death of nature, yet *fall into the second death,* which is of sin, and afterwards into the eternal death of hell; so that they will not only not taste of the tree of life, which is in the Paradise of delights, but will be cast into the abyss of pains, where will be given to them to eat of the tree, if it may so be termed, of death, whose fruits are, "fire," "brimstone," worms, serpents, weeping and gnashing of teeth, and will drink of the most bitter "wine of the wrath of God," even to the dregs. (7)

2. But *those who overcome,* although they suffer some detriment by the first death, because they are sometimes wont bodily to die in the battle, as it happens to the holy martyrs, yet they will *receive no damage by the second death,* namely, of sin, nor of hell, from which death God delivers them, crowning them with a crown of life, namely,

(5) Apoc. ii. 4.   (6) Apoc. ii. 10.   (7) Apoc. xiv. 10.

with an immortal crown, which always lives, and with a life so blessed, that it will be the crown of their victory. Hence it is that the first death of the body does not endamage them, but is profitable to them, and they rejoice in it, making use of it as of a passage to life, for as the Wise man says, "the souls of the just are in the hands of God, and the torment of death shall not touch them."(8)

3. Finally, in the day of judgment He will likewise deliver them from the first death of the body; for those which were overcome shall rise again to such a life as shall be a second death, and shall be " cast into the pool of fire and brimstone," where they "shall be tormented day and night for ever and ever." (9) But the conquerors will rise again to a new glorious life, on whom "the second death " will have " no power," (10) because their bodies will not only be immortal, but also impassible, resplendent, and joyful with this new life.

Colloquy.—O my Saviour, open the ears of my soul, that I may hear what Thy divine " Spirit says unto the churches;" and help me to fight against my enemies and Thine with so great fervour, that though the body die, yet the soul does not die, nor eternal death touch me ; but grant me that I may persevere faithfully in Thy holy service, even " unto death," that I may receive of Thee " the crown of life." Amen.

POINT III.

Glory is the third reward which Christ our Lord promises to *those who resist their enemies* and who avoid their perverse company, saying to them:—" To him that overcometh I will give *the hidden manna,* and will give him a *white counter,* and in the counter a *new name* written,

(8) Sap. iii. 1.

(9) Apoc. xx. 10.   (10) Apoc. xx. 6.

which no man knoweth but he that receiveth it." (11)   In which words are to be pondered,—i. what *Manna* this is, —and ii., what *white counter*,—iii., what *new name*, and *who he is that receives* and knows the same.

i. First, this manna is the *sweetness of the divinity which is tasted in glory;* and like another manna, after a most eminent manner contains all kinds of delights and sweetness of taste, (12) which riches, dignities, friends, and all things created can possibly bring, and which all the senses can possibly receive, with which Almighty God discovers the sweetness with which He delights His sons; but the same is called hidden manna, because it is hidden and unknown to men on earth, although it be manifest and very evident to the just in heaven, yea, even here they have some taste of it, for which cause David said;— " O how great is the multitude of Thy sweetness, O Lord, which Thou hast hidden for them that fear Thee!" (13) They are many by reason of the variety of celestial favours which they contain, and they are great by reason of the excellency that each of them have. O how sweet is the wisdom of Almighty God to him that sees it, and how sweet His goodness to him that loves it! So much sweetness as our will can desire, so much and much more will He give us in the glory of His divinity.

ii. The " *white counter*" which is given in glory, is a most precious inward testimony which Almighty God gives to the Blessed, by which he knows that he is approved and elected to enjoy Him for ever with exceeding security, and that he shall never be reprobate nor excluded that glory, nor will have given to him the black counter, which is given to the accursed in sign of their eternal reprobation and condemnation. And it is called "a white counter," because the Holy Ghost gives the same to those

(11) Apoc. ii. 17,   (12) Sap. xvi. 20.   (13) Ps. xxx. 20.

"who have made " their souls "white in the blood of the Lamb." (14)   And it is a precious counter which is given together with this delicious manna, to enrich the invited, and to assure them of the perpetuity of their banquet. And if in this life the testimony which the Holy Ghost gives the just that his name is "written in the book of life," (15) so rejoice him, what joy will it be to see himself now, not with doubtful or uncertain testimonies, but with evident and certain, that he shall everlastingly enjoy the sweetness which he has tasted. So that in the day of judgment, to the elect and conquerors who have overcome, Christ our Lord will give a white counter, which is that public and approved sentence with which He will say;— " Come ye blessed of my Father, possess you the Kingdom prepared for you from the foundation of the world;" (16) but to the reprobate who were overcome, He will give the black counter of the sentence of their condemnation.

Colloquy.—Wherefore, O my soul, take heed how thou livest, because in the hour of death thy cause is so sifted and examined, and the examination shall be but one, because the judge is but one. If, therefore, thou hast lived ill, He will declare His sentence with the black counter of condemnation; but if thou hast lived well, He will declare His suffrage in thy favour, giving thee the white counter of approbation and salvation.

iii. Thirdly, the " name " that is written in this counter is the name of the Son of God and of the heir of His Kingdom, which is declared by this approbation, for then the Holy Ghost will give interior testimony in the behalf of the elect, that they "are the sons of God; and if sons,

(14) Apoc. vii. 14.   (15) Rom. viii. 16. Apoc. xx. 15, et xxi. 27.
(16) Mat. xxv. 34.

heirs also, heirs indeed of God, and joint heirs with Christ."(17) And this name is called a "new name," because the perfect adoption of sons, and the inheritance of celestial glory, is anew given to them, and shall perpetually be preserved in this novelty, whose excellency is so great that it is not possible to know it nor to esteem it as it deserves, but then when it is received in bliss and glory. O happy they who conquer sins, since they are to receive so great a recompense for their victory! O how joyful will they be with that meat of manna! And how rich and contented with that "white counter" of perpetual approbation, and how honoured and glorious with that "new name" of the sons of God; insomuch that the damned themselves with a certain obscure light which they shall have of all this in the day of judgment, shall say with loud voices:—"We fools esteemed their life madness, and their end without honour. Behold how they are numbered among the children of God, and their lot is among the saints."(18)

Colloquy.—O most glorious saints, whose lot was so happy that the "white counter" of everlasting approbation fell to you; obtain for me of the celestial Father, who has accepted you for sons and heirs, that I may live after such sort on earth, that I may obtain with you the same lot above in heaven. Amen.

POINT IV.

Glory is the reward which Christ our Lord promises to him that overcomes and *keeps His works to the end;* namely, His precepts which He commands to be kept, and doing the works which Himself did, to whom He says;—"I will give him power over the nations, and he shall rule them with a rod of iron, and as the vessel of a potter shall they

(17) Rom. viii. 16.   (18) Sap. v. 4.

be broken; as I also have received of my Father, and I will give him the morning star." (19)

1. Concerning which is to be pondered first, the great honour which Christ our Lord does to those saints who in this life were oppressed and afflicted by sinners, changing the lots of the one and of the other. For to the just He will give *dominion and power over the nations* who afflicted them, although they be kings and princes, whom they shall hold under their feet, and will rejoice for the justice and severity with which Almighty God chastises them with a rigorous rod of iron, breaking them like vessels of clay which are unprofitable, for which cause David says;—" The saints shall rejoice in glory, they shall be joyful in their beds. The high praises of God shall be in their mouths, and two-edged swords in their hands, to execute vengeance upon the nations, chastisements among the people. To bind their kings with fetters and their nobles with manacles of iron. To execute upon them the judgment that is written, this glory is to all His saints." (20)

Colloquy.—O true glory, glory solid and ineffable, ordained by God Himself to honour His saints! O my God, "how exceedingly honourable" are Thy friends become, "their principality is exceedingly strengthened!"(21) To whom Thou givest the power which Thou receivedst of Thy Father, because they lived subject to Thy government. I give Thee thanks for the honour Thou dost to them; grant me that I may imitate their life, that I may be made partaker of their glory. Amen.

2. " *The morning star* " which here is promised is *Jesus Christ*, God and Man, who calls Himself by the same

(19) Apoc. ii. 27.   (20) Ps. cxlix. 5.

(21) Ps. cxxxviii. 17.

name; for as He is God, He was begotten of His Father "in the brightness of the saints, from the womb before the day star;" (22) and as Man, He was born in the world, and afterwards rose again as the beginning of light and first fruits of the Resurrection. This star Christ gives to those who overcome and imitate Him in His works, that they may see Him and enjoy Him, and come to that pass that in imitation of Him they may be stars of the firmament, and may have part in His glorious Resurrection, and rising again in glorified bodies like His.

Colloquy.—O most loving Jesus, who art born like the morning star, to drive from the world the darkness of ignorance, and the sorrowfulness and bitterness of all sin; make me a star in Thy Church militant, that, shining by the light of life and doctrine, I may afterwards become a shining star in Thy Church triumphant, world without end. Amen.

POINT V.

Glory is the fifth reward which Christ our Lord promises to those who have not defiled the garments of their soul, and whose works have been full before God, to whom He says;—" He that shall overcome, shall thus be clothed in white garments, and I will not blot out his name out of the book of life, and I will confess his name before my Father and before His angels." (23) In which words are included three excellencies of glory with which Almighty God rewards those that overcome.

i. The first is, to "clothe them with white garments, adorning their souls with the most rich garments of grace and light of glory, with a certain divine purity, replenishing them with perpetual gladness. And clothing their bodies likewise with the most precious garments of impas-

<hr>

(22) Ps. cix. 3.   (23) Apoc. iii. 2, 5.

sible immortality, and of resplendent impassibility, and of most beautiful splendour, much more bright than the sun itself, accomplishing in them that which is written. For this cause shall they receive a double garment "in their land," (24) namely, of health and of justice.

Colloquy.—O sweet Redeemer, I give Thee thanks for this garment of glory which Thou hast prepared in heaven for those who shall clothe themselves with the garment of Thy grace here on earth; clothe me, dear Lord, I beseech Thee, with this Thy garment, that I may hereafter be worthy to be clothed with Thee in the other. Amen.

ii. The second excellency is, that their names shall not be blotted out of the book of life; that is to say, He will assure them that for ever they shall be with Him in His glory, and as from His eternity He wrote them in His understanding and will, electing them that they might be blessed, so will they remain for all eternity; and by consequence assures them that they shall never be "cast into the pool of fire" into which they will be cast, who are not "written in this book." (25)

iii. The third excellency is, that *He will confess them and praise them before His Father*, and His angels, (26) glorying to have them in His company, and publishing the services which they havè done Him, that they may be honoured of God. Which thing He will yet do more amply in the day of judgment, before all men, and even beforethe wicked themselves, as well to confound them, as that they may see how faithfully He performs what He promised to honour those who serve Him with fidelity.

Colloquy.—O eternal God, who disdainest not to be called the God of Abraham, and of the other just,

<hr>

(24) Isa. lxi. 7.   (25) Apoc. xx. 15.   (26) Luc. ix. 26.

who are pilgrims below on earth, because Thou hast "prepared for them" a most rich and noble "city"(27) above in heaven; I give Thee thanks for this honour which Thou dost them, and I humbly beseech Thee not to disdain to accept me for Thy servant, that Thou do not cast me for ever forth of Thy Kingdom. Amen.

POINT VI.

Glory is the sixth reward which Christ our Lord promises to *those who persevere in keeping the good they have received*, saying:—"He that shall overcome I will make him *a pillar in the Temple of my God*, and he shall go out no more: and I will *write upon him the name of my God*," *and the name of the new city of my God*, "the new Jerusalem which cometh down out of heaven, from my God, and my new name." (28)

1. Those who overcome the enemies of Jesus Christ, and are *as pillars which support the faith* and the Church, with their life and doctrine, shall be honoured as pillars in heaven, all praising them for the sanctity and fortitude which they had on earth: and, therefore, Almighty God will there make them pillars of His celestial Temple, to adorn and deck it, working and decorating them much better than Solomon did the pillars of his temple, with a thousand ornaments of graces and virtues. (29) Moreover, they will be firm and immutable pillars, inasmuch as they will never stir from the place which God shall give them, nor will ever go out of heaven to return to their former state. For this is the difference betwixt them and the just, who here are pillars of the Church; for these, in that they are mutable of their own nature, sometimes fall from their state; and, therefore, Christ our

<hr>

(27) Heb. xi. 16.   (28) Apoc. iii. 12.   (29) 3 Reg. vii. 15.

Lord said:—" Hold that which thou hast, that no man take thy crown: He that shall overcome, I will make him a pillar in the Temple of my God, and he shall go out no more." (30)

Colloquy.—O sweet Redeemer, pillar of the militant and triumphant Church, who hast built Thy " house" on earth, upon " seven pillars"(31) of great strength and stability; grant me that I may stand with such stability in Thy holy service, that I may come to be a pillar in Thy holy Temple. Amen.

2. Christ our Lord, the more to honour these celestial pillars, promises that *He will write upon them three names*, that is to say,—the name of God,—of the new city Jerusalem,—and His own new name, which is Jesus and Saviour: to signify, that God takes them for His own, who are the work of His own hands, of which He glories, and that they are perpetual citizens of the celestial Jerusalem, enjoying everlastingly the happy vision of peace, which His name signifies: and finally, the same Jesus imprints in them the fruits of His name, manifesting in them the riches of the salvation which He gained for all. O how beautiful will these celestial pillars be, with the writing of these three glorious names!

Colloquy.—O God of my soul, imprint Thy name within my heart, so that it be never blotted out by my offence. O sweet Jesus, engrave Thy sweet name within my bowels, imprinting in me the effects of Thy salvation. O city of Jerusalem, which descendest from heaven, making thyself known here on earth, vouchsafe to accept me for thy citizen, now by loving confidence, and afterwards by eternal possession. Amen.

(30) Apoc. iii. 11, 12.   (31) Prov. ix. 1.

POINT VII.

The heavenly glory is the seventh reward which Christ our Lord promises to those *who shall overcome lukewarmness of life*, which provokes Him to vomit, saying:—" He that shall overcome I will give unto him, to sit with me in my throne, as I also have overcome, and have sat with my Father in His throne."

1. In these words are to be pondered the sovereign excellency which the saints will have in glory, for the *great conformity which they will have with Christ our Lord in it*, which, although it never attain to equality, yet to manifest the greatness of it, it is expressed by words which signify equality, and therefore Christ says:—" Vincenti dabo." He that shall overcome I will give to him to sit in my Kingdom, not as a servant, who serves, but sitting in great tranquillity and majesty, like a prince and great person in my court. And he shall sit not afar off from me, but " mecum," with me in my company, and in my presence, conversing with me familiarly, and participating in my goods. Again he shall sit with me,—not barely so,—but " in throno meo," " in my throne," so that there will not be betwixt us any separation, and he shall also have part in the honour which is done to me: that is to say, I will give to him the dignity of God, in such a degree as he is capable of, that he may enjoy that excellency which Lucifer aimed at by evil means, but obtained not, when he said:—" I will ascend into heaven, I will exalt my throne above the stars of God, I will sit in the mountain of the covenant, I will ascend above the height of the clouds, I will be like the most High." (32)

Colloquy.—O most high God, I give Thee all

(32) Isa xiv. 13.

thanks that I possibly can that Thou grantest to men who overcome pride, that which Thou deniedst to Lucifer and his angels, who were vanquished thereby. "Thou raisest up the" needy from the dust, and liftest "up the poor from the dunghill, that he may sit with princes, and hold the throne of glory."(33) In this life he stood on foot, watching and labouring; in the other life he shall sit down and rest. Here he was in the lowest place, prostrated on the dust and filth of the earth; there he shall be in the highest place, elevated to the throne and greatness of heaven. Here he was like to the highest in virtues, and there he shall be like him in the rewards which he deserved for them. O eternal King, if in this mortal life Thou honour so highly those that serve Thee, that Thou sayest to them:—"You are gods, and all of you the sons of the most high:(34) how much more wilt Thou honour them in that immortal life, giving to them the dignity of gods, in such manner as they are capable thereof?—Happy are they who serve Thee, since they attain to so great excellence.

2. Then will I ponder the comparison that Christ our Lord proposed, the more to declare the greatness of this reward, saying:—"I will give" to him, "to sit with me in my throne, *as I also have overcome, and am set down with my Father in His throne,*" (35) that is to say, I have suffered great labours and persecutions from the Devil, and from his ministers, and have gotten the victory over them all, and for this victory my Father has exalted me above all the heavens, and has set me upon His right hand in His throne. In this manner, therefore, those who suffer for my sake, and fight until they overcome, I will do them that honour which my Father did to me, according to the

---

(33) 1 Reg. ii. 8.

(34) Ps. lxxxi. 6.   (35) Apoc. iii. 21.

merits of every one, placing them upon my right hand, and in my throne, giving them the pre-eminence of glory which their services have deserved.

Colloquy.—O happy labours, with which so sovereign recompences are obtained! O sweet victory, though a little painful to the flesh, unto which is due so glorious a throne for the spirit! Animate thyself, O my soul, to fight for Christ until thou obtain the victory, since He promises to thee that thou shalt reign with Him in the throne of His glory.

THE CONCLUSION OF THAT WHICH HAS BEEN SAID.

Of that which has been said in these points I conclude an admirable sentence, which comprehends *fire things* that have been the matter and arguments of what has been meditated in this whole book, and are of great power and efficacy to draw our affection to the divine service, viz., that all the labours of this life are not equal, and to be compared neither to the pains of hell which I have deserved for my sins, nor to the joys of heaven, which is promised me; nor to those many things which my Redeemer did and suffered for my sake, nor with the infinite goodness and majesty of God, whom I serve, with which the innumerable benefits which He has done me, and which I hope that He will do me, granting to me the rewards of glory. And this confidence to obtain those rewards ought principally to rely upon the goodness and charity of Almighty God, who promises them, and on the merits of Jesus Christ, who purchased them, and upon the desire which He showed to make me partaker of them, and upon the manifold means that He has given me to obtain them; and upon the possession which the same Saviour has taken, not only for Himself, but also for all those who desire to be united to Him, as lively members to their head, mindful of that which St. Paul says, making a sum of all these titles of confidence in these words:— " God who is rich in mercy for His exceeding charity, wherewith He loved us, even when we were dead by sins, quickened us together in Christ, by whose grace you are saved, and hath raised us up together, and hath made us sit together in the heavenly places, through Christ Jesus, that He might show in ages to come the abundant riches of His grace, in IIis bounty towards us, in Christ Jesus." (36)

Colloquy.—O God most rich in mercies, with what can we requite Thee for the innumerable benefits which Thou hast done us, and for the inestimable riches of mercy which Thou hast imparted to us? Thou hast loved us with immense charity, and out of the same hast given to us Thy beloved Son, our Redeemer. Being dead by sin, Thou hast gratuitously given us the life of glory; Thy Son dying for us, Thou hast revived us by His death, being raised afterwards from death to a glorious life, Thou assurest us that we shall rise again with Him, to be made partakers of His glory; and ascending into heaven, to sit upon IIis right hand, Thou givest us a pledge that we shall sit with IIim on His throne. And all this Thou dost, not for our goodness, but for Thine own! nor for our merits, but for the merits of Thy Son, to manifest in Thine elect the excellency of Thine infinite mercy, the inestimable riches of Thy grace, and the immense dignity of the Saviour that merited the same. And since these things moved Thee to begin the work of our salvation, let the self-same move Thee to perfect

(36) Ephes. ii. 4.

it in us, to the end that there may be many to fill the seats of heaven, and employ themselves in singing Thy praises, and the praises of Thine Only-begotten Son, Jesus Christ, and of the Holy Ghost, world without end. Amen.

AD MAJOREM DEI DEIPARÆQUE VIRGINIS GLORIAM.

INDEX

OF THE

PRINCIPAL PASSAGES OF SCRIPTURE EXPLAINED IN THIS WORK.

GENESIS.

PROVERBS.

ECCLESIASTES.

CANTICLES.

WISDOM.

INDEX

OF THE

SUBJECT MATTERS CONTAINED IN THE SIX VOLUMES.

Capitals, as I. II , indicate which Part, or Vol.—Arabic, as 1, 2, which Meditation. —And Small Roman, as i. ii , which Point. Thus, III. 7. ii. means : Third Part, seventh meditation, and second point.

A.